GW00546702

Creating the Infrastructure for Cloud Computing

An Essential Handbook for IT Professionals

Enrique Castro-Leon
Bernard Golden
Miguel Gómez
Raghu Yeluri
and Charles G. Sheridan

Intel
PRESS

ISBN 13 978-1-934053-27-0

This book is printed on acid-free paper.

Publisher: Richard Bowles
Editor: David J. Clark
Program Manager: Stuart Douglas
Text Design & Composition: STI
Cover: Ted Cyrek
Illustrations: InfoPros

Library of Congress Cataloging in Publication Data:

Printed in China

10 9 8 7 6 5 4 3 2 1

IMPORTANT

You can access the companion Web site for this book on the Internet at:

www.intel.com/intelpress/virtn

Use the serial number located in the upper-right hand corner of the last page to register your book and access additional material, including the Digital Edition of the book.

Contents

Chapter 2   **A Reference Architecture for Cloud Computing   25**

Contributed by Enrique Castro-Leon, Parviz Peiravi, Raghu Yeluri and Jim Blakley

Chapter 15   The Intel Cloud Builder Test Bed   369

Chapter 16   Virtual Machine Live Migration across Heterogeneous Systems   413

Contributed by Sudhir Bangalore and Kamal Natesan

Chapter 22   Energy Management in a Virtualized Cloud Environment   545

Chapter 23 Suspend-to-RAM Support in Servers   595

Chapter 24 Virtualized Low Cost Infrastructure for Small and Medium Businesses   609

Foreword

It is now almost five years since Amazon Web Services (AWS) introduced its Elastic Compute Cloud (EC2) and Simple Storage Service (S3), Web based infrastructural offerings that have grown rapidly to serve both enterprise and consumer focused application owners. With many tens of thousands of servers, AWS is certainly the leader in the segment, and it is worth pausing to consider what made their revolutionary concept possible. I am firmly of the belief that the entire concept of cloud computing would not exist were it not for two key forces in innovation:

■ The incredible power and innovation of the open source movement. AWS uses the Xen hypervisor to run its compute cloud, and its entire infrastructure portfolio is built using open source software. The rate of innovation in open source, and the collaborative, community-centric model of technology development are enabling the single most powerful transformation of IT after the adoption of the x86 processor.

Indeed, the adoption of the x86 processor is both a requirement for and a consequence of cloud computing: With an industry standard processor architecture, compatibility between applications and hardware becomes a non-issue. Complex, proprietary computing systems, the pride of every legacy application owner, will play mainly specialized and niche roles. Moore's Law and x86 will deliver the future computational grid for all applications.

■ Moore's Law, and a community-centric, technology-first development model are the ingredients of the cloud. Together they offer the lowest risk and therefore lowest cost strategy, combining an industry standard processor architecture with an open industry-standard software base that prevents customers from being locked in, catalyzes innovation, and enables the development of a new foundation for the future of IT.

Cloud computing, both private and public, is radically transforming every aspect of IT. It is revolutionary because, courtesy of virtualization, the IT infrastructure can now become dynamic, responsive and more utility based. At the same time, because the term is overly broad, and the market has yet to mature, there is a general lack of a common framework to model and understand the potential that cloud brings to the enterprise. As a result almost every discussion of cloud computing involves a long detour while the participants debate about the definition of the word cloud. Frequently there is an assumption that all clouds are like AWS, which is today used more for Web based applications than legacy enterprise applications. The assumption is wrong. Moreover it is my firm belief that for every enterprise application in use today, a cloud provider and service model exists that can deliver the application more effectively than the existing legacy infrastructure stack supporting the application today.

As a strong advocate of cloud computing, I am sometimes challenged by IT traditionalists, who offer a range of objections to the utility notion of IT: clouds cannot be secure, they do not offer service guarantees, and users could lose their data if the cloud fails or goes out of business... and so on. At the heart of these objections lie a few major concerns that I believe must be placed up front in the debate:

Cloud computing challenges existing IT practice and practitioners, requiring that they adopt new technology and processes. But anyone who has run a successful IT group knows that "new technology", "new process" and "reliable enterprise IT services" have almost never been used in the same sentence before. Cloud challenges every tenet of successful IT today including control, visibility, process, and security.

Cloud computing is the only way forward for IT. It is quite simply impossible for enterprise IT groups to continue to pay an order of magnitude more for compute, storage, networking and other infrastructure capabilities than their competitors who are adopting cloud computing. The agility and ease of consumption of cloud based resources can transform the competitiveness of any business, and the granular, metrics based accountability enables business owners to finally understand the true cost of their applications.

Whilst it may appear that the above points are irreconcilable, there is indeed an evolutionary path forward and hence my confidence in stating that every enterprise can make some use of the cloud today. A broad range of service offerings are available from multiple providers, from the large and well known Amazon Web Services and its EC2 compute cloud and S3 storage service to boutique providers allowing enterprises to outsource their entire IT process to a modern, isolated, cloud based infrastructure with granular controls and consumption based charging. What is missing is an understanding of what is available, and a methodology for mapping these offerings onto today's IT processes and application needs.

Digging into my assertion, namely that there is a cloud for every application that can meet the application's needs, the key challenge is to understand the different infrastructure service models on offer, and map them to application needs. These needs necessarily include complex compliance, security, SLA and other requirements.

Many cloud providers can offer better control over and insight into a highly regulated and secured IT environment than any privately owned enterprise IT group. These enterprise-focused cloud providers today allow their customers to build rich, isolated, private enterprise infrastructures that are verifiably secure. You choose your core infrastructure, and layer on top security, compliance testing, auditing, granular access controls and rich management capabilities. Many are certified to host highly regulated applications and data and use hardened facilities, with redundancy, replication, and high availability. To these features providers add elastic computing, network and storage, with granular access control, and powerful network capabilities such as intrusion detection, firewalling, load balancing and Payment Card Industry (PCI) Security Standards compliance. In short, everything you could want for your enterprise applications.

It is my belief that in this book you will discover a model of cloud computing that enables you to transform your IT practices, whilst respecting the implicit constraints that every IT practitioner must adhere to: security, availability and performance. In these pages you will come to understand the key choices to be made when using clouds:

- Elasticity and scaling: By virtue of their scale and geographical distribution, clouds can make applications and data available under conditions that would render any private IT resources useless, including attacks and failures. In addition the infrastructure can scale on an elastic basis, permitting you to use just the right amount of resource to match your application needs.

- Because of their rich connectivity and geographical distribution, clouds are better placed to deliver applications to geographically dispersed end users with great performance.

- Data and application security. Of course in all enterprise centric clouds the focus on security is implicit, but there are additional opportunities: You can encrypt your data. Combined with secure access control, opaque object name spaces, and a high degree of automation, you can make the likelihood of data leakage effectively zero. Fewer humans, simpler, infrastructure services, and secure isolation at multiple layers can offer better security.

This book provides a foundation for organizations to understand and execute a cloud computing vision that is right for their circumstances and opportunities. I am firmly of the belief that cloud computing is, for every organization, a "when," not an "if," and that the right time for every organization to begin is now. Enjoy the book, and use it as a foundation for your cloud computing initiative.

Simon Crosby

CTO, Citrix Systems

Preface

Cloud computing represents a paradigm shift in how IT services are integrated, packaged and delivered, a change that promises large gains in efficiency and flexibility at a time of increasing demand on the data center, outsourcing and unbearable cost constraints. The tools, building blocks, solutions, and best practices for cloud computing are evolving, and challenges to deploying cloud solutions need to be considered.

The cloud is one ounce of technology and a pound of process and business transformation. The role of technology in the cloud is significant, some in use today, some very advanced, but it pales compared with the creativity of enterprising cloud pioneers putting it to use. Although we tried very hard to capture as much insight as we could on the second part, industry events are still unfolding, and any attempt to write the "definitive book" on the subject will be met with ignominious obsolescence in a few years or even months. In any case, once the cloud becomes mainstream it will also become part of the standard IT practice and will cease to be a distinct subject, much in the same way distributed programming used to be in the early 1980s: today with every operating system supporting TCP/IP, support for distribution is assumed.

All this said, the book is heavy on the technology, partly because it reflects the background of the authors, partly because at the time of writing the industry is at a singularity or inflection point characterized by rapid change and innovation. As Simon Crosby remarks in the foreword, there are authoritative figures in the industry stating a thousand credible reasons why the cloud is not a very good fit for fulfilling an enterprise's IT needs, all the while there is a large number of cloud related startups coming into the arena in the middle of a structural economic recession. The book speaks to technologists, application and data center architects and decision makers intent in putting cloud technology to productive use. The authors hope that some of the technological capabilities described, and initial proof of concept ideas will feed into the industry's creative frenzy in effect in midflight as we speak.

This book project started at the tail end of our first book, *The Business Value of Virtual Service Oriented Grids*. Our initial goal was to expand on virtualization strategy aspect especially to document the transformation of data center consolidation at the time. At that point the concept of cloud computing was emerging and soon its gravitational pull proved irresistible; the initial thematic did not seem as compelling to the audience we were trying to address as cloud computing. Hence the project slowly and eventually morphed into a cloud computing project. The recurring abstraction throughout the book is that of a *virtualized cloud data center*.

Physically, a virtualized cloud data center is not much different from a traditional corporate owned, vertically integrated data center, or even a hosted facility. The main difference is that virtualized cloud data centers are architected to function as "service factories." Instead of applications being physically bound to the hardware on which they run, a virtualization layer has been added that allow applications to "float" across physical hosts. It can't be said it happens easily today, but that's what technological evolution is enabling. The implications of this capability are enormous. For instance a number of applications can be collocated in the same physical platform to improve utilization efficiency. Hardware can now be scheduled separately from application capabilities for the purposes of maintenance, security, performance, locality or other criteria.

For implementation purposes, the granularity can be smaller than whole applications, which brings us back to the notion of servicelets or microservices discussed in our previous book. Cloud applications become agglomerations of servicelets, some in-house, some outsourced and assigned to hosts that meet the business requirements for the application.

For most of the contributors to this book the controversy of whether or not the cloud is a viable alternative for delivering IT is irrelevant. Consistent with Intel's traditional participation, the focus is on data center infrastructure components that support the cloud. For the architects, engineers and researchers involved in cloud projects the cloud is a concrete reality they live every day through their work in their labs, architecting microprocessors, server platforms and putting together conceptual cloud solutions to certain business needs.

As the authors went through their research and compiled the material certain insights and patterns became obvious.

■ For instance the resource pooling capabilities of clouds make them inherently power and energy efficient, conferring strategic cost advantages to data center operators who adopt cloud computing. However realizing energy efficient requires more than deploying technology; it also implies varying degrees of process maturity.

■ Another example is related to data center cooling. In the average data center today it takes as much power to cool a data center as to power the server equipment in the first place, partly because of operating rules that go back decades to the mainframe era. A number of experiments, reported in Chapter 12, indicate that server equipment can operate at elevated ambient temperatures over 35 degrees C without deleterious effects. Allowing the ambient temperature to rise would reduce cooling costs. In practice this is not possible today because operating equipment beyond the recommended thermal envelope would void manufacture warranties.

■ Yet another example is predicting the performance impact of redistributing application components to the cloud. It turns out that Intel engineers were researching this problem as early as 2006 in the context of data center consolidation even before the cloud became a popular term.

From an infrastructure perspective, the possibilities of data center efficiency in energy usage brought by virtualized cloud environments cannot be underestimated. Well-known research reported by J. Koomey[1] indicates that the aggregate use of electricity in data centers doubled from 2000 to 2005

---

1   Jonathan G Koomey 2008 Environ. Res. Lett. 3 034008.

represents about 1 percent of the world's electricity consumption, not an insignificant figure. Volume servers represent about 28 percent of electricity consumption in data centers. Traditional, corporate owned data centers have historically been run at abysmally low 10 to 20 percent utilization rates. These numbers are a consequence from the way the equipment is operated. Servers are typically run 24–7 and sized for peak workload demand plus an allowance for workload growth during the useful life of the equipment. As we shall see in the book, for servers provisioned to service cloud workloads in virtualized environments it is possible to at least quadruple the initial utilization factors, to the range of 60 to 80 percent. The net effect is quadrupling the application yield without significantly increasing energy input and carbon emissions. We dedicate several chapters to the solution architecture and the practices to achieve these goals.

As previously mentioned, the impetus behind cloud computing is the ever-increasing demands placed on data centers often already at near capacity and resource-constrained. These demands include growing needs to manage business growth and increase IT flexibility.

In response to these challenges, cloud computing is evolving in the forms of both public clouds, deployed by Internet and telecommunications companies, hosting service providers and others, and private or enterprise clouds, deployed by enterprises behind a firewall for an organization's internal use.

Public clouds are being driven by exponential growth of Internet data and traffic as the Internet matures and Internet-based services proliferate. By 2015, over 2.5 billion people with more than 10 billion devices will access the Internet. That's over twice today's demand, requiring a cloud infrastructure with one billion virtual servers.[2] The monumental requirements associated with the data center build-outs needed to satisfy this growing demand can only be met with the increased efficiency, performance, and flexibility of cloud architectures.

Private clouds are being driven by the expanding business demands on enterprise IT. More and more data centers find themselves facing real limits, whether based on lack of power, lack of room, lack of server capacity, or lack of network bandwidth. Expanding traditional infrastructures to

---

2   Sources: IDC "Server Workloads Forecast" 2009; and IDC "The Internet Reaches Late Adolescence" Dec 2009

meet these challenges quickly uncovers multiple inherent inflexibilities. We cover a number of issues related to public and private clouds in Chapter 3 summarizing the experience from a set of our top enterprise IT customers.

Cloud computing is a step beyond data center virtualization. Initially, virtualization technologies allowed data centers to consolidate server infrastructure to save cost. Next, flexible resource management technologies added the ability to more dynamically allocate data center resources. This further reduced costs and also increased data center flexibility and performance, ushering in a new era of technology development and deployment. Software vendors have begun to design robust management features and technology optimizations for enterprise and public clouds based upon virtualization. Hardware vendors have extended their management tools and reliability features to include increased flexibility.

The era of cloud computing can be seen as the next natural step, where significant automation and scalability become possible. Cloud computing offers a path to optimized use and rapid deployment of resources, improved operational efficiency, and potential for significant cost savings. While the scope of this book does not span manageability as a main subject, the chapters on data center efficiency cover various aspects of server power management in data centers.

When fully realized, cloud computing infrastructures can provide competitively significant IT agility, flexibility, and adaptability through systems that are efficient, simplified, and a level of security that matches the application objectives.

Cloud computing technology is maturing at a fast pace and many cloud services and vendors are entering the market to enable the development of private clouds for enterprise IT. Several public cloud providers are expanding their services to support enterprises. From conversations with vendors, analysts and customers, we've identified critical attributes in cloud computing infrastructures and solutions, namely federation, automation, and client-awareness.

■ Federated means communications, data, and services can move easily within and across cloud computing infrastructures. To accomplish truly federated systems, smooth interoperability across many platforms and solutions must be a reality.

Today, the industry is just reaching the point that enterprises can move or migrate workloads within and between their own data centers.

Data center operators are far from being able to have data and services seamlessly and securely scale beyond their borders to span public and private clouds when desired. A level of federation that enables the movement of workloads and data from one service provider to another would be valuable; burst implementations between internal private cloud and public cloud providers if additional capacity is needed; and secure and reliable data flow across vendors, partners, and clients.

■ Automated means that cloud computing services and resources can be specified, located, and securely provisioned with very little or zero human interaction. Today, the industry faces many gaps in automation. According to an IDC's Data Center Survey in 2009, virtualization thus far has failed to reduce complexity. The number of server instances that can be managed by the average systems administrator has increased from 37 to only 41 comparing non-virtualized servers to virtualized servers.

Moreover, virtual machines are generally very statically provisioned versus automatically responding to user needs. Data center management remains very manual today where the patching of servers doesn't scale reliably. Highly desirable would be a level of automation enabling dynamic allocation of resources to agreed-upon service levels and optimizing the data center for maximum resource utilization and power efficiency. This includes automation of provisioning, resource monitoring, reporting of consumption for bill back, and workload balancing.

■ Client-aware means that cloud computing solutions adapt seamlessly to the end user's device and use model regardless of the type of client system used. Today, there are certain frameworks that allow some level of data center intelligence and scaling to support the client being served.

Unfortunately these frameworks are neither consistently applied nor ubiquitous. Many of today's Internet services support the lowest common denominator device even if the user is accessing the service with a powerful desktop computer.

Conversely, other services are difficult to use on a handheld device because they were written for a PC. Again, highly desirable capabilities with data centers and service providers would be access and optimal experience across a range of devices, by making the cloud knowledgeable about client device attributes.

These attributes include the device's capabilities, location, policies, and connectivity. At the same time, client device capabilities can affect the overall performance of cloud solutions: intelligent performance on the client device can deliver better end user experiences through local computing power; security capabilities on the client device can ensure security policies are applied at the device; and pervasive communication (using any choice of connectivity, such as LAN, WAN, Wi-Fi[†], or personal area network) enables work-from-anywhere flexibility.

Borrowing on established principles in computer science, there is a hint of a self-referential approach in the book in that its structure mimics the system it describes. For instance, instead of the traditional approach of having one or more authors write the content, the writing of the book was "cloudburst" to more than two dozen of different experts. This way it was possible to short the knowledge procurement process by years and present it to the audience much sooner than otherwise possible. This approach also provides multiple points of view and much better insight into cloud concepts than one person's point of view. Each chapter is credited to their contributors to the extent possible.

Evolving the infrastructure to realize the full potential of cloud computing will not be trivial. It will require cooperative development and specific focus by many providers and customers across the IT landscape. We believe that to move towards this vision of cloud computing, individual organizations and the IT industry as a whole need to focus on four principles:

■ Efficiency: While the need for computing throughput increases exponentially, resources are limited. These resources include space, power, cooling capacity, qualified IT professionals, dollars for infrastructure, and dollars for operations. Doing more with existing or available resources will require increased efficiency from infrastructure and processes.

■ Simplification: Generally, the growth of a system inherently increases complexity, and this is certainly true of IT infrastructures. Multiple architectures complicate management. Increased server utilization raises network bandwidth requirements. And systems from different vendors typically present integration complications. For cloud computing environments to deliver on their promise, simplification must underlie cloud architectures and practices.

■ Security: Both business risk and compliance requirements make data security paramount. In an environment with abundant traditional security issues, cloud computing creates new challenges because it moves data in new ways, often outside of traditional physical boundaries. The successful implementation of cloud computing requires new security models to meet new challenges.

■ Open standards: When multiple providers (of solutions, hardware, software, integration, or processes) act independently, poor interoperability and lack of flexibility are the natural results—and are in direct contradiction to the main promises of cloud computing. The evolution of cloud computing requires open standards that are carefully constructed and create greater interoperability.

We cover aspects of efficiency, simplification and open standards in this book, less on security, not because it is not important, but because we did not have much visibility into the subject at the time of writing. In any case, Intel is making an effort to establish a continuum from silicon to platforms to software architecture to data center design.

An example of this effort is the Intel® Cloud Builder, covered in Chapter 15. Cloud Builder a program designed to ease the deployment of cloud infrastructure for service providers, telecom companies, hosting companies and enterprises. The program, created by Intel in conjunction with leading cloud independent software vendors, including Canonical, Citrix, Enomaly, Microsoft, Parallels, Red Hat, Univa, VMware, Xen, and others, documents a number cloud reference architectures to be used as templates to build cloud solutions.

The book is roughly structured in four parts:

1. The first chapter covers context for virtualization and cloud computing.

2. General architectural principles for the data center infrastructure supporting cloud applications are covered in Chapters 2 through 6.

3. General principles for architecture instances by major industry segments are covered in Chapters 7 through 9.

4. Specific reference implementations are covered in Chapters 10 through 25.

The book is not meant to be read from cover to cover especially when readers are likely to lead very busy lives. The structure of the book is reminiscent of Julio Cortázar's 1963 novel *Rayuela* ("Hopscotch"). The novel carries 155 chapters out of which 99 are "optional." The author suggests different chapter sequences to fulfill different goals by "hopscotching" through the content with each chapter containing explicit instructions about where to proceed next. Some say that this novel anticipates the concept of hyperlinks by several decades.

The content of this book is certainly quite different and there are no instructions about where to go next. The reading instructions are quite simple and do not need a detailed instruction sequence. The reader can go through the first three parts with some detail, and selectively pick the case studies of interest in part 4.

Acknowledgements

As mentioned above, the backgrounds of the different contributors are rich and varied, from platform architects in product development groups to integration engineers and architects to Intel IT practitioners as well as researchers from Intel Labs. Here is a very likely nonexhaustive list of contributors: Nishi Ahuja, Stephen Anderson, Robert Armstrong, Sudhir Bangalore, Nicolas Barcet, Charlton Barreto, Mary Bass, Chris Black, Jim Blakley, William Carter, Enrique Castro-Leon, William Carter, Reuven Cohen, Trevor Cooper, Billy Cox, Martin Curley, David Filani, Ravi A. Giri, Bernard Golden, Ricki Godfrey, Miguel Gómez Rodríguez, Gopi Govindaraju, Paul Guermonprez, Jackson He, Andy Hoffman, Jim Kenneally, Dustin Kirkland, Ed Jimison, Cong Li, Hong Li, Ignacio Biasco López, Milan Milenkovic, Kamal Natesan, Daniel Nurmi, Judy Ossello, Parviz Peiravi, Luc Provoost, Rekha Raghu, Murali Rajappa, Richard Reiner, Randy Schneider, Dror Shenkar, Charles G. Sheridan, Xavier Simonart, Jake Smith, Catherine Spence, Robin Steinbrecher, Jim Sutorka, Robert Villanueva, Sinisa Veseli, Mark Wright, Pat Wendorf, Rick White, Rich Wolski, Raghu Yeluri, Aamir Yunus, and Tianfei Zhu.

This book could not have been created without the multi-year effort of Intel's IT organization and the support of the Data Center Group business unit tea through funding, risk taking, product development. Their whitepapers and industry engagements provided the impetus for the development of many of the principles in cloud computing of this book. Specifically we would like to acknowledge: Rich Uhlig, Dylan Larson, RK Hiremane, Brad Shafer, and Jake Smith.

The support from Hugh Mercer, program manager, and the contributions from a set of our top enterprise IT customers are acknowledged.

The staff at Intel Press is acknowledged for their guidance and infinite patience in the publication process: Bruce Bartlett, David Clark, Stuart Douglas, Mary Taylor, and Joe Zawadsky.

Chapter 1

From Virtualization to Cloud Computing: The Evolution of the Data Center

Contributed by Bernard Golden

I think it's becoming more and more accepted that virtualization and cloud computing will become more of the norm, and what will matter the most during the "switch" is the ability to control and deploy the systems that run the infrastructure.

—Alicia Glick

One of the biggest advantages to virtualization is going to be how much complexity and cost the company never saw because virtualization is in place.

—Art Wittmann

Many users of computer technology—and for that matter, many technology creators and administrators—complain about the rapid pace of change in information technology. Some even blame technology companies, comparing the constant stream of new products to the fads common to the fashion world.

It's true that the dizzying array of products can seem overwhelming. And it's also true that this ongoing development is often exacerbated by technology vendors, each anxious to stake its place in the sun, each eager to emphasize how its products are the latest and the greatest.

The most recent example of a new technology trend bursting upon the scene is *cloud computing*. Setting a record for going from "what is it?" to "I've got to have it," cloud computing for many people seems to represent a revolution in how computing will be done in the future.

It's important, however, to understand that, despite its sudden arrival, cloud computing is actually the latest manifestation of well-established trends, each of which has brought new benefits and new challenges to those working in IT. Crucial to understand is that cloud computing signifies a movement away from IT-centric product focus and signals a re-engagement with computing users, made possible by those long-established trends.

We will see that cloud computing is part of a continuous development, a continuous improvement in computing and how it is the logical outgrowth of what has gone before—with its own significant characteristics, of course. We will examine four stages of data center development and comprehend the benefits and challenges each stage embodies.

Underlying Trends

One might reasonably ask, why the excitement about cloud computing and why now? To understand what exactly has led to cloud computing at this time, it's critical to recognize the technology trends underlying cloud computing's development.

Perhaps the single most important trend driving all the stages of data center transformation is the technology progression referred to as Moore's Law. Based on an observation by one of the founders of Intel, this law refers to tendency of computer chips to double their capacity roughly every 18 months. This tendency means that software applications unachievable at a reasonable economic investment at one point in time often become trivially inexpensive to implement just a few years later.

Complementary to the power curve of Moore's Law has been the increasing concentration by the industry on a smaller number of chip architectures. Simply put, the industry has moved more and more to standardizing on certain chip architectures.

This second factor has further reduced costs and also led software users and vendors to accomplish more with less, since resources can be concentrated on fewer areas.

Combined, the mutually reinforcing trends of lower costs for processing power and increasing standardization have resulted in what has come to be referred to as commodity chips. In particular, servers based in the x86 microprocessor architecture have become ubiquitous, serving as the basis for a very high percentage of total computing being done in data centers today. Of course, one shouldn't apply the concept of commodity too recklessly: even though servers based on the x86 architecture have become a de facto standard, the market in no way resembles typical commodity situations. Commodity markets are usually associated with a standardized product with little differentiation, little ongoing improvement, and rock-bottom prices, yet there are considerable opportunities for server manufacturers to add differentiation. By contrast, though we speak of these servers and the chips that power them as a commodity, it's important to keep in mind that they continue to increase their processing power thanks to Moore's Law. In fact, far from being a static commodity, chips continue to deliver dramatically better performance over time—to a degree unprecedented in human history. It is no exaggeration to say that the human mind, conditioned as it is to incremental change in single or double digit percentages, has an immense challenge in comprehending the enormous and rapid improvement in computing power available due to Moore's Law.

Associated with this move to standardized hardware has been the move to standardized operating systems. Before hardware standardization, each hardware manufacturer had its own operating system designed to optimize its chip architecture. With the increasing success of commodity servers came the growth of standardized operating systems: Microsoft[†] Windows and Linux.

The two developments of standardized hardware and standardized operating systems set the stage for an explosion of computerization. What was once a formidable and expensive task—automating business processes through computerization—became commonplace. In fact, the use of computerization exploded so that the typical enterprise began implementing a cornucopia of applications.

Indirectly, this explosion of applications accounts for the wrenching change that has gone on in data centers, as their operators struggled (and continue to struggle) to keep up with the implications of the improvement. In examining the development of data center use, we can identify four stages, each with its own benefits and challenges:

1. One application/one server

2. Server consolidation

3. Server pooling

4. Cloud computing

One Application/One Server

Standardized computing, consisting of commodity hardware and standard operating systems, enabled businesses to migrate their processes from manual systems to automated processes. This migration is the quintessential component for IT-driven business transformation.

While the early days of computing limited applications to areas like payroll and accounting, the vastly lower cost of commodity computing meant that it was financially feasible to apply computerization to many other business processes.

The result was predictable: an explosion of application implementation as every business unit sought to get its processes automated. Applications for sales force automation, customer relationship management, enterprise resource planning, partner management all became feasible at around the same time— and all became part of an overloaded IT group's implementation schedule.

The net result of this for data centers was, simply put, a hardware land rush. There was a simple formula at this stage of technology adoption: every application got its own server. The reasons for this were many:

■ Technical challenges of hardware sharing. Even though the hardware and operating systems were standardized, the rest of the software stack—the application servers, databases, integration packages—were not. Applications dictated the software components needed on a machine for the application to run (and be supported) successfully. Most of these components did not "play well" together. Similar components often assumed primary control of critical hardware resources, thereby causing conflict over hardware access. Even the same application in different versions could not gracefully share access to hardware resources. Consequently, it was usually easier to place each application in its own machine, and the physical server became the smallest quantum for application deployment.

■ Budget practices. Applications are usually funded by business groups that aim their investment at project-specific needs. Trying to coordinate several projects to fund one piece of hardware is much more difficult than allowing each to purchase an application-dedicated server. Consequently, most applications ended up as a lone resident on a server.

■ Lack of system robustness. Early in its lifetime, Microsoft Windows, the most commonly used operating system for applications, was not very robust when compared with mainframe operating systems and commercial grade Unix-based deployments. Moreover, applications could (and did) crash the operating system. Running multiple applications on a single server meant larger populations of users had their work interrupted as a result of server crash. Segregating applications one to a server reduced the disruption due to lack of robustness.

■ Hardware performance. Hardware was not as powerful as it is today. Even if utilization was low, this equipment would have struggled in a cloud multitenant environment. The industry crossed this threshold around 2005 to 2006 when data center consolidation became a practical consideration, covered in the next section.

Key Benefits

The key beneficiary of this move to "one application/one server" was business units. Investment led to business performance improvement as processes became more efficient, required less headcount, and allowed redirection of employee effort toward increasing sales rather than shuffling paper. Use of computerized systems increased standardization of processes, raising customer satisfaction. Capture of data in computerized format enabled rapid access to records and analysis of business performance.

The reduced cost and increased efficiency of one application/one server gave business units an enormous boost in output and productivity. Many economists attribute the rapid productivity growth in the United States during the decade of the 1990s to the investment in these type of applications.

Key Challenges

This very positive move to increased computerization carried two primary challenges with it:

- Large and increasingly inefficient hardware investment. One implication of "one application/one server" is that there are lots of servers. As application implementation increased, companies experienced "server sprawl," a pungent way to describe the march of thousands upon thousands of servers into company data centers. In fact, many companies installed so many servers they ran out of data center space—and had to build new data centers. Moreover, the ongoing march of Moore's Law meant that later in the process the servers being installed were so powerful that the single applications running on them used very little of the server capacity—an extremely wasteful practice.

- IT operations headcount growth. It takes a lot of people to manage a ton of servers. Company IT staffs burgeoned in order to manage the huge server farms installed to support business applications. And people are very expensive.

- Concerns over sustainable computing. The rise of social computing created considerable demand for data centers. Energy consumed by the data center became a measurable fraction of the electricity consumed by nations. It became obvious that the one server/one application paradigm was not sustainable.

The net result of this move to the "one application/one server" world is that companies ended up with massive numbers of lightly loaded servers, all watched over by an army of IT staff. With no reduction in the growth of applications forecast, the situation was coming to a head: something needed to be done. Which brings us to the next phase of data centers—server consolidation.

Server Consolidation

As the cliché goes, if something can't go on, it won't. Clearly, the exponential growth in numbers of servers and system administration personnel couldn't be sustained. A different approach that did not require so much hardware investment was needed—badly.

Enter virtualization.

Virtualization is, at bottom, a way for multiple software components to share a single piece of hardware. The most common form of virtualization is server consolidation—enabling multiple operating systems to be installed on a single server, with each operating system isolated from the others, able to support its own specific software stack, without being affected by the other operating systems or the software components installed in those operating systems. The virtualization is implemented by a software layer referred to as a hypervisor—its job is to coordinate and keep safe the hardware sharing among the guest operating systems. Hypervisors coordinate safe access to key system resources (such as processor(s), memory, storage, and network) and ensure that data is isolated from access by unauthorized systems. Of course, this is a radical simplification of what virtualization does and how it operates, but this description captures an important characteristic of virtualization: it enables hardware sharing by enforcing secure access privileges to key hardware resources.

The effect of virtualization is that much higher utilization of servers is possible. Whereas the "one application/one server" model resulted in many servers running at 10 percent utilization—or less—virtualization resulted in utilization rates upwards of 60 percent—or 600 percent greater than the previous operating model.

Key Benefits

Raising utilization rates by such a large degree obviates the need for lots and lots of hardware. Moving beyond the "one application/one server" model meant that servers could be loaded with 5, 10, even 20 "virtual machines." Every virtual machine meant one less hardware device purchased, one less rack unit needed, along with savings in power, cooling, and space.

Just as fewer resources are required for a world of few devices, so too are fewer system administrators. There's less hardware to keep track of, to maintain uptime for, to monitor for availability and performance.

All of these benefits deliver significant financial payoff to the IT organization. It needs to fund and manage less hardware. It needs to manage less as well. Fewer IT staff are required. Savings in power and cooling redound to IT as well. In short, virtualization is a tremendous financial windfall for IT.

Key Challenges

Server consolidation presents relatively few challenges and those that exist are very manageable.

- Additional investment in virtualization software. The hypervisor software needs to be procured and a cost is associated with that. On the other hand, the savings in hardware procurement avoidance as well as reduced power and cooling generally results in a very large payback amount and a very short payback period—often on the order of less than 12 months.

- Business unit reluctance to share resources. Because projects traditionally budgeted for hardware in their project plans, many business units asserted that the purchased servers were "theirs." Asking them to share hardware was not always enthusiastically received, not to mention a challenge to typical budget practices that find it difficult to incorporate shared payment for common resources.

- Human capital investment. New technologies require training and time to improve skills—often referred to as the learning curve. Since server consolidation introduces a new software layer—the hypervisor—naturally additional human capital investment is required. Fortunately, the change server consolidation introduces is confined to the server management group, minimizing the overall investment necessary.

On the other hand, while fewer operations personnel are required for a consolidated environment, this form of virtualization does little to improve the standard practices for software installation, network and storage assignment, and so on. Application provisioning still require high levels of manual interaction by expensive personnel, clearly an undesirable situation. Addressing this brought forward the next phase of data center management: infrastructure automation.

Infrastructure Automation

While server consolidation very effectively raises the utilization rates of server hardware, it leaves most of the rest of the infrastructure and operations processes untouched—and does not affect the large costs associated with manual system administration. This is particularly troubling in the environment in which demand continues to grow, while cost pressures cause IT to remain flat or even shrink.

Because virtualization abstracts software from association with any particular hardware, it's easy to see that the same virtual machine (VM) that can be placed on one server may also be placed on another—after all, there is no dependency upon hardware, because the hypervisor inserts a layer of software between the guest VM and the physical device.

Inspired by the vision of this abstraction, virtualization has been extended in a number of ways:

- Virtual machine migration. A virtual machine can be moved from one server to another, and in fact can be migrated while operating, making it possible to move a working application from one server to another with no disruption in service.

■ Shared storage. Virtual machines cannot depend upon local disks, since the virtual machine may not be able to contact a disk on another server, should that server be down. The move to supporting virtual machine migration drives adoption of shared storage in the form of network attached storage (NAS) or a storage area network (SAN). These technologies have also implemented virtualization, abstracting data from dependence upon any particular storage mechanism, allowing transparent data migration.

■ Network agility. Clearly, a virtual machine that moves around a set of servers must be able to take its network connectivity, its IP address, and any network dependencies like VLAN or VPN configurations with it. Network equipment providers have implemented abstraction capabilities throughout the network to support system agility.

■ Total system management. Even though each compute resource has been virtualized, it is still problematic if each one has its own management structure requiring interaction through its client. The multiplicity of system interfaces also causes problems when problems are being traced, because of the lack of a central source of information. To address this, server virtualization products have been extended to manage storage and networks; in addition, third-party management tools are available that treat all resources as part of an overall pool to be management as a whole. This total system management simplifies system administration and reduces operations costs.

Key Benefits

Treating the entire compute infrastructure as a single pool of resources extends the benefits of server consolidation enormously. Instead of one area of IT infrastructure benefiting from cost reduction, costs can be reduced throughout. Furthermore, much of the manual management work necessary to administer each separate physical device is moved to a management infrastructure that enables remote administration. Furthermore, the remote administration enables treating each resource as a general pool that can be assigned—and reassigned—automatically. This latter capability is sometimes described as an "agile infrastructure," one in which system loads can be created or moved very rapidly, allowing IT operations to direct resources at the most appropriate compute needs.

Making the infrastructure agile also raises system availability, since hardware failure no longer results in system outages. Instead, virtual machines and their associated storage and network resources are re-hosted on other physical devices, enabling better uptime results.

Finally, agile infrastructure makes infrastructure maintenance easier. Instead of having to schedule downtime during off-hours (that is, nights or weekends) to replace servers or make hardware changes, system loads can be migrated to different hardware to allow the devices needing repair or replacement to be working on during normal business hours.

Key Challenges

Every improvement brings change, and infrastructure automation is no exception. Moving to an automated environment requires investment as well as re-engineering IT operations processes. Organizations moving to automated infrastructures typically find these aspects challenging:

- Additional virtualization software cost. The functionality described above goes well beyond the ability to place multiple virtual machines on a single server. Supporting virtual machine migration, integrated management, and the like requires much more sophisticated virtualization software, which is significantly more expensive than base virtualization functionality.

- Additional hardware cost. Most of the infrastructure automation products available expect that the infrastructure will consist of recent-vintage equipment. Many organizations find that upgrades of some or much of their infrastructure equipment, including network switches, network cards, storage hardware, need to be upgraded. Servers supporting a virtualized environment require a large memory footprint. The cost of the memory can overshadow the cost of the base hardware. The bottom line is that a substantial hardware investment is commonly required to move to an automated infrastructure.

- Organizational conflict and split incentives. Most IT operations organizations are divided along functional lines: a server group, a network group, a storage group. Each manages and controls its own resources. Automated infrastructure requires that all of these resources be coordinated and managed in an integrated fashion. The resource groups are concerned that losing direct control will make it more difficult to meet SLA requirements. Concern is also present about losing power, since each group will no longer have a separate fiefdom. Finally, in an integrated environment, even one with an integrated management capability, there is the question of who's responsible for a system problem, which raises the potential for finger-pointing in difficult situations. Split incentives occur when the cost of a decision made by an organization is borne by another organization. The classic situation is IT operations taking measures to improve application uptime. These measures increase power consumption, impacting the facilities management budget.

■ Vendor issues. Just as IT operations groups are usually organized along functional lines, so too are vendors—each has a server division, a network division, and so on. An IT organization that seeks to move to an automated infrastructure may find that its vendors do not present a coherent story or are unable to deliver an integrated solution. This makes it difficult to ensure successful implementation of the automated infrastructure.

Infrastructure Automation Conclusion

Infrastructure automation builds upon and increases the value of virtualization by extending it throughout all the compute resources within the data center: servers, storage, and network. Infrastructure automation can improve IT operations efficiency significantly by decreasing the amount of labor required to provision and manage compute resources.

On the other hand, infrastructure automation is a localized efficiency—it improves the operations of the data center, but does little to make the overall IT organization more efficient. Requests for resources by applications groups still get handled in an extended, manual process characterized by multiple meetings, repeated e-mails, budget approvals, and so on. The net effect of infrastructure automation is that a leisurely process is married to a highly efficient one, with the final outcome being only slightly shorter than when the entire process was completely manual.

Pressure to improve the overall process is significant and building. It is only increased by the change in applications IT organizations are deploying—larger amounts of data, unpredictable loads, and, at times, exponential growth. It's clear that the only way to address this pressure is to implement end-to-end automation that optimizes the entire process. Which brings us to cloud computing.

Cloud Computing

Cloud computing is the latest—and hottest—technology trend going. Many people see it as crucial to the next step in enterprise computing, and an inevitable development in internal data centers. But what is it?

It doesn't take long in examining the buzz around cloud computing to realize the definition of cloud computing is, well, cloudy. There are tons of definitions around, and each day brings someone else's definition to the mix.

At HyperStratus, instead of adding to the cacophony of definitions, we refer to one promulgated in the February 2009 report by the UC Berkeley Reliable Adaptive Distributed Systems Laboratory. This organization, also known as the RAD Lab[1], identified three characteristics of cloud computing:

■ The illusion of infinite computing resources available on demand, thereby eliminating the need for cloud computing users to plan far ahead for provisioning;

■ The elimination of an upfront commitment by cloud users, thereby allowing companies to start small and increase hardware resources only when there is an increase in their needs;

■ The ability to pay for use of computing resources on a short-term basis as needed (for example, processors by the hour and storage by the day) and release them as needed, thereby rewarding conservation by letting machines and storage go when they are no longer useful.

What do these three characteristics mean in real-world environments?

---

1   Intel Corporation is a sponsor of the RAD Lab.

The Illusion of Infinite Computing Resources

In typical data centers, an application's resources are relatively fixed. There is little opportunity to adjust the amount of compute resources devoted to an application in a short timeframe. Consequently, calculating the amount of resources to devote to the application is performed in a process known as *capacity planning*. Since it is difficult to truly forecast what usage patterns will be during an application's lifetime, it is to be expected that the capacity planning exercise will be a rough guess. Consequently, application planners have two options available:

■ Overprovision. This option requires purchasing more equipment than the forecast calls for. Doing this means the application will always have adequate resources available, but also means that for some or all of its life extra capital will be tied up in unneeded equipment.

■ Underprovision. This option purchases just the amount of equipment called for in the capacity planning exercise. However, it faces the risk that too little equipment will be available if demand grow significantly. Consequently, because the lead time on obtaining new hardware resources is typically lengthy, this options will often find applications running slowing or being unavailable due to overload.

One might summarize these two options thusly: overprovision, and throw away money; or underprovision, and throw away users.

Cloud computing addresses this issue by offering a very large pool of compute resources that can be assigned on a dynamic basis to applications as needed.

This "infinite scalability" obviates the challenge of capacity planning. It's not necessary to forecast future system load; if system load increases, more resources are requested and added to the application's resource pool. The drive for the adoption of cloud computing comes from improved efficiency at the industry level for two reasons: first, capacity planning risks are spread out over a much larger user community and second, the service organizations providing cloud computing can in principle bring expertise and deliver economies of scale out of reach to departments focused on line of business activities. In other words, cloud computing moves the capacity planning role and responsibility from the application to the cloud provider. This enables capacity planning to be performed over a larger overall pool of application load, enabling demand smoothing over a larger number of total compute resources.

No Upfront Commitment

Because the amount of compute resources that will be required by an application is unforeseeable, it's important that no commitment to consume a particular level of resources be required. Otherwise, cloud computing would be no different than the old days of capacity planning, with the same choices: overprovision and throw away capital, or underprovision and throw away users. Consequently, for cloud computing to fulfill its vision, long-term commitments to specific resource use levels must not be required.

In a world of no long-term resource commitments by applications, the cloud provider takes on the responsibility for delivering sufficient resources. The user, being able to leverage the "infinite scalability," is freed from long-term decisions. One might expect that other responsibilities will fall on the user—perhaps a higher cost for shorter-term use, an upfront payment for access to the cloud system, and so on.

One important point about the lack of commitment is the fact that users are able to obtain resources for as long—or as short—as necessary, which is to say that the scalability discussed in the previous section is therefore bidirectional; in other words, an application can, as demand falls, be scaled down in terms of the overall amount of compute resource devoted to the application. Absent a lack of commitment, organizations might be reluctant to consume additional resources for fear of taking on a lengthy financial burden for resources needed on a transitory basis.

Pay-as-You-Go Resource Use

Since no commitment beyond actual need is required in cloud computing environments, payment must be tied to something other than ownership or long-term contractual commitment.

Within cloud computing environments this implies payment tied to direct resource use, known as *pay as you go*. Typical payment schemes are charged on the basis of processor-hour, monthly storage per gigabyte, and so on. Tying costs to resource use offers a number of benefits:

■ It ties costs to consumption. Many IT organizations assess costs in an opaque fashion, making it difficult for user organizations to understand the basis for the assessed costs. Tying payment to transparent measures of resource consumption make it much easier to understand the cost rationale for IT services.

■ It ties costs to value. Many user organizations feel that the costs of their IT resources are disproportional to the value they receive from their applications. When costs are directly tied to resource consumption, the connection between application cost and the value received by running the application is much clearer.

■ It leads to better use of computational resources. Since the value associated with individual compute resources can be transparently examined, it is much easier to determine whether applications are cost-justified. Should an application consume more resources than the value generated by application operation, it is easy to shut down the application and stop wasting money on low-value compute activities. Of course, the lack of long-term commitment discussed in the previous section makes this application culling possible.

■ It improves the economic ecosystem efficiency overall. Service providers essentially pool services across their customer base leading to reduced stranded capacity. Also, successful service providers become experts at what they do and hence are able to deliver a service more efficiently at a lower cost than what a similar service would cost in house. It's a win-win situation where service providers make a profit while delivering a service at a lower cost than what it would cost to deliver it in house.

The Benefits of Cloud Computing

The RAD Lab's cloud computing characteristics imply several benefits for application developers and users:

■ The tradeoff between provisioning and budget discipline is no longer necessary. Because cloud environments offer, effectively, infinite resources on demand, application creators need no longer attempt to forecast future application load; instead, they can deploy at a resource level appropriate to initial demand, secure in the knowledge that increased application load can be easily met through additional resource allocation.

■ Cloud scalability fosters a new breed of applications. Applications that require massive amounts of compute resources are one type of system that space-constrained internal data centers struggle to support. Another type of application poorly suited to traditional data center environments are those that have very large variability in load; because of the difficulty of adding and subtracting compute resources in traditional environments, application creators typically had no opportunity to deploy high load-variability applications. In cloud environments, these kinds of applications—very large analytical or data mining systems are a common example—can easily be accommodated.

■ Cloud computing will foster new business models. This book has not yet been written. We are in the middle of a significant transformation in the industry, and we won't know what works and what does not until the dust settles. This situation should not preclude experimentation. Visionary organizations can make educated guesses, and due to the pay-as-you-go nature of the cloud, experimentation does not require large capital outlays. This approach will optimize the upside while minimizing the down side. Visionary organizations will likely realize a first mover advantage, leaving the laggards catching up.

■ Both users and IT organizations benefit from cloud computing. IT organizations can ensure that resources are consumed only by organizations willing to directly pay for their use; this provides an efficient rationing mechanism and obviates the need for IT to adjudicate among competing demands for IT resources. From the perspective of IT users, cloud computing provides transparency in IT costs; more importantly, it allows IT users to control the decision about resource consumption. Assuming the user organization is willing to pay, resources are available. This offers user organizations the opportunity to map their use of compute resources to their business needs in a fine-grained fashion—certainly the ideal of cost/benefit balance.

Implementation Challenges of Cloud Computing

The vision of cloud computing is clear: control of resource provisioning is shifted to the application group—the IT organization responsible for the application—away from the operations group—the IT organization responsible for overall resource provisioning. A different way of saying this is that the operations groups retains responsibility for ensuring overall capacity is sufficient for the total demand load of all applications, but individual application groups now have the responsibility (and right) to make individual provisioning decisions as they see fit.

Obviously, this is a vastly different approach to managing infrastructure—one that is revolutionary, carrying enormous benefits, but one that disrupts the traditional organization and processes of IT organizations. One very exciting aspect of cloud computing is that it focuses IT more on responding to application—also known as end user—needs, rather than internal IT needs. The phases of virtualization described as server consolidated and infrastructure automation focus primarily on improving IT operations efficiency—admirable, no doubt, but with little effect on application availability and efficiency. Remember, applications are the real point of IT: delivering functionality that improves business operations, reduces costs, and increases opportunities. An IT organization that increases its efficiency but fails to increase the usefulness of applications is failing at its raison d'être.

The primary challenge of cloud computing is how to move from today's IT operations-centric view of infrastructure to one that is application-centric. To accomplish this, several things are necessary.

Real-time Capacity Planning

Unlike older systems, in which total physical demand provisioning was a relatively relaxed effort with extended timeframes made necessary by the lengthy delivery cycles of vendors, cloud computing requires real-time capacity planning. Because application groups can "click a mouse button" to access more resources, it's crucial that IT operations ensure sufficient physical resources are available in a real-time fashion.

This need for real-time capacity planning will stress IT operations as it's never been stressed before. It will have little insight into total system demand, since total demand can vary according to individual application group decisions. It must commit to application group's demands never coming up "empty" when additional resources are requested.

A good metaphor for what IT operations must put into place is the "just-in-time" inventory systems common to automobile manufacturing today. Previous generations of auto manufacture relied on massive local inventories of parts to ensure production was never interrupted. The just-in-time revolution substituted accurate forecasting and advanced logistics to pare physical inventories and reduce costs. Real-time capacity planning for IT operations will impose the same conditions.

Orchestration

Orchestration is the term applied to a coordinated set of actions needed to provision a cloud-based application infrastructure. In the past, creating an application infrastructure required the involvement of several different groups: servers, network, storage, security, and perhaps even others. This imposed time delays and coordination challenges.

Orchestration moves all of the different manual processes into a single automated process that coordinates all individual resource provisioning. It is what brings to life the "click a mouse button and provision a system" vision of cloud computing. Simple. Fast. Easy.

As the saying goes, making it look easy is hard work. Orchestration is no different.

At the lowest level, orchestration depends upon a completely automated infrastructure that may be provisioned without needing any manual effort. So, in that respect, orchestration depends upon the functionality described in the previous section of this chapter. That automated infrastructure must be implemented throughout the entire portion of the data center in which cloud computing is to exist.

At the next level up, orchestration requires a client application through which to interact with the automated infrastructure and define resources to be provisioned. This is typically delivered as a Web page with a portal infrastructure behind it, interacting with the whatever management software drives the automated infrastructure. An approved user defines the desired system resources by filling out the Web page, selecting the configuration for the virtual machine needed by the application. The configuration includes information on the needed number of processors, amount of storage, any specific network requirements (for example, a particular VLAN the application needs to reside within), amount of memory to be available to the virtual machine. Particularly sophisticated orchestration systems can define and create multiple virtual machines as part of an application topology. The virtual machines would typically each be assigned a role: one might act as a database server, several might act as web servers, and one or more might act as middleware machines in which application logic would execute. In essence, the orchestration system embodies the knowledge that system administrators would apply in creating application resources. As might be imagined, the effort necessary to capture that knowledge and implement it as a set of automation rules is not trivial.

Chargeback

Chargeback accomplishes the task of assigning infrastructure costs to the application group that uses that infrastructure. Chargeback has a long and controversial history within IT. In mainframe settings, chargeback was common and direct. With the rise of distributed computing, it is much harder to assess and assign costs to any particular application, since multiple applications may share a machine. Moreover, it's difficult to assign more general costs like floor space and power, especially since those costs are often paid by a non-IT group. Virtualization has made chargeback somewhat easier, since in a virtualized world, applications tend to reside in a single virtual machine, which can simplify cost assignment.

Chargeback takes on increased urgency in a cloud computing environment. This is because the ease of requesting resources via the orchestration system is likely to drive up the overall demand for resources. In a financial climate in which IT operations groups are unlikely to receive increased budgets, increased demand will cause contention for resources, making it vital to implement a rationing mechanism. Chargeback provides that mechanism, since application groups can identify exactly how much the compute resources they've requested cost when running in a production mode. The importance of chargeback is highlighted by the fact that the UC Berkeley RAD Lab Report referenced earlier in the chapter identifies "pay-as-you-go" as one of three key characteristics of cloud computing.

Like orchestration, chargeback is not easy to implement. Tracking down all of the costs to be included in chargeback calculations is difficult, particularly given the fact that many of them fall into different budget areas. To mitigate this problem, a limited form of chargeback that merely assigns direct costs for an application's virtual machines, network, and storage may be used as a substitute for a complete chargeback system.

Overall, the challenges posed by implementing a cloud computing environment should not be underestimated. Both infrastructure and process change are needed, requiring financial investment as well as organizational restructuring. An IT organization's resources may dictate whether it takes on the effort and investment in order to implement an internal cloud; if it is reluctant or unable to make the necessary resources available, it is more likely to turn to an external provider for its cloud needs. If an external cloud provider is used, that does not mean that the items identified just above are no longer needed; it just means that another organization takes on the responsibility for implementing them.

Cloud Computing: The Future

Much of the attention paid to cloud computing has focused on its agile provisioning—the way it can speed up initial system provisioning from weeks (or months) to mere minutes. There is no doubt that it delivers on quick provisioning, thereby addressing a traditional pain point for application groups. This quick provisioning enables them to commence work on new applications rapidly, or to respond to changed business conditions nimbly—certainly a huge advantage in today's tumultuous business climate, and definitely an improvement upon typical provisioning conditions.

However, less attention has been paid to the innovation opportunities available through the "infinite scalability" cloud computing provides. Applications that heretofore would never have been considered due to budgetary restrictions, data center space restrictions, or inability to manage highly variable loads can now be accommodated in the "infinitely scalable" cloud. Examples of these kinds of "infinitely scalable" enabled applications include massive business intelligence analysis, intermittent application loads, and highly seasonal processing requirements. The current data deluge being experienced by most businesses, along with the growing trend of mobile and location-aware applications, means that more of these type of applications will be needed by most mainstream businesses. Cloud computing can help.

Summary

The role and capability of the data center has been transformed over the past two decades. It experienced rapid growth during the 1990s and the first few years of this century as business processes were migrated to automated software systems running on commodity hardware. The "one application, one server" practice that originally enabled business unit flexibility and enforced system partitioning eventually led to server proliferation and rapidly escalating costs.

Server consolidation, made possible by virtualization, reduced the overall number of servers, making the data center infrastructure much more efficient. Virtualization achieved rapid ROI by slashing power costs, trimming required floor space, and reducing hardware costs.

Despite the benefits of server consolidation, it left most of the manual system administration practices untouched. It also did little for the other device endpoints within the data center—the network switches and shared storage. The next stage of data center efficiency improvement focused on extending virtualization to all device endpoints as well as automating system provisioning and management—the administration of the infrastructure. This stage, which may be called "automated infrastructure," improves the operational efficiency of the data center, and extends the cost savings of server consolidation.

Notwithstanding the data center efficiency improvements, virtualization qua virtualization does little to address the most pressing strategic challenge facing most companies: an increasingly hectic business environment demanding faster responsiveness and improved agility. Even though the provisioning and administration functions of the "back office" data center are automated, the process for application groups obtaining resources continues to be a protracted, meeting-ridden affair.

Cloud computing is a logical extension of the technology of virtualization, integrated with application group self-provisioning, enormous scalability, and agile responsiveness borne of a no need to make long-term commitments for compute resources.

It must be noted that cloud computing builds upon the experience and technologies of the two previous phases. Cloud applications will continue running in data centers in commodity servers. The ownership patterns may be different because the service may be provided by an external provider, or the internal architecture of the services may also be different in the case of internal clouds, where there is a transformation away from a hard binding between physical servers and applications to a pooled, dynamic environment. Likewise, virtualization is not going away; it becomes a foundation technology to build the emerging cloud infrastructure. Hence our intent is to give these technologies equal air time in the book.

Cloud computing represents the next logical evolutionary step for the information technology industry. The acceptance of cloud technology is a reflection of the current state of available technology components and IT process maturity. Cloud computing promises to make the efficient data center agile enough to meet today's chaotic business environment. However, despite its obvious benefits, cloud computing imposes challenges as well—translating manual processes to automated ones is often difficult and always expensive. It remains to be seen which "flavor" of cloud computing—internal, external, public, private—becomes the widest used; there is no doubt at all that the conditions dictating cloud computing will engender its success.

Chapter 2

A Reference
Architecture
for Cloud Computing

*Contributed by Enrique Castro-Leon, Parviz Peiravi, Raghu Yeluri
and Jim Blakley*

It is undeniable that cloud computing activities have come to the forefront in the IT industry to the point that Gartner declares "the levels of hype around cloud computing in the IT industry are deafening, with every vendor expounding its cloud strategy and variations, such as private cloud computing and hybrid approaches, compounding the hype." As such, Gartner has added cloud computing to this year's Hype Cycle report[1] and placed the technology right at the peak of inflated expectations.

Making Sense of the Cloud Evolution

Michael Sheehan in his GoGrid blog[2] analyzed search trends in Google[†] Trends[3] as indicators technologies' mindshare in the industry. Interest in cloud computing seems to appear out of nowhere in 2007, and interest in the subject keeps increasing through the end of 2009 and seems to have reached a plateau

---

1   http://www.gartner.com/it/page.jsp?id=1124212

2   http://linux.sys-con.com/node/587717

3   http://www.google.com/trends?q=Cloud+Computing%2C+Grid+Computing%2C+virtualization

in 2010. The trending for keywords *cloud computing, grid computing,* and *virtualization* is shown in Figure 2.1. The graph suggest that as the industry participants become familiar with the subject and the volume of new entrants starts tapering down, the search volume peaks. The news reference volume lags and keeps increasing, for instance because it takes time for product vendors to bring new offerings into the marketplace to meet demand. New products result in press releases, which brings up the news reference volume.

Also worth noting is the trend of virtualization, one of the foundational technologies for cloud computing. Interest in virtualization increased through 2007 and reached a plateau in 2008. Likewise, the trend in terms of news reference volume has remained constant in the past two years.

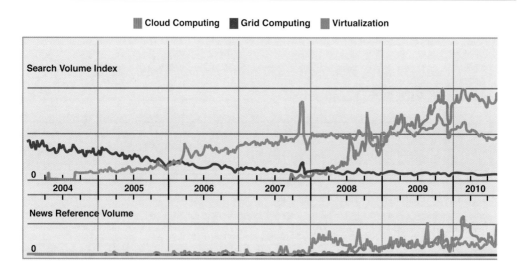

Figure 2.1   Google Trends Graph: References to Cloud Computing, Grid Computing and Virtualization

Given this information, is cloud computing at its peak of hype, about to fall short of expectations and bound to fall into the trough of disillusionment? According to Gartner, the goal of this exercise is to separate hype from reality and enable CIOs, CEOs, and technology strategists to make accurate business decisions regarding the adoption of a particular technology.

Cloud computing does not stand for a single technology in the sense that mesh networks, speech recognition, or wikis do. Rather, cloud computing represents the confluence of multiple technologies including grid computing, virtualization, and service orientation. Hence the Gartner Hype Cycle may not be an accurate model to be useful in predicting how the technology will evolve and will be adopted in the industry.

If the Gartner Hype Cycle theory is to apply to cloud computing, it cannot be in isolation. In addition to the three enabler technologies mentioned above, we need to add the Internet for making possible the notion of federated computing. From this perspective, what we may be witnessing is actually the Hype Cycle's Slope of Enlightenment. The search volume index for the Internet is shown in Figure 2.2.

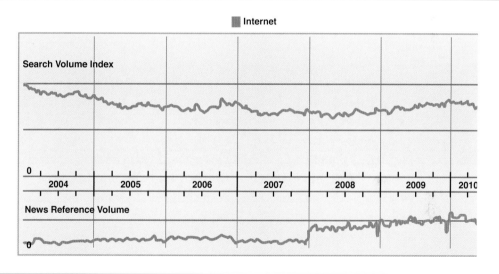

Figure 2.2   Google Trends Search Volume Index for the Internet.

The graph by itself does not look very interesting until we note that it is actually a picture of the Trough of Disillusionment: the time frame is actually too short to be meaningful. We can claim that the Peak of Inflated Expectations actually occurred in the years 1994 through 2001, that is, the period of the infamous Internet boom.

Historical Context for the Cloud Evolution

Beginning at the end of 2007 we see the convergence of grid, virtualization, and services into the cloud and the Internet infrastructure build-out beginning to pay off. Grid computing moves from niche applications, starting with scientific computing, to technical and engineering computing, to computational finance into the mainstream enterprise computing. Cloud computing would not be possible without the dark fiber laid out in the 1990s.

The technology trigger period is actually much longer than what the Gartner graph suggests. For a number of watershed technologies there is usually a two or three-decade incubation period before the technology explodes into the public consciousness.

This pattern took place with the radio industry from the 1901 Marconi experiments transmitting Morse code over radio to the first broadcasts in 1923. With the automotive industry the incubation period spans from the invention of the first self-propelled vehicles in the late nineteenth century to 1914 with Henry Ford's assembly line manufacturing and the formation of large scale supply chains. For the Internet the incubation period took place during the government Internet with the creation of ARPANET in 1969 and the trigger started with the commercialization of the Internet marked with the official dissolution of ARPANET in 1990.

The trigger point for a technology is reached when a use case is discovered that makes the technology self-sustaining. For the automobile it was the economies of scale that made the product affordable and Ford's decision to reinvest profits to increase manufacturing efficiencies and lower prices to spur demand. For the radio industry it was the adoption of the broadcast model supported by commercial advertising. Before that there was no industry to speak of. Radio was used in small scale as an expensive medium for point-to-point communication.

Consistent with the breadth of the technologies involved, the commercial development of the Internet developed along multiple directions during the speculative period in the 1990s. The Peak of Inflated Expectations saw experimentation of business models, with the vast majority proving to be unsustainable. The speculative wave eventually went bust shortly after 2000.

Hence we'd like to claim that the recent interest in cloud computing, taken in the context of prior developments on grid computing, the service paradigm, and virtualization and over the infrastructure provided by the Internet, is actually the slow climb into the Slope of Enlightenment. Experimentation will continue, and some attempts will still fail. However the general trend will be toward mainstreaming. In fact, one of the success metrics predicted for the grid was that the technology would become so common that no one would think about the grid anymore. This pattern is already taking place with federated computing and federated storage.

The Reference Architecture Model

Our organization has a strong interest in usage models revolving around technologies under development at Intel Corporation. These technologies revolve around computers and networking, foundational technologies for cloud computing. It is hard to tell at this juncture whether specific usage models today will still be around ten or even five years into the future. Longevity notwithstanding, our tactical goal is to do a mapping from usage model to an existence proof for building an application that uses Intel technology in its constituent parts.

On this note, a number of teams within Intel and fellow travelers in the industry have been conducting a number of exploration activities in cloud computing. Our main tool to present the results of these explorations to the industry is the *reference architecture*. The reference architecture model represents an attempt to synthesize this experience and provide templates for other industry participants to replicate the processes used and hopefully obtain similar results.

A reference architecture is essentially an instantiation of the scientific method in common use for the past five hundred years. Figure 2.3 summarizes the essential steps of the scientific method.

Under this method, we start with a number of questions, as general as "is cloud computing for real or a fad, and if it's the former, what strategies are appropriate to maximize the business return for the community?" Questions can be more specific, such as "what technologies would be appropriate to bring into this context?" or even "what should be an appropriate power management strategy?"

From these questions we built a number of hypotheses and carried out a number of experiments. To make the experiments fact based, the teams seek participation from cloud players in the industry: end users, service providers, cloud operators, or involved products or technologies widely deployed in cloud space.

The teams are forward looking, working with emerging technologies that have not had the benefit of a long historical record or wide deployment. The main instrument for carrying out these experiments is the *proof of concept* or PoC for short. A proof of concept brings together a set of emerging technologies, an organization interested in bringing that technology to market in the form of business solution and a potential end user for the solution. The proof of concept is set to validate a number of hypotheses. This exercise can't be a free-for-all because it is of necessity budget constrained. There is significant thinking behind the formulation of the hypotheses. The results need to be meaningful to the business questions that motivated the proof of concept in the first place.

The proof of concept is carried out and the team performs deep analyses on the results during and after the experiments. If the results are as expected, the experience is shared with the industry through various media, including conference papers, white papers, and press releases. Beyond reporting, the experience from proof of concept gets incorporated into future products and the business solutions involving these products.

Figure 2.3 shows a feedback loop when the experiments don't go as planned. Reality is more nuanced. Teams rarely wait until the end of the proof of concept to reconsider and start again. Doing so would be enormously expensive. Instead there is a continuous process of re-evaluation as the proof of concept takes its course. Emerging technologies being as they are, they bring surprises and discoveries as the proof of concept is carried out. Readjustments take place as normal operating procedure.

Beyond hypotheses, other artifacts of the scientific methods are models and scientific theories. A hypothesis is a limited statement linking cause and effect. We build models when knowledge is limited and hence hypotheses have limited validity. A scientific theory represents a group of hypotheses validated through repeated experimental tests.

Cloud computing as an emerging endeavor built by humans does not have the immutability of physical systems. The teams working in cloud computing have made no attempt to establish a scientific formalism beyond building models. The goal is to establish a degree of predictability that will allow participants build useful business plans and products that meet user needs over the product life cycle, and at the very least, allow other teams to independently replicate and verify the results. The degree of predictability we seek for cloud analysis is about the same as the models used for software engineering or investment models. Variances will occur, but at least they provide the basis for rational decision making.

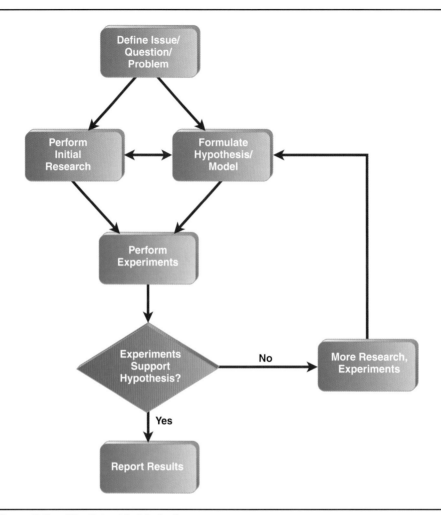

Figure 2.3 The Scientific Method.

The process followed is a combination of inductive and deductive approaches. The inductive process tries to derive some general conclusions from a series of experimental results. Conversely, the deductive approach uses general principles to instantiate them into particular cases.

A proof of concept provides answers to specific hypotheses. The usefulness of proofs of concepts would be limited if we could not take the results beyond the original context. Proof of concept participants use their experience to make generalized inferences about the proof of concept discoveries, based on a model. This model is captured in a *reference architecture*. Generating the reference architecture is the inductive portion of the process.

The usefulness of the reference architecture is that it becomes an abstraction for a class of applications and solutions for which the original proof of concept provided one data point. The reference architecture, once available, can be used as a template to generate solutions in related contexts, allowing the initial experience from the proof of concept to be used to build solutions to a broader class of problem beyond the initial proof of concept.

Cloud Reference Architecture Framework

Because of the complexity of cloud computing we have elected to analyze cloud architectures from two perspectives, one horizontal and the other vertical. The horizontal perspective tends to align with technology or an infrastructure, each of which can be multipurpose and server multiple application domains. The orthogonal, vertical view is to look at a specific application domain and how a specific cloud solution addresses the needs of the particular application. A *cloud reference architecture* provides the horizontal view, whereas a *cloud application reference architecture* delivers a vertical view.

An example of technology focus horizontal assessment activities are studies to determine the general applicability of a generation of server CPUs such as the Intel® Xeon® 5500 or 5600 series to cloud computing or the application of a technology featured in a CPU generation, such as Intel® Intelligent Node Manager for power management or the features associated with the Intel Trusted Execution Technology.

An example of an industry focus vertical activity would be the application of Intel Intelligent Node Manager to address needs of the telecommunications industry.

When we look at the level of detail for each discourse, we can also distinguish two coverage levels:

■ A *descriptive* treatment, the *architecture overview*

■ A *prescriptive* treatment, the *architecture guide*

Architecture overviews address the *what* question for a given horizontal or vertical plane. It is helpful to decision makers in defining strategies and in integrating technology roadmaps with business planning. These discussions may involve C-level executives, their staff, as well as their peers in the industry. In other words, a cloud overview helps frame the discovery and exploration phases of the technology, mapping technology to strategic business goals for the whole organization.

A cloud overview covers aspects of business architecture starting with the status quo and explores changes brought by the adoption of cloud computing technologies. Actual planning activities depend on the nature of the organization involved.

- Product manufacturers and vendors and software vendors will want to use a cloud overview to explore systemic changes in the industry and optimize product strategies to maximize revenue in view of these changes for a particular organization.

- IT organizations and service providers will be interested in investigating how cloud computing will change their cost and sourcing strategies.

- Government and public services organizations might be interested in optimizing procurement processes in view of anticipated changes in the industry brought by cloud computing.

On the other hand, architecture guides, being prescriptive in nature, are compiled to address the *how* question, such as, for example, how a specific technology gets instantiated into specific data center infrastructure strategies and policies.

An architect can take a guide, incorporate the overview document to provide guidance, and coordinate with stakeholder engineering teams to build an infrastructure aligned with the strategic goals of the organization, or take the strategic guidance for a specific application and again work with engineering and planning teams to build a cloud-based application to address the needs of the organization for the particular vertical segment.

A particular cloud reference architecture may take on a number of usage classes of interest to the organization. Specific topics may include areas where the organization has had traditional strengths with the goal of exploring how these core areas might change with the adoption of cloud technology. Another cloud application reference architecture may be appropriate to explore new areas and opportunities opened by cloud computing on behalf of the subject organization.

Table 2.1   Taxonomy for Enterprise Cloud Reference Architecture

		Cloud Reference Architecture	Cloud Application Reference Architecture
Overview	**Audience**	CIO, CTO, Marketing, Management	
	Purpose	Thought leadership, education	Technology and platform positioning
	Example	A set of our top enterprise IT customers virtual private cloud reference architecture (Chapter 3)	Cloud storage power management reference architecture (Chapter 7)
Guide	**Audience**	Engineering, architecture	
	Purpose	Platform and technology diffusion	Technology diffusion
	Example	Intel Cloud Builder Reference Architecture for Enomaly, Univa, and Canonical/ Eucalyptus (Chapter 15)	Intel Intelligent Power Node Manager recipes (Chapter 22)

Overview discussions take place between CTOs, CIOs, IT architects and IT managers with a target to explore a specific usage model or class of use cases. The focus of an overview is technology and technology building blocks. The building blocks are represented by generic technology capabilities, not necessarily instantiated into specific products.

Using a self-referential approach, we have structured this chapter to reflect the Cloud Reference Architecture Framework. At this point we have completed describing the *overview* aspects of the cloud solution development methodology in use at Intel. In the remainder of the chapter we'll drill down to the *guide* level and offer a prescription on how to carry out a customer proof of concept engagement.

To illustrate the abstract concepts in this chapter[4], we have also included examples for each of the four cases, as listed in Table 2.1: Intel invited CTOs and CIOs from a number of large corporations and government organizations to provide their perspective on the evolution of cloud computing. A synthesis of the evolution of virtual private clouds is presented in Chapter 3. Chapter 15 follows through with a number of aspects instantiated by leading independent software vendors. In Chapter 7 we discuss how Intel platform

---

4   We are using a self-referential approach in the structure of this chapter where the structure of the description mimics the structure of the subject. For a deeper treatment, with a discussion on the expressivity and the pitfalls of this approach, the book by Douglas R. Hofstadter, *Godel, Escher, Bach: An Eternal Golden Braid* (New York: Basic Books, 1999) presents a fascinating discussion on the subject.

power management technology gets mapped into the needs of cloud-based storage in the context of energy efficiency driving cloud activities. Finally, Chapter 22 describes how Intel® Intelligent Power Node Manager and Intel® Data Center Manager, specific technology instances aimed at server platform power management, get integrated in a telecommunications application.

Process for Carrying Out Proofs of Concept

Up to the point where a technology-based product is about to ship there has been an intense collaboration between platform engineering development teams and business planning teams to ensure alignment between platform features industry trends and corporate end user requirements.

The collaboration continues after the product ships with the emphasis of the activities shifting from completing the development to meet the launch date to finding innovative usages for the technology of high value to users deploying it. The new platform capabilities enable new usages that are unlikely in current industry practice. For this reason the proof of concept is the main instrument for early adoption. It is essentially the implementation of a single idea in a controlled environment that yields a first proof point or existential validation of the initial idea. For instance, the proof of concept with Telefónica started with the conjecture that using Intel Intelligent Node Manager in addition to placing servers in a low energy state such as S5 would expose new value vectors for Intel Intelligent Node Manager, namely by allowing customers to realize energy savings. The proof of concept yielded a concrete proof point: when the two technologies are applied to Telefónica's rate profile application for premium mobile content they can reduce their daily electricity consumption by 27 percent using a pool of servers of size 2.

The process we use for architecting proofs of concept is not much different from the scientific method, where we formulate a conjecture or hypothesis, asserting the business value of specific emerging technologies in the context of a number of use cases, and then we design and carry out a number of experiments with the goal of proving the hypothesis. Since the output of the proof of concept is a series of assertions about business value, if the results of the proof of concept are successful, the results can be easily mapped to build a business strategy and associated marketing campaign without a big semantic discontinuity.

The work products for end user platform integration include

■ Joint press statements with the end user

■ White papers documenting the work done

■ Technical journal papers documenting discoveries where appropriate

■ The supporting test reports

■ Strategy documents mapping technology to business value

■ Internal demonstrators and integration reports to engineering teams

■ Recommendations to engineering teams to refine next generation products

■ Building demos including complete end-to-end applications and showing them at trade events

There is really no archetypal proof of concept process; proofs of concept come in all sizes and each is unique to some extent. It is useful to segment a proof of concept engagement into three major stages, namely engagement planning, execution, and closure. A proof of concept can be internal to Intel, carried at an Intel facility. When technical and business circumstances allow it, proofs of concept are carried out jointly with external participants. The application and domain expertise of the participants brings additional checks and balances that make the results more useful and credible to eventual stakeholders benefiting from the results.

For cloud-related proofs of concept, the state of the art is not yet at a stage where we bring in a new application domain and, through the application of the current body of knowledge, map out a cloud-based solution to address pain points in the target domain. In fact, at the current state, and possibly for the next two or three years, the industry will be building this body of knowledge.

If we look at cloud computing as an applied engineering discipline, the approach that yields the best business outcomes and is also fast is the inductive process, where we build early experience in as many application domains as possible by doing, namely, by carrying out proofs of concept.

Once we have built a body of experience across a number of application domains and documented results through a number of cloud application reference architecture reports, it will be possible to perform a synthesis of the knowledge gained and derive some general principles to be embodied in a set of standard cloud practices.

This approach is well aligned with the goals of standardization and interoperability across multiple vendor offerings that are central to cloud computing technology.

Proof of Concept Engagement Planning

Proof of concept planning starts with an exploration discussion followed by a series of technical disclosures. To make this discussion more concrete, let's assume that the proof of concept centers on the application of advanced server platform power management. For this case, the proof of concept participant and Intel hold an initial conversation about the capabilities brought up by power management and complementary technologies. The customer talks about their current, as-is situation.

The technology disclosures start with a power management demonstration including power management aggregation using Intel® Data Center Manager. The workload is usually a synthetic workload, MaxPower or SPECpower for simplicity.

After a familiarization with the capabilities facilitated by platform power management, the joint team works to single out a power-related pain point amenable to a solution through the application of Intel power management technology, possibly even involving the application that exemplifies the pain point.

A technology mapping to solution follows: the team identifies current that exhibit the pain points and the future usage scenarios where the pain points have been addressed. Some simplification may be needed at this point where the team builds the use cases specific to the proof of concept.

The next step is to build the solution architecture: devising an approach to power-enable the application. Implicit in the use cases to be implemented is a hypothesis or series of hypotheses to be proved by carrying the experiments in the proof of concept. Metrics and key performance indicators (KPIs) need to be singled out and documented so the team can determine whether the experiments to be carried out are successful.

The steps above now allow defining the work products that will come out of the proof of concept and a rough inventory of the equipment to be used. The number of platforms involved in a proof of concept usually ranges between one and four servers.

A go or no go decision can be taken at any time during planning, the earlier the better for the purposes of resource planning.

Proof of Concept Engagement Execution

If the parties involved commit to go ahead with the engagement, detailed project planning follows.

The main project execution activities comprise

- *Building the project execution plan.* For simplicity, projects are usually structured in a number of phases.

- *Building the project schedule.* The team discusses the milestones in the execution plan and starts attaching dates to each one of the phases. The committed schedule becomes Plan of Record (POR).

- *Figuring resource planning.* With milestones and dates in place is now possible to compute the intensity at which resources will be applied in terms of engineering, architecture, and planning headcount. Date revisions are possible if the team determines that the project is short in certain resources. To the extent possible, the bulk of application-specific activities need to be carried out at the customer premises by their engineers.

- *Planning the engineering activities.* Engineering activities include the ordering or allocation of the equipment, equipment provisioning, configuration and preparation at an Intel lab, shipping the equipment, carrying the technical activities proper and capturing test reports.

- *Project management.* To ensure a consistent pace in execution progress it is crucial to have regular project development team (PDT) meetings with participation from Intel and customer stakeholders. From past experience a beat rate of one to two weeks between meetings represents the best compromise between time spent and results. One or more site visits may be necessary.

Proof of Concept Engagement Closure

Closure activities encompass activities that follow the technical execution of the project. Activities include

■ Gathering test reports to compile the proof of concept final report. The report becomes a content repository from which to build other pieces of content such as conference and journal papers and press articles.

■ Securing marketing releases from the customer

■ Building a technical communications plan

Post-Engagement Activities

These activities are not part of the proof of concept proper. Specific post-engagement activities depend on the initial goals of the project. If the initial goal was to demonstrate the technology in an end-to-end solution context, these activities would include marketing communications, webinars, conference and journal papers or even a reference architecture report, essentially a template built from generalizing the proof of concept results that would allow architects and engineers to replicate the solution in similar contexts. Internally, the experience of the proof of concept is shared with product groups as needed for the purposes of continuous improvement.

Summary

Many industry leaders and the authors as well believe that cloud computing as a trend represents a fundamental shift in the industry. One indicator for this trend is the Google Trends data. Far from being a late surging phenomenon, we believe cloud computing is the conclusion of a number of historic transformations that started in the early 1990s with grid computing followed by the infrastructure build-out during the Internet boom. The subsequent Internet crash and the subprime market crisis that started in 2008 actually brought opportunities for the adoption of cloud computing by the industry.

While the need for IT capabilities did not really go away, IT organizations faced a budgetary crunch. At the same time the visibility into the future was nonexistent, muddled by potential market discontinuities. When long term infrastructure was hard to justify, the pay-as-you-go instant deployment features of clouds seemed a perfect match to the difficult business conditions.

The challenge of infrastructure investment does not go away; it just gets deferred to other players, namely, IaaS, PaaS and SaaS providers. In principle the arrangement is potentially more efficient for the industry as a whole presumably because service providers can spread risks across a large pool of service customer versus a single IT organization owning a large infrastructure that might not get use. Also, because of the division of labor, service providers can build expertise and hence economic efficiency in ways that a single IT organization cannot.

Likewise, for infrastructure technology providers it is not immediately obvious how existing technology can be applied to this brave new environment, much less to figure out which capabilities might be needed in the future. We suggest that an inductive approach can yield the fastest approach: it is basically learning by doing and documenting each experience as a template to be applied in similar circumstances. The format for each template is the reference architecture. Our expectation is that a portfolio of templates set up horizontally across broad use technology and vertically across application domains will get the process of mapping technology capabilities to cloud computing needs very quickly.

The proof of concept is the tool of choice to carry out the learning by doing part described above. We conclude the chapter with a description of the proof of concept methodology in use by a number of technical and business teams within Intel in combination with participating industry leaders.

Chapter 3

A Reference Architecture for Enterprise Virtual Private Clouds

Contributors: Raghu Yeluri, Parviz Peiravi, Enrique Castro-Leon, and Ralph Biesemeyer

Intel is strategically committed to bring up the technology to build the underpinnings of the cloud, from data centers to client devices that function as delivery points for cloud-based applications. This infrastructure can't be built in a vacuum. As a grounding exercise, Intel convened a board of advisors represented by CTOs and CIOs from Fortune 500 companies to formulate a set of requirements for what they deemed a near-term cloud deployment, for cloud usages applicable to large enterprise deployments not necessarily in effect today, but yet attainable with technologies, architectural elements, and services currently available in the industry. A benefit of this exercise is the identification of integration gaps and technologies and processes amenable to industry standardization to facilitate interoperability and accelerate and lower the cost of future deployments.

We synthesize these cloud services, technologies, and processes into a prescriptive *solution reference architecture*, or SRA as described in Chapter 2.

Work in progress encompasses translating these architectural frameworks into specific proofs of concept to test out specific hypotheses. Proofs of concepts lead to small scale production pilots, possibly at some of the participating companies' data centers, to eventually incorporate these practices into production environments.

The solution reference architecture herein described focuses on one particular usage model for enterprise clouds known as *cloud bursting*.

The general premise for cloud bursting is to use the cloud to act as an overflow resource when the in-house infrastructure becomes overloaded. Doing so saves an IT operator from provisioning the infrastructure for peak usage with the resulting poor utilization. We cover two variants of cloud bursting:

- Dynamic or manual scaling of applications.
- Live migration of workloads between the enterprise infrastructure and the remote cloud.

Key architectural considerations for successful design and implementation of cloud bursting include:

- Security and isolation
- Performance of the WAN and the Internet in the presence of VPN and encryption
- Aspects of interoperability, automation, and programmability of the management frameworks
- Data locality and regulatory compliance

Significant detail work will be needed to instantiate the reference architecture into a specific application domain. This task is beyond the scope of this exercise.

Cloud Computing Technology

Let's recap some cloud concepts for the purposes of this chapter. It is not difficult to identify a number of present trends in information technology:

- Evolution toward a more distributed computing environment
- Increasing interest for the utility model (elastic resources and pay-as-you-go charging)
- High bandwidth data links
- Falling cost of storage devices
- Proliferation of handheld devices supporting Web applications
- Ever increasing adoption of Web 2.0 based technology with SaaS based applications along with virtualization

Cloud computing is a popular topic today, as a phenomenon setting the tone and direction for the future of enterprise computing. Cloud computing refers to the delivery of software and other technology services over the Internet by a service provider, as illustrated in Figure 3.1. The most powerful incentive driving the adoption of cloud computing is the reduction of capital expenditures and operational costs along with fast time to market and enhanced flexibility, scalability, and high availability.

Essential characteristics of cloud environment include:

- On-demand and self-service

- Ubiquitous network access

- Location independent and dynamic resource pooling

- Rapid scalability and elasticity

- SLA driven measured service

- Choice and agility

Deployment includes private internal clouds, public external clouds, and hybrid cloud models.

The definitions of cloud computing, including private and public clouds, infrastructure as a service (IaaS), and platform as a service (PaaS), are taken from work by the National Institute of Standards and Technology[1]. NIST defines four cloud deployment models:

- Public clouds. A cloud infrastructure made available to the general public or a large industry group.

- Private clouds. A cloud infrastructure operated solely for an organization.

- Community clouds. A cloud infrastructure shared by several organizations.

- Hybrid clouds. A cloud infrastructure that combines two or more clouds.

---

1   Peter Mell and Tim Grance, "The NIST Definition of Cloud Computing," http://csrc.nist.gov/groups/SNS/cloud-computing/

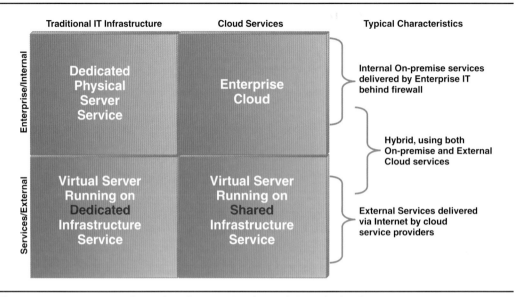

Figure 3.1   Service Relationships between Traditional IT and Cloud Services

Service delivery models include software as a service, platform as a service and infrastructure as a service (IaaS). While not all PaaS and SaaS implementations create an explicit IaaS layer, for the purpose of this SRA, we are assuming that an IaaS implementation is the base on which all additional services are created.

For the purposes of this reference architecture, we'll emphasize aspects of IaaS, with some PaaS details. The fundamental IaaS capability made available to cloud consumers is a cloud service. Examples of services are computing systems, storage capacity, and networks that meet specified security and performance constraints. Examples of consumers of cloud services are enterprise datacenters, small businesses, and other clouds. Refer to National Institute of Standards and Technology (NIST-1), for detailed definitions for these delivery models.

The scope for the reference architecture described in this document covers what we call enterprise virtual private clouds or EVPCs. EVPCs cover internal, on-premise services delivered by enterprise IT behind the firewall as described below.

Enterprise Virtual Private Clouds

Enterprise virtual private clouds (EVPCs) constitute a variation of the private cloud service deployment model where the cloud resources inside the enterprise and the cloud resources in the service provider cloud are encapsulated to appear as a single homogenous computing environment, thereby bridging the ability to securely utilize remote resources as part of a seamless global compute infrastructure.

The resources at the service provider would be part of the same management, security, and trust domain of the enterprise. All the procedures and policies governing security, compliance, and manageability that are well honed and optimized for the enterprise can now be applied to the quarantined virtual infrastructure that has been assigned for enterprise use at the service provider. Figure 3.2 shows the taxonomy of the cloud service delivery models and where EVPCs fit.

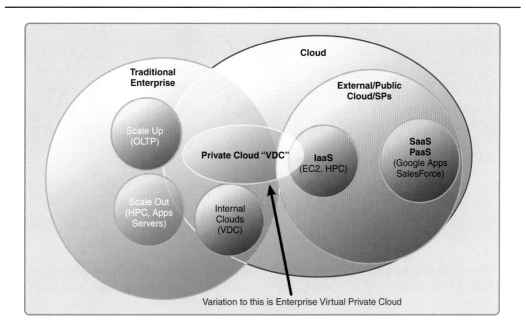

Figure 3.2   Cloud Deployment Model Taxonomy

A Cloud Computing Usage Model

For clarity of exposition, we have mapped the reference architecture to four distinct use cases over three application types and two software technology frameworks as captured in Tables 3.1, 3.2, and 3.3.

We'll initially describe four use cases as part of the EVPC reference architecture in three application types.

The first two of the four use cases include WAN-based clouds and cloud bursting, applicable to legacy and enterprise applications, including Web 2.0 applications.

The last use case refers to high performance computing (HPC) applications over corporate-owned services and external services, respectively. These use cases are direct descendants of grid computing during the 1990s, and are not covered in this chapter for brevity.

Each of the use cases can be implemented with open source software or commercial software. Open source software may be an attractive alternative in cases where licensing terms may be onerous, for instance a license owner insisting on long-term license terms that do not match the bursty usage models typical of clouds, or IT's desire to host a cloud service internally in cases where the only alternative is the externally hosted version of the service.

Table 3.1   Enterprise Virtual Private Cloud Use Cases

Use Case	Description
Load balancing between virtual data centers over WAN	Elastic Load balancing applications/workloads between virtual data centers within a WAN-based enterprise cloud. This would be between two virtual data centers in two different physical enterprise virtual data centers.
Enterprise cloud bursting	Elastic load balancing/bursting applications between enterprise cloud and cloud service provider over the Internet.
HPC load balancing over WAN, intra-company	Elastic load balancing HPC application within a LAN and WAN-based enterprise cloud. This would be between two virtual data centers in two different physical enterprise virtual data centers.
HPC bursting over WAN, inter-company	Elastic load balancing/bursting HPC application between enterprise cloud and cloud service provider over the Internet/WAN.

Table 3.2   Enterprise Virtual Private Cloud Application Types

Application Types	Examples
Enterprise and Web 2.0 applications	Standard three-tier applications and social networking or collaboration applications
High performance computing	Drug discovery, seismic analysis, crash simulations, computational fluid dynamics (CFD), EDA, molecular dynamics simulations, ray-tracing for rendering, Monte Carlo simulations, and so on
Legacy	Custom/In house developed, standalone applications

Table 3.3   Software Technology Frameworks

Framework	Representative example
Open source software	Eucalyptus[†] and Xen[†]
Commercial software	VMware[†]

Essential Architecture for EVPC Deployments

EVPC deployments supporting the usages described above require some basic elements, illustrated in Figure 3.3: a virtualized data center, one or more remote clouds, some means of connectivity, and devices used to access applications.

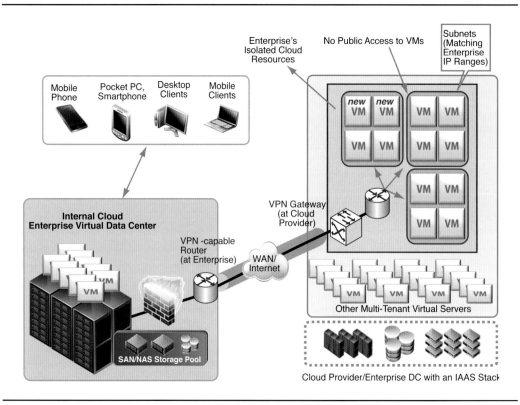

Figure 3.3   Essential Architecture for Enterprise Virtual Private Clouds

Let's look at how these diverse elements relate to each other.

■ The lower left side of Figure 3.3 is the representation of the enterprise virtual data center, which is assumed to be a virtualized data center. The top right is a representation of a remote cloud—either a different data center in the enterprise, or multi-tenant cloud resources at a cloud service provider, that is, a public cloud.

■ The two data centers are connected via an enterprise WAN in the case of two different internal clouds or the Internet (when the remote cloud is at a cloud service provider. For secure access, a VPN connection is enabled between the endpoints, either IPSec or SSL-based. Depending on the specific use case, a Layer 3 or a Layer 2 VPN might be utilized.

- The service provider would provide logically isolated, but not necessarily dedicated resources for the enterprise tenant. This means that the enterprise tenants' virtual machines and workloads might coexist with other tenant virtual machines and workloads on the same physical resources. The isolation is typically network isolation to ensure that the tenants' network traffic flows are secure and isolated from each other. Physical isolation is enabled by the hypervisor via the virtual machine sandbox. Storage is partitioned to support for multi-tenancy. The network isolation model is not consistent across the various cloud service providers: Providers like Savvis, OpsCloud, AT&T, provide VLANs for each enterprise tenant (4-5 VLANs per enterprise). However, providers like Amazon offer a proprietary Layer 2 isolation.

- Typically, the external cloud resources are considered as a logical extension to the enterprise resources, and thus adhering to the management, security and trust models and policies of the enterprise. There is no specific external or public access to the virtual machines and workloads in the overflow capacity, and public access is through the existing enterprise external points. This way the enterprise security, firewall, IDS/IPS controls and monitoring can be enforced on the overflow capacity traffic as well. In this model the cloud is used essentially as a back office extension.

- All traffic over the WAN or Internet with VPN is encrypted for security. The latency of the WAN or Internet and the additional latency due to encryption and decryption may not be acceptable to certain workloads and hence a performance assessment may be necessary to determine suitability.

Architectural Considerations for Enterprise Virtual Private Clouds

We will do a quick introduction of the concepts and elaborate in subsequent sections.

- *Security and isolation.* In the end-to-end view of this deployment model this is extremely critical. Enterprises would be hesitant in trusting a third party service provider to host the applications (or components of applications), and accessing the enterprise data either by reaching into the enterprise, or maintaining a cache/hot dataset at the service provider. Additionally, a service provider needs to provide sufficient proof that the services provided meet the compliance and audit requirements of the enterprise. Security in transit, at rest, and also access control needs to be addressed thoroughly to allay customer concerns and facilitate the migration and use of the overflow capacity. Bilateral trust between two cloud data centers would be a requirement for this to be embraced by enterprises. Unfortunately, the applicable technologies and standards are still in their infancy.

■ *Network performance and data architecture.* Network latency and bandwidth are big concerns when applications "burst" into the overflow capacity. The connectivity between the clouds will inevitably look like a horizontal hourglass. Even with the best WAN networks and WAN optimization and acceleration, the throughput and latency can become a real concern. Also, the connectivity between the data centers will almost always have a VPN connection with encryption, which adds to the latency. Optimized data architecture involving data cache in the overflow capacity, replication of the shadow databases in overflow capacity, and so on are architectural patterns that can be considered to address these partly. In cases where huge data sets (of a terabyte or more) are required along with the compute components at the service provider, it is not cost effective to move it electronically, and the current practice of physically shipping data on removable media still makes the most sense. This usage model works best for applications that work with smaller data sets, or for applications that are not overly latency sensitive (latency less than 10–15 milliseconds would be unrealistic for this model currently).

■ *Management and federation.* Seamless management, resource allocation/optimization, and lifecycle management between an enterprise virtual data center and the overflow capacity in the cloud remote data center is a requirement for enterprises to leverage EVPCs. Interoperability of the cloud platforms and programmability of these platforms determines the extent to which enterprises can utilize the same management platform to manage both resources. IaaS services are defined, developed, published, provisioned, and managed by what are called cloud application programming interfaces (APIs).

Numerous proprietary and open APIs have been proposed to provide management, security, and interoperability among IaaS services, including Amazon.com Inc.'s Elastic Compute Cloud API, VMware Inc.'s DMTF-submitted vCloud[†] API, Sun Microsystems' Open Cloud API, Rackspace US Inc.'s API, and GoGrid Cloud Hosting's API. Key to the adoption of EVPCs however, is being able to move quickly and easily among different cloud service providers, without a vendor lock-in and this means standardization of these APIs.

■ *Reliability.* For the bursting of production applications into the overflow capacity, one legitimate concern for enterprises would be the reliability of mechanisms to instantiate the applications in the overflow capacity from scratch when needed. The question is, will the application component instances start correctly? In order to mitigate this risk, enterprises would have a small number of these application components already instantiated in the overflow capacity. This way enterprises can constantly assess the quality of service coming from the overflow capacity and ensure that the instances are patched and configured correctly at all times. This design decision is very critical consideration in the overall ROI calculations of bursting into the cloud.

■ *Data locality and compliance.* Lack of transparency from cloud providers on the exact physical location of their data represents a significant concern for enterprises contemplating the use of external clouds. There are country and regional constraints on how far and where the data can or cannot migrate. Depending on the type and kind of data processed by the cloud application, there might be legal restrictions on the location of the physical server where the data is stored. What is really lacking is a simple API-based mechanism with the cloud platforms to query the precise location of the tenant data. Migration of workload, even if the associated data doesn't move, to a public cloud, would increase the complexity associated with meeting legal and regulatory requirements for sensitive information. How can an enterprise be certain that the VMs that were instantiated in the overflow capacity at the service provider have been shut down and the ephemeral storage has been cleaned out correctly?

Cloud Service Provider IaaS Stack Overview

A solution stack perspective of the spatial model described in the previous section provides a different and useful point of view. This is a solution stack view from a service provider perspective, and it is different from an enterprise solution stack. Enterprise virtual data centers interface with this solution stack to use the IaaS services made available to them by the service provider via a service catalog.

There are four distinct actors for the service developer IaaS stack. These actors interface with the stack and platform via the interfaces and tools represented in the top section of Figure 3.4.

1. *Service consumer.* For this reference architecture, this would be an enterprise needing the various IaaS resources for enterprise use.

2. *Service provider.* This would be the provider of the "remote cloud" (service provider).

3. *Cloud service developer.* This would be a developer at the service provider who would create the service offerings provided to enterprise customers. These services would include the standard offerings provided through the self service portal and custom offerings developed for specific enterprises when the standard offerings can't meet the requirements of that enterprise. (The services the service developer builds are fundamental IaaS services like "4 vCPU compute server with 40 GB of memory." These are then published to the service catalog).

4. *Service provider administrator.* This would be a system administrator at the service provider. This administrator might have a portal interface to monitor and manage the infrastructure.

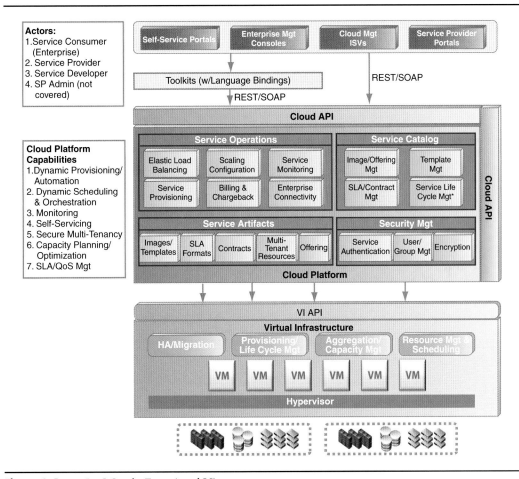

Figure 3.4 IaaS Stack, Functional View.

The virtual infrastructure layer in Figure 3.4 hosts the virtual machines and the physical mapping to the infrastructure resources. It is owned by the service provider and managed by the service provider administrator. The service developer and the service consumer have no awareness, knowledge or visibility of the virtual infrastructure layer. The service provider services are instantiated as one or more virtual machines at this layer. This layer has the logic for resource allocation, management, scheduling, resource pooling, capacity management, and so on. VMware vSphere[†] and vCenter[†], Xen and Xen Center[†], Microsoft Hyper-V are examples of the virtual infrastructure layer described here.

The cloud platform layer in Figure 3.4 is owned by the service provider and managed by the service provider administrator. The service developer and service consumer are aware of the cloud platform via interactions through the cloud API. The cloud platform provides a higher level abstraction and gives a streamlined virtual view of the infrastructure resources, abstracted away from the underlying physical resources without physical resource pools, servers, storage LUNs, and so on. The main cloud infrastructure management products offer similar core features:

■ Dynamic provisioning and automation, including on-the-fly creation and provisioning of new objects and the destruction of no longer needed objects, such as servers, storage, or applications.

■ Dynamic scheduling and orchestration

■ Monitoring

■ Self servicing

■ Secure multi-tenancy

■ Capacity planning and optimization

■ SLA/QoS management

■ Support different cloud types

These capabilities are very much standard across various cloud platform offerings (VMware vCloud, Canonical/Eucalyptus, Enomaly† and so on.) Differentiation takes place in the richness of implementation, and the support of interoperability and programmability and the cloud APIs. In particular, the selection of cloud APIs is a critical choice in the implementation of cloud services as it determines which cloud service providers will be able to host a given cloud service. IaaS services are defined, developed, published, provisioned, and managed by these cloud APIs.

Having a programmable interface to the IaaS infrastructure means an ability to write applications such as Web servers and application servers using this interface to manage the use of the cloud. Figure 3.5 shows the drilldown of the functional abstractions for the cloud APIs. These are well aligned with the DMTF cloud standards incubator work[2].

---

2   Please refer to DMTF clouds standards work at www.dmtf.org

Underlying these cloud APIs are the cloud resource models. Agreement on these abstractions and the underlying resource models is the first step towards standardization of the interfaces. These functional interfaces accept and respond to messages on any protocol like HTTP, REST, SOAP, and so forth. They fall into four categories:

1. *Service Operations.* Example interfaces: load balancing, scaling configuration, billing and chargeback, monitoring, service provisioning, enterprise connectivity.

2. *Service Catalog.* Image management, template and contract management, lifecycle management.

3. *Service Artifacts.* Encompasses data structures passed through the functional interfaces.

4. *Security Management.* Encompass functions for defining and managing security, including user/role management.

The DMTF Incubator Task Force is hard at work fleshing out the data models and the specific use cases, and interaction models for each of these categories and their respective interfaces.

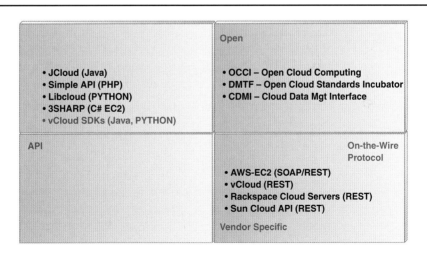

Figure 3.5 IaaS Mgt Interface APIs

Figure 3.5 gives a snapshot view of the developments with the IaaS cloud APIs. Many cloud providers have licensed their specific APIs freely allowing anyone to implement a similar cloud infrastructure. Despite the availability of open cloud APIs, cloud community members have been slow to uniformly adopt any single vendor interface. The Open Source community has attempted responses, but this has done little to stem the tide of API proliferation. In fact, Open Source projects have increased the tally of interfaces to navigate in a torrent of vendor specific APIs.

What is needed instead is a vendor neutral, standard cloud API for cloud computing that all vendors can implement with minimal risk and assured stability. This will allow customers to move their application stacks from one cloud service provider to another easily and at minimal cost based on changing business needs.

In Figure 3.5, the x-axis displays "on-the-wire" protocols to the right, and full APIs with language bindings for service developers to use on the left.

Most of the pioneering cloud service providers have provided their own vendor-specific APIs for their cloud platforms initially, close to the "on-the-wire" protocols such as REST and SOAP. Each of these cloud operating environments has submitted their APIs for standardization to DMTF, OCCI and others standards organizations. Specific instances are VMware submitting their vCloud API to DMTF, Fujitsu submitting their cloud API also to DMTF for standards consideration. In order to get the mindshare of the developers, all these cloud service providers offer various language bindings. Examples: 3 SHARP for Amazon for C# developers, Java[†] and Python[†] vCloud SDKs from VMware, and most of them are committing the bindings into Open Source.

The big open question with these language bindings is whether they are fully functional, and if developers can interface completely with these bindings, versus having to drill down to the lower level API based on REST/SOAP.

In the next few sections we will cover clouds for enterprise and Web 2.0 applications and support for legacy applications.

Cloud Computing for Enterprise and Web2.0 Applications

The main usage model we'll explore for supporting these applications will be through the practice called cloud bursting. This section begins with a description of cloud bursting, and the problems it addresses, followed by a "walk-the-flow" of the use case with a specific workload and a solution stack, namely VMware's vCloud. A short enumeration of the vCloud solution stack components is followed by a description of a reference architecture view for instantiating the cloud bursting use cases taking advantage of the vCloud solution stack. The section ends with an exhaustive look at the issues, challenges and gaps in deploying cloud bursting in the enterprise.

In order to illustrate the components of the stack and the interactions between the enterprise virtual data center and the service provider cloud, we use Microsoft Exchange[†] as the enterprise workload. It may not be the ideal workload for cloud bursting, but because it is widely used and understood application, it is used in the reference architecture to explore the cloud bursting life cycle, and also illustrate the solution stack interactions.

About Cloud Bursting

Cloud bursting refers to the notion of either dynamically or manually deploying or migrating entire application components, or parts of application (packaged as virtual machines), that normally run on internal organizational compute resources, to another (internal or external) cloud to address a spike in demand, for business continuity or for capacity optimization.

The general premise of cloud bursting is to allow the cloud to act as over-flow resources for the following situations

- An enterprise's infrastructure becomes overloaded, for instance by demand spikes.

- Resource arbitrage: when it becomes cheaper for some of the applications to be executing on the overflow capacity.

- For the purposes of disaster recovery and failure mitigation.

Cloud bursting must be deployed in an active failover model where the overflow capacity has few instantiations of applications or components already executing on the service provider side, and when the overflow capacity is needed, new instantiations can be brought up reliably, or instantiations in the overflow capacity can service the requests with a 100-percent guarantee.

Ultimately, the opportunity is that we can now scale not just based on basic aspects such as load, but based on real world metrics such as the quality of experience and service (QoS).

Cloud bursting aligns the traditional safe enterprise computing model with cloud computing; in essence, bursting into the cloud when necessary or using the cloud when additional compute resources are required temporarily.

Cloud bursting addresses three basic needs for an enterprise virtual data center.

1. Companies infrequently need additional capacity to handle demand spikes, which typically manifest as overload; investing internally to handle peak loads leaves unused capacity and stranded investment.

2. Companies are hesitant to move all infrastructures to a cloud computing provider due to security and stability concerns. Cloud bursting alleviates some of inhibitions towards cloud by providing a hybrid model for enterprises. Also, the cloud service provider may be used to host important but non line-of-business applications such as human resources and expense reporting applications, when LOB applications need the extra infrastructure for special occasions.

3. There would be a need to move or migrate an executing workload from one cloud to another based on usage of resource and performance (network bandwidth, storage, management, security, and so on). In this scenario, the bursting is not triggered by load overflow; rather it is a need for live migration to optimize the resource utilization.

This requires the ability to automate the cloud's data center and orchestrate the local and the remote resources, policies, and so on from inside the local data center. It requires that the enterprise service consumer manage both the deployment of applications and resources in the enterprise virtual data center but also within the cloud platform of the cloud service provider through the cloud API using the service provider's self service portal.

All demand spikes on the enterprise virtual data center infrastructure are not the same, and there are different characteristics that determine the spikes:

■ Periodic peaks. These occur multiple times during certain times of the year, for instance closing the books every quarter, and have 2x–4x amount of loads. Peak-to-average ratio of load is 3 to 4, and cloud bursting could be a good option.

■ Random peaks. These are hard to plan for; especially if the usage is long downloads like software, catalogs, pricing sheets, and so on. Enterprises typically smooth these spikes out to enhance utilization and reduce infrastructure costs. Bursting to a cloud service provider helps to smooth and also reduce costs.3

■ One-time, unforeseeable events. These have unpredictable timing and amplitude. Launch of new products, special announcements, hurricanes, earthquakes, and scandals increase demand on enterprise Web sites and can create a demand peak at the origin site. Similarly, time-sensitive events drive demand and workload load peaks, and the overflow capacity can help.

Today, enterprises handle these by over provisioning the infrastructure. Enterprises can take advantage of cloud bursting to the overflow capacity, and not have to deploy enterprise infrastructure for this aggregate demand.

There are two specific use case variations to cloud bursting that are considering in this reference architecture and they are described in the following section.

Cloud Bursting Use Cases

Table 3.4 outlines the two cloud bursting use cases. The typical one is the first, namely dynamic or manual scaling. The second use case, live migration is equally, if not more compelling for enterprises from a load-balancing, disaster recovery, business continuity, and resource optimization perspective. All cloud operating environments and service providers are building out their software stacks to enable dynamic or manual scaling, though the richness of the implementations vary significantly. Live migration between clouds is fraught with significant challenges with latency, performance, distance limitations between the enterprise virtual data center and the cloud service provider, and network, storage and data migration issues. Let us look at the first use-case, scaling, in more detailed in the following section.

---

3   Armbrust et al, *Above the Clouds: A Berkeley View of Cloud Computing*, Berkeley RAD Lab, 2009.

Table 3.4 Cloud Bursting Use Cases

Use Case	Applicability
Enterprise cloud bursting—scaling (dynamic or manual spawning of applications)	Dynamic or manual spawning of application stack instances (virtual machines) in response to load or for capacity optimization between:
	Two clouds (across WAN) - between two enterprise virtual data centers
	Two clouds (on the Internet) - between enterprise virtual data center and cloud service provider (enterprise virtual private clouds)
Enterprise cloud bursting—live migration between internal and external clouds	Move a single VM or multiple VMs while providing continuous availability between:
	Two clouds (across WAN) - between enterprise virtual data centers
	Two clouds (on the Internet) - between enterprise virtual data center and cloud service provider (enterprise virtual private clouds)
	Two options for live migration.
	Option 1: Migration of compute VMs to remote DC, data tier still in the enterprise tier.
	Option 2: Migration of compute VMs and also the associated data/storage

Dynamic and Manual Scaling under Cloud Bursting

There are two models for scaling that apply:

- ■ *Proactive.* In this model, the service consumer, that is, the application owner or administrator in the enterprise, scales nodes or servers based on an anticipated uptick in traffic, whether by time-of-day or triggered by special events. The service consumer fully understands the load patterns and current capacity, and proactively launches the extra servers and virtual machines in the overflow capacity (or some cases, use pre-deployed VMs in the overflow capacity) to meet the needs, for instance the early morning e-mail rush on Microsoft Exchange servers, or, end of the quarter finance close load on servers.

■ *Reactive.* In this model, service consumer configures the management platform to dynamically instantiate servers/VMs in the overflow capacity based on unscheduled surges in traffic or requests. This model could be a target of malicious attacks, and hence strong, controlled scaling safeguards (governors) are needed to avoid creating hot spots in the infrastructure and to manage denial of service (DoS) attacks.

Considerations for this use case include the following:

■ Data and applications will be crossing company boundaries and possibly political/country boundaries. It is imperative that this be done within the appropriate laws and regulations.

■ An assessment on latency and bandwidth requirement is needed.

■ Contractual service level issues need to be addressed.

■ Key performance indicators need to be in place to ensure that service level agreements are met.

■ Predictions and forecast of future events are required with possible effect on SLA, provisioning, load balancing, and so on.

Cloud Bursting Life Cycle

Figure 3.6 illustrates the setup, configuration, and steps that enterprises would have to go through to enable for cloud bursting. There are four distinct steps:

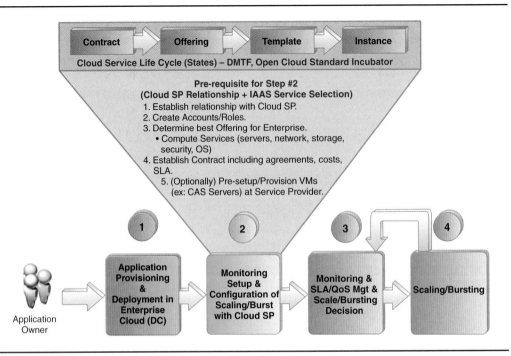

Figure 3.6   Cloud Bursting Life Cycle

1. *Application provisioning and deployment.* A given application is deployed on a virtualized infrastructure in the enterprise virtual data center. This is a significant task and it requires deliberate planning and design of the virtual infrastructure, provisioning of compute, network and storage resources, and deployment of application set. In the context of this SRA, this is a prerequisite step to enable for cloud bursting to an external cloud at a service provider.

2. *Monitoring setup and configuration of bursting to cloud service providers.* The primary actor for this step is the service consumer, who is also the enterprise application owner/application administrator. There are multiple involved steps in this phase.

- It requires calculating the SLA/QoS metrics to determine when to apply bursting. This could be queuing delays, service response or CPU utilization. This presumes the existence of an application performance monitoring facility to capture the metrics. In a VMware environment, this could be accomplished with tools like AppSpeed in conjunction with tools like VMware Orchestrator.

- Configuring bursting policies is not trivial. Good knowledge of application performance, choke points, and scaling architecture of individual application components (how many users/requests does a given application component can support) are needed to figure out the scaling policies. The scaling component of the enterprise management platform would provide interface for you to specify how long you would monitoring the QoS or load metrics before scaling and bursting decisions are made, and, how many instances have to be created to meet the demand surge.

- The service consumer may deploy applications on-demand to the cloud service provider, but most providers will likely require the application be deployed before it is needed. The service consumer would use the cloud APIs or the self-service portal to pre-stage the applications at the service provider.

A pre-requisite for this step is to have a contractual agreement and access to a cloud service provider's services. This not a simple process, and is assumes that the necessary due diligence and selection processes have been followed in the selection of a cloud service provider. The service consumer would work with the service developer on the cloud service provider side to create specific IaaS custom services with the appropriate SLAs, and make them available in the service catalog if these are not standard offerings from the service provider already. The service consumer uses the self-service portal in order to create, select and provision the services required for cloud bursting this application. The Cloud Incubator Task Force has been developing a "service life cycle" that an enterprise would follow to contractually engage to use the services and specific offerings from a cloud service provider.

3. *Management of monitoring and scaling.* Enterprise application performance monitoring tools (like VMware AppSpeed and VMware Orchestrator) can actively monitor performance metrics of the application in a closed loop, as described in Step 2 above. The orchestrating engine determines the bursting need, based on the metrics monitored.

4. *Scaling and bursting.* If the decision is made to burst, VPN connection is initiated between the enterprise virtual data center and the cloud service provider, and using the cloud APIs, the additional application components (VMs) are started (or downloaded, deployed, and started in case they are not pre-staged). The policies determine how many application VMs are created and when they are scaled back.

How Cloud Bursting Works: Microsoft† Exchange Scenario

We use the Microsoft Exchange application as a representative environment to show how a cloud bursting scenario can be instantiated. We begin with a high-level overview of the Microsoft Exchange 2007 servers and a conceptual description of how cloud bursting would work for Microsoft Exchange components, followed by a detailed walk-the-flow of how this can be accomplished with a VMWare vCloud solution stack.

Exchange Server 2007 provides or distributes its features and functionality through five defined server roles: Mailbox, Hub Transport, Client Access, Edge Transport and Unified Messaging. A server role provides a defined set of Exchange 2007 functionality and can be deployed standalone on a hardware server system (bare metal or virtualized) or, with certain restrictions, be combined with other roles. Exchange Server 2007 supports the following five separate server roles to perform the tasks of an enterprise messaging system:

■ Client Access servers (CAS). Supports Post Office Protocol 3 (POP3) and Internet Message Access Protocol 4 (IMAP4) clients, as well as Exchange ActiveSync, Office Outlook Web Access, and Outlook Anywhere and new Outlook 2007 client functions.

■ Edge Transport servers. Handle message traffic to and from the Internet and run spam filters. Microsoft IT also installs Forefront Security for Exchange Server on all Edge Transport servers for virus scanning.

- ■ Hub Transport servers. Perform the internal message transfer, distribution list expansions, and message conversions between Internet mail and Exchange Server message formats. At Microsoft, all Hub Transport servers also run Forefront Security for Exchange Server for virus scanning.

- ■ Mailbox servers. Mailbox servers maintain mailbox store databases and provide Office Outlook clients and Client Access servers with access to the data.

- ■ Unified Messaging servers. Integrate voice and fax with e-mail messaging and run Outlook Voice Access.

There are clear recommendations from Microsoft on hosting these server roles in virtualized servers, including sizing guidance on number of virtual CPUs, memory, and I/O requirements. The guidelines also specify the ratio of mailboxes types and sizes, the number of users, and the number of CAS and hub transport servers. The virtualization design of Microsoft Exchange is out of scope of this document.

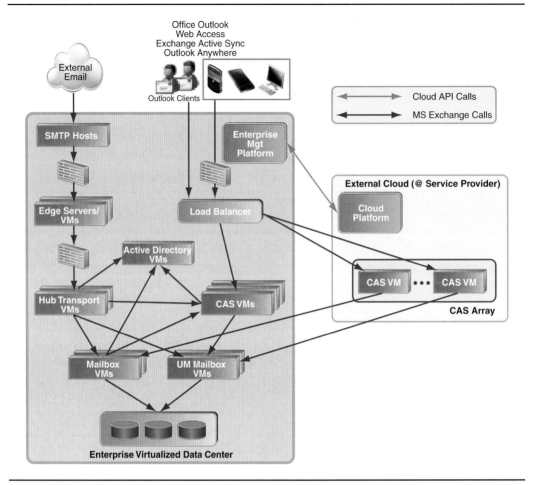

Figure 3.7   Cloud Bursting w/ Microsoft[†] Exchange

Figure 3.7 illustrates how cloud bursting of Microsoft Exchange component, Client Access Servers (CAS), works. A typical scenario for bursting would be to manage the peaks in users of the CAS VMs by instantiating extra VMs in the overflow capacity (or directing the traffic to the CAS VMs that are already in the overflow capacity), and scale them down once the demand spike subsides.

There can be multiple events within an enterprise that result in unexpected spike in demand. There are significant architectural, performance, security, and manageability challenges for this to work for enterprises.

These are highlighted in the section dealing with issues, challenges, and gaps for cloud bursting in the use case deep dive.

Here is a summary of how cloud bursting works.

- Must have the application or components of the application deployed and available inside the remote cloud at the service provider. For applications that are not latency sensitive, it might be possible to reach into the enterprise virtual data center for the data. However, as a general practice, data replication may be needed at the service provider.

- Also, while it may be possible to deploy applications on-demand to the cloud service provider, it is likely that the application be deployed before it is needed for performance reason. The enterprise management platform and the cloud platform will need to address operational aspects such as patch management, license management, and so on.

- An intelligent load balancer needs to be present to direct requests to a secondary site applications or application components as needed. This can be an application embedded load balancer, or it could be part a global load balancer that can be controlled by policy.

- The application manager needs to determine when the application infrastructure is near capacity. This trigger point may be determined by a single metric such as application response time, concurrent connections or aggregate server load, or it could be a combination of factors. The goal is to determine the threshold at which requests are redirected to the cloud instead of the local application instance.

The next section illustrates how the use case and the cloud bursting life-cycle steps can be instantiated using the VMware vCloud software stack.

A Cloud Bursting Solution Stack with VMware vCloud

Figure 3.8 is a representation of the VMware vCloud solution stack. VMware vCloud is a common set of cloud computing services for businesses and service providers supporting most any application or operating system and with the ability to choose where applications get deployed, on or off premise. The core components of the vCloud are VMware vSphere, the vCloud API, and additional cloud computing services like the vCloud services that are brought to end customers both via internal clouds built on VMware and the vCloud service providers. The vCloud set of services is important to enterprise customers as it enables them to build internal clouds and seamlessly deploy test labs, disaster recovery or simple flex capacity off premise, to the cloud, as needed.

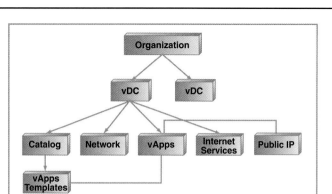

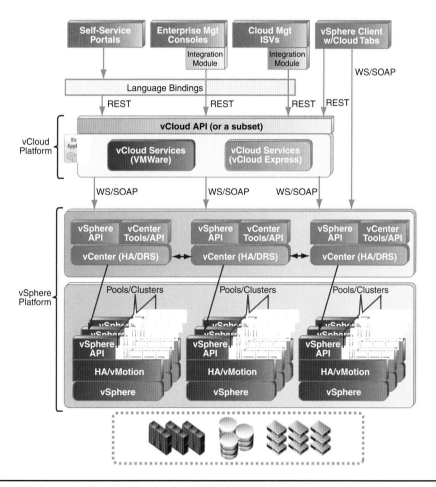

Figure 3.8   VMware vCloud Solution Stack.

As shown in Figure 3.8, the bottom layer is the vSphere platform with the VCenter management servers providing the interface for the virtualization management, including provisioning, resource management, life-cycle management, and so on. The vCenter management servers are linked for a comprehensive view of all the pools and clusters, and avoid a single point failure. The vCloud platform logically resides above the vCenter layer, and provides the cloud platform capabilities, including multi-tenancy, provisioning, resource allocation and optimization, as well as automation. This platform also implements vCloud API, the cloud APIs from VMware. The vCloud APIs provide the interface for

■ Providing and consuming resources in the cloud

■ Deploying and managing virtualized workloads in the cloud

■ Migrating virtualized workloads between clouds

There would be an instantiation of this vCloud Services that VMware would deliver. This would be part of the solution stack for the enterprise. There is an implementation of the vCloud API by the service providers, called vCloud Express. vCloudExpress is the instantiation of vCloud APIs for enterprise customers, and is analogous to using other cloud services like Amazon Web Services, Rackspace servers, and so forth. The vCloud APIs are based on the Representational State Transfer (REST) architectural pattern, and use HTTP.

Reference Architecture for Cloud Bursting with vCloud

Figure 3.9 shows reference architecture for cloud bursting between an enterprise virtual data center and an external cloud at a service provider, for Microsoft Exchange workload. For simplicity, we assume that both the enterprise and the service provider clouds are VMware-enabled. Future extensions to this reference architecture would address the cloud bursting use cases across heterogeneous clouds.

Here are the main components of the architecture:

- The enterprise instantiation of Microsoft Exchange is on the vSphere platform on a heterogeneous resource pool of Intel x86 servers, connected with 10 GbE network and Fibre Channel over Ethernet storage traffic over a unified fabric connected to a Fibre Channel SAN storage. The focus of this architecture is not to pick the optimal storage configuration, but a shared storage model that would enable us to have VM mobility and resource optimization in the data center resource pools.

- vCenter with vCloud Services as the enterprise management platform, with vSphere client (with appropriate extensions for vCloud) as the single management console.

- Microsoft Exchange virtual servers deployed on vSphere with fault tolerance as a high-availability feature, and separate VMware vShield zones for the edge server virtual machines. Edge servers are the external facing servers bringing in the SMTP mail to the Microsoft Exchange servers.

- Low-latency VPN connectivity to a vCloud Express-enabled cloud service provider that has the virtual private cloud isolation environment for the enterprise with subnet ranges specified by the enterprise.

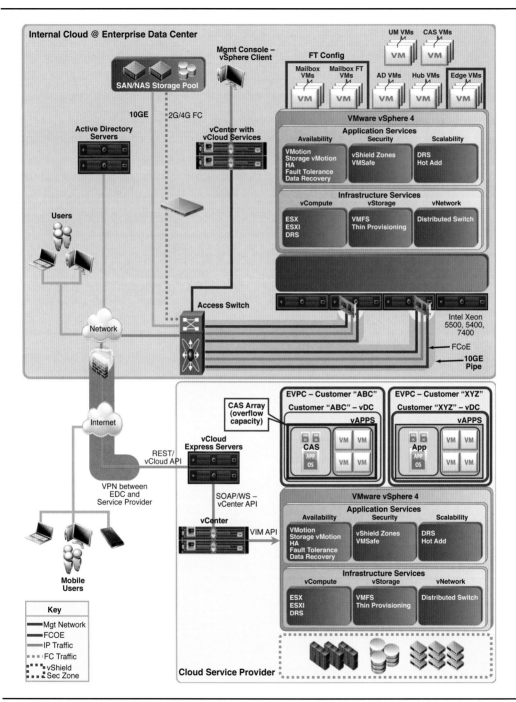

Figure 3.9 Cloud Bursting Reference Architecture with vCloud

■ Depiction of the vCloud Express servers that respond to the REST APIs, and the associated connectivity to the vCenter Servers at the service provider to initiate and manage the enterprise tenant provisioning and utilization of the infrastructure resources.

■ Multi-tenant customers and their virtual data centers (VDCs) hosted at the service provider, with vApps, the existing VMs and the overflow CAS VM array that has been created as part of the cloud bursting solution from the enterprise. A vApp is a pre-built software solution, consisting of multiple virtual machines, packaged and maintained as a single entity. VApps are self-describing and self-managing on the platform they run and typically comprise multitier applications.

If enterprises use vCenter as their virtualization management platform, they can continue to manage the enterprise infrastructure along with the resources in the overflow capacity, with enhancements that VMware is building into vCenter. These extensions would use the vCloud APIs to upload, provision, orchestrate, and provide life cycle management to virtual machines seamlessly in the overflow capacity at the service provider with the same level of trust and security.

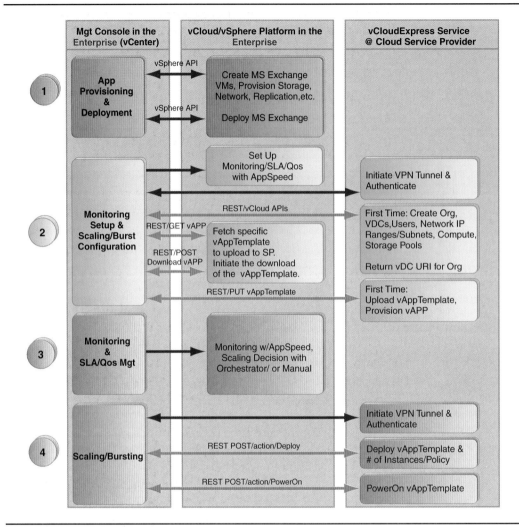

Figure 3.10   End-to-end Walk-the-flow for Cloud Bursting with vCloud

Alternatively, an enterprise would develop an integration module to their favorite enterprise systems management platform or tool like HP Operations Manager or IBM Tivoli, that would provide the seamless integration with the external IaaS services at different service providers using the RESTful vCloud APIs, or the various language bindings that are becoming available from VMware and the third parties (Java, Python, C++/C#).

Figure 3.10 shows the end-to-end process flow for how to set up, configure, and initiate cloud bursting using the vCloud stack between the enterprise and the external service provider cloud for the Microsoft Exchange example. It shows the vCloud API calls that used for configuring and bursting into the overflow capacity.

Issues, Challenges, and Gaps for Cloud Bursting

Cloud bursting is a very compelling usage model for enterprises to really leverage the elasticity of the clouds, and this has significant implications on load balancing, disaster recovery, capacity, and demand planning. However, there are critical architectural issues that span standards, data architecture, metrics and manageability, network performance, security and multi-service sourcing. The following section articulates some of these.

Security

There are multiple aspects of security that are of concern with cloud bursting. From a network isolation side, there is no uniform model across all cloud service providers. Some assign a separate, private VLAN for each of the tenants (Savvis, Terremark, Verizon, OpsCloud), and there are others like Amazon that provide a proprietary Layer 2 isolation mechanism to accomplish the network isolation. Enterprises would have to determine the service provider based on the business need, and their company information security policies. If security enclaves are a requirement for confidential data and applications, cloud service providers with higher focus on security should be selected. If the focus for cloud bursting is for enterprise 3 tier applications, and horizontal scale is important, cloud service providers like Amazon would be a good choice.

The enterprise workloads and virtual machines coexist at the cloud service provider along with other virtual machines that belong to other tenants. The platform level isolation in the infrastructure is provided by the hypervisor via the virtual container (VM) mechanism. Though the security model at the hypervisor is solid, there is still some potential vulnerability. This could be a source of concern for enterprises. There are technologies in the server platforms (Intel's Trusted Execution Technology, or Intel® TXT with the Intel®

Xeon® 5600 processor series family, Intel AES-NI for improving performance of encryption, and so on) that, in conjunction with the hypervisor software, can provide additional security via the attestation of the hypervisor.

Clouds must leverage a unified identity and security infrastructure to enable flexible provisioning, yet enforce security policies throughout the cloud. As clouds provision resources outside the enterprise's legal boundaries, it becomes essential to implement an information asset management system to provide the necessary controls to ensure sensitive information is protected and meets compliance requirements.

Ideally, the enterprise user manages a single ID, with an infrastructure federating other identities that might be required by cloud services. This might need the implementation of SAML, for federating of identity.

Standards

Cloud bursting requires interoperability and portability across clouds. Without them the benefits of the cloud remains just a promise. The standards need to exist not just for deployment, but for management and gathering of data, the data needed to realize clouds based on business and operational metrics. Standards are needed for network protocols, virtual machine representation, APIs, and identity and security. Each of these standards is at various levels of maturity, with virtual machine representation and packaging taking significant lead with DMTFs OVF. The vision, once these details have been worked out, is that of a completely ubiquitous computing environment that seamlessly blends all forms of clouds and their physical instantiations, is unfriendly to vendor lock-ins, addresses flexible migrations, and is much more palatable for the enterprises.

Metrics and Manageability

Context awareness is the foundation of a dynamic infrastructure. A dynamic infrastructure in turn requires integration and collaboration in the network and application network infrastructure, underscoring the relevance standards and interoperability. The manageability solution should be capable of interpreting myriad variables encompassing both operational metrics and business metrics.

Operational metrics should include more than

■ CPU or memory resources or connections or response time

■ Physical conditions on the network and in the data center

These metrics should also include those describing costs, inclusive of the cost of data center power and power optimization, if possible. Business metrics should include cost thresholds, SLAs, and key performance indicators (KPIs) specific to the business objectives. These metrics make up the *context*, and context is what makes cloud bursting valuable architecture and usage for enterprises.

On the manageability front, there is no consistency and no canonical model for describing and enforcing SLAs in a cloud environment. Questions such as:

■ How does an enterprise know proactively that its SLAs are met in a multi-tenant environment at the service provider?

■ How can the enterprise and service provider describe these critical SLAs?

■ Is there standard way of defining SLAs that enterprise can migrate between service providers?

Regulatory Compliance and Data Locality

The advantages to cloud bursting for organizations need to be tempered when addressing regulatory requirements. The financial advantages of cloud bursting for organizations requiring additional capacity to address spikes are well understood. However, regulatory issues that surround such implementations hinder adoption of this method to address cost-effective capacity increases when necessary only for short periods of time. Regulations such as PCI-DSS and HIPPA have specific requirements difficult to comply with in cloud environments.

One of the biggest concerns for enterprises is the lack of transparency from cloud service providers on the exact physical location of their data. With cloud bursting also, this data locality could be a problem. There are country and regional constraints on how far and where the data can or cannot migrate.

What is really lacking is a simple API-based mechanism with the cloud platforms to query the precise location of the tenant data. Depending on the type and kind of data processed by the cloud application, there might be legal restrictions on the location of the physical server where the data is stored.

In essence, enterprises have large amounts of sensitive data requiring access monitoring and protection. Data (and information generated from the data) is the lifeblood of many enterprises; the loss of control is not an acceptable outcome. The migration of workloads to public clouds would increase the complexity associated with meeting legal and regulatory requirements for sensitive information.

Performance

Though cloud bursting promises to maximize agility and efficiency, which in turn minimizes cost, the challenge is to determine the best way to deal with data distributed applications require or generate. There is a number of strategies for dealing with cloud bursting, each with different implications for cost, performance, and architecture.

Irrespective of the strategy chosen, the WAN/Internet bandwidth and latency plays a significant role in the overall viability of bursting applications from the enterprise virtual data center and the external cloud at the service provider. On top of this, VPN links add an incremental overhead, though there exist VPN products that featuring very low latency. Encryption, with SSL or IPSec, is a requirement to connect the cloud burst data centers, adding extra overhead.

■ *Remote access to data.* The obvious and straightforward approach to access and update enterprise data may be for application instances running in the external cloud to directly access a single-instance data store—essentially reaching into the enterprise via the VPN connectivity. The viability of this approach depends on the pattern and intensity of reads and writes from the cloud data center to the enterprise and the bandwidth, latency, and protocol support of the data networking or storage networking approach used to connect the cloud application to the enterprise-based data—whether it be block-oriented, network-attached, content-addressed, or simply a database server. In general, JDBC/ODBC connectivity begins to time-out or results in "retries" when the latency gets beyond 20–25 milliseconds, and if WAN/LAN connectivity has a latency around 10–15 milliseconds, it might be acceptable for these applications.

■ *Data in the cloud.* There would clearly be applications that are very latency-sensitive, and for these the above model doesn't work—the I/O intensity and/or network latency are too high for remote access. For these applications, the needed data that isn't already in the cloud must be placed there at the beginning of the cloud bursting process, and any changes must be consolidated in the enterprise store at the end of the cloud bursting. How much data needs to get to the cloud service provider, and how quickly? For some computations, a large data set may required, or because the pattern of reads is unpredictable. If this is the case, even with fast file transfer techniques, either there will be

— Delays in the startup of cloud bursting from the attempt to pass a lot of data through a small pipe or by using physical disk delivery, the Amazon model.

— An alternative is to build a large bandwidth pipe between the data centers to quickly migrate the data, at a cost: laying fiber, deploying optical transport equipment, and paying for rights of way and rights of entry, that can run into the millions of dollars.

These models assume that the current application architecture stays the same for cloud applications. New application architectures are clearly emerging that take into account the inherent limitations and costs of the high bandwidth networks, and these might be better fit for cloud bursting usage.

Chapter 4

Data Center Platform Power Management

Contributed by Enrique Castro-Leon, Xavier Simonart, Luc Provoost, Martin Guttmann, Todd Christ, and Murali Rajappa

Power management and energy efficiency constitute two important benefits from operating a cloud infrastructure. This is beneficial to both cloud operators from the standpoint of lower operating expenses to end users through lower capital expense costs. This subject has been researched intensely at Intel as a platform infrastructure provider. We'll share this experience in the next two chapters. Chapter 4 covers server platform aspects of power management. In Chapter 5 we generalize these concepts and apply them to virtualized cloud data centers.

Server platform power management refers to two fundamental capabilities enabled by sensors and controllers placed in every managed server. The instrumentation allows management applications monitoring the hardware obtain readings for power consumption in that machine directly in watts. It also implements a capability for these applications to set power consumption targets. To enable control policies, the data presented by the platform and power targets must be in direct physical units, namely, watts and in real time. The frequency at which these measurements can be taken are determined by the platform architecture and network bandwidth. Data stored in a device for offline retrieval only would make it difficult to implement control loops.

For the same reason, changing power settings must not require a system restart. This scenario would be typical of parameters defined by the BIOS firmware.

The range of power control is defined by the architecture and the configuration of the server. For current generation platforms, the authority range is in the order of 20 to 30 percent of a server's peak power consumption.

The Need for Power Management

When it comes to information technology and business alignment, the IT industry has been going through a number of paradigm shifts since the era of the mainframe started in the 1950s.

As shown in Figure 4.1, in the early days the focus of computing was on mainframes. Because of the expense of the technology, only the largest organizations were able to afford it. Applications were relatively few because the expectation was for business to adapt to the technology and not the other way around. The prevailing paradigm was that of the glass house where mainframes were used to run the world's largest banks and governments.

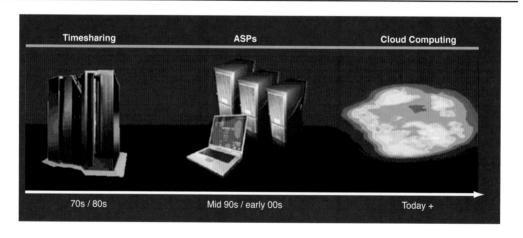

Figure 4.1   Evolution from Mainframes to Cloud Computing

The wide adoption of the PC in the industry and especially of client-server computing based on the Intel® architecture led to a radical reduction in the cost of computing, bringing the benefits of IT to much smaller firms and customers around the world, including those in emerging markets. A large market for hardware, software, and services also emerged opening opportunities for new players. In this environment a large portion of deployments moved from mainframe computer to client-server and multi-tier distributed computing. The now "traditional" three-tier computing originated in this era.

All was not well, however. Mainframes were replaced with standards-based computers that could be built by system integrators with components from a diversity of suppliers. These computers were two orders of magnitude less expensive than the mainframes they replaced. Large organizations deployed them by the tens of thousands, a computer for most every application. Even small businesses were able to deploy a few of them in a back room. Unfortunately, these large deployments led to another challenge, affectionately called "server sprawl."

Server sprawl neutralizes the benefits from the initial ease of allocation of relatively inexpensive computers to applications: the sheer numbers, the diversity of hardware and software makes a collection of computers hard to manage and maintain. The power consumed by so many machines has come to the forefront in the past few years as well. As in the mainframe era, IT organizations found the enormous power of client server computing came at a cost incompatible with their budgets. In addition, the honeymoon period where business had to fit the requirements of technology was long past. The pendulum was beginning to swing in the opposite direction for IT to become responsive and accountable to the needs of business.

The State of Data Center Power Today

If we go back 10 to 15 years, power used to be an afterthought for servers deployed in data centers. Even today, some of the old practices still persist. For instance, in many facilities the power bill still comes bundled with the facilities charge.

What has happened is that even though servers have become much more efficient, packaging densities have increased much faster and so the power densities. As a result power has become a significant component of operational costs.

Furthermore, a large number of established data centers were not originally architected to factor in increased power densities, and are quickly reaching their load bearing limits, both in terms of available infrastructure to power more servers and to keep the physical infrastructure from exceeding thermal limits.

Yet the power infrastructure in data centers today typically is not well used. It is difficult to forecast power consumption accurately for server deployments, let alone monitor the actual power consumption. Data center planners need to significantly overprovision power to provide enough of a cushion because the falling short is not an option. This is not efficient use of infrastructure and capital resources.

One important requirement is whatever method we use to solve this problem, it needs to be interoperable across equipment providers.

Server Power Management

The recently introduced Intel® Xeon® 5500 Series processor, formerly code named Nehalem, brings a number of power management features that not only improve on energy efficiency over previous generations, such as a more aggressive implementation of power proportional computing. Depending on the server design, users of Intel Xeon 5500 Series–based servers can expect idle power consumption that is about half of the power consumed at full load, down from about two thirds in the previous generation (Bensley).

A less heralded capability for this new generation of servers is that users can actually adjust the server power consumption and therefore trade off power consumption against performance. This capability is known as *power capping*. The power capping range is not insignificant. For a dual socket server consuming about 300 watts at full load, the capping range is in the order of 100 watts, that is, for a fully loaded server consuming 300 watts, power consumption can be reduced to about 200 watts. The actual numbers depend on the server implementation.

The application of this mechanism for servers deployed in a data center leads to some energy savings. However, perhaps the most valuable aspect of this technology is the operational flexibility it confers to data center operators.

This value comes from two capabilities: first, it allows data center operators to match server power demand to supply, and second, servers implementing power capping offer actual power readouts as a bonus: their power supplies are PMBus enabled and their historical power consumption can be retrieved through standard APIs.

With actual historical power data, it is possible to optimize the loading of power limited racks, whereas before, the most accurate estimation of power consumption came from derated nameplate data. The nameplate estimation for power consumption is a static measure that requires a considerable safety margin during operations. This conservative approach to power sizing requires overprovisioning of power. The approach was acceptable when energy costs were a second order consideration. That is not the case today.

This technology allows dialing the power to be consumed by groups of over possibly thousands of servers, allowing a power control authority of tens of thousands of watts in data centers.

Technologies for Power Management

Intel has been working on power management for many years and has developed an extensive portfolio in this area. Since CPUs are possibly the most energy intensive components in a server, it is logical that a power management portfolio start with the CPU. Emerging technologies such as solid state drives are also being applied to reduce baseline power consumption. Future developments may also encompass memory power consumption. Some of these technologies are depicted in Figure 4.2.

The Intel® Intelligent Power Node Manager captures the CPU power management capability and implements power monitoring and control for a single server.

Intel Intelligent Power Node Manager is implemented as firmware stored in the Serial Peripheral Interface flash device in the baseboard. It is executed by the Management Engine (ME), a microcontroller embedded in the processor chipset.

The Intel Intelligent Power Node Manager features are available through an ordinary TCP/IP network using the industry standard Intelligent Platform Management Interface (IPMI). The IPMI protocol defines power-specific data formats in the IP packets used for power management data exchange.

A common arrangement is to have IPMI available through the Ethernet management port connected to the Baseboard Management Controller or BMC. The Ethernet port can be implemented as an extra Ethernet port or dual-ported with one of the server's data ports. From the IPMI perspective, the BMC functions as a proxy for the ME.

In order to make this single server (node) power monitoring and control mechanism for data center applications housing up to tens of thousands of servers, an aggregation mechanism is needed to manage power in servers arranged in logical groups. A server group may be defined by the application they run or by the organization that runs them.

The aggregation capability is provided by a software development kit (SDK), namely the Intel® Data Center Manager (Intel® DCM) SDK. The Intel DCM SDK implements an adapter that allows it to communicate with a number of nodes enabled for Intel Intelligent Power Node Manager and bind them together as a logical group. A summary of Intel DCM capabilities is in the next section, with a more in-depth treatment in Chapter 8.

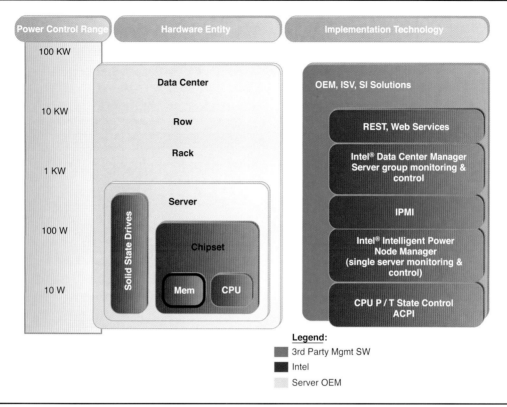

Figure 4.2   Technology Portfolio for Power Management

The features of Intel DCM are available to higher level management applications through a REST/Web services interface. A reference management application providing a user interface is available with the SDK for testing purposes and small scale deployments.

Intel provides interfaces or APIs available to third party integrators at most any of the levels of integration depicted in Figure 4.2. Each interface represents the usual tradeoff between integration effort and fine grained control. For instance, using Intel DCM makes it easy to manage machines as groups. By the same token, it is more difficult to control the behaviors of individual machines.

At the other extreme, using IPMI allows very fine grained control of individual machines. However, programming IPMI fields is probably as laborious as programming in assembly language, and without the policy templates provided by Intel DCM, implementing group policies require a significant engineering effort.

The scale on the left of Figure 4.2 captures the range of power control possible under current technology. Intel Intelligent Power Node Manager can trim power consumption of a processor by a few tens of watts. This translates to about a hundred watts for a single server. When totalized over thousands of servers deployed in a data center, these numbers can add to hundreds of kilowatts. There is also a multiplicative effect in with the data center PUE[1]: the heat not emitted by servers due to power capping means the data center does not need to be cooled as much either.

Given the reduction in power consumption possible under power capping, the question arises about operating servers under a permanent capping regime. Following this policy is not advisable. Capping is attained by slowing down the processors, which in turn has a potential effect on performance. While this may be immaterial during periods of low demand, applications may need to muster all the performance available to meet workload peaks and yet stay within contracted service level agreements. The relation is complex, to the extent that we have dedicated a section to this interesting subject.

How Server Platform Power Management Works

No power management technology allows reducing power consumption all the way down to zero watts, short of turning off the machine. Even when the machine is turned off and unplugged, the machine still consumes trace amounts of power: it uses the baseboard battery to keep the real time clock (RTC) ticking.

Effectively, powering down a machine by pushing the power button (ACPI *mechanical off*) or unplugging or even unracking a machine constitute legitimate measures to reduce power consumption. However doing so may be impractical unless the machine will not be used for weeks or months. When it comes to having a machine offline there are many modalities. The modalities usually represent a tradeoff between power consumption and time to recovery.

---

1   PUE stands for Power Usage Effectiveness, a figure of merit for data center efficiency defined by the Green Grid Industry consortium, http://www.thegreengrid.org.

Faster recovery times require that the recovery process be done under program control. For technology available today the lowest energy state that allows recovery under program control is by putting a server in ACPI sleep state S5. A server in S5 can be restarted through an IPMI wakeup command or by sending a wake-on-LAN (WOL) IP packet.

Table 4.1 Server Behavior for Selected Low Energy States

Low Energy State	RTO Considerations	RPO Considerations
ACPI G3, Mechanical off	Tens of minutes to days to recover	Re-provisioning or rebooting needed
ACPI S5/G2	5–20 minutes to recover	Reboot needed
S4	2–10 minutes to recover	Reload state at shutdown from hibernation file
S3	10 seconds to 1 minute to recover	Memory stays charged with data preserved. However, application data does not get updated while the server is asleep.
S2	Very fast for practical purposes. Some extra time relative to S1 required to restore CPU context. Application may require resynchronization.	CPU suspended; data in cache and registers lost.
S1	Instant for practical purposes. The application may need to resynchronize.	CPU suspended, retains cache context. However memory is not updated while the CPU is suspended.
S0	Instant for practical purposes. Workload can pick up as fast as the application allows. The application needs to implement logic to remove workload from the designated server. OS services and application background tasks continue running.	No loss of data; workload needs to be limited if the server is to be considered idle.
Capped under Intel® Intelligent Power Node Manager	1 s (single server) to 30 s (group) to recover	No loss of data; server keeps running while capped

The concepts of *recovery time objective* (RTO) and *recovery point objective* (RPO) used in the *business impact analysis* (BIA) of data center outages also apply to individual servers or groups of servers. An application or solution engineer charting a power management strategy representing the best tradeoff between recovery times, that is, the time it takes to bring a server back on line from the low energy state, and power consumption while the server is in a low energy state. The RPO is represented by the application state retained, from none during S5 or mechanical off, requiring a full reboot to reloading memory from a hibernation file under ACPI S4, to full state if the server is just idling (ACPI S0). A stricter RPO requires spending more power during the low energy state. See Table 4.1.

Inner Workings of Intel® Intelligent Power Node Manager

Power control in the CPU is done through voltage and frequency scaling. If we slow down a CPU, its power consumption will go down. The same will happen if we reduce the voltage applied to a CPU. Power consumption is approximately linear with frequency and proportional to the square of the voltage.

The voltage and frequency scaling is not applied as a continuum, but done in a series of discrete steps, each with an associated voltage and frequency. The Intel Xeon 5500 series processor supports as many as 13 steps depending on model. These steps are defined under the Advanced Configuration and Power Interface standard (ACPI) and are colloquially identified as *P-states*. P0 is nominally the normal operating state with no power constraints. P1, P2, and so on represent increasingly aggressive power capped states.

Figure 4.3 shows an example for the 5500 processor family. Each column in the figure represents a specific processor model. The model furthest to the right has a base frequency for the P0 performance state of 2.93 GHz. States P1 and P2 are clocked at 2.80 and 2.66 GHz respectively. Additionally, this particular CPU exposes three additional frequency above the base frequency available under the Intel® Turbo Boost Technology. When the operating system requests the CPU to run at P0, the CPU will dynamically increase the frequency. The particular frequency chosen and the duration ("residency") at that frequency is a function of the number of active cores, the CPU current and power consumption and the CPU temperature.

While the manipulation of P-states can be used to vary the power consumption of a server up or down, it is still not possible to measure the actual power consumption of a server. Taking power measurements at the power supplies allows measuring power consumption for the whole server. Power supplies built to the PMBus standard have such capability.

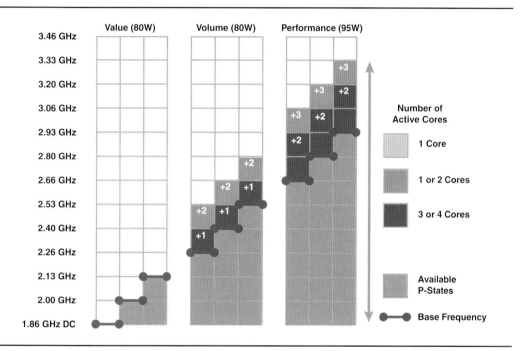

Figure 4.3   Typical P-states and Turbo Frequency Upside for Intel® Xeon® 5500 Series Processors

The Intel Intelligent Power Node Manager firmware, which can take power readings from a PMBus power supply, can now establish a classic control feedback loop where comparing a set target power against the actual power indicated by the power supplies, as shown in Figure 4.4. The Intel Intelligent Power Node Manager code manipulates the P-states up or down until the desired target power is reached. If the desired power lies between two P-states, this code rapidly switches between the two states until the average power consumption meets the set power. This is an implementation of another classic control scheme, affectionately called bang-bang control for obvious reasons.

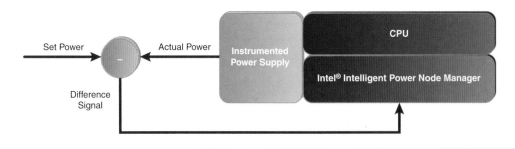

Figure 4.4   Intel® Intelligent Power Node Manager Control Loop

Figure 4.5 provides an expanded detail of the control loop. Here we can see that the Intel Intelligent Power Node Manager firmware implements the difference engine. Intel Intelligent Power Node manager directs the operating system or the hypervisor to change to a target P-state.

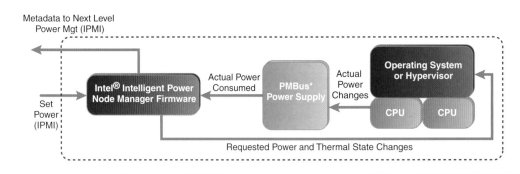

Figure 4.5   Expanded View of the Intel® Intelligent Power Node Manager Control Loop

Note that the target P-state is set through an in-band mechanism, that is, through the operating system. Intel Intelligent Power Node Manager does not set P-states directly. It sends requests to the operating system or hypervisor through an API. This is necessary to coordinate power policies with other power policies that the operating system or hypervisor might be carrying out.

Changes in processor P-state induce changes in the level of power consumption registered by the PMBus enabled power supplies.

Managing Power Consumption in Server Groups

From a data center perspective, the ability to regulate power consumption of just a single server has a small impact and is not intrinsically useful. Harnessing the "power of the masses" represents a key capability. We need the means to control servers as a group, and just as we were able to obtain power supply readouts for one server, we need to monitor the power for the group of servers to allow meeting a global power target for that group of servers. This function is provided by the Intel Data Center Manager software development kit and shown in Figure 4.6.

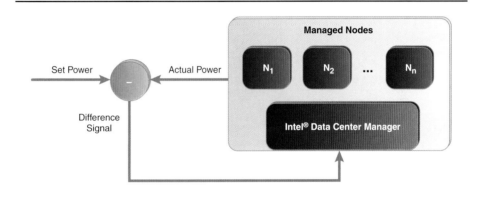

Figure 4.6   Power control loop in a group managed by Intel® Data Center Manager.

Note that Intel Data Center Manager implements a feedback control mechanism very similar to the mechanism that regulates power consumption for a single server, but at a much larger scale. Instead of watching one or two power supplies, Intel Data Center Manager oversees the power consumption of multiple servers or "nodes" whose number can range up to thousands. At this level Intel Data Center Manager is in charge of implementing the difference engine.

Figure 4.7 depicts an expanded view of the Intel Data Center Manager control loop as well as the relationship with the Intel Intelligent Power Node Manager control loop underneath. No specific agents need to run in each node. Intel Data Center Manager communicates with the board management controller (BMC) in each node for setting power targets and for doing readouts of the actual power consumed. Intel Intelligent Power Node Manager firmware takes care of ensuring that the individual server meets the assigned power consumption target.

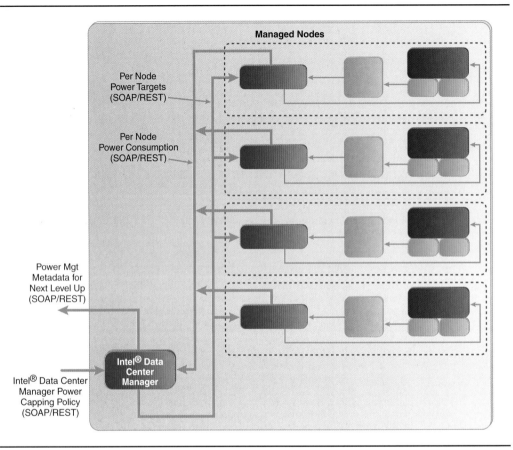

Figure 4.7   Intel® Data Center Manager Power Control Loop, Detailed View.

Intel DCM was purposely architected as an SDK as a building block to enable system integrators to build more sophisticated and valuable capabilities for the benefit of data center operators. One possible application is shown in Figure 4.8, where Intel DCM has been integrated into a building management system (BMS) application. Most servers enabled for Intel Intelligent Power Node Manager also come with inlet temperature sensors. This allows the BMS application to monitor the inlet temperature of group of servers, and if the temperature rises above a certain threshold, it can take a number of measures, from throttling back the power consumed to reduce the thermal stress on that particular area of the data center to alerting system operators. The BMS can also coordinate the power consumed by the server equipment, for instance with the CRAC fan speeds.

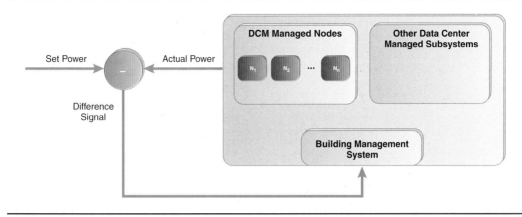

Figure 4.8   Data Center Application Control Loop

Server Power Management Use Cases

The abstractions implemented by Intel Data Center Manager on top of Intel Intelligent Power Node Manager allow the implementation of power management use cases that involve up to thousands of servers. Some of these cases are covered in this section. These use cases are actually part of a much larger continuum of usage models. For a more in-depth treatment of this continuum, please refer to Chapter 18.

Active Power Capping to Reduce Stranded Power

Stranded power is power capacity allocated statutorily but never used or used infrequently. For instance, if a rack is rated for 12 kW consumption, it will require the assignment of two 6 kW branch circuits. Yet the actual power consumption may rarely exceed 6 kW. Hence this particular workload could be served by a single 6 kW circuit except for the rare occasions where there are peaks that go beyond 6 kW.

For this situation, Intel power management can implement a guard rail capability to limit excursions beyond 6 kW. Hence one branch circuit is all it takes to feed the rack and the second one may be released for other uses. For this particular example, the existing power provisioning can now be used to feed twice the number of servers.

Optimization of Rack Loading

In some server hosting environments customers are given a power quota for a leased rack, say 2 kW. The customer can fill it in any way possible as long as the 2 kW limit is not exceeded. This quota can be fulfilled on basis of nameplate power plus a de-rating factor and a safety margin. Unfortunately this estimation method is overly conservative and results in over-provisioning. This is another manifestation of stranded power. Also, because rack loading needs to be done on the basis of peak consumption, doing so severely limits the number of servers even though those peaks are almost never reached and, if they are, they rarely overlap.

Intel power management can address this issue; it has been used in proof of concept experiments to increase rack loading by 40 to 60 percent in racks operated under fixed power budgets.

Power Workload Optimization

The power workload optimization use case is an extension and evolution of rack loading optimization. Experiments performed indicate that where for I/O and memory intensive workloads, a power cap of 40 watts can be applied with little impact on performance.

Power and Thermal Monitoring and Event Management

The notion of events enable management software using the Intel Data Center Manager SDK to take action on specific conditions.

The implementation of the reduction of stranded power above would use events: if the collective consumption of the rack is about to exceed 6 kW, the guard rail kicks in and Intel Data Center Manager instructs Intel Intelligent Power Node Manager running in the servers to roll back power consumption just enough to keep power consumption from exceeding the threshold

SLA-Driven Power Allocation to Workloads

Management software regulating power-aware scheduling of workloads may allocate these workloads to server groups under specific power consumption profiles, enforced by specific Intel Data Center Manager policies attached to the group.

For example, picture three service classes for workloads: representing high, medium, and low priority workloads. The high priority workloads run on unconstrained servers; they can take all the power they need to run as fast as they can. Medium priority workloads are assigned to power capped servers. These will run slower but they will still run. A server running a low priority workload may be put to sleep if the power it would use needs to be reallocated elsewhere.

Power Forecasting in Data Center Operations Planning

Having a record of power consumption is useful for planning purposes even if no active power management is enforced.

The historical record can be used to institute tighter bounds on power allocation for the groups of servers involved, increasing the utilization of the existing data center electrical power infrastructure.

Knowledge of historical power consumption records can be used to put together accurate power forecasts into the future that will allow negotiations with utility suppliers for power contracts. Advance knowledge of power consumption allows utilities to schedule generation accordingly and deliver power at lower prices.

Power Metering and Chargeback Services

Power as a fraction of operating costs has increased from noise level item to a major consideration. Hence the historical trend is to meter the cost component of power at increasingly finer granularity. A few years ago, and even in some facilities today, the cost of power was included in the facilities charge to IT. As the cost of energy becomes a larger portion of data center TCO, pressure will mount to make this charge explicit as a component to the cost of operations. Doing so is difficult today, because power metering is done at the utility feed level. Intel Data Center Manager brings the granularity of metering one step finer, at the level of individual servers. With Intel Data Center Manager, hosting operators now have the option of billing for the cost of electricity on a per server basis.

Business Continuity

A good example would be a case where a chiller would go out in a data center. Without power capping, IT would need to take extreme actions such as hard shutdown of servers to prevent damage. Intel Intelligent Power Node Manager would allow a power cap to be applied to the servers, reducing their power consumption, and either allowing the servers to continue to operate during the outage or at least give IT more time to shut some or all of the servers down gracefully.

Effect of Power Capping on Performance

Robert A. Heinlein popularized the term TANSTAAFL ("There ain't no such thing as a free lunch") in his 1966 novel *The Moon Is a Harsh Mistress.* The first question that comes to our mind when first exposed to Intel Intelligent Power Node Manager technology is the following: this technology works by slowing down the CPU; does TANSTAAFL apply here? It certainly does, in terms of some additional application deployment complexity and indeed some performance impact.

On the flip side, the benefit of Intel Intelligent Power Node Manager comes in form of power scalability, and making the tradeoff between power and performance explicit to applications, management consoles, and ultimately, to the user.

When Intel Intelligent Power Node Manager is enabled in a system, the application or the management entity can select the optimal operating point for power consumption whenever is beneficial to do so or turn it off at will with no overhead cost whatsoever.

Intel Intelligent Power Node Manager is useful even when it is not actively power capping but is used as a guardrail, ensuring that power consumption will not exceed a threshold. The predictable power consumption has monetary value because it provides data center operators a ceiling in power consumption. Having this ceiling helps operators optimize the data center infrastructure and reduce stranded power, a power delivery capability that needs to be there for occasional use, and yet none of the putative effects on server performance are realized because Intel Intelligent Power Node Manager does not kick in during normal operations.

The bottom line, as we shall see from the ensuing discussion, is that the performance impact can vary from zero when Intel Intelligent Power Node Manager is used as a guardrail to a percentage equal to the number of CPU cycles lost due to power capping when Intel Intelligent Power Node Manager is applied at 100-percent utilization. When applied during normal operating conditions, the loss of performance is smaller than the number of cycles lost to power capping implies because the OS usually compensates for the slowdown. If the end user is willing to re-prioritize application processes, under some circumstances it is possible to bring performance back to the uncapped level or even beyond.

Power Capping

A discussion about the performance tradeoff in Intel Intelligent Power Node Manager usually refers to the effect of the application of power capping. As we saw earlier, power capping is attained through voltage and frequency scaling. Power consumed by a CPU is proportional to frequency and to the square of the voltage applied to the CPU. This is done in discrete steps (P-states as defined by the ACPI standard). An Intel Xeon 5500 Series CPU can support up to thirteen P-states depending on the particular SKU.

The highest performing (lowest numbered) P-states are also the most energetic. Starting from a fully loaded CPU, the DBS assigns lower energy P-states as workload is reduced through the Intel® SpeedStep Technology. An additional dip takes place as idle is reached as unused logical units in the CPU are switched off automatically as shown in Figure 4.9.

Please note that the data in this section is not intended for benchmarking the absolute SPECpower performance of the platforms quoted. The runs for this benchmark, or as a matter of fact, for any of the benchmarks runs mentioned in this chapter, were not done under the controlled conditions prescribed by the benchmark.

Running the SPECpower benchmark application allows throttling the performance yield from full CPU utilization down to zero and contains a mix of workloads that give the CPU a good workout and hence provides insight into the performance versus power behavior of server platforms.

Performance versus Power

The SPECpower plots in Figure 4.9 depict data for three server platforms; the highest (blue) plot is that of a prototype Intel Xeon 5500 Series system. The lower two represent two shipping systems. The SR1600UR is a general purpose, dual CPU rack mount server code named Urbanna, whereas the S5500WB is a low power baseboard mounted in a 1U chassis, code named Willowbrook. The S5500WB has been optimized for deployment in Internet portal data centers; it is generally provisioned with lower power CPUs and all components not essential for IPDC applications have been removed from the baseboard.

The plots in Figure 4.9 were done by adjusting the yield with the knobs provided by the benchmark software and recording the ensuing power consumption.

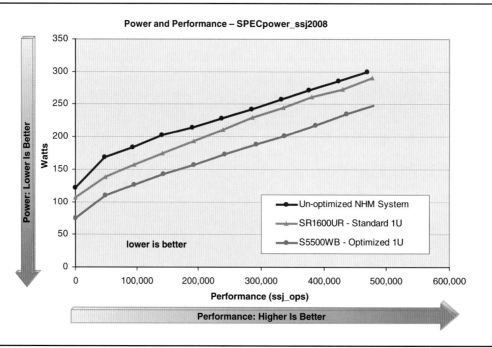

Figure 4.9   Single Node Power Proportional Computing

Intel Intelligent Power Node Manager allows manipulating the P-states under program control instead of autonomously as under the Intel SpeedStep Technology. Since the CPU is running slower, this has the effect of potentially removing some of the cycles that otherwise could be used by applications, but reality is more nuanced.

It helps understand the dynamics involved if we look at what happens at both ends of the curve. On the right side the CPU is running at nearly 100 percent utilization. Under these circumstances, most of the cycles are taken by the application; cycles taken by OS tasks will likely represent a small percentage of the total CPU cycles. Hence, if power capping is applied, a reduction in CPU speed will yield and almost one-to-one reduction in application performance.

On the left side, the CPU is idling and power consumption is already at the floor level. An application of Intel Intelligent Power Node Manager will not yield any additional power consumption reduction. The effect of Intel Intelligent Power Node Manager on performance is irrelevant because the application is idling.

The more interesting cases take place in the mid-range band of utilization, when the utilization rate is between 10 and 60 percent. Taking utilization beyond 60 percent is not desirable because the system would have difficulty in taking up load spikes and hence response times may deteriorate to unacceptable levels. Running servers at below 10 percent makes them targets for consolidation exercises.

In Figure 4.10, the effect of applying Intel Intelligent Power Node Manager from any starting point generally moves that point downward and slightly to the left. The effect is more pronounced toward the right side of the graph and nil on the left.

We ran a number of applications in the lab and observed their performance behavior under Intel Intelligent Power Node Manager. Surprisingly, the performance loss is generally *less* than frequency scaling would indicate.

There are two potential mechanisms at work:

1. One possible explanation, applicable to *CPU-intensive applications* is that when utilization is in the mid-range, there are idle cycles available. The OS scheduler compensates to some extent for the slower cycles by increasing the time slices to the applications, using up otherwise idle cycles, to the point that the apparent performance or throughput of the application is little changed.

2. A second possible mechanism is that the CPUs are usually not the performance bottleneck in the system and applying power capping will not have appreciable effect on performance until the CPU itself becomes the bottleneck. The situation is especially applicable to *data-intensive applications* where the CPUs spend a lot of time just waiting for I/O completion or waiting behind a database lock. It also takes place in *memory-intensive applications* where the CPUs spend considerable time waiting for data being retrieved from memory.

We conducted a number of experiments with applications or workloads exhibiting these two profiles and observe behaviors consistent with the two mechanisms described above. The results presented in this section are not meant as incontrovertible scientific proof; they should be taken as a report of observed facts to encourage interested readers to conduct a deeper exploration on the behaviors of their favorite application.

The Effect of Intel® Intelligent Power Node Manager on CPU-Intensive Applications

The software suite in the SPECpower benchmark is an example of a CPU intensive workload. It also features a throttling knob, the target load that allows adjusting the workload imposed on the server and therefore the performance yield. This benchmark defines the extreme end in terms of performance sensitivity to power capping in the applications that we have observed. All other applications observed exhibit less variability in terms of performance yield.

Figure 4.10 depicts a series of parametric curves plotting SPECpower yield in server side Java operations or SSJ Ops against platform power, each with defined by a throttle setting. In the topmost curve we let SPECpower run unbridled. Starting on the right with the uncapped server, we apply increasingly aggressive capping and measure the actual power consumption until the bottom of the control range is reached. The curve starts at 270 watts and 360,000 SSJ Ops and ends at about 200 watts and 225,000 SSJ Ops. For the subsequent curves we adjust the yield to 90, 70 percent and so on down to 10 percent.

The 40 percent curve is flat at the bottom at 90,000 SSJ Ops: after it reaches this level the yield stays flat even as the CPU slows down: somehow the benchmark gets a constant number of CPU cycles even as the CPU itself slows down. The relationship is obviously complex and nonlinear. The set power is not necessarily the same as the actual power. The two numbers are usually close but not the same because of imperfections in the control feedback loop. The hook at the low end in the 90 percent curve is an anomaly where the server is commanded to go to the lowest power setting, and it responds by actually increasing both power and yield slightly.

Some of the observed behaviors may be due to interactions between the behavior of SPECpower and the priority that the operating system gives to the processes running the benchmark, interactions that are not obvious from the available data.

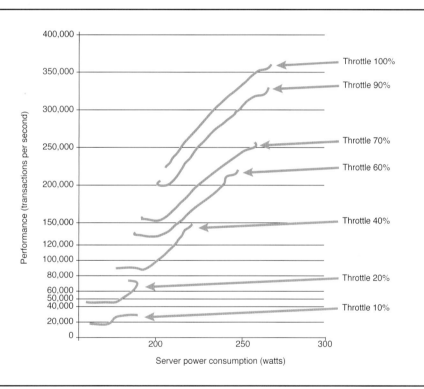

Figure 4.10 Performance versus Capping, CPU-Intensive Workload

To study the effect of workload priority under capping, we conducted a proof of concept experiments in collaboration with the automobile manufacturer BMW using a mix of applications run at a BMW site. The goal was to explore the boundaries of the extent to which that application could be re-prioritized under power capping to restore the original, uncapped throughput.

If it is possible to apply capping and yet restore the original, uncapped throughput, this begs the question of running under a capped regime at all times. Unfortunately, TANSTAAFL still applies here. Yes, the application is still yielding the same performance under power capping. However, since there are fewer cycles available due to frequency scaling, there will be less headroom should the workload pick up suddenly and the application performance may become unacceptable. In this case the remedy is simply to remove the cap. The management software needs to be aware of these circumstances and initiate the appropriate action. Hence it is possible to reduce power consumption running under a capped regime. The tradeoff is some operational complexity to monitor SLA and pull back on the level of capping should a workload spike take place.

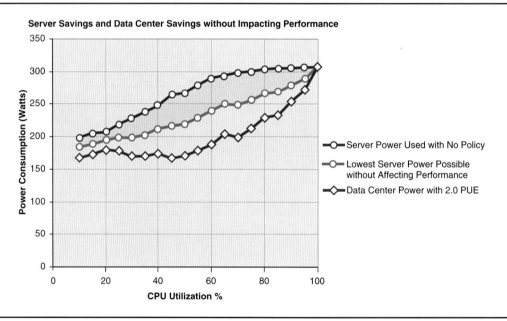

Figure 4.11   BMW Proof of Concept: Power Consumption against CPU Utilization

In the first series of experiments we plotted power consumption against CPU utilization by throttling the workload up and down, shown in the middle graph of Figure 4.11.

In the second series, shown in green, for each dot in the original curve we apply an initial power cap. This yields a performance reduction.

The workload is throttled up until the uncapped performance is restored. This process is repeated with increasingly aggressive power caps until the original performance cannot be reached. The capped level is shown plotted in green. The difference between the red and green curves represents the range of power capping possible that allows restoring the original, uncapped performance by re-prioritizing the workload after capping. If we apply the data center PUE factor, the power savings due to Intel Intelligent Power Node Manager are even greater, as shown in the bottom graph of Figure 4.11.

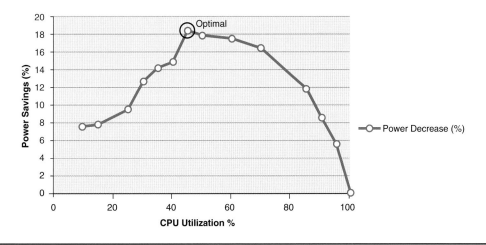

Figure 4.12   Maximum Power Savings versus Utilization without Affecting Performance

Figure 4.12 depicts the difference between the red and the green graphs. As expected, at 100 percent utilization the headroom is zero; the CPU is already fully utilized; any frequency scaling represents a one-for-one reduction in throughput, and no amount of workload throttling can bring the performance back to the uncapped level. At the other end of the spectrum the CPU is idle and the capping range is zero again. The sweet spot is somewhere in the middle.

Note that operating in the green line has the CPU running at close to 100 percent utilization and capped. Hence there is no headroom left for any load spikes. Any uptick in the workload will lead to immediate deterioration in performance or response time.

The Effect of Intel® Intelligent Power Node Manager on I/O- and Memory-Intensive Applications

To investigate the effect of power capping with I/O-intensive applications, an engineering team at our lab ran an Intel IT workload making heavy use of the Microsoft† SQL Server database software.

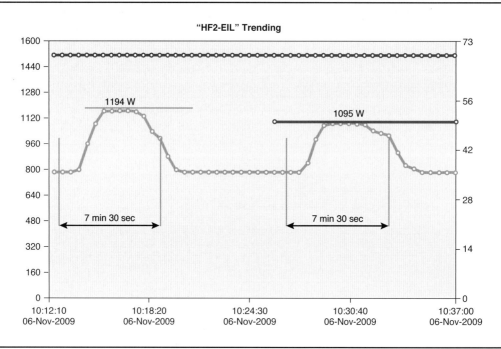

Figure 4.13   Two Intel IT Runs for an Intel IT Microsoft† SQL Server Workload

Figure 4.13 shows the power consumption plots for two successive runs of the workload. The workload ran on four Intel SR2600 2U servers provisioned with Intel Xeon 5500 Series processors. The first run was performed without any power capping in effect. Peak power consumption was 1194 watts, and ran for about 7 minutes and 30 seconds. The second run was performed with power for the server group capped at 1095 watts. The second run lasted exactly the same time, in spite of the CPU turning at a slower speed from capping. The most plausible explanation for this behavior is that because of concurrency, the extra time from the CPU running slower gets taken from the dead time waiting behind database locks.

This behavior is possible under moderate to low utilization factors. Performance deterioration is still possible during periods of high workload demand, in which case higher performing CPUs are still useful.

The next four benchmarks were running by manipulating P-states directly through standard in-band controls present in the Linux operating system and bypassing Intel Intelligent Power Node Manager Control to highlight the effect of P-state changes.

The four benchmarks in this experiment include

■ SPECjbb2005 - from the SPEC suite

■ STREAM - a memory bandwidth intensive application

■ OpenSSL - a CPU intensive, small memory usage application

■ OpenSIPS - a UDP SIP based proxy

The benchmarks were run in a pre-production dual socket SuperMicro server provisioned with Intel Xeon 5500 Series CPUs running at 2.93 MHz. Power was measured with an external Hameg programmable power meter.

The results are plotted in Figure 4.14. Each graph depicts the relative performance for each benchmark at each P-state, from P0 to P7. Of particular note are the STREAM results. The performance yield hardly changes as the marches through the different P-states. The benchmark puts a very light load in the CPU as evidenced by the small change in power consumption from 285 watts to 255 watts. An optimal power policy for this type of workload is a minimum power usage policy. The application of this policy would not have a performance impact at all.

The OpenSIPS benchmark loads the processor lightly and is not as memory intensive as STREAM. The capping range is only slightly larger at about 40 watts. Under Node Manager, the control range would have been even more compressed as the lower numbered P-states might not be reached due to low CPU utilization.

The OpenSSL lies at the other extreme of STREAM, and hence exhibits the largest power and performance variance of about 75 watts and 45 percent, respectively. This behavior is similar to the behavior we observed with SPECpower at 100 percent target load.

The results for SPECjbb2005 lie somewhere in between. The benchmark is designed to emulate a Java 5.0 3-tier transactional enterprise application, inspired by the TPC-C benchmark, and perhaps it is indicative of the capping range and performance variance for this type of applications.

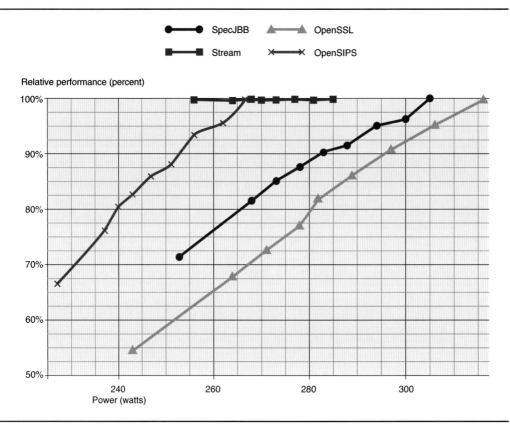

Figure 4.14   Effects of P-State Changes on Server Performance

Summary

Whenever a specific parameter becomes relevant to data center management, the first order of the day is to measure the parameter in an economical way. Power has become a first order operating expense consideration in the past few years. Intel Intelligent Power Node Manager and associated interfaces provides a uniform, commonly accessible way for applications to obtain real time platform power consumption data without the need to attach special purpose instrumentation, an impractical requirement during normal operations.

Once a monitoring capability exists for platform power consumption, it becomes useful to have a common means to control the monitored variables. This capability is also available from Intel Intelligent Power Node Manager. Hooks into Intel Intelligent Power Node Manager technology are available to manufacturers and system integrators at multiple levels of abstraction to bring opportunities to industry players to create value.

We covered the power management technology in the context of increasing process maturity that brings increasing capability in terms of the ability to continue operations under impaired power conditions and ultimately reduce energy consumption. We have just begun exploring the potential of this technology, and we provide some data points from proofs of concept performed as leading indicators for cost reduction.

Through composition we have taken a simple capability, namely a controlled dynamic voltage and frequency scaling capability, and combined it with composition mechanisms to implement sophisticated uses that can lower power consumption in large data centers by hundreds of kilowatts.

Chapter 5

Virtualized Cloud Power Management

Contributed by Enrique Castro-Leon, Miguel Gómez, Jim Blakley, Aamir Yunus, Herman Wong, and Rekha Raghu.

In the previous chapter we covered some fundamental concepts of power management applicable to server platforms and the data centers in which they are deployed. In this chapter we'll conduct a deeper analysis on a number of topics in virtualized cloud data centers providing analytical tools for readers interested in architecting solutions related to their present environment. We'll start with power considerations for virtualized environments, refine the notion of power versus energy management, define concepts of efficiency applicable to virtualized pools, and introduce the approach of composite usage models as an optimizing analytic tool to tailor power related technical solutions to match a specific business goal.

Power Management in Virtualized Cloud Environments

Given the recent intense focus in the industry around data center power management and the furious pace of the adoption of virtualization, it is remarkable that the subject of power management in virtualized cloud environments has received relatively little attention.

It is fair to say at the time of writing that power management technology has not caught up with the needs of the virtualized data center. For historical reasons the power management technology available today had its inception in the physical world where watts consumed in a server can be traced to the watts that came through the power utility infrastructure. Unfortunately, the semantics of power in virtual machines have yet to be comprehensively defined to industry consensus.

For instance, assume that the operating system running in a virtual image decides to transition the system to the ACPI S3 state, sleep to memory. What we have now is the state of the virtual image preserved in the image's memory with the virtual CPU turned off.

Assuming that the system is not paravirtualized, the operating system won't be able to differentiate whether it's running in a physical or virtual instance. The effect of transitioning to S3 will be purely local to the virtual machine. If the intent of the virtualized application was to transition the machine to S3 to save power, it does not work this way. The virtual machine still draws resources from the host machine and requires hypervisor attention. Transitioning the physical host proper to S3 may not be practical because other virtual machines might still be running, not ready to go to sleep.

Server consolidation is another technology for reducing data center power consumption by driving up the server utilization rates. Consolidation for power management is a blunt tool, where applications that used to run in a physical server are now virtualized and compressed into a single physical host. The applications are sometimes strange bedfellows. Application profiling might have been done to make sure the applications can coexist, as an a priori, static exercise, with the virtual machine instances treated as black boxes.

Server consolidation technology makes no attempt to look at the workload profiles inside each virtualized instance and in real time. Power savings come from an almost wishful side effect of repackaging applications formerly running in a dedicated server into virtualized instances.

A capability to map power to virtual machines, in both directions, from physical to virtual and virtual to physical would be useful from an operational perspective. The challenge is twofold, first from a monitoring perspective because no method has as yet been commonly agreed upon to prorate host power consumption to the virtual instances running within, and second from a control perspective. It would be useful to schedule or assign power consumption to virtual machines, allowing end users to make a tradeoff between power and performance. Fine-grained power monitoring would allow prorating power costs to application instances, introducing useful pricing checks and balances encouraging energy consumption instead of the more common method today of hiding energy costs in the facility costs.

Let's look at a similar dynamic in a different context: In some regions in the globe water used to be so inexpensive that residential use was not metered. The water company would charge a fixed amount every month and that was it. Hence, tenants in an apartment would never see a water bill. The water bill was a predictable cost component in the total cost of the building and included in the rent. Water was essentially an infinite resource and reflecting this fact, there were absolutely no incentives in the system for residents to rein in water use.

As population increased, water became increasingly a more precious and expensive resource. The water company started installing residential water meters, but bowing to tradition, landlords continued to pay the bills, which was still a very small portion of the overall operating costs. Tenants still had no incentive to save water because they did not see the water bill.

Today there are very few regions in the world where water can be treated as an infinite resource. In our initial example, the cost of water increased so much faster than other cost components to the point that landlords decided to expose this cost to tenants. Hence the practice of tenants paying the specific consumption for the unit they occupy is common today. Also, because this consumption is exposed at the individual unit level, the historical data can be used as the basis for the implementation of water conservation policies, for instance charging penalty rates for use beyond a certain threshold.

The use of power in the data center has been following a similar trajectory. For many years the cost of power had been a noise level item in the cost of operating a data center. It was practical to include the cost of electricity in the bill of the cost of the facilities. Hence IT managers would never see the energy costs. This situation is changing as we speak. See for instance this recent article in *Computerworld*.[1]

---

1   http://www.computerworld.com/s/article/9126920/Power_struggle_What_role_should_IT_play_in_
    reining_in_energy_costs_

Server platforms enabled with Intel® Intelligent Power Node Manager allow compiling a historical record for power usage. The historical information is useful for data center planning purposes by delivering a much tighter forecast, beneficial in two ways: by reducing the need to over-specify the power designed into the facility or by maximizing the amount of equipment that can be deployed for a fixed amount of power available.

From an operational perspective we can expect ever more aggressive implementations of power proportional computing in servers where we see large variations between idle power consumption and power draw at full load. As mentioned earlier, this variation used to be less than 10 percent. Today 50 percent is not unusual. Data center operators can expect wider swings in data center daily and seasonal power demand cycles. These swings bring additional management challenges. Server power management technology provides the means to manage these swings, stay within a data center's power envelope, and yet maintain existing service level agreements with customers.

There is still one more complication: with the steep adoption of virtualization in the data center in the past two years starting with server consolidation, an increasing portion of business is being transacted using virtualized and possibly cloud resources. Under this new environment, using a physical host as the locus for billing power may not be sufficient anymore, especially in multi-tenant environments, where the cost centers for virtual machines running in a host may reside in different departments or even in different companies.

It is reasonable to expect that this mode of fine-grained power management at the virtual machine level will take root in cloud computing and hosted environment where resources are typically deployed as virtualized resources. Fine-grained power monitoring and management makes sense in an environment where energy and carbon footprint is a major TCO component. To the extent that energy costs are exposed to users just as the MIPS consumed, this information provides the checks and balances and the data to implement rational policies to manage energy consumption.

Based on the considerations above, we envision power monitoring and control practices to evolve under the following three scenarios.

■ Undifferentiated, one bill for the whole facility. Power hogs and energy efficient equipment are thrown in the same pile. Metrics to weed out inefficient equipment are hard to come by.

■ Power monitoring at the physical host level implemented. Exposes inefficient equipment. Many installations are feeling the pain of increasing energy cost, but organizational inertia prevents passing costs to IT operations. Power monitoring at this level may be too coarse grained, too little, too late for environments that are rapidly transitioning to virtualization with inadequate support for multi-tenancy.

■ Fine-grained power monitoring. Power monitoring encompasses virtualized environments. This capability would align power monitoring with the unit of delivery of value to customers.

We expect these scenarios to be correlated with practices under the Data Center Power Management Capability Maturity Model. The first scenario would prevail in Stage 1 and 2 shops; the second scenario would be typical of Stage 3. The technology to support the most advanced scenario is still being perfected today. Combined with the process maturity needed to implement it, we don't expect this scenario to be implemented earlier than Stage 5 shops.

Before we continue it will be useful to formally define two concepts that we touched earlier in this chapter, namely *power capping range* and *power dynamic range*, followed by a discussion on the subtle differences between *power* management and *energy* management.

Power Capping and Power Dynamic Range

Up to this point we have been using power capping and power dynamic range informally. These numbers constitute important indicators for power management performance applicable to a single server or to a server pool. Let's use some mathematical rigor for a more precise definition of what these figures of merit mean.

The *power capping range* is the ratio of power consumed under full load over power consumed when the machine or group is capped to the lowest possible power consumption:

$$\rho_{capping} = \frac{P_{load}}{P_{capped,load}}$$

where P_{load} represents group power consumption under workload; $P_{capped,load}$ represents the same, but under maximum capping action.

The reciprocal, $1/\rho_{capping}$ represents how much power consumption is lowered when the machine or group are capped for lowest power consumption. The capping range applied to a group of machines is the average for all machines in the group:

$$\rho_{capping} = \frac{\Sigma_i P_{i,load}}{\Sigma_i P_{i,capped,load}}$$

Likewise, the *power dynamic range* is the ratio of power consumed under full load over power consumed when the machine or group is idling. It is similar to $\rho_{capping}$, except that the denominator used is the idle power, not the capped power:

$$\rho_{dynamic} = \frac{P_{load}}{P_{idle}}$$

Where P_{idle} represents the idle power consumption. A machine with a $\rho_{dynamic}$ number of 2:1 means that its idle power consumption is one half of its peak power consumption. The group version is defined similarly:

$$\rho_{dynamic} = \frac{\Sigma_i P_{i,load}}{\Sigma_i P_{i,idle}}$$

Note that these ratios are particular to a machine and a machine configuration. For $\rho_{capping}$, the addition of an unmanaged component, for instance memory and hard drives, will add the same quantity in the numerator and denominator, and hence will tend to lower the ratio. Conversely, when memory becomes a managed component, it may improve the figure of merit.

The $\rho_{dynamic}$ ratio is also dependent on the machine's target idle state. As an example, assume a machine consuming 300 watts at full load and 25 watts in S5 (soft off) state. For this particular situation,

$$\rho_{dynamic} = \frac{P_{load}}{P_{idle}} = \frac{300}{25} = 12$$

that is, the machine exhibits a $\rho_{dynamic}$ ratio of 12:1 for S5. Using the reciprocal metric, we can say that the machine consumes only about 8 percent of its peak consumption during S5.

Here are some examples from the Intel Cloud Builder[2] engagement with Microsoft. The measurements were taken from a pool of two machines running Microsoft Windows[†] 2008 with the Hyper-V role enabled. The syn-

---

2   http://software.intel.com/en-us/articles/intel-cloud-builder/

thetic workload MaxPower was loaded on the virtual machines until the host reached peak power consumption. Runs were made on an Intel Server Board S5500WB, a low power baseboard mounted in a 1U chassis, code named Willowbrook. Each server is provisioned with 24 GB of memory and one internal hard drive.

Figure 5.1 shows the calibration power run trace for the machine named ComputeNode3. After the machine reached a peak consumption of 309 watts, an aggressive cap beyond the current control range was applied.

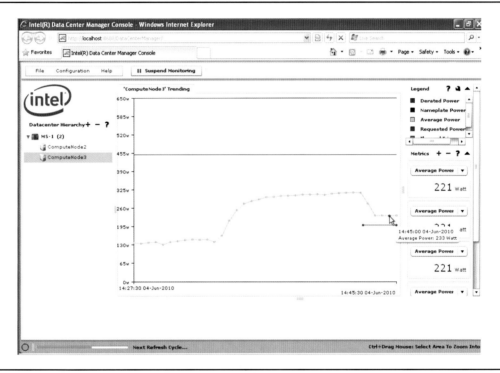

Figure 5.1   Power Run Trace for Compute Node 3

The capping ratio for this machine is

$$\rho_{capping} = \frac{P_{load}}{P_{capped,load}} = \frac{309\ watts}{233\ watts} = 1.32$$

The numbers for ComputeNode2 were 252 watts and 191 watts, respectively. Hence the collective capping ratio for the two nodes would be

$$\rho_{capping} = \frac{(309 + 252)}{(233 + 191)} = 1.32$$

Note the significant variation in power consumption even though the two machines were configured identically.

Power Management versus Energy Management

Discussions about power management actually involve two main aspects, *power management* proper and *energy management*. A metric for power management allows us to track operational "goodness," making sure that power draw never exceeds limits imposed by the infrastructure. The second metric tracks power saved over time, which is energy saved. Energy not consumed goes directly to the bottom line of the data center operator.

Energy represents a capability to deliver a certain amount of work, whereas power represents an instantaneous measure of a capability of *intensity* to carry out that work. In electrical terms power is measured in watts. Energy represents power applied over a time interval. Hence energy is measured in watt-hours.

Power consumed by a server can vary instantaneously and continuously. The language of calculus is useful for expressing this time-varying relationship: the energy consumed by a server is represented by the integral of its power consumption over that particular interval:

$$E = \int P(t)dt$$

A power saving mechanism can also yield energy savings. To understand the dynamic between power and energy management let's look at the graph below and imagine a server without any power management mechanisms whatsoever. The power consumed by that server would be $P_{unmanaged}$ regardless of any operating condition. Most servers today have a number of mechanisms operating concurrently, and hence the actual power consumed at any given time t is $P_{actual}(t)$. The difference $P_{unmanaged} - P_{actual}$ is the power saved. The power saved carried over time, t_1 through t_2 yields the energy saved during that particular interval.

Mathematically, the energy saved is represented by the equation

$$E = \int_{t_1}^{t_2} (P_{unmanaged}(t) - P_{actual}(t))\, dt$$

The graphical representation of this equation is shown in Figure 5.2. From this analysis it becomes clear that in order for a power saving mechanism to yield meaningful energy savings, power savings need to be maintained for a long time and the difference between $P_{unmanaged}$ and P_{actual} needs to be as large as possible.

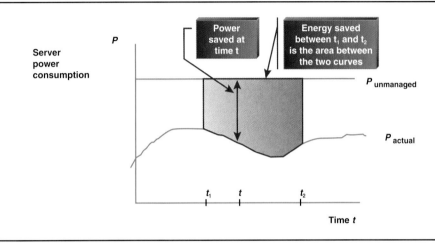

Figure 5.2   Power and Energy Saved from Application of Management Technology

Note that a mechanism that yields significant power savings may not necessarily yield high energy savings. For instance, as previously mentioned, the application of Intel Intelligent Power Node Manager can bring down power consumption by about 100 watts, from 300 watts at full load to 200 watts in a dual-socket 2U Intel® Xeon® processor 5500 series through the use of voltage and frequency scaling. However, if Intel Intelligent Power Node Manager is used as a guard rail mechanism, to limit power consumption if a certain threshold is violated, Intel Intelligent Power Node Manager may never kick in, and hence energy savings will be zero for practical purposes. The reason why we do this is because Intel Intelligent Power Node Manager works best only under certain operating conditions, namely high loading factors, and, because it works through frequency and voltage scaling, it brings a power consumption versus performance tradeoff.

Power Proportional Computing

Another useful figure of merit for power management is the dynamic range for power proportional computing. Energy proportional designs have been proposed to achieve a significant saving in energy consumption in the data center.

The relationship is not necessarily linear but assume it is to simplify the discussion. Hence, the power consumption of this server can be represented by this model:

$$P_{actual} = P_{baseline} + P_{spread}L$$

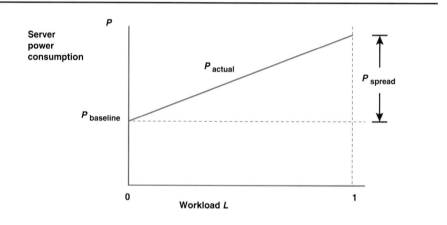

Figure 5.3 Power Proportional Computing.

This model is represented graphically in Figure 5.3. The x-axis represents the workload that can range from 0 to 1, that is, 0 to 100 percent. $P_{baseline}$ is the power consumption at idle, and P_{spread} is the power proportional computing dynamic range between $P_{baseline}$ and power consumption at 100 percent workload. A low $P_{baseline}$ is better because it means a low power consumption at idle.

As previously mentioned, for a Intel Xeon processor 5500 series-based server, $P_{baseline}$ is roughly 50 percent of power consumption at full utilization, which is remarkable, considering that it represents a 20 percent over the number we observed for the prior generation servers using the Intel Xeon processor 5400 series[3]. The 50 percent figure is a number we have observed in our lab for a whole server, not just the CPU alone.

With the typical 5 to 10 percent loading, the actual power consumption from servers will also be less than the peak. However, even when loading factors are low, power consumption remains significant portion of peak.

As mentioned above, a low $P_{baseline}$ is better. Current technology imposes a limit on how low this number can be. Progress has been considerable. Just a few years ago it was close to 90 percent of full power, and today it stands at about 50 percent. That's the current limit if we look at a server as our unit of analysis.

If a 50 percent $P_{baseline}$ looks outstanding, we can do even better for certain application environments such as load-balanced front end Web server pools and the implementation of cloud services through clustered, virtualized servers. We can achieve this effect through shutting down or *parking* idle servers. For instance, consider a pool of 16 servers. If the pool is idle, all the servers except one can be parked. The single idle server is consuming only half the power of a fully loaded server, consuming one half of one sixteenth of the cluster power. The dormant servers still draw about 8 percent of full power. Hence, after doing the math, the total power consumption for the cluster at idle will be about 8 percent of the full cluster power consumption. For a clustered deployment, the power dynamic range has been increased from 2:1 for a single server to about 10:1 for the cluster as a whole.

Luiz Barroso in his classic 2007 paper[4] posited that given that servers in data centers were loaded between 10 and 50 percent of peak, it would be beneficial from an energy perspective to have servers with a large power dynamic ratio, the ratio of power consumed at full workload to power at idle. Figure 5.4 represents the state of the art today with a dynamic ratio of about 2:1.

---

3   This particular experiment was conducted with an S5000SL platform provisioned with two Intel ®Xeon® E5440 processors and configured with 8 GB of memory and one SATA hard disk drive.

4   http://www.barroso.org/

Let's assume these servers deployed in a traditional data center, that is, a nonvirtualized data center with the operating system still running on bare metal. For these centers, common utilization rates hover around 15 percent and efficiency runs at about 20 percent. The operating band depicted is more conservative than what Barroso indicated, with a CPU utilization that rarely surpasses 40 percent.

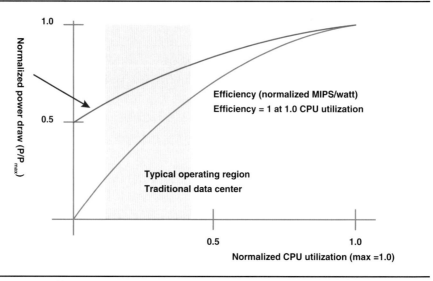

Figure 5.4   Efficiency as Function of Workload Demand

A 20 percent efficiency is rather low compared with the efficiency obtained at higher load factors toward the right side of the graph.

Figure 5.5 shows what happens if we improve the dynamic ratio to 5:1. A 5:1 dynamic ratio means $P_{baseline}$ is only 20 percent of peak power when idle. This is not possible today for single servers, but it is attainable for cloud data centers and as a matter of fact, for any environment that allows servers be managed collectively as pools of fungible resources and where server parking is in effect: a lower $P_{baseline}$ means efficiency ramps up much faster with workload.

The improved dynamic ratio also dramatically improves the operating efficiency in the operating band of the data centers, but it gets even better: the servers in the active pool are kept in the sweet spot of utilization in the range of 60 to 80 percent. If the CPU utilization in the active pool gets below

60 percent, the management application starts removing servers from the active pool to the parked pool until the utilization starts inching up. If the CPU utilization gets close to the upper range, the management applications starts bringing back servers from the parked pool into the active pool to provide relief and bring the utilization numbers down.

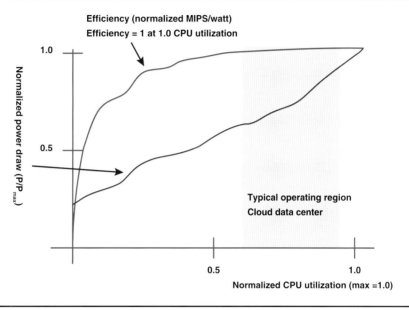

Figure 5.5   Power Proportional Computing with Cloud Clusters

Optimizing Power Performance in Virtualized Cloud Data Centers

Two approaches are commonly applied to reduce lighting energy use in residential or commercial buildings: turning lights off and using dimming mechanisms.

Turning lights off yields the greatest power savings, assuming the room is not to be used. A small amount of residual power is still being drawn to power pilot lights or motion sensors to turn on the illumination if someone enters the room.

Dimming the lights reduces power consumption when a room is in use it is possible to reduce the illumination level while allowing people to occupy the room for the intended purpose. For instance, illumination in certain areas may not be needed because mixed daylight is in use, zonal lighting on work areas is sufficient, or because the application calls for reduced lighting, such as in a restaurant or dining room. Power saved through dimming will be less than turning lights off.

Similar mechanisms are available in servers deployed in data centers. Applying server parking would be the equivalent of turning lights off in a room. The capability for "dimming lights" in a server is embodied by the Enhanced Intel® SpeedStep® technology and Intel Intelligent Power Node Manager technology. Enhanced Intel SpeedStep technology reduces power consumption during periods of low workload and Intel Intelligent Power Node Manager can cap power, that is, reduce power consumption at high workload levels under application control.

There is also a richer set of options for turning off servers than there are for turning lights off. The ACPI standard defines at least three states suitable for server parking: S3 (sleep to memory), S4 (hibernation where the server state is saved in a file) and S5 (soft off, where the server is powered down except for the circuitry to turn it on remotely under application control). The specific choice depends on hardware support; not all states are supported by a specific implementation. It also depends on application requirements. A restart from S3, if supported by the hardware, can take place much faster than a restart from S5. The tradeoff is that S3 consumes more energy than S5 because of the need to keep the DIMMs charged.

A widespread use of server parking is not feasible with traditional where a hard binding exists between the application components and the hardware host because bringing any of the hosts offline could cripple the application. This binding gets relaxed for virtualized cloud environments that support dynamic consolidation of virtual machines into a subset of active hosts.

With the binding between hosts and virtual machines, it is feasible to move virtual machines around effectively defining a sub-pool of active hosts grown or shrunk to optimize utilization levels as shown in Figure 5.6. The active pool contains the servers running application virtual machines. During periods of decreasing demand, when server utilization goes below a predefined threshold, the management application consolidates virtual machines into a smaller pool of active servers. Vacated hosts are parked, the equivalent of turning lights off in a room, and as in the lighting example, once a server is in parked state the server can't run applications.

Conversely, during periods of increasing demand, if the load average increases above a predefined threshold, the management application restarts one of the dormant servers in the parked pool and spreads out the virtual machines to provide relief to machines in the active pool.

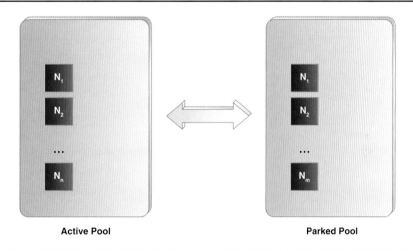

Active Pool   **Parked Pool**

Figure 5.6   Dynamic Reconfiguration plus Server Parking

Composite Usage Models

Combining the application of Intel Intelligent Power Node Manager power capping with ACPI S3 or S5 server parking is an example of a *composite usage*. A composite power usage is analogous to approaches used in other knowledge domains, such as in the making of single malt or single grain whiskies versus blended whiskies or varietal wines versus blended wines involving the blending of different products to achieve a specific flavor or effect. In medicine, it is not uncommon for physicians to combine several drugs to treat serious conditions and produce certain desired therapeutic effects.

The motivating use case for the composite approach in this section is to extend the power dynamic range to a degree comparable to the daily cycle dynamic range typical of common workloads. From our observations, a dynamic range of at least 5:1 is desirable because it can bring power consumption down to the ballpark level of utilization in traditional data centers around 20 percent.

Placing servers in a low energy state essentially changes the configuration of a pool of servers servicing a cloud workload, and hence we name this approach *dynamic reconfiguration*.

We have measured a number current generation servers in the lab. We found for S5 power consumption in the range of 5 to 8 percent of peak server power consumption while S3 power consumption hovers around 10 percent of peak power. The asymptotic value for achievable dynamic range is the reciprocal of these numbers, or about 12:1 for S5 and 10:1 for S3. In practice it will be less than that because at least one of the servers in the pool must remain active to be able to wake up the rest of the pool, unless a separate console is in use to perform this action.

Under the TANSTAAFL principle, application of a composite usage is not free. It introduces complexity, which requires certain process maturity. In addition, each technology element brought into the mix brings side effects. These side effects need to be evaluated to ensure they won't interfere with the application, and when interference exists, measures are needed to neutralize the side effects.

The *main benefits* of dynamic reconfiguration are twofold:

■ Dynamic reconfiguration can potentially bring the average power consumption of a cluster of servers down to a level commensurate with workload demand. If the average workload demand is about 20 percent, we would expect the average power draw to be also about 20 percent of peak usage for the cluster, even though servers individually can't go below 50 percent of power usage, even at idle.

■ Second, dynamic reconfiguration can bring significant reductions in energy use by lowering the average power demand.

The main observed *side effect* of dynamic reconfiguration is a slower demand for demand spikes. The reason is that if when an uptick in demand takes place and a server in the pool needs to be restarted, it might take as long as 15 minutes to bring a server from S5 to an operating state.

Let's run the following scenario as an example. Imagine a pool of servers supporting an application. Furthermore, assume each server has a performance has a performance yield of 1,000 transactions per second (TPS) and that recovery time from S5 is 15 minutes.

The tuning of this installation would start with the examination of a daily cycle looking for the fastest occurrence of a demand spike. Let's say that the trace shows a bump in demand from 8,000 to 13,000 TPS in 2 minutes. The goal here is to have just enough servers running to meet the demand at any given time to save as much energy as possible.

Before the bump occurs, the system operator is happy running with 8 servers. As soon as the bump hits, there is trouble: two minutes after the bump, there is a demand for 13,000 TPS but the extra servers do not come online until 13 minutes later. Meanwhile, with 8 servers servicing a demand meant for 13, customers start experiencing longer and longer wait times until the SLA goes down the drain.

A solution for this situation is to have extra servers powered on, with enough numbers to ride the worst bump. In this case we'd need at least 5 extra servers online at all times only because they are needed for only one or two instances during the day. If demand is met with only 3 or 4 servers for most of the day, an extra 5 seems a price too steep to pay just to ride out the spikes.

Now assume that by using S3 instead of S5 the recovery time is reduced to 1 minute. Since recovery is so much faster, it may be possible to have only one or two servers in reserve and still meet the SLA.

What we have done is essentially create a third sub-pool of servers in standby to meet SLA requirements. Another approach to minimize the impact of maintaining the reserve sub-pool is to use these servers for low priority workloads and run them under an aggressive power cap to minimize their power draw. The management of the reserve pool is not static; if it looks like the reserve pool is getting exhausted due to a demand spike, the management application will start replenishing it to maintain a safety margin, with less urgency, because the servers in the reserve pool can be brought to work very quickly.

The pattern that emerges from this example is the notion of platoons: different contingents or sub-pools of servers backing each other to implement a global power management policy. For this reason we call this scheme for distributed power management *platooning*.

Figure 5.7 captures a generalized platooning framework, with parked states toward the right and active states toward the left and some in-between states. There is a choice of parking states offering different tradeoffs between power consumption and recovery time. Power capping can be applied to define other sub-pools and to trim power consumption as needed.

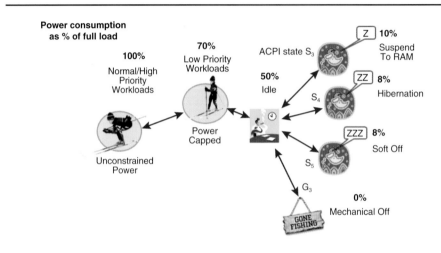

Figure 5.7   Generalized Platooning Framework

Platooning requires actively managing the server pools in each partition, either by transitioning the servers across different states, and hence moving them across platoons, or by moving workloads across platoons through the use of virtual machine migration technology.

In theory a platooning scheme can be made as complex as needed to meet most any power performance behavior. In practice a lot of weight needs to be given to simplicity. A scheme with three or more platoons can become difficult to manage: as platoons are added to achieve certain behaviors, additional platoons may need to be defined to counteract possible secondary effects.

Figure 5.8 summarizes the results of a platooning experiment performed during the Telefónica proof of concept. For a more detailed recount, please refer to Chapter 22. The setup for dynamic reconfiguration is the simplest possible: the application runs on two servers. At any given moment the application may be running on both servers, and hence the active pool contains two servers and the parked pool is empty, or it may be running with one server, in which case there is one server in each pool.

The time scale in the graphs is the same, a daily cycle starting at 4:00 AM and ending at 4:00 AM the next day. The top graphs capture the power consumed by the pool taken from Node Manager. The bottom graph represents the workload demand. The workload can vary by as much as 10:1 through the day, exhibiting two peaks.

The topmost line in the upper graph represents the baseline case where both servers were running throughout with no other mechanism than Enhanced Intel SpeedStep technology. Note that there is a slight reduction in power consumption during low demand, but not as large as the swing in workload demand and the expected variation from Enhanced Intel SpeedStep technology would indicate. What may be happening here is that even when the demand is small the application keeps running background tasks that keep the servers running at the most energetic P-states.

The lower curve in the top graph is a trace with dynamic reconfiguration and server parking in effect. The management application monitors KPIs for the application, essentially the wait time for service. If the wait time becomes shorter than required by the SLA, the management application deems the number of servers over-provisioned and shuts down one of the two servers.

As the workload picks up and waiting times for the application deteriorate, the application manager restarts the server to make sure the wait times do not deteriorate beyond those required by the SLA. The lower graph indicates that there is a significant reduction in power consumption vs. the baseline case. The difference in energy consumed is about 27 percent, a significant amount.

The shape of the power consumption curve begins to resemble the shape of the demand curve. The match is not perfect because of the small number of servers. When the second server is restarted, the supply is initially over-provisioned. For larger pools, the supply curve becomes a staircase approximation of the demand curve. It is also feasible to use power capping to adjust the performance level to better match the supply curve.

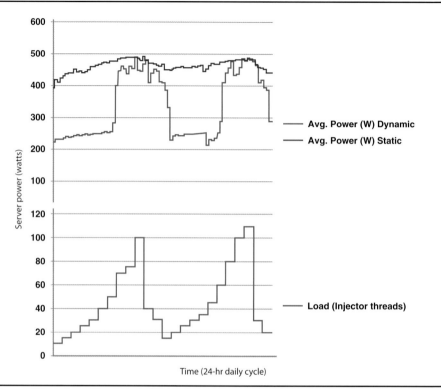

Figure 5.8   Comparison of Power Consumption under Autonomic versus Dynamic Reconfiguration Schemes for a Server Pool

This example illustrates how a composite usage, namely the reduction of energy use, not just power demand, can yield a benefit not anticipated in the original design for Intel Intelligent Power Node Manager, which was intended essentially to provide power management, not energy management.

Summary

In this chapter we defined the power capping range and dynamic range metrics as indicators of the power performance capability of a server platform or a pool of servers implementing a cloud service. We also establish the distinction between power management and energy management.

The capability of a platform for power proportional computing is relevant for achieving energy savings by taking advantage of the low utilization factor of many workloads as they go through their daily ups and downs. Machines with a high capping ratio perform well in this environment, but this may not be sufficient. We introduce the notion of composite usages where we combine one or more usages paired with their respective technologies to amplify the power proportional computing effect, for instance, combining Intel Intelligent Power Node Manager power capping with server parking, putting a server to sleep. An extra benefit from this approach is it is possible to attain significant energy savings. The Telefónica proof of concept indicated an energy reduction of 27 percent with the smallest possible pool size of two. Gains are likely larger with larger pool sizes.

Composite usages have side effects; they bring operational complexity, and hence composite schemes need to be architected with care. In the example mentioned, the composite scheme reduces the system's capability to follow workload spikes. Possible solutions are to add reserve machines that can come online fast, which requires more power, or use a more energetic parking state, which also requires more power.

Chapter 6

Mapping a Cloud Taxonomy to IT Strategy

Contributed by Hong Li, Catherine Spence, Robert Armstrong, Ricki Godfrey, Randy Schneider, Jake Smith, Judy Ossello, Enrique Castro-Leon, and Rick White

The cloud taxonomies covered in Chapters 2 and 3 provide insight into the understanding and evolution of cloud technology. However, the use of taxonomies has practical implications in helping IT organizations chart out a strategy for vendor evaluation and selection. In the case study covered in this chapter we show the elaboration of well-known taxonomic elements such as SaaS and IaaS into an ecosystem analysis providing inferences about various vendor offerings.

The cloud computing market is evolving rapidly, with a fast-growing number of external cloud services and enabling technologies. This creates a need for tools to better understand the market, define an internal IT and external cloud computing strategy, and facilitate adoption of cloud computing services targeted to specific needs. The analysis allows framing these needs and assessing the suitability of cloud vendor offerings to address these needs as well as the evaluation of internal and external cloud alternatives.

Taxonomies, that is, classifications based on a hierarchical structure, have traditionally been used to understand technology market segmentation and geographic breakdown, evaluate suppliers, and map potential usage to the available technologies. Another important advantage of taxonomies is that they provide a common terminology to facilitate understanding and communication.

From the perspective of cloud adoption, the cloud ecosystem, including service providers, end users, developers, and administrators, has a natural evolving order that can be represented by taxonomy. However, though several cloud taxonomies already exist, none of them in isolation provides a comprehensive analysis of the entire market as needed by Intel IT.

This shortcoming provided the motivation for a number of planning teams to convene and come up with a common, standard terminology across the stakeholder teams and make sense of the rapidly evolving cloud market as well as to identify key suppliers and products to address the stakeholders' needs. Steps included defining the primary categories of cloud computing service, segmenting these into subcategories, and creating an ecosystem analysis of the suppliers within each category.

Intel IT Capability Frameworks

Intel IT has developed several capability frameworks that assist in planning and decision making. These constitute a tool to facilitate understanding and alignment of top-level IT capabilities across the enterprise and the supporting ecosystem. We based our cloud computing taxonomy segmentation partly on these frameworks.

At its core, a *framework* is defined as a fundamental structure or set of assumptions and practices that constitute a way of viewing reality. A well-known framework for optimizing IT operations is ITIL. Frameworks are used to provide context and process around the reality of our business.

The capability frameworks have become a valuable tool to assist in inevitable tradeoff decision making associated with strategic planning by providing:

- A simple picture of the structure of the enterprise and the IT systems that support it

- Understanding and alignment of top level IT capabilities across the enterprise and supporting systems

Intel IT currently has four frameworks, three of which are published as the IT Frameworks proper, and the Capability Maturity Framework, or CMF, used to score the health of the information systems capability within the ECF framework. The three IT Frameworks (ECF, xECF, and ISF) are used to score the current of business processes, applications, data, and infrastructure. Figure 6.1 depicts the relationship between the frameworks.

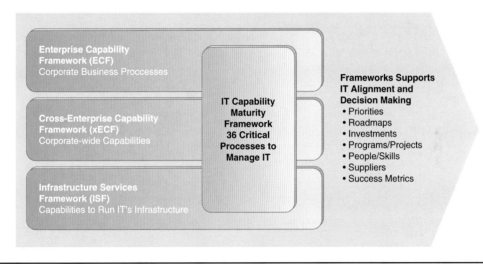

Figure 6.1   The Four IT Frameworks

Each framework provides a unique perspective of IT capabilities. Let's take a look.

■ The *Enterprise Capability Framework* (ECF) represents capabilities to run business specific functions. This framework holistically describes all the business capabilities

■ The *Cross-Enterprise Capability Framework* (xECF) represents horizontal, technical capabilities building blocks, not infrastructure components, used across business units such as Microsoft SharePoint[†] services and instant messaging.

■ The *Infrastructure Services Framework* (ISF) represents capabilities to run infrastructure. Servers, data centers, laptops, and networks all reside in this framework.

■ The *Capability Maturity Framework* (CMF) is complementary to the ECF, xECF, and ISF and enables IT to measure the maturity of a capability or service in order to help make decisions on the best IT investment proposals, deliver competitive advantage, and manage IT investments for optimal business value.

The capabilities described in these three main frameworks enable IT to deliver the business processes as seen by the customer business units. Using a restaurant analogy, the Intel IT "restaurant" provides a menu of available "dishes" offered by a wait-staff (ECF); ingredients, kitchen equipment, and recipes (xECF); and the foundation infrastructure to prepare food as well as keep customers comfortable within the "dining room" (ISF).

Making Sense of the Cloud Vendor Ecosystem

A departure point for Intel IT was an existing cloud computing approach from prior experience on growing the cloud from the inside out. Intel IT had been developing an enterprise private cloud with strong considerations to extend the private cloud to, and support interoperability with, the Internet or external cloud. A benefit of this approach is to allow Intel IT to dynamically transfer workload in and out of the enterprise, with actions driven by key performance indicators related to cost, security, and compliance.

While the jury deliberates, Intel IT has opportunistically been taking advantage of external cloud offerings that deliver value such as increased agility and cost savings, for instance by sourcing a number of human resources applications such as expense reporting and job postings to external providers. An Intel cloud computing taxonomy can help identify trend lines and specific additional offerings to meet enterprise needs.

The planning teams took advantage of characteristics of the cloud as discussed earlier: the cloud as a computing paradigm where services and data reside in shared resources in scalable data centers, and those services and data are accessible by any authenticated device over the Internet. To recap, some key attributes that distinguish cloud computing from conventional computing are:

- Abstracted and offered as a service.

- Built on a massively scalable infrastructure.

- Easily purchased and billed by consumption.

- Shared and multi-tenant.

- Based on dynamic, elastic, flexibly configurable resources.

- Accessible over the Internet by any device.

A long term trend in IT in the past few years has been a move toward server, data, and application consolidation. One example is driving all human resources applications out of the same employee roster database. Because of separate and organic development, the initial state might have been each application running out of a unique database for each application such as payroll, expense reporting, and benefits administration.

This style of transformation is well known with SOA projects where the entity designated for common access exports commonly agreed interfaces. Cost reduction comes from removing the need to maintain and update redundant capabilities. The paradigm applied is known as *inside-out*[1]. Cloud computing brings the complementary paradigm, *outside-in*. The challenge under this new paradigm is to figure out how to integrate pre-built vendor offerings into business applications, especially legacy applications.

- We identified primary categories of cloud computing service. Figure 6.2 shows these categories arranged according to their value and visibility to enterprise end users. Though most of these category names were already in use within the industry, our taxonomy defined two new categories: *cloud clients* and *service as a service*. The new categories address the areas of user experience and interoperability, respectively.

- *Software as a service (SaaS)* is a model of software deployment in which an end user or enterprise subscribes to software on demand. SaaS applications are built with shared back-end services that enable multiple customers or users to access a shared data model.

---

1 "Scaling Down SOA to Small Businesses." Enrique Castro-Leon, Jackson He and Mark Chang, IEEE Int'l Conference on Service-Oriented Computing and Applications, Newport Beach, CA in June 2007 (SOCA 2007). Also in *The Business Value of Service Oriented Grids*, Chapter 2, Castro-Leon, He, Chang and Peiravi, Intel Press (2009)

■ *Platform as a service (PaaS)* is the delivery of a cloud computing platform for developers. It facilitates development and deployment of applications without the cost and complexity of buying and managing the underlying hardware and software layers. PaaS provides all the facilities required to support the complete life cycle of building and delivering Web applications and cloud services over the Internet.

■ *Infrastructure as a service (IaaS)* is the delivery of technology infrastructure, such as network, storage, and compute, as a service, typically through virtualized cloud data centers. Users subscribe to this virtual infrastructure on demand as opposed to purchasing servers, software, data center space, or network equipment. Billing is typically based on pay per use, that is, on the resources consumed.

■ *Service as a service* is the delivery of a horizontal service, such as billing, as a service. These services can be used, usually on a subscription basis, as a component within other cloud services such as SaaS, PaaS, or IaaS offerings.

■ *Cloud software* is purchased or packaged software that is uniquely used to build and run cloud services, for example cloud management software. Our goal was to include the market subsegments, ISVs, and products not typically found in a traditional enterprise or consumer ISV taxonomy.

■ *Cloud client* technology comprises client-centric services, runtimes, and runtime optimizations that can impact the overall cloud computing user experience.

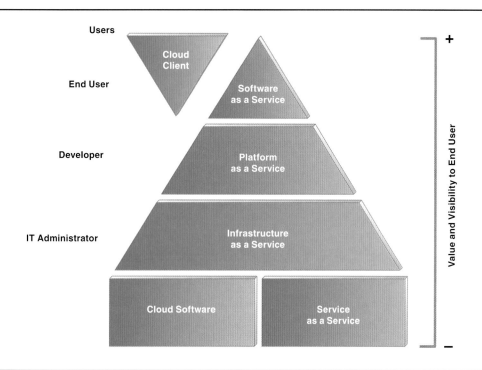

Figure 6.2   Primary Categories for Cloud Services

We expanded our cloud taxonomy by dividing the main categories into subcategories, as shown in Figure 6.3, based on the Intel IT capability frameworks and existing cloud taxonomies. This provided an additional layer of detail, which enabled us to cluster and compare ISVs with similar characteristics, delivered market insights, and helped to ensure that our taxonomy spanned the entire breadth of cloud computing offerings.

We mapped key ISVs to each of the taxonomy subcategories, and then added analysis such as each ISV's strategy, market position, revenue, and ecosystem alliances. Our goal was to identify market leaders and fast-moving, potentially disruptive innovators.

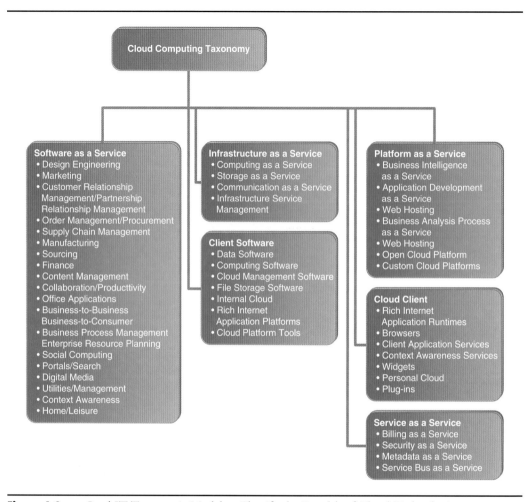

Figure 6.3   Intel IT Taxonomic Model to Classify the Breadth of Cloud Technologies

Table 6.1 shows a generic extract from our detailed ecosystem analysis for several subcategories within the SaaS category.

Table 6.1   Sample Outcomes from an SaaS Ecosystem Analysis

Enterprise Line of Business	Provider	Description
Marketing	ISV-1	Has a suite of products that provide core marketing capabilities for managing campaigns and complex marketing mixes.
	ISV-2	Provides focused software as a service (SaaS) marketing products. Venture capital–backed company with limited customer penetration.
	ISV-3	Strong customer portfolio including airlines, financial, telecom, software, and retail; revenue increased substantially last quarter.
	ISV-4	Targets the financial industry and retail/consumer packaged goods markets.
	ISV-5	Offers good breadth of functionality for basic and advanced campaign management, and for basic and advanced analytics. Has taken the lead on loyalty management, while many other vendors have still not disclosed firm plans.
	ISV-6	Strong hosted on-demand offering, which is attracting medium-sized businesses looking for cost effective solutions.
Customer Relationship Management	ISV-7	Full suite of customer relationship management (CRM) tools designed for any size customer, used by several large companies.
	ISV-8	Strong customer portfolio, significant increase in revenue for most recent quarter.
	ISV-9	Leading SaaS CRM vendor, leveraging their existing CRM suite for on-demand customer needs.
	ISV-10	Billed as the alternative to a full enterprise resource planning (ERP) suite but with solutions for small and medium businesses to larger companies. Strong customer base with a solid partner program supported around the world. Also contains a strong human resources software capability.
	ISV-11	Many new customers added, many of them larger than previously typical for this company. The company's strong ecosystem has assisted sales.
Partner Relationship Management	ISV-12	Revenue grew modestly in most recent quarter. Strong customer base. Sales slowly increasing; a company to watch.
	ISV-13	Strong channel supporting their core products. European company with strong ties to all key back-end products.
	ISV-14	Provides hosted services model using Web services capabilities. Joint marketing effort has been very well received.

Note: For illustration purposes only. Confidential information or information unique to specific suppliers has been removed or changed.

Using the Cloud Taxonomy and Ecosystem Analysis

Intel teams are using the taxonomy and analysis in discussions directed to identifying available and emerging cloud computing solutions.

The high level taxonomy forms the basis for these discussions across multiple stakeholders, helping introduce cloud computing concepts and categories, define common terminology, and position our inside-out strategy. The more detailed analysis is then used to focus on a cloud subcategory and identify top ISVs within the category. The resulting ISV list can be used in combination with industry analyst reports and other publicly available information to discover innovative solutions for further research and development projects, which in turn may influence Intel IT production roadmaps and Intel® platform technology enabling strategies.

For example, Intel IT is already using a variety of SaaS offerings. As we think about the future of our application portfolio, we are considering which applications we should host internally and which make sense in the SaaS model. We have found that good candidates for SaaS are applications with industry-standard workflows and well structured data exchanges, which do not involve intellectual property or sensitive data. Our ecosystem analysis spreadsheet makes it easier to identify SaaS solutions with these characteristics; we can then compare these solutions with traditional packaged enterprise solutions to assess possible efficiencies and cost savings.

Chapter **7**

Reference Architecture for Cloud Storage

Contributed by Enrique Castro-Leon

Rapid growth in demand for storage has data literally spilling out of the traditional confines of the corporate data center into the cloud. This has created opportunities for storage services through the deployment of storage appliances. What has not changed is the need for these appliances to be energy efficient. This chapter describes a template for quickly incorporating the energy-efficient features inherent in Intel microarchitecture processor-based servers into cloud storage appliances through the concept of cloud plug-ins. This is an instantiation of a Cloud Application Reference Architecture introduced in Chapter 3.

In cloud computing the concept of *appliance* represents a useful working abstraction, specifically a virtualized appliance.

An appliance is a piece of equipment or tool that performs a specific role. In cloud computing a virtualized appliance is an application bundled with all the hardware and software components needed to run it. This appliance can be provisioned on very short order because all the constituent elements have been pre-cut, pre-measured and pre-negotiated for deployment.

Appliances can come in different models chosen to deliver specific service levels. A private cloud storage service can be implemented through a storage appliance. If the service level agreement specifies that the storage must be on the company's premises, one alternative implementation calls for hosting a physical storage appliance in a company data center. For a less stringent service level, the storage appliance can actually be a proxy for an outsourced storage service provider. The service provider may in fact deliver the service out of the same physical appliance. The cost to the consumer will likely be lower because the physical appliance may be shared among multiple tenants.

Traditional SAN-based data center storage would still be an option, but because this storage capability is custom designed and labor intensive, it would be the most expensive option of all. Eventually this type of deployment will be used only for applications with specialized needs that justify the cost and custom work. This is the norm today because no other alternatives are commonly available.

Storage Yesterday

The notion of cloud storage is not new. It was pioneered in the early 1990s by IBM and Sun Microsystems. The goal for this initiative was to realize economies of scale through provider specialization. A company with deep expertise in providing and deploying storage services can do it much more efficiently than custom, one-of-a-kind deployments in corporate data centers.

The idea was slow to a start because the network infrastructure at that time was inadequate to provide this kind of service to the satisfaction of customers. Network bandwidth, latency, reliability, and security did not meet the application requirements. While these services were ahead of their time, they were also one-of-a-kind, negating the potential benefit of an appliance-like service.

Customers were not willing to share a common infrastructure, first because there was no precedent to reassure them that this was an acceptable option and second because security was really insufficient and mechanisms in place were not acceptable. Customers demanded true physical isolation for each service instance. The requirement for separate infrastructure effectively negated the potential economies of scale of a shared infrastructure.

Storage Today

According to IDC[1], the size of the data universe, that is, the aggregation of all the data stored by humankind, is growing at a yearly rate of 60 percent. For corporate data, think of e-mail. A few years ago a 30-megabyte mailbox provided ample space to store a year's worth of mail. Today, three e-mail messages with presentation attachments can exhaust that quota. If the message is sent to ten recipients, the data center will need to allocate nominally 300 megabytes for that message. The actual space requirements can be much larger. The mail store may be housed in a server using RAID hard drives, and hence the physical storage will be larger. Storage requirements grow by multiples if we account for a number of backups and archival copies. New technologies, such as statutory requirements for storing surveillance data or the deployment of RFID also generate massive amounts of data. Special techniques, such as de-duplication or data reduction at the source provide some relief, but do not address the fundamental problem.

Consumers are also facing data storage challenges. Digital pictures are getting bigger from less than a megabyte per file a few years ago to over twenty megabytes per frame for a picture in raw format today. Uncompressed TIFF files are even larger. Building a movie library in HD format can easily take 20 to 50 gigabytes of storage per movie.

Because the current trend is unsustainable, we are reaching a true inflection point. Data will eventually overflow data centers. The current custom-made on-the-premises approach will eventually become unworkable.

Table 7.1 summarizes challenges and opportunities for consumers. In spite of a proliferation of backup solutions, the risk of data loss is ever-present.

Table 7.1   Storage Challenges and Opportunities for Consumers

Challenges	Risk of data loss
	Proliferation of storage media
	Increasing data volume
	Media obsolescence
Opportunities	A la carte storage services
	Data stewardship

---

1   John F. Gantz et al., *The Diverse and Exploding Digital Universe*, IDC March 2008

Consumers need to deal with two or three types of flash media storage, about half a dozen different optical media and formats, plus storage silos in cell phones, PDAs, desktop and laptop computers, and Web-based storage.

With proliferation comes obsolescence. Computers today no longer come with floppy drives. Retrieving data from old DC-2120 tapes is becoming an impractical task. Even with a tape drive and a copy of Windows 98†, a consumer may find the drivers for that tape unit may have been misplaced, rendering it unusable.

With challenges come opportunities. One approach to minimize the risk of data loss is the notion of a data presence service where disembodied data is stored outside the consumer's premises and essentially accessible through any connected device anywhere, whether a cell phone, PDA, desktop, roaming netbook, or laptop computer. Data is processed for display according to the capability of the presentation device.

Offsite storage not only addresses the availability problem, but also the customer's needs for disaster recovery. Perhaps the best backup solution is to do no backup at all. The customer registers with a storage provider specifying a desired service level, and the storage provider implements a data migration and replication scheme that meets the target service level using a combination of on and off premises storage.

The opportunities that cloud computing brings are for providers to recombine and integrate lower-level cloud-based storage service products to address needs of specific audiences, as shown in Table 7.2. These service offerings can be built relatively quickly because it is no longer necessary to build them from the physical infrastructure up.

Table 7.2   Storage Challenges and Opportunities for Consumers

Challenges	Exponential growth of digital footprint
	Cost of in-house data storage
	Energy usage
Opportunities	Virtualization driving usage and delivery
	Service oriented IT with SLA-driven products
	Retention, privacy, access, management, security
	Service decoupled from underlying technology
	Organization-wide, uniform policies
	Advanced information capture, search, discovery, classification

Due to the growth of the digital footprint, the need for storage is increasing exponentially, in spite of new technologies such as de-duplication.

The status quo, storing data in-house, does not constitute a sustainable approach. In some cases it may be overkill, and hence more expensive than it should be, and in other cases, such as for critical applications, it may fall short and does not meet business requirements.

There is another consideration that is becoming more relevant day by day: energy efficiency, in terms of watts per bit, keeps increasing with advances in technology, but not fast enough. Energy efficiency is an essential issue and we'll cover it at length in the remainder of the chapter.

What opportunities are there? It is important to look at issues from a fresh perspective; for instance virtualization is allowing the implementation of logical isolation across tenants sharing a common physical resource. The level of isolation is not as absolute as physical isolation. On the other hand, many shades of gray are possible where the level of isolation is mapped to a specific service level, allowing the customer to trade off a level of assurance and the fee for the service. This is not possible today in an environment where applications are bound to physical servers.

Virtualization precisely introduces an abstraction layer that helps decoupling the service from the underlying implementation technology. Service and technology updates become possible without the need for a "fork-lift" upgrade. The service paradigm also allows rethinking the way storage is delivered to corporate customers. In principle, a pay-as-you-go service, allocated and released on demand, metered and securely managed, carries the potential of keeping customers happy while at the same time lowering upfront capital costs because of lessened need for overprovisioning.

There will be more disintermediation with respect to specific hardware; storage services will be characterized by service specifications defining retention, privacy, access, management, and security. IT organizations will have the choice of continuing to provide on-the-premises services or outsource as needed at multiple levels of abstraction. It is becoming possible to switch across service providers or even move from in-house to outsourced providers on the fly as business conditions dictate.

Storage Tomorrow

It would be naïve to expect storage moving to the cloud under the same old paradigms. For one thing, distinctions between consumer and corporate storage are likely to blur. Some service providers may cater to both markets. More likely due to the expected disintermediation, lower level storage providers may end up storing data from both worlds as higher level storage providers channel data to their infrastructure providers. The infrastructure providers won't know if the data is corporate data or data stored on behalf of the customers' clients.

The proliferation of service classes will increase the storage efficiency of the industry as a whole, with an improved matching of needs against cost and less overprovisioning. Cloud-based storage technologies represent an excellent fit for this new environment.

Cloud Storage Use Cases

Complex environments are usually analyzed in terms of layered models. Use cases are particular to each one of the layers.[2] A cloud storage application can be decomposed into five distinct layers, from the physical infrastructure at the bottom to the actual delivered service at the top.

These layers are

■ Storage virtual infrastructure services

■ Business services

■ Application and data storage services

■ Storage-based applications

■ Storage consumer application

The layers are illustrated in Figure 7.1 below.

In a cloud environment we assume storage has been virtualized. At the infrastructure level storage can be implemented on company data centers or outsourced to cloud storage providers. To the layers above there is no difference except for the service level agreements involved such as through-put, latency and uptime.

---

2   Castro-Leon et al., *The Business Value of Virtual Service Oriented Grids*, Intel Press (2009) ISBN 1-934053-10-4.

From a business model perspective, the infrastructure services can be used by corporate IT for in-company use. A storage provider may have a similar infrastructure, not primarily for own use but to turn around and market a storage service product. The provider may choose to host their infrastructure in-house or outsource to an infrastructure storage provider. Yes, in the cloud world there is no requirement for a service provider to host their physical infrastructure.

The storage service can be sliced and diced on an SLA basis to support diverse families of application support capabilities, from rich Internet applications to an e-mail store. A data presence service is a cloud concept. The assumption is that consumers will store "disembodied" data in the cloud, such as media files in standard industry formats such as JPEG. This data will be available to them any time from any device they happen to have at the moment, from desktops at home to PDAs to cell phones if they are mobile. Data will be delivered in a form appropriate to the end point device in use at the moment.

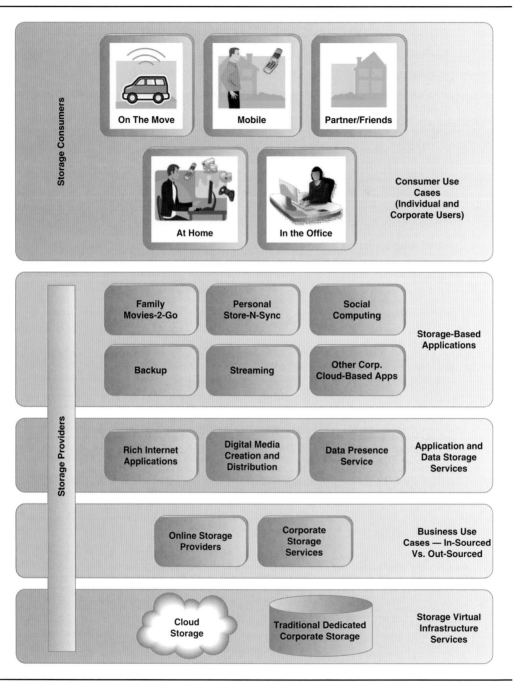

Figure 7.1   Hierarchical Model for Cloud-based Storage

In the upper layer for storage providers we find application offerings, either a la carte from cloud service providers to individual and corporate consumers or as packaged corporate applications for use by employees.

At the bottom layer, whether storage is on the data center premises or outsourced, storage eventually gets instantiated in physical servers. Even though the areal data storage density, that is, the number of bits per unit area, has increased by a factor of about 10,000 in the past 15 years[3], due to the increase in data volume and new application demands, the trend of the overall power consumption in the data center is increasing. This is a good segue into power management aspects of cloud storage.

Cloud Storage Application Power Management

Cloud storage is hosted in data centers, so this capability is inextricably linked to power issues in the data center today. Recapping from Chapter 5, the data center power infrastructure needs to be dimensioned to meet peak demand. Unfortunately, this approach leaves data centers grossly overprovisioned. The power drawn by a server is a function of workload. In typical data centers server utilization factors are low, in the order of 5 to 10 percent[4].

There are two problems here:

■ At any time power consumption is typically in the low end of the range. Yet the data center power infrastructure needs to be sized to peak power consumption to avoid service interruptions. Also power consumption needs to be projected into the future and the estimates require an extra cushion added because of the statistical uncertainty of the forecast.

■ Second, the low end of power consumption is not really low enough. The most efficient servers available today consume about half of peak power even when they are idle.

Let's focus on the first problem for now. The second problem is covered in Chapter 22, "Energy Management in a Virtualized Cloud Environment."

---

3   http://www.tomshardware.com/reviews/15-years-of-hard-drive-history,1368-6.html

4   This fact is documented widely in the in the industry and has been driving the adoption of virtualized servers. See for instance "Virtualization and Automation Drive Dynamic Data Centers," a white paper by CA.

Because of peak sizing, in a data center there is a significant overprovisioning, just in case that power level is reached under some extraordinary conditions. However, this power level is seldom reached, if ever. This unused capacity is called *stranded* or captive power. The undesirable side effect of stranded power is the additional capital expense allocation needed to meet it.

Another consideration is the difficulty of estimating the actual power consumed by a server without actually measuring it. The power consumption is a function of workload, as mentioned above, but it is also determined by the configuration: the amount of memory and the number of hard drives in the system. Hence the power consumption figures provided in the manufacturer specifications include ample margins. These numbers are usually derated to get closer to the actual figure. The derated estimates still contain a generous margin of error, which is not very helpful in determining the actual power consumption, let alone matching the actual power consumption to the data center infrastructure capability.

Intel® Data Center Manager can address exactly this issue. Having been purposely architected as an SDK, it can be quickly integrated as a module to augment the capability of a management console or as a matter of fact, any application fulfilling the role of a power management policy engine. One possible application is shown in Figure 7.2, where Intel® Data Center Manager has been integrated into a cloud storage appliance application.

A number of Intel® Intelligent Power Node Manager-enabled servers are also fitted with inlet temperature sensors. This allows the application to monitor the inlet temperature of a group of servers, and if the temperature rises above a certain threshold, it can take a number of measures, from throttling back power consumption to reducing thermal stresses. At this level the application code is in charge of the difference engine described in Chapter 4.

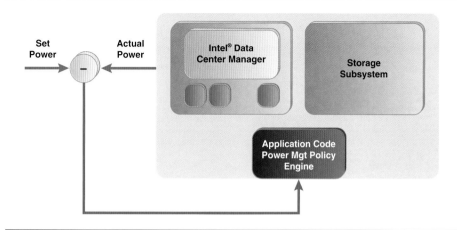

Figure 7.2 Storage Appliance Control Loop

An application interfacing with Intel Data Center Manager no longer needs to manage individual server nodes; the application code's power policy engine designates a power consumption target to Intel Data Center Manager through the Intel Data Center Manager API. Intel Data Center Manager in turn breaks down the power target into power targets to the individual nodes under its command.

The application code also needs to mind the power consumed by the storage subsystem. Less sophisticated implementation may have a monitor-only capability; the application code reads out the power consumed by the storage subsystem by querying the intelligent PDU that feeds it and then sets the server power in a way that the total consumption for the appliance matches the overall set power.

Figure 7.3 provides a more detailed view of this process. In this figure we see the appliance control algorithm implemented by the application's power policy engine. The constituent components are loosely coupled through Web services APIs.

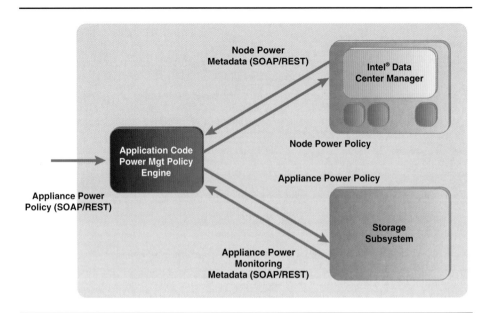

Figure 7.3   Expanded View of Appliance Power Control

One potential concern with three nested loops operating concurrently is the potential for oscillatory or unstable behaviors. This issue does not arise in practice; the time constants across the three levels are fairly spread out: the time constant involved with the Intel Intelligent Power Node Manager loop is in the order of milliseconds, whereas the Intel Data Center Manager constant is in the order of a few seconds. Finally, the time constant associated with power management for an appliance is in the order of tens of seconds. Because of the time constant spreads, it is possible to optimize each loop individually to ensure that no under-damped, oscillatory behaviors occur.

A Reference Architecture for Cloud Storage Appliances

We now have the elements to put together a power management capability for a cloud storage application, with the application built using storage appliances. We have done an overview of the foundation technologies and how these technologies are integrated into a power management capability that encompasses the whole application and how power management for the application gets integrated into the data center power infrastructure.

In this section we provide a synthesis of the concepts in the form of a reference architecture. The reference architecture provides a concise representation of the power management concepts. The concepts are generic and hence we can recast them into a template, ready to be instantiated for other applications.

A Cloud Application Overview Reference Architecture

A goal for compiling a reference architecture is providing a constructive proof, mapping desired use cases to technology components. For each use case that delivers a certain business value to an end user, we want to enumerate a set of constituent necessary building blocks that combined allow an end user to carry out that particular use case.

Figure 7.4 illustrates this process. The top row captures five example use cases. The examples listed are not exhaustive by any measure.

- Rack optimization allows users to maximize the number of servers loaded in a rack when the rack is under a specific power budget.

- Branch circuit optimization addresses the demand side, minimizing the number of feeder circuits for a rack, thereby minimizing stranded power.

- Server Parking lowers Pbaseline and extends the power proportional computing dynamic range for virtualized clusters used to implement cloud computing applications. Platooning enables not just power management, but can reduce energy consumption.

- Instrumented power supplies allow not only making power management decisions based on actual, real-time power consumed but enable fine-grained power metering such as *chargeback*. A chargeback capability is well aligned with the pay-as-you-go nature of cloud computing.

- Power and thermal monitoring enable building historical records for power consumption useful for power planning. Knowledge of actual power consumed helps in maximizing the use of the data center electrical infrastructure, scheduling workloads to take advantage of off-peak rates and provides a factual basis for negotiating optimal rates with utility companies. This is usually a win-win situation; utilities can deliver scheduled generation at a lower rate than the cost of generation on demand basis.

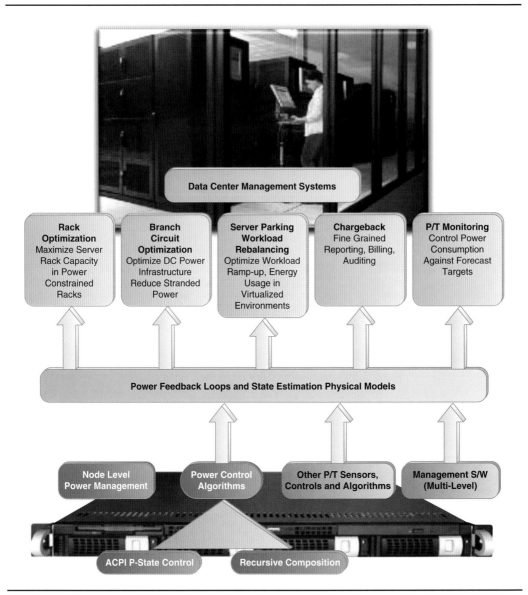

Figure 7.4   Mapping of Technology to Use Cases

The basic architectural pattern for power management is to combine the foundation technologies such as P-state control and PMBus-instrumented power supplies through recursive composition to increase the scope of a particular technology from a single CPU or server to an arbitrarily large domain including the whole data center.

This pattern is similar to patterns seen in operating system design: transactions of arbitrary size are rooted in atomic CPU instruction set architecture (ISA) constructs such as test-and-set or spin locks. These instructions are used to build more complex database locks which in turn ensure the ACID properties of transactions.

Likewise, less accurate or reliable clocks in computers can be combined into an arbitrarily reliable distributed clock when the clocks of a large number of computers are coordinated through software.

Implicit in this process is the feedback loop and a physical model within which the feedback loop operates. This model is relatively simple at the lowest level, where the difference between the actual and desired power is fed into Intel Intelligent Power Node Manager, which in turns manipulates the CPU P-states to minimize that difference.

Complexity increases at the higher levels: Intel Data Center Manager needs to divide a power quota over the servers under control in real time.

Control involving the whole data center may need to involve the calculation of computational fluid dynamic models. These models would allow computing temperatures through the data center starting from temperature and airflow data in servers and other locations.

Power-Enabling Cloud Storage Appliances through Plug-ins

In Figure 7.5 we have integrated all the technology components discussed so far into an abstract cloud storage power management architecture. This architecture supports the use cases mentioned above as well. The numbered paragraphs below correspond to the like number in Figure 7.5.

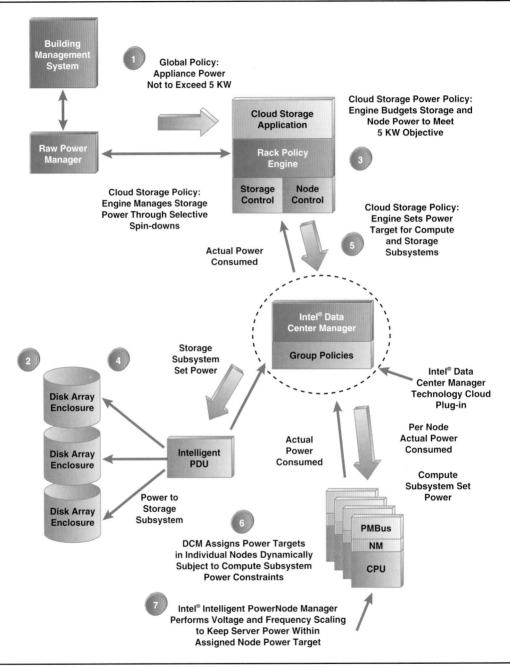

Figure 7.5   A Cloud Storage Application Power Management Reference Architecture

1. The cloud storage application may be implemented with multiple physical appliances arranged in a row. We postulate a management application regulating the power behaviors of the appliances in that particular row, the *row power manager*. The row power manager may be connected to the *building management system* (BMS) application, whose role, among others, is to oversee power management across the whole data center.

   The row power manager implements a number of policies that get mapped into specific directives to each storage appliance. For instance, if a row is being powered by a single 5-kW branch circuit, the row power management imposes a 5-kW power guard rail for each of the storage appliances. Without it, an extra branch circuit is required leading to significant stranded power.

2. In addition to the application of power management-specific technologies, there are emerging technologies that bring reduced power consumption. A case in point is the replacement of hard drives with solid state drives (SSDs). SSDs consume less than 1 watt at idle and less than 5 watts compared to 10 to 15 watts typical of mechanical hard drives. Hence using SSDs will yield a lower Pbaseline.

3. The rack policy engine in the storage appliance oversees its power consumption by monitoring the power draw from the power distribution unit (PDU) feeding the hard drives and the power consumption by the server subsystem as reported by the instance of Intel Data Center Manager regulating the power consumption of the servers.

4. The implementation of the storage appliance may provide a monitor-only capability for the storage subsystem, in which case the appliance policy engine needs to meet the power quota for the appliance by regulating the power consumed by the servers in the appliance.

5. The rack policy engine in the storage application assigns a power target to Intel Data Center Manager. This power target can change dynamically depending on workload conditions and the policies set at the higher levels.

6. Intel Data Center Manager takes the overall power quota for the server subsystem and divides it across the servers in the appliance.

7. Intel Intelligent Power Node Manager instances set the P-states accordingly to meet the quota imposed by Intel Data Center Manager.

The role that Intel Data Center Manager plays in component number 5 in Figure 7.5 is crucial in this reference architecture: it allows power-enabling a cloud appliance at a fraction of the cost that it would take to implement node control algorithms within the application. In our experience, interfacing an application to the Intel Data Center Manager usually takes less than a weeks' time even with implementation team not previously exposed to the API; all it takes is a few Web services calls. Most of the effort goes into validating the new capabilities. Because of the small effort involved in the interfacing, Intel Data Center Manager, for practical purposes, functions as a *plug-in* module to quickly add a power management capability to a cloud-based application; in this case, a cloud storage application. This capability is added without need of re-architecting the original application in any fundamental way.

Figure 7.6 provides a detailed view of the inner workings of each component in Figure 7.5, showing the interactions inside each subsystem depicted in Figure 7.5. Please note that each component in Figure 7.6 is represented singly even though hundreds or even thousands of them are present in most data centers.

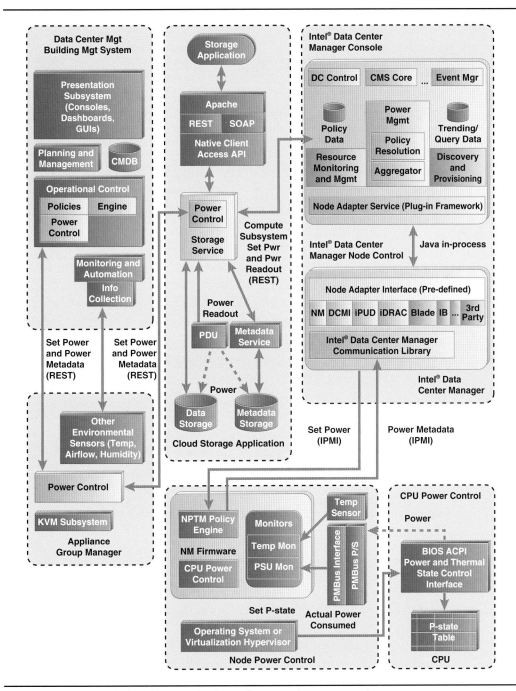

Figure 7.6 Detailed Architectural Scheme for Power Management in a Cloud Storage Application

Summary

According to the UC Berkeley Reliable Adaptive Distributed Systems Lab[5], cloud computing has three essential characteristics:

- The illusion of infinite computing resources available on demand
- The elimination of an upfront commitment by cloud users
- The ability to pay for use of computing resources on a short-term basis as needed

Many applications today, for instance those involving highly confidential data or corporate secrets, may not be appropriate for cloud deployment. However, opportunities exist today to deploy storage infrastructure as a cloud supporting broad classes of storage-based applications such as backup, personal data presence services, and media distribution.

In the emerging cloud environment, storage infrastructure is still ultimately hosted in data centers. The patterns of ownership are different however, as these resources are typically owned or leased by service providers, not under corporate ownership serving the parent company. The storage in these data centers serves multiple service customers in different companies and even service companies, building on this infrastructure and providing a value-added service directly to individual consumer subscribers.

The justification for this process of intermediation is increased ecosystem efficiency: a large corporation reduces capital and operating expenses by outsourcing storage to a service provider. The service provider can deliver the service at a lower cost than the corporate in-house alternative because it amortizes the equipment over a large audience and because storage is their main business; they have built expertise that gives them a cost advantage.

A certain level of technology maturity is needed to justify this business model, from having the appropriate process to the availability of a network infrastructure able to keep bandwidth and latency within limits tolerable to the customers.

With advancing technology maturity, at some point delivering this service through storage appliances becomes economically viable, because appliances can be deployed as single logical functional groups with predictable specifications, behaviors and cost, therefore enabling the service provider to offer fairly precise service levels.

---

5   Armbrust et al., *Above the Clouds: A Berkeley View of Cloud Computing*, TR UCB/EECS-2009-28, February 10, 2009

Energy costs constitute a significant portion of the operational expenses. For instance, the electricity bill of an appliance drawing 5 kW will be about USD 5,000 per year assuming a 100 percent duty cycle and an energy cost of USD 0.12 per kWh.

A small upfront investment to make these appliances highly power and energy efficient makes economic sense because this investment can be amortized over multiple instances of the appliance. This work is much harder to justify if it needs to be done for every deployment in the one-of-a-kind environment under the more traditional solution approach.

The benefit from this investment comes in many ways:

- The impact on the data center infrastructure within which the appliance is deployed. If the power consumption of the appliance can be made more predictable and consumption peaks mitigated, the traditional approach of gross overprovisioning for expected peak demand is not needed anymore.

- Even if the pain of the utility bills does not go away, because power is now a significant TCO component, it makes sense to measure it and control it. With power consumption data in hand, service providers now have the option of prorating this cost to individual customers according to specific business policies.

- An economic benefit is that data center operators will be able to extend the life of their current data center infrastructure.

- The intrinsic energy cost avoidance conferred by the by the application of power management policies such as selective node shutdowns and hard drive spin-downs.

The power management mechanisms described in this chapter deliver an extend power dynamic range with workload level under the power proportional computing paradigm. This behavior is highly aligned to the pay-per-use nature of cloud services.

Chapter 8

Platform Group Power Management in Cloud Data Centers

Contributed by Enrique Castro-Leon, Dror Shenkar, and Susmita Nayak

Power and cooling literally constitute a burning issue in data centers today. According to IDC[1], while data center capital expenditures have moderated, operating expenditures are on the upswing, and a major component of TCO comes from energy costs: every dollar invested in hardware represents requires fifty cents in power and cooling over the server's lifetime. The cost of energy has prompted some of the largest data center operators, such as Google, to deploy their largest data centers in Hood River, Oregon, near the Bonneville power dam where electricity is plentiful and the cost is one of the lowest in the continental United States. Operators in other countries like Japan and even smaller operators in the United States that don't enjoy the economies of scale of Google still need to deploy their data centers in dense urban centers with limited power supply.

In Chapter 4 we presented an overview of the inner workings of the Intel® Intelligent Power Node Manager technology. For additional details see paper by Satya et al. on power management[2]. Fundamentally, Intel Intelligent Power Node Manager allows an IT operator to set server

---

1   Scaramella et al., Solutions for the Datacenter's Thermal Challenges, IDC Jan 2007

2   Satya S L, Siva Sathappan, Tabassum Yasmin, Mrittika Ganguli, Naresh K. Sehgal, *Power Management in IA Servers,* Intel white paper (2009)

platform power consumption targets by adjusting the power consumed by the processors in the servers. The CPU power adjustment in turn is attained by setting the voltage and clock frequency fed into the processor as defined by the ACPI P-states that govern the processor.

There may be a slight loss of performance as the P-states are ratcheted down to the lower states. The data center operator, through a management console or management application, sets the power consumption capping level by observing the actual historic power consumption trend of the server and setting a target that offers the best compromise between power consumption and performance. For example, an IT operator can direct a server to keep power consumption under a certain threshold during periods of low demand without impacting the performance of the workload. Even during an aggressive power capping regime, the performance penalty may be smaller than expected. Most servers are operated at less than sixty percent workload. If fewer cycles are available due to frequency scaling, the operating system can increase the priority of the workload therefore increasing system utilization, minimizing the performance impact.

It is reasonable to expect that future platforms will come with additional control points, for instance by adding memory banks to the list of controllable devices.

Once we have acquired the ability to determine the capability to regulate the power consumed by a single server, it is possible to aggregate this capability to also control the power consumption of a group of servers. This capability is available through the Intel® Data Center Manager (Intel DCM) software.

The notion of group is useful: data centers have physical power and cooling constraints at rack, row, and PDU level. Also IT users managing thousands of servers in data centers normally think and manage at the rack or group level. Intel DCM extends server power management capabilities to racks and server groups.

Intel DCM is offered as a software development kit designed to integrate with existing management consoles, be it consoles from commercial independent software vendors, original equipment manufacturer consoles or even IT in house management software or command line–based utilities.

The Intel Data Center Manager API provides a Web services API offering a high level alternative to integrating the Node Manager functionality in terms of IPMI byte-codes. Integrating at the IPMI level does not make economic sense in terms of cost of labor and time to market unless extremely fine grained control is required, much in the same way that today assembly language coding is not used for general software development.

Software development with IPMI is as complex as programming real-time systems, subject to subtle timing considerations, requiring extreme care to avoid race conditions that lead to inconsistent results. Most of these hazards have been factored out and debugged in the Intel Data Center Manager API.

A graphical user interface is available with Intel DCM demonstrating leading usage models for the convenience of developers and system integrators and for self-contained deployments involving a small number of servers.

Intel DCM plays an ever more useful role with the introduction of the newer platforms to harness the capabilities of power proportional computing. Under power proportional computing the power consumed by a server is at a minimum when the server is idling and greatest with a server running with the CPUs at 100-percent utilization.

Up to the early 2000s, idle power was as high as 90 percent of the power consumed at full load. While platform peak power consumption, that is, power consumption at high load factors, has changed little over the years, idle power has been gradually reduced over successive server generations from about two thirds of full power to about one half on some implementations of the current generation.

Power regulation under Intel Intelligent Power Node Manager can bring the power consumption at full load to close to the idle power consumption. A practical limit for the Intel® Xeon® 5500 and 5600 Series processors is a capping range of about one third of the power consumption at full load.

Figure 8.1 illustrates the relationship between the underlying platform, Intel Intelligent Power Node Manager, the IPMI interface, Intel Data Center Manager SDK, and the Intel DCM Reference GUI.

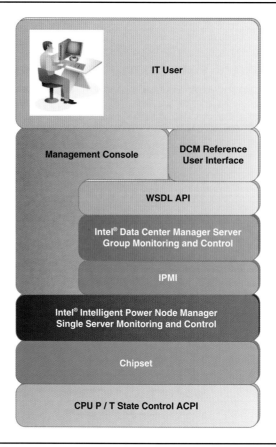

Figure 8.1   Intel® DCM Conceptual Architecture

Intel® Data Center Manager Reference User Interface

Now let's take a closer look at the Intel Data Center Manager GUI screen for a representative view of the available features as shown in Figure 8.2.

The configuration of server groups is captured on the left pane. Note that the server groups can be hierarchical. For this particular configuration, four servers are installed in a rack, divided into two sub-groups, two servers running a high priority workload and two servers running a low priority workload. Priority is an input provided by the IT user to Intel DCM when setting a policy and is a proxy for the workload SLA.

The light blue band represents the focus of the plot. The focus can be changed with a simple mouse click. The current focus in the figure is the whole rack. Hence the power plot is the aggregated power for all four servers in a rack. If the high priority sub-group were selected, then the power shown would be the power consumed by the two servers in that sub-group. Finally, if a single server is selected, then the power indicated would be the power for that server only.

Four lines are represented in the graph. The top line is the *plate power*. It represents an upper bound for the server's power consumption. For this particular group of servers the plate power is 2600 watts. The servers are identical, and hence rated at 2600/4 = 650 watts.

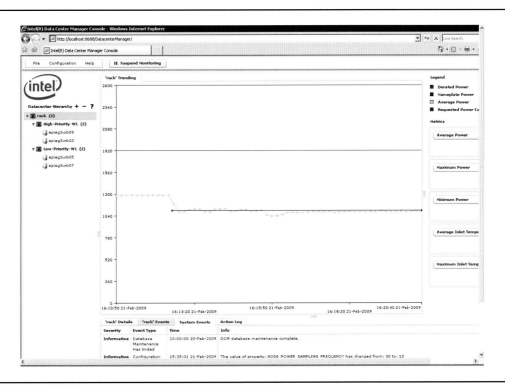

Figure 8.2   Intel® Data Center Manager Reference GUI

The next line down is the *de-rated power*. Most servers will not have every memory slot or every hard drive tray populated. The de-rated power is the operator's best guess for maximum power consumption taking the actual configuration the server into account but without the instrumentation to measure actual power consumption. The de-rated power is still a conservative guess for the lowest upper bound for power consumption, considerably higher than the actual power consumption of the server. We don't want actual power to exceed de-rated power during operations because this could cause a breaker tripping event.

As a rule of thumb, de-rated power is set to about 70 percent of the name-plate power. For this example, the de-rated power has been set at 1820 watts for the rack or 455 watts per server.

Finally, the gold line represents the actual power consumed by the server. The dots represent successive samples taken from readings from the instrumented power supplies.

The servers are running at full power using the SPECpower benchmark. The rack is collectively consuming a little less than 1300 watts. At approximately 16:12 a policy is introduced to constrain power consumption to 1200 watts. Intel DCM instructs individual nodes to reduce power consumption by lowering the set points for Intel Intelligent Power Node Manager in each node until the collective power consumption reaches the desired target.

Intel Data Center Manager keeps track of the average, maximum, and minimum power during the observation period. For servers with front panel inlet temperature sensors, Intel Data Center Manager also keeps track of the observed average, maximum, and minimum inlet temperatures.

Group Dynamic Power Control with Intel® Data Center Manager

When we instructed Intel Data Center Manager to hold a power cap for the group *rack (2)*, as shown in Figure 8.3, Intel Data Center Manager makes an effort to maintain power at that level, in spite of unavoidable disturbances in the system.

The source of the disturbances can be internal or external. An internal disturbance can be the server fans switching to a different speed causing a power spike or dip. Workloads in servers go up and down, with a corresponding uptick or dip in the power consumption for that server. An external disturbance could be a change in the feed voltage or an operator action. In fact at T = 16:14 we introduced a severe disturbance: we brought the workload of the bottom server, *epieg3urb07* down to idle. Figure 8.3 depicts Figure 8.2 with markers for the two events.

Note that it takes a few seconds for transients to die out to reach and for power to reach the new level. Likewise, when the bottom server is brought to idle, it also pulled back the power consumption for the group. However, the group power went back to the target power consumption after a couple of minutes.

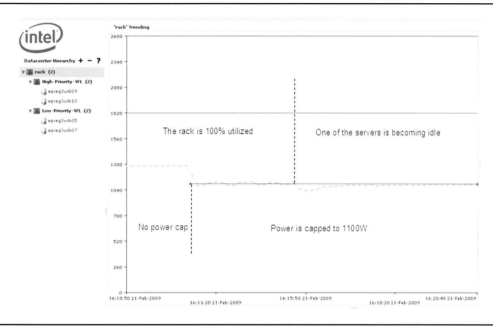

Figure 8.3   Plot of Group Power with the Power Capping Followed by Pulling the Bottom Server to Idle

If we look at the plot of the individual servers, as shown in Figure 8.4, we can see Intel Data Center Manager at work maintaining the target power. Note that right after the capping policy is introduced, Intel Data Center Manager reduces the power for each one of the servers in the group, but not by the same amount. The power consumed by each server exhibits local peaks and dips, yet Intel Data Center Manager keeps group power relatively level at the set target.

When the second event takes place and the bottom server is idled, Intel Data Center Manager instructs Intel Intelligent Power Node Manager to relax the P-states in the remaining servers. Power consumption for each of the remaining servers in the group goes up almost to the original, unconstrained power. It is possible that the P-states in the idled server were relaxed as well, with power settling at the lower, idle power level.

The behavior of power control is analogous to the behavior of the cruise control in a vehicle: the cruise control system controls the vehicle's speed by manipulating the engine throttle and measures the vehicle's speed at the wheels. It adjusts the fuel flow until the measured speed reaches the set speed. Disturbances in the road will change the vehicle's speed. The vehicle will slow down when the vehicle starts climbing an uphill. The cruise control opens the throttle at this point allowing the vehicle to accelerate until it reaches the original cruise speed.

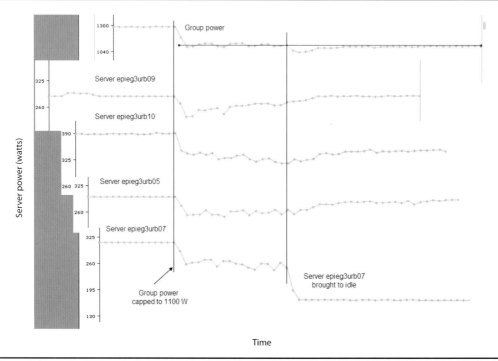

Figure 8.4   Behaviors of the Individual Servers in the Group

In addition to the inherent lag in recovering from disturbances, the control authority of the cruise control system has design limits. If an incline in the road is too steep, the vehicle may not have enough horsepower to reach the set speed. If the cruise speed is set too slow, the cruise control might not be able to maintain the target speed.

Use Cases for Intel® Data Center Manager

Chapter 18 contains an extensive list of use cases for platform power management technology. While some of them are specific to Intel Intelligent Power Node Manager, quite a number depend on the Intel Data Center Manager SDK to implement. In this section we describe the subset implemented with the help of Intel Data Center Manager.

Increasing Server Rack Density

Forecasting the power requirements for a server over the product's lifetime is not an easy exercise. Server power consumption is a function of server hardware specifications and the associated software and workloads running on them. Also the server's configuration may change over time: the machine may be retrofitted with additional memory, new processors, and hard drives.

This challenge is compounded by more aggressive implementations of power proportional computing. As mention earlier, servers of a few years ago exhibited little variability between power consumption at idle and power consumption at full power, but this is changing: while power proportional computing has brought down the average power consumption, it also has increased its variance significantly. Data center administrators can now expect wide swings in power consumption during normal operation.

Undersizing the power infrastructure can lead to operational problems during the equipment's lifetime: it may become impossible to fully load racks due to supply power limitations or because hot spots start developing.

One possible strategy is to forecast power consumption using an upper bound. The most obvious upper bound is to use the plate power, that is, the power in the electrical specifications of the server. This is a number guaranteed to never be exceeded. Throwing power at the problem is not unlike the approach of throwing bandwidth at the problem in network design to compensate for lack of bandwidth allocation capability and QoS mechanisms. This approach is overly conservative because the power infrastructure is designed by adding the assumed peak power for each server over the equipment's lifetime, an exceedingly unlikely event.

The picture is even worse when we realize that IT equipment represents only 30 to 40 percent of the power consumption in the data center as depicted in Figure 8.5. This means that the power forecasting in the data center must not only include the power consumed by the servers proper, but also the power consumed by the ancillary equipment, including cooling, heating, and lighting, which can be over twice the power allocated to servers.

Establishing a power forecast and sizing up a data center based on nameplate will lead to gross overestimation of the actual power needed and unnecessary capital expenses[3]. Yet some oversizing of the power infrastructure is needed as insurance for the future because of the large uncertainty in the actual power consumption forecast. It does not necessarily reflect current need.

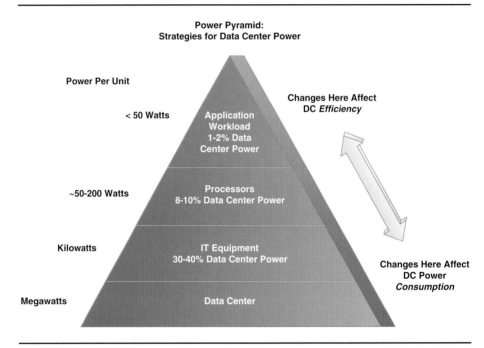

Figure 8.5 Power Allocation in the Data Center

A more realistic factor is to de-rate the plate power to a percentage determined by the practices at a particular site. Typical numbers range between 40 percent and 70 percent. Unfortunately, these numbers represent a guess representative over a server's lifetime and are still overly conservative.

---

3   *Determining Total Cost of Ownership for Data Center and Network Room Infrastructure*, APC Paper #6 and *Avoiding Costs from Oversizing Data Center and Network Room Infrastructure*, APC Paper #37, http://www.apc.com

Intel Data Center Manager provides a one year history of power consumption that allows a much tighter bound for power consumption forecasting. At the same time, it is possible to limit power consumption to ensure that group power consumption does not exceed thresholds imposed by the utility power and the power supply infrastructure.

Initial testing performed with Baidu and China Telecom indicates that it is possible to increase rack density by 40 to 60 percent using a pre-existing data center infrastructure.

Managing Power and Thermal Exceptions

Intel Data Center Manager can provide real-time information to optimize data center operations. It provides a comprehensive list of publish/subscribe event mechanisms that can form the basis of a sophisticated data center management infrastructure integrating multiple applications where applications get notified of relevant thermal and power events and can apply appropriate policies.

These policies can span a wide range of potential actions, such as dialing back power consumption to bring it down below a reference threshold or to reduce thermal stress on the cooling system. Some actions can be complex, such as migrating workloads across hosts in a virtualized environment, powering down equipment or even performing coordinated actions with building management systems.

Intel Data Center Manager also provides inlet temperature or front panel thermals along with a historical record that can be used to identify trouble spots in the data center. This information provides insights to optimize the thermal design of the data center. The actions needed to fix trouble spots need not be expensive at all; they may involve no more than relocating a few perforated tiles or installing blanking panels and grommets to minimize air leaks in the raised metal floor. Traditionally, the hardest part has been identifying the trouble spots, involving time consuming temperature and air flow measurements. Intel Data Center Management provides much of this data ready made from operations without the need to bring a consulting team.

Deployment scaling can range from a small business managing a few co-located servers in a shared rack in a multi-tenant environment to organizations managing thousands of servers.

Dynamic Power Allocation

Intel Data Center Manager supports the notion of server groups. Because groups can be nested and each group can carry its own policies, it is possible to coordinate policies to attain power allocation to carry out specific SLA goals. Policy coordination needs to be done with care to prevent situations where they are in conflict with each other or would require settings beyond the control authority possible with the underlying Intel Intelligent Power Node Manager technology.

The general approach for the power allocation use case is to cap power to groups running low priority loads and make this power available to high priority loads.

Here is an example scenario implemented in the Intel Enterprise Integration lab to demonstrate the use of Intel Data Center Manager power policies to increase rack density and balance power across servers based on workload demand. The experiment was implemented with dual CPU server white boxes, code-named Urbanna with Intel® Xeon® 5500 Series processors in a 2U rack form factor. The power managed server operating system installed was Red Hat† Enterprise Linux 5.2 running SPECpower as a synthetic benchmark.

Consider an example 3000-W rack that hosts 4 servers provisioned based on power supply nameplate of 650 W (rack nameplate 2600 W). The servers in the rack have been partitioned in two groups of two servers each:

- Group A runs a customer facing workload with high service-level agreement. The workload has 50 percent system utilization between 5 p.m. and 9 a.m. and 100 percent utilization between 9 a.m. and 5 p.m.

- Group B runs an internal IT batch job. The workload has an average of 50 percent utilization throughout the day.

Due to a high priority service level agreement for Group A, the IT administrator wants a minimal impact to performance on this workload, but also wants to add more servers to this rack. Here is how IT user can accomplish this using Intel Data Center Manager power policies:

- Use Intel Data Center Manager to determine trending, that is, historical consumption patterns over a pre-specified observation period. In this example we find that the rack consumes 1150 W at peak times (9 a.m.–5 p.m.) and 980 W off-peak (5 p.m.–9 a.m.).

- Use Intel DCM to apply a power policy of 1100 W at the rack level effective over the whole day. Configure the policy further and set Group A to high priority and Group B to low priority.

This scenario is illustrated in Figure 8.6. Note that if we sized up the branch circuit feeding the four servers using the 2600 watt nameplate power, we'd be overprovisioning the power for these servers by 50 percent. Even if we used the de-rated power of 1820 watts, we'd still be overprovisioning by almost 30 percent. In this figure we see that setting a power cap slightly above the historical peak consumption of 1300 watts will have Intel Data Center Manager limiting power excursions beyond 1300 watts, and hence the power quota assigned to these servers can be safely brought down further below 1820 watts. A small safety margin would still be necessary. The actual number would depend on the data center practices in effect.

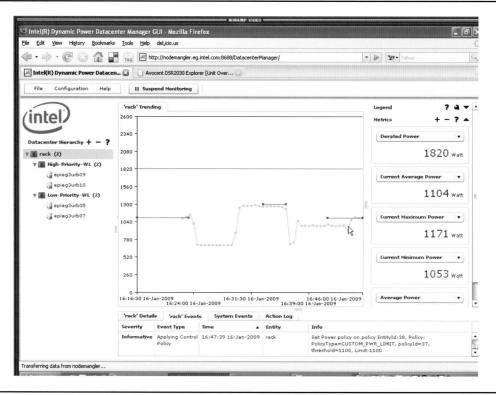

Figure 8.6   Example Power Allocation Scenario, Plot of Global Rack Level Data

As we enter the peak period on the far right of the graph, the operator instructs the group to maintain a 1100 W rack power policy. At the same time, Intel Data Center Manager senses that Group A needs more power and hence increases the power allocation from 520 W at non-peak time to 676 W as illustrated in Figure 8.7.

As an example of a coordinated power policy, in order to prevent consumption from exceeding the 1100 W group cap, Intel Data Center Manager reduces the power quota allocated to Group B (observed decrease from 480 W to 424 W in Figure 8.8). There was no observed performance impact to Group A workload. Note that the power consumption for the group has been allowed to increase, reflecting the high priority of this workload.

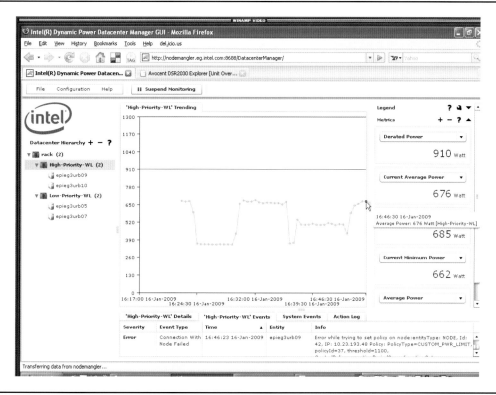

Figure 8.7   Example Scenario, Plot Of Group A (High Priority) Power Consumption

From above example, we also note that provisioning the rack based on 1100 W allows IT user to reclaim about 1500 W (down from 1820 watts) when designed to rack nameplate value. The freed power can be reallocated to host more servers on the rack.

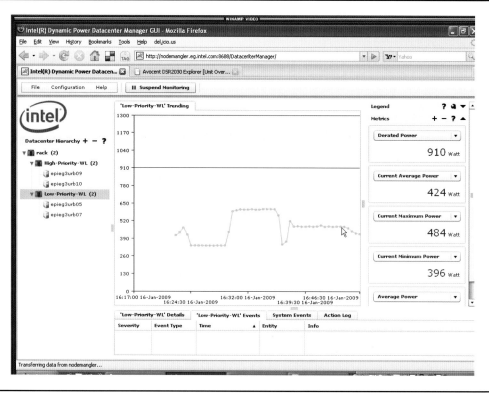

Figure 8.8   Sample Scenario, Power Consumption Plot For Group B (Low Priority)

Power Shedding

This is a more radical version of the power allocation use case in the previous section to carry out business continuity and disaster recovery processes. These measures are applicable during power outages, cooling failures and brownouts. For instance, during a power outage and the data center operating under emergency power, the data center operator may enact a policy that includes clamping server power usage to the maximum on medium priority workloads and an orderly shutdown of nonessential applications. The policy allows prioritizing the limited available power to critical workloads and extended operation time if the stored fuel supply is limited and hard to replenish.

Power Forecasting

Knowing about the past makes it easier to plan for the future. The power monitoring capability in servers with instrumented power supplies managed under Intel Data Center Manager provides data center planners with much more accurate data about historical consumption patterns in a data center allowing tighter power forecasts, much closer to the actual power growth patterns. A smaller power supply infrastructure may be sufficient to meet the data center needs over its lifetime. Improved knowledge about power growth patterns may even make possible scheduling capital investments as milestones over the life cycle of the data center. This spending deferral improves the capital spending scenario even further.

Power Metering and Chargeback

The last usage scenario we will consider in this chapter is metering and chargeback. The historical power consumption data provided by Intel Data Center Manager enables finer grained methods for power metering and chargeback impossible to implement before. Furthermore, it is possible to combine this power data with other data center statistics to obtain a variety of figures of merit, including watts per square feet and MIPS per watt.

As a matter of practice, it is not uncommon for power costs in a data center to be managed on the basis of one bill or one bill per utility feed for a whole data center.

Under these conditions there is no reason to deviate from the common practice of bundling the power bill with the cost of operating the facilities. Because of bundling, data center operators saving energy becomes an abstract concept and a pain point only during the process of yearly budgeting. Keeping the business running takes precedence over saving energy. There is also little incentive to remove older, energy hogging servers because their effect can be hidden under the global power budgeting process.

With metered power supplies it is now possible to expose energy costs and assign these costs to individual servers. For virtualized environments, methods are under development to break these costs even further, down to the application level.

Whether departments are in a large organization or individual tenants in a hosted environment, the capabilities of Intel Data Center Manager enable finer grained power monitoring capabilities. This will make it easier for organizations to implement strategies to save energy.

Data center operators will be able to reduce the number of branch circuits needed to feed a certain number of servers. In power restricted environments, hard power caps may not be necessary, but because historical data is now available, data center operators can now charge for power at penalty rates for power consumption above a pre-agreed threshold and provide economic incentives to keep excessive power consumption in check.

Summary

A coordinated hierarchy of power monitoring and control mechanisms are available with Intel-based servers that start with CPU power control through voltage and frequency scaling in servers fitted with the Intel® Xeon® 5500 and 5600 Series processors. These mechanisms are available through ACPI standard APIs under the control of the operating system and at various abstraction levels.

Voltage and frequency scaling are not useful unless these capabilities are used to control the actual power consumed by a server. This capability is implemented by the Intel Intelligent Power Node Manager technology. Firmware running in the chipset can read power consumed from instrumented PMBus† power supplies and adjust voltage and frequency scaling in the form of ACPI P-states to track a predefined target power consumption.

Intel DCM implements the next level up in the hierarchy enabling assigning targets for power consumption to a *group* of servers. Intel DCM achieves this capability through composition; that is by monitoring the power consumption of each node in the group and adjusting their consumption to meet the overall target consumption.

Intel DCM was purposely architected as a software development kit to support higher level management applications that set power to entities at higher levels of abstraction, for instance by application or at a larger scale, including whole data centers or eventually for coordinating the power consumption of server equipment with building management systems.

Chapter 9

Client Virtualization in a Cloud Environment

Contributed by Charlton Barreto

Computation models seen in client space are arguably much more diverse than those in the server space proper. For servers, there are essentially two, the earlier model of static consolidation and the more recent dynamic model where virtual machines are lightly bound to their physical hosts and can be moved around with relative ease.

Virtualized clients also have two main models, depending on whether the application execution takes place in servers in a data center or on the physical client. Beyond that we have identified at least seven distinct variants, each architected to address specific management, security, and TCO needs and with usage models that have specific business scenarios in mind.

At least for server-based clients, their presence may be an indication of technology convergence between clients and server products in cloud space, a continuation of the trend that started when clients were used as presentation devices for traditional three-tier applications.

Client Virtualization

Server-based computation models comprise session virtualization or terminal services and are captured in Table 9.1.

Table 9.1   Server-based Client Virtualization Computation Models

	Terminal Services/ Session Virtualization	Virtual Hosted Desktops/ Virtual Desktop Infrastructure
Application data storage	Server, NAS or SAN	Server, NAS or SAN
Mobility/ Off-network operation	No	No
Local device connection (bar code readers, PDAs, cell phones)	Limited	Limited
Acceptable clients	Terminal Desktop PC Laptop PC	Terminal Desktop PC Laptop PC
Major providers	Citrix, Microsoft	VMware, Citrix

Client-based models comprise OS streaming, remote OS boot, application streaming, virtual containers, and rich distributed computing, summarized in Table 9.2.

Classifying blade PCs, such as those provided by Hewlett-Packard or ClearCube, depends on whether users are assigned to blades in a one-to-one or one-to-many basis. If each user is assigned a single PC blade, the model most closely resembles rich client except it can only be used in a fixed location and is constantly connected to the network. If an individual PC blade services multiple users simultaneously, the model more closely resembles virtual hosted desktop.

Each of these computation models have appropriate uses based on the business scenario, user needs, and infrastructure requirements. Intel's position is that the client-side execution models provide the best user experience and can be deployed to meet IT requirements for security and manageability.

Table 9.2   Client-based Virtualization Computation Models

	OS Streaming	Remote OS Boot	Application Streaming/ Application Virtualization	Virtual Containers (evolving model)	Rich Distributed Computing/ Rich Client
Application data storage	Server, NAS or SAN	SAN	Client, Server, NAS or SAN	Client, Server, NAS or SAN	Client, Server, NAS or SAN
Mobility/ Off-network operation	No	No	Yes, with local caching option	Yes	Yes
Local device connection (bar code readers, PDAs, cell phones)	Yes	Yes	Yes	Limited	Yes
Acceptable clients	Desktop PC Laptop PC	Desktop PC	Desktop PC Laptop PC	Desktop PC Laptop PC	Desktop PC Laptop PC
Major providers	Citrix	Lenovo	Microsoft, Citrix, Symantec, AppStream	Kidaro, VMware Aternity, more developing solutions	Traditional PC software providers

Infrastructure Requirements

Each compute model places unique demands on the enterprise infrastructure. Moving large amounts of client computation, graphics, memory, and storage into a data center will likely require additional infrastructure build-out, unless the current equipment is grossly underutilized. Infrastructure issues to be considered include

- Server computation capacity
- Network bandwidth, both wired and wireless
- Storage of user operating systems, applications, data, and customization profiles
- New connection brokers or remote access gateways
- New management tools
- Power delivery for additional computation, graphics, memory, and storage now in the datacenter

- Cooling capacity of the datacenter
- Physical space within the datacenter
- Physical distance between the datacenter and associated clients

Client Devices and Compute Models

Conversations around compute models often get intertwined with the device on which they will be deployed. The analysis becomes easier if devices and models are treated separately. For example, the business scenario may dictate server-based computing for a certain application, such as a patient information database. However, this "thin client" model need not be deployed on a thin terminal. A desktop or laptop PC may actually be a more appropriate device, depending on a user's total application and mobility needs.

Mixed Compute Models

In most cases, IT will deploy a mix of computation models depending on needs for data security, performance, and mobility. Individual users may have a hybrid of models. For example, a construction estimator in the field may use a cellular modem to access the centralized job scheduling tool via a terminal server session, but also have Microsoft[†] Office locally installed for word processing and spreadsheet work. The complete application and business needs of the user should be carefully parsed to understand which applications and data make sense to centralize versus install locally. Only in certain cases does a 100-percent server-side model make business sense.

Security Considerations

There is no such thing as perfect security. Protection is always a matter of degrees. For simplicity, let's constrain security considerations to software-based attacks (viruses, worms, software vulnerability exploits) and remote hacking, assuming that the user is not a malicious attacker. Let's exclude hardware-based attacks, such as videotaping screen images or attaching purpose-built attack hardware. No compute model is inherently immune to that class of attacks.

Benchmarking Applications

There are no industry standard benchmarks for alternative compute models. Under the current state of the art it is not meaningful to carry out performance comparisons across computation models. Performance comparisons can be attempted between models if a common workload is measured, but even under these conditions, issues such as network loading, number of simultaneous users, server and network speed, workload content and other factors can make simulation results much different than real-world deployments. IT managers should evaluate performance claims carefully to understand the applicability of such claims to their situations.

Streaming and Application Virtualization

Streaming and *application virtualization* are not synonyms, even though they are often used interchangeably. Streaming refers to the delivery method of sending the software over the network for execution on the client. Streamed software can be installed in the client operating system locally, or in most cases, it can be virtualized. With application virtualization, streamed software runs on an abstraction layer and does not install in the operating system registry or system files. When shut down, a virtualized application may be removed from the client, or stored in a special local cache for faster launches or off-network use. The abstraction layer may limit how the virtualized application can interact with other applications. An advantage of application virtualization is that it can limit the continuous accumulation of randomness in the operating system registry and system folders that lead to system instability over time.

Application versus Image Delivery

A helpful way to think of the models and how they fit with customer requirements is to determine whether the problem needs to be solved at the application level or image level, as shown in Table 9.3. In this case, an *image* is the complete package of the operating system and required applications. Some computation models solve application problems, some solve image problems. It is important to understand the customer's need in this area.

Table 9.3 Application-level versus Image-level Models

Application level models	Terminal services
	Application streaming
Image level models	Virtual hosted desktops
	OS streaming
	Blade PCs
	Remote OS boot
	Virtual containers

Public versus Private Images

When centrally distributing a complete desktop image with either virtual hosted desktop or operating system streaming, it is important to comprehend the difference between a common public image and a customized private image.

Public images are standardized operating system and application stacks managed, patched, and updated from a single location and distributed to all authorized users. Files and data created by the applications are stored separately. Customization of the image is minimal, but since all users access a single copy of the OS and application, storage requirements are relatively small.

Private images are operating system and application stacks personalized to each user. Although users enjoy a great deal of customization, each private image must be stored and managed individually, much like managing rich, distributed clients. Current products do not allow private images to be patched or updated in their stored locations, but rather require them to be actively loaded and managed in-band, either on the server or the client. The storage requirement of private images is much higher, since each user's copy of the operating system and application must be stored.

Dynamic Virtual Clients

Dynamic virtual clients represent a category of client-side models that follow the paradigm of a centrally managed application delivered with client-side execution and mobility. Dynamic virtual client models share the following characteristics:

- Centrally-managed and application and/or OS images
- Client-side execution, not server-side
- Off-network mobility

Currently, four models fall into the dynamic virtual client category:

- Application streaming/virtualization
- Operating system streaming
- Remote operating system boot
- Virtual containers

Hence we use the dynamic virtual client to collectively refer to the above four models.

Server-based Models

Let's describe the server-based models in Table 9.1 in more detail.

Terminal Services

Terminal services represent the quintessential server-based model, as illustrated in Figure 9.1. Here, the client is merely a display and input device. All computation is done centrally on the server and all data is stored in a data center. Nothing is persistent on the client. It is the most proven, reliable server-side model, harkening back to the days of mainframe computing. Remote Display Protocol (RDP) or Independent Computing Architecture (ICA) are used to deliver an image of the server-based application to a terminal viewer on the client, and return keystrokes and mouse clicks to the server.

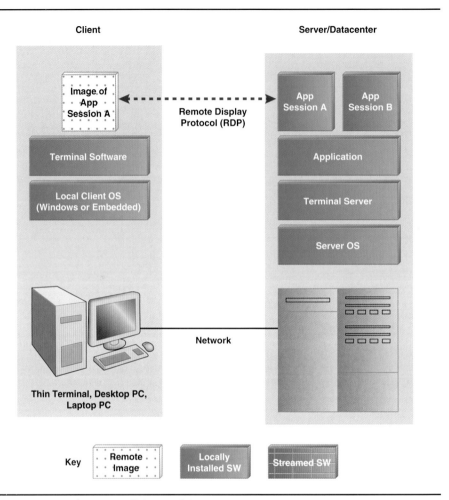

Figure 9.1 Architecture of Terminal Services

Most enterprises of significant size use terminal services for some applications and users. Bank tellers accessing the transaction system, call center workers entering orders into a database and healthcare professionals working with text-based patient records are examples where terminal services may be a good solution. The benefits and limitations of terminal services are summarized in Tables 9.4 and 9.5, respectively.

Table 9.4   Benefits of Terminal Services

Security	The OS, applications, and data never leave the data center, reducing the likelihood of a client-initiated attack or loss.
Manageability	Applications and data are centralized, allowing simpler administration and more reliable backup. Application management, validation, and support are simplified. Driver and DLL conflicts with the OS on the client are reduced.
Cost of Incremental deployments	Most enterprises already have some terminal services. Expanding to a few new applications may require little new infrastructure or software. Compared to virtual hosted desktops, terminal services require fewer servers to support a population of users.
Simplicity	Terminal services are very mature and well-understood. Implementation is fairly straightforward for IT. User adds, moves, and changes are simple.
Access	If enabled, users can access their applications from any network connected client. Users do not need to be at "their" workstation.
Disaster Recovery and Business Continuity	In event of lost of client function, users shift to another client or site.
Client power consumption	If deployed on thin client terminals, client power consumption will be lower than most desktop PCs. (Note: power savings on the client may be offset by increased power consumption and new capacity in the data center.)

Table 9.5   Limitations of Terminal Services

Performance	System responsiveness starts to degrade as the number of users per server rises.
	Remote Display Protocol (RDP) creates a serious graphics bottleneck. Video, Flash, and animated GIFs do not work effectively over RDP. This can be overcome with proprietary hardware or software acceleration products, but adds cost and/or additional complexity to the solution.
	Server-based models, since all input and display are transferred over the network, require a constant stream of low-latency bandwidth to maintain display, keyboard, and mouse responsiveness.
Software Compatibility	Applications must support a multiuser mode and run on a server operating system, such as Microsoft Windows† Server 2008. Not all software runs under terminal services.
	Some software is ill-suited to terminal services, due to its inherent limitations, such as VOIP, streaming media, compute-intensive, or graphics-intensive applications.
	Workflows or applications requiring specialized peripherals such as barcode readers or synchronization with a mobile device (phone, PDA, mobile internet device) may not work in server-side models, or may require custom engineering.
Mobility	Application delivery via terminal services requires a persistent connection to the network with sufficient bandwidth.
	Wireless laptops or tablets can be used with terminal services, but the application cannot be used outside the LAN or VPN.
Cost of New Deployments	New deployments of terminal services to large numbers of users is a significant expense, including space, servers, software, and networking.
	The cost of space, power delivery and cooling are higher in an advanced data center than cost in a typical office space.
	Acquisition cost of thin client terminals is similar to many desktop PCs.
	Principled Technologies reports that initial costs of terminal services are about the same as virtual hosted desktops, but higher than streaming or well-managed PCs .
Disaster Recovery and Business Continuity	In event of lost of server function, workloads must shift to a redundant server or data center.
	Loss of network function renders clients inoperable.
User Satisfaction	Users are conditioned to the PC experience—performance, customization, flexibility, and mobility. Inappropriate or draconian use of terminal services can result in high user dissatisfaction and complaints.

Virtual Hosted Desktops

The newest entry into server-side computing is *virtual hosted desktops*, more commonly known by VMware's acronym, Virtual Desktop Initiative (VDI). Given that additional vendors are creating similar products to VDI, such as Citrix's XenDesktop Server, we will use the generic term virtual hosted desktop and acronym (VHD) for this discussion. See Figure 9.2.

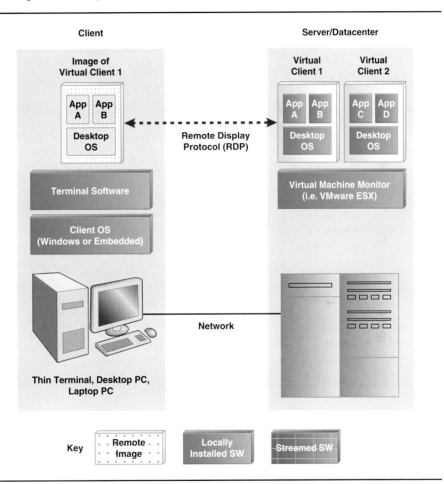

Figure 9.2   Architecture of Virtual Hosted Desktops

Similarly to terminal services, VHD is a server-side compute model. All computation and storage are centralized, with images of the user's desktop pushed over the network to the client via RDP or other protocol. The major difference is that VHD offers each user his or her own complete virtual machine, including the OS, applications, and settings. The benefits and limitations of virtual host desktops are summarized in Tables 9.6 and 9.7, respectively.

Table 9.6   Benefits of Virtual Hosted Desktops

Security	The OS, applications, and data never leave the data center, reducing the likelihood of a client-initiated attack or loss.
Manageability	Desktop image and data management are centralized, allowing simpler administration and more reliable backup. Software image management, validation, and support are simplified. Driver and hardware conflicts with the client OS are reduced. If using public images, IT needs to only manage and store one master image of each OS and application in the data center. This significantly reduces the image management and storage challenges.
User Customization	Each user interfaces with a full virtual machine on the server, allowing PC-like experience. If private images are enabled, user can have personalization and customization capabilities that are identical to a rich PC. Even with public images, some level of user preferences and look-and-feel customizations can be engineered with appropriate use of Active Directory profiles and "personality" features in the various solutions.
Access	Centralized computing can allow users access from any network connected client. Users do not need to be at "their" workstation to get access. VHD virtual machines can be targeted to either a specific user or machine.
Hardware/Software Image Validation	With VHD, all virtual machines run on a standard image of virtualized hardware, provided by the VMM vendor. This provides a single "platform" target for all OS and application images, which reduces validation efforts.
Disaster Recovery and Business Continuity	In event of lost of client function, users shift to another client or site.
Client Power Consumption	If deployed on thin client terminals, client power consumption will be lower than most desktop PCs. (Note: power savings on the client may be offset by increased power consumption and new capacity in the data center.)

VHD is designed to replicate the user experience of a rich PC with all the management and security of server-side models.

Table 9.7   Limitations of Virtual Hosted Desktops

Performance	Performance characteristics similar to terminal services
Manageability	Although software images no longer reside on the client, IT still must manage, update, and patch all the virtual desktop images now stored in the data center. The business may be trading one management challenge for another.
	If using private images, IT cannot realize a "manage once, run everywhere" vision. To patch or update a private image, it must be loaded onto a client, patched, and then returned to storage. They cannot be patched while stored.
Software and Peripheral Compatibility	Some software is ill-suited to server-based computing, due to its inherent limitations, such as VOIP, media, compute-intensive, or graphics-intensive applications.
	Workflows or applications that require specialized peripherals (barcode readers) or synchronization with a mobile device (phone, PDA, mobile internet device) may not work in server-side models, or may require custom engineering.
Mobility	Desktop delivery via VHD requires a persistent connection to the network with sufficient bandwidth.
	Wireless laptops or tablets can be used with VHD, but the application cannot be used outside the LAN or VPN.
Cost	Deployments of VHD to large numbers of users a significant expense, including data center space, servers, software, storage, and networking.
	The cost of space, power delivery, and cooling are higher in an advanced data center than cost in a typical office space.
	VHD is the most server-intensive delivery method, due to the burden of the server VMM and multiple concurrent copies of the client OS and applications. It takes more servers to support a population of users with VHD compared to terminal services or streaming.
	If using private images, each user's personalized OS, applications, and associated data must be stored in the data center, increasing storage capacity requirements.
	Acquisition cost of thin client terminals is similar to many desktop PCs.
	Initial costs of VHD are about the same as terminal services, but higher than streaming or well-managed PCs (source: Principled Technologies)
Disaster Recovery and Business Continuity	Similar to terminal services
User Satisfaction	Similar to terminal services

Compared to terminal services, VHD is relatively new and only just beginning to be deployed in volume. However, the industry buzz around VHD is high and research indicates that many enterprises are experimenting with it today.

Client-based Models

Now let's cover client-based models as initially described in Table 9.2.

OS and Application Streaming

Streaming both the OS and applications combines the simplicity of a stateless client with the performance of local execution. Here, the client is essentially "bare-metal" with no OS or applications installed, as illustrated in Figure 9.3.

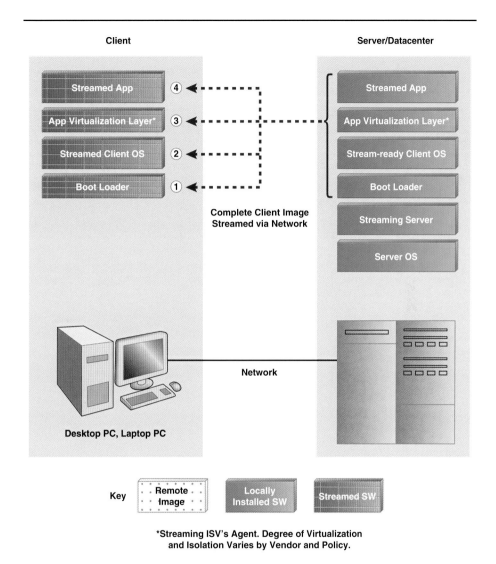

Figure 9.3   OS and Application Streaming Architecture

At power-up, the operating system and applications are streamed to the client over the network, where they execute locally on the client's own CPU, graphics, and so on. Application data is usually stored in a data center. The client may be PC with no hard drive, using main memory exclusively.

With streaming technology, the software does not stream to the clients in the same form as it comes from the software vendor. The software first goes through a process called *sequencing,* where it is divided up into prioritized blocks and placed in a specific order for streaming to the client. The basic launch and initiation software go first, followed by high-demand services and capabilities. Some less frequently used capabilities may remain in the data center until requested in order to reduce network traffic. A small minority of applications cannot successfully complete the sequencing process because of the way they were coded or are linked to other software. In these cases, another means of delivery must be used. The benefits and limitations of OS and application streaming are summarized in Tables 9.8 and 9.9, respectively.

Table 9.8 Benefits of OS and Application Streaming

Security	Application data can be stored and protected in the data center.
	Any local corruption of applications or operating systems is removed and all patches updated when the system is re-imaged at each boot-up.
	Applications can be isolated or "sandboxed" in protected containers, limiting data exposure to other applications or the OS.
Manageability	OS, applications and data are centralized, allowing simpler administration, easy software migrations, and more reliable backup.
	If using public images, IT needs to only manage and store one master image of each OS and application in the data center. This significantly reduces the image management and storage challenges.
	Not having a permanent OS or application installation on the client simplifies software image management and support issues.
	Software licensing can be centrally managed. Streaming provides better insight into actual application usage, enabling greater licensing optimization.
	Stateless clients (diskless PCs) make adds, moves, and changes very simple.
Performance	Since the OS and applications execute on the local processor, memory and graphics, performance is virtually identical to traditional locally installed applications.
	Compute- and graphics-intensive applications, as well as video, Flash and streamed media perform well.
	Caching options can be set to accelerate initial boot-up and application launches without locally storing data.
	Network load is highest at initial boot-up, but once OS is running, network demand drops to very low levels. With server-based models, RDP requires a constant stream of screen images and keyboard/mouse traffic over the network.
Infrastructure Cost	Since computation and display remain on the client, fewer and less-expensive servers are required than server-side models.
	If using public images, IT need only store one master image of each OS and application in the data center. This significantly reduces storage requirements.
	Streaming technology has the lowest initial deployment costs of the centralized compute models (source: Principled Technologies).
Disaster Recovery and Business Continuity	In event of lost client function, user can shift to a different site or client (private images may complicate this if image is assigned to a device, not a user)
	In event of lost of server or network function, client may be able to continue to work for a while if local caching is enabled. No new boots can be performed if OS streaming server or network down.

Table 9.9   Limitations of OS and Application Streaming

Security	At runtime, data and applications are resident on the client, and therefore susceptible to client-side attacks or theft.
Performance	Streaming download speeds can be affected by physical distance from the server, network load, and number of users.
	Some applications, particularly web-based applications, assume certain components are locally installed. These interactions must be accounted for in the application packaging architecture.
Cost and Manageability	If using private images, each user's personalized OS, applications, and associated data must be stored in the data center, increasing storage capacity requirements.
	If using private images, IT cannot realize a "manage once, run everywhere" vision. To patch or update a private image, it must be loaded onto a client, patched, and then returned to storage. They cannot be patched while stored.
Software Sequencing Process	A small percentage of software, due to its internal architecture, cannot successfully complete the sequencing process and cannot be streamed.
	The sequencing process can be time and labor-intensive during the initial setup and debugging period.
	Interactions between streamed/virtualized applications may result in behavior not encountered when the applications were locally installed. These issues must be root-caused and debugged.
Hardware/Software Image Validation	Unlike VHD, the streamed OS interacts directly with the physical hardware. As they do with a locally installed OS, IT must validate and tune streamed operating systems with each target hardware configuration.
Disaster Recovery and Business Continuity	In the event of a lost client function when private images are in use, IT may have to manually configure a new device to get the user up and running.
	In the event of a lost server or network function, local caching may prevent immediate loss of productivity, but the client cannot operate independent of its network drive for long.
	No new boots can be performed if OS streaming server or network is down.
Mobility	Currently, no commercially-available product enables off-network or mobile use of a streamed OS.

Remote Operating System Boot

Remote operating system boot is similar to operating system streaming in that it delivers a complete operating system and application image to a "stateless" PC whose hard drive has been deactivated or removed, as illustrated in Figure 9.4. The equipment manufacturer Lenovo provides a solution called *Secure Managed Client* that uses the iSCSI hard-drive protocol over the network to boot the system directly from a storage area network (SAN) device. The PC treats the SAN just like its local hard drive.

Unlike operating system streaming, remote operating system clients boot directly from the SAN, and the image is unmodified from the "gold" image that would be used on a local disk. On one hand, these differences can lower the cost of the solution. However, if the image is not optimized for delivery over the network, boot times will be extremely dependent on the speed of the network connection. The benefits and limitations of remote operating system book are summarized in Tables 9.10 and 9.11, respectively.

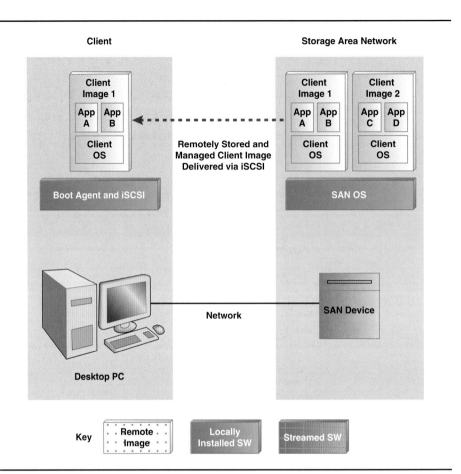

Figure 9.4 Architecture of Remote Boot

Table 9.10 Benefits of Remote Operating System Boot

Security	Application data can be stored and protected in the data center.
	Any local corruption of applications or operating systems is removed and all patches updated when the system is re-imaged at each boot-up.
Manageability	OS, applications, and data are centralized, allowing simpler administration, easy software migrations, and more reliable backup.
	If using public images, IT needs to only manage and store one master image of each OS and application in the data center. This significantly reduces the image management and storage challenges.
	No permanent OS or application installation on client simplifies software image management and support issues.
	Software licensing can be centrally managed. Streaming provides better insight into actual application usage, enabling greater licensing optimization.
	Stateless clients (diskless PCs) make adds, moves, and changes very simple.
Performance	Since the OS and applications execute on the local processor, memory and graphics, performance is virtually identical to traditional locally installed applications.
	Compute- and graphics-intensive applications, as well as video, Flash, and streamed media perform well.
	Network load is highest at initial boot-up, but once OS is running, network demand drops to very low levels. With server-based models, RDP requires a constant stream of screen images and keyboard/mouse traffic over the network.
Infrastructure Cost	Since computation and display remains on the client, fewer servers are required than server-side models.
	Since clients boot directly from the SAN rather than a streaming server, and no image sequencing is required, remote OS boot can cost less than OS streaming models.
Disaster Recovery and Business Continuity	In the event of lost client function, user can shift to a different site or client (private images may complicate this if image is assigned to a device, not a user)
	In the event of loss of server or network function, client may be able to continue to work for a period of time if local caching is enabled.

Table 9.11   Limitations of Remote OS Boot

Security	At runtime, data and applications are resident on the client, and therefore susceptible to client-side attacks or theft. Stored data can be protected in the SAN or locally on an encrypted hard drive.
Performance	Since the image is not sequenced for optimal network delivery, remote OS boot becomes extremely dependent on the speed and latency of the network. (Since SMC has not shipped at this time, the actual performance and difference versus OS streaming is not yet measured)
	OS boot speeds can be affected by physical distance from the server, network load, and number of users.
Hardware/Software Image Validation	Unlike VHD, the remotely booted OS interacts directly with the physical hardware. As they do with a locally installed OS, IT must validate and tune remotely booted operating systems with each target hardware configuration.
Disaster Recovery and Business Continuity	In the event of lost client function while private images are in use, IT may have to manually configure a new device to get user up and running.
	In the event of loss of server or network function, local caching may prevent immediate loss of productivity, but client cannot operate independent of its network drive for long.
	No new boots can be performed if SAN or network is down.
Mobility	Currently, no commercially-available product enables off-network or mobile use of remote OS boot.
Vendor Lock-In	At this time, only Lenovo offers an integrated remote OS boot solution. The PCs, SAN, and software must all be particular Lenovo systems for it to function.

Application Streaming/Virtualization

In this model, the operating system is locally installed, but applications are streamed on-demand from the datacenter to the client, where they are executed locally, as shown in Figure 9.5. Streamed applications frequently do not install on the client operating system, but instead interface with an abstraction layer and is never listed in the operating system registry or system files (hence the term *application virtualization* that some vendors use).

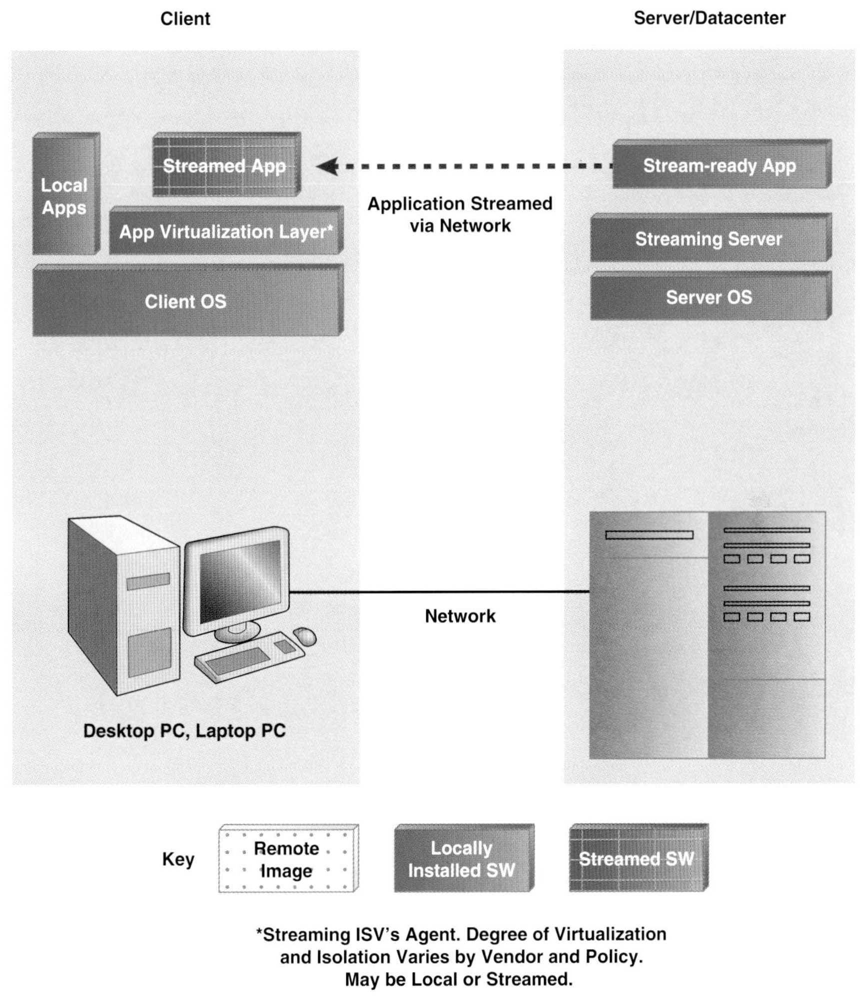

Client

Server/Datacenter

Local Apps

Streamed App

App Virtualization Layer*

Client OS

Application Streamed via Network

Stream-ready App

Streaming Server

Server OS

Network

Desktop PC, Laptop PC

Key

Remote Image

Locally Installed SW

Streamed SW

*Streaming ISV's Agent. Degree of Virtualization and Isolation Varies by Vendor and Policy. May be Local or Streamed.

Figure 9.5 Architecture of Application Streaming/Virtualization

This simplifies the interactions between the streamed application, other locally installed software, and the operating system, virtually eliminating software conflicts and image management problems. It also can effectively "sandbox" applications in isolated containers, allowing better security. Applications virtualized in one container may not interact with other applications in the same way they do when they are both locally installed or virtualized in the same container (that is, cut-and-paste or web-based applications may not work properly). This can be mitigated by packaging related applications in bundles. Independent software vendors also have different levels of "permeability" of their virtualization layer, where the restrictions of interactions through the layer can be scaled up or down. The benefits of application streaming/virtualization are summarized in Table 9.12.

Table 9.12 Benefits of Application Streaming/Virtualization

Security	Application data can be stored and protected in the data center.
	Any local application corruption is removed and all application patches updated each time the application is initiated from the streaming server.
	Applications can be isolated or "sandboxed" in protected containers, limiting data exposure to other applications.
Manageability	OS, applications, and data are centralized, allowing simpler administration, easy software migrations and more reliable backup.
	If using public images, IT needs to only manage and store one master image of each OS and application in the data center. This significantly reduces the image management and storage challenges.
	No permanent OS or application installation on client simplifies software image management and support issues.
	Software licensing can be centrally managed. Streaming provides better insight into actual application usage, enabling greater licensing optimization.
	Application virtualization may enable legacy applications to run on a newer OS, even if the application has compatibility problems if locally installed.
	Since they are abstracted from the OS registry, virtualized applications reduce conflicts, corruption, and randomness in the OS registry, significantly reducing application conflicts and software problems.
Performance	Since the OS and applications execute on the local processor, memory and graphics, performance is virtually identical to traditional locally installed applications.
	Compute- and graphics-intensive applications, as well as video, Flash, and streamed media perform well.
	Caching options can be set to accelerate initial application launches without locally storing data.
	Network load is highest at application launch, but once application is running, network demand drops to very low levels. With server-based models, RDP requires a constant stream of screen images and keyboard/mouse traffic over the network.
	Streaming only the applications reduces the network load versus streaming whole OS.
	User experience for OS boot is the same as standard PC since it is locally installed.

	Since computation and display remain on the client, fewer and less-expensive servers are required than server-side models.
Infrastructure Cost	If using public images, IT needs to only store one master image of each OS and application in the datacenter. This significantly reduces storage requirements.
	Streaming technology has the lowest initial deployment costs of the centralized compute models (source: Principled Technologies).
Disaster Recovery and Business Continuity	In the event of lost client function, user can shift to a different site or client
	In the event of loss of server or network function, client can continue to work off-line with cached content.
Mobility	Streamed applications can be cached for off-network use on mobile clients.

Streamed applications can be cached on a laptop and taken off the network. When the laptop reconnects with the network, the application can re-synchronize with the server to check licensing, version, and usage information, and download any new application data to the data center. This is currently the only centralized model that allows this level of mobility.

The limitations of application streaming are summarized in Table 9.13.

Table 9.13 Limitations of Application Streaming

Security	At runtime, data and applications are resident on the client, and therefore susceptible to client-side attacks or theft. Stored data can be protected in the data center or locally on an encrypted hard drive.
Performance	Streaming download speeds can be affected by physical distance from the server, network load. and number of users.
	Virtualization may limit interactions between applications compared to applications that are locally installed (that is, no cut-and-paste between applications). This issue varies by ISV, as each handles it differently.
	Some applications, particularly web-based applications, assume certain components are locally installed. These interactions must be accounted for in the application packaging architecture.
Software Sequencing Process	A small percentage of software, due to its internal architecture, cannot successfully complete the sequencing process and cannot be streamed.
	The sequencing process can be time- and labor-intensive during the initial setup and debugging period.
	Interactions between streamed/virtualized applications may result in behavior not encountered when the applications were locally installed. These issues must be root-caused and debugged.
Disaster Recovery and Business Continuity	With a local OS, the client is not a stateless, "bare-metal" device. Although application data is stored centrally, getting users working again in a new site is more complex than other models.

Blade PCs

Blade PCs repartition the PC, leaving basic display, keyboard, and mouse functions on the user's desk and putting the processor, chipset, and graphics silicon on a small card (blade) mounted in a rack on a central unit. PC blades, unlike server blades, are built from standard desktop or mobile processors and chipsets. The central unit, which supports many individual blades, is secured in a data center or other IT-controlled space. In most cases, remote display and I/O are handled by dedicated, proprietary connections rather than using RDP over the data network. The architecture of blade PCs are illustrated in Figures 9.6 and 9.7.

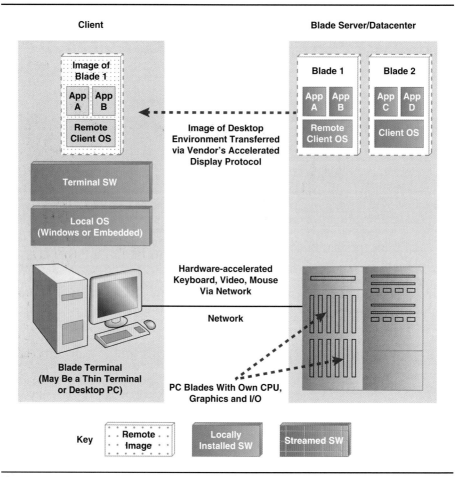

Figure 9.6   Architecture of Blade PC (One-to-One Model)

Blades promise a higher level of manageability and security than distributed PCs through restricted physical access, software image policies, and limits on the types of activities users can do on the client device. OS, application, and data storage are centralized in a storage network.

Blade PC vendors initially targeted a user-to-blade ratio of one-to-one, where each user was dynamically assigned a blade and they had exclusive use of it. However, as blade solutions and virtualization software has advanced, most vendors are now enabling one-to-many capabilities.

The proprietary nature of blade PCs mean IT organizations must make a long-term commitment to a vendor-specific architecture once they get on this path. Switching vendors or compute models requires a complete "forklift upgrade" in most cases.

The benefits and limitations of the blade PC model are summarized in Tables 9.14 and 9.15, respectively.

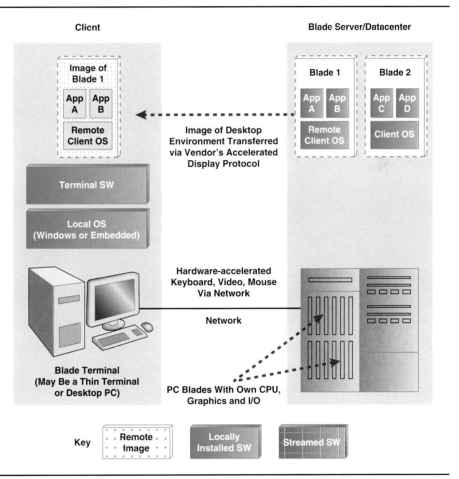

Figure 9.7 Architecture of Blade PC (One-to-Many Model)

Table 9.14 Benefits of Blade PCs

Security	There is much lower risk of a security breach or data loss via the client with the OS, applications, and data locked down in the data center or "blade closet."
Manageability	OS, application, and data management are centralized, allowing simpler administration and more reliable backup. PC blades offer a common hardware stack, which simplifies validation, image management, and support. Users can be dynamically assigned any PC blade that is available. User adds, moves, and changes are simplified.
User Customization	If enabled for private images, each user can have a unique OS and application image, allowing PC-like personalization of preferences and settings.
Access	Centralized architecture can allow users access from any blade-connected client, or in some cases, any Internet-connected client. Users do not need to be at "their" workstations to get access.
Disaster Recovery and Business Continuity	In the event of lost of client function, users shift to another client or site, or are assigned to another blade.
Client Power Consumption	Since compute power is located on the blades, power consumption, heat, and fan noise at the client device will be lower than most desktop PCs. (Note: total power consumption of the clients, blades, and associated storage may be comparable to standard PCs.)

Table 9.15 Limitations of Blade PCs

Performance	In one-to-many deployments, application performance may degrade depending on the number of users and workloads.
Manageability	Although software images no longer reside on the client, IT still must manage, update, and patch all the centralized desktop images now stored in the data center. The business may be trading one management challenge for another.
Vendor Lock-In	Blade PCs are not standardized and each vendor has a proprietary implementation. Once IT has selected a vendor's blade architecture, switching costs are extremely high. IT may be limited in available management tools, and becomes dependent on their vendor's tools and development schedule.
Mobility	No mobile option exists for blade PCs. They are only suitable for users with a persistent network connection.
Cost	Due to their nonstandard architecture, blade PCs are more expensive per user than other models [source: Principled Technologies]. OS, applications, and data must be accommodated in the storage area network. New hardware, networking, and building space may be required.
Disaster Recovery and Business Continuity	In the event of loss of blade PC rack or storage function, workloads must shift to a redundant blade PC rack. Loss of network function renders clients inoperable.

Virtual Containers

Virtual containers form a compute model that is still in its early stages, and is rapidly evolving. In some form, it is available through products like VMware ACE[†], Microsoft MED-V/Kidaro[†], RingCube vDesk[†], Wanova[†], InstallFree[†], or the early virtual appliances developed for Intel® vPro™ technology. In this model, virtual machine images, including the OS and applications, are created and managed centrally by IT. But instead of running the virtual machine on the server (the VHD model), the virtual machine is streamed to the client for local execution on a client-based virtual machine monitor (VMM), as illustrated in Figure 9.8. This provides centralized management of the image and, depending on storage policy settings, centralized security of application data. Since execution is on the client, even compute- or graphics-intensive applications are responsive, and users can enjoy off-network mobility.

Virtual containers can be general-purpose user environments, such as a standard Windows OS and productivity applications, or they can be purpose-built, single function "virtual appliances" that provide services like compliance monitoring or highly-secure applications. The early virtual appliances developed for Intel vPro technology are examples of purpose-built virtual containers.

Virtual containers enable some valuable usage models for IT:

■ Since the VMM abstracts hardware variations away from the operating systems, the requirement for testing and validation of the image against dozens of hardware combinations is eliminated. Theoretically, the image can now run on any PC. Users could use the corporate image on their home PC or a laptop they provided.

■ IT can deploy a centrally-managed, locked-down corporate image that runs alongside a more open "personal image." Even if the corporate image is the only image on the PC, there is still significant value since virtualization eliminates most of the hardware/software validation testing.

■ IT can deploy a virtual container with a "partner image" or "contractor image" with applications and security clearances to access only the required corporate resources. Policy can be set to easily revoke virtual containers if a contractor no longer needs access.

■ Highly secure applications, such as critical R&D or patient records, can be deployed in an isolated virtual container.

■ Virtual appliances can be deployed that provide services to the systems, such as firewall or compliance management, but are less vulnerable to tampering or attack since they run outside the user's virtual machine.

Many variations exist in the architecture and deployment of the virtual containers model, and we are a few years away from a dominant method. Some implementations create the whole image on the server and stream it as a unit to the client. Other implementations create a hollow virtual machine on the client, and then fill it with a centrally-managed streamed OS and streamed applications on demand. Some architectures assume the VMM has been pre-installed on the client, while others bring the VMM down to the client with the virtual container. Intel has a preference for "hypervisor" implementations where all operating systems run on the VMM, which allows us to bring Intel® Trusted Execution Technology (Intel® TXT) and Intel® Virtualization Technology (Intel® VT) to bear. "Hosted OS" virtualization does not allow as much opportunity to optimize for Intel technologies.

The benefits and limitations of the virtual containers model are summarized in Tables 9.16 and 9.17, respectively.

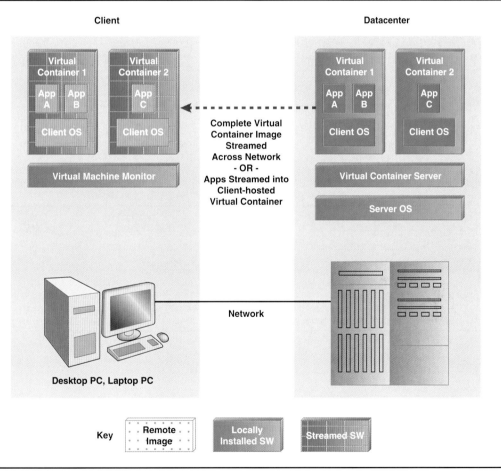

Figure 9.8   Architecture for Virtual Containers

Table 9.16 Benefits of Virtual Containers

Security	Virtual containers are isolated from each other. Software in one virtual container cannot view, capture, or modify software in another container. This contains virus and intrusion threats, and can isolate highly secure applications from other software.
	Security policies can be set for the needs of the virtual container, allowing IT more control over lock-down, access policy, data storage, and authorization/revocation rights.
	Purpose-built virtual appliances can provide valuable security services from outside the user's environment.
	Security patches and updates can be deployed on a central corporate image and easily distributed to virtual containers on the clients.
Manageability	OS images, application management, and data management are centralized, allowing simpler administration, easy software migrations and more reliable backup.
	Since virtual containers run on a VMM, not the physical hardware, image validation only needs to be done against the VMM, not dozens of unique hardware configurations.
	Virtual containers are highly portable. Installation may be as simple as streaming a file to the client or inserting a USB flash drive.
Performance	In theory, performance is virtually identical to traditional locally installed applications since the applications execute on the local processor, memory, and graphics. VMM efficiency and performance will be a factor.
	Compute- and graphics-intensive applications, as well as video, Flash, and streamed media should perform well.
	RDP is not used to push application screen images over the network, so network loading is reduced.
Mobility	Since virtual containers execute locally, they can be cached and taken off the network for true mobility.
	Users could carry their virtual container image on a USB drive and run it on any PC (home, office, partner site, and so on).
Infrastructure Cost	Since computation and display remains on the client, fewer servers are required than server-side models.

Table 9.17 Limitations of Virtual Containers

Security	At runtime, data and applications are resident on the client, and therefore susceptible to client-side attacks or theft. Stored data can be protected in the data center or locally on an encrypted hard drive.
	The VMM layer introduces a new layer that must be protected. A security breech in the VMM could expose data from all virtual containers. ("Blue Pill" is a well-documented sample attack on a VMM. It does not work on a VMM protected by Intel® TXT and Intel® VT)
Performance	Running multiple virtual machines on a VMM may cause performance degradation. VMM efficiency and hardware-assistance will be key to achieving "near native" application performance.
	Virtualization may limit interactions between applications. This may be by design in some cases, but may be an unintended consequence in others.
Maturity	The virtual containers model is still in its infancy. The technology, deployment and management tools, and IT processes are not fully developed.
Industry-wide Technical Challenges	The industry needs to solve several fundamental technical challenges before the vision of virtual containers can be fully realized. This includes virtualization of graphics, wireless, power management, docking stations, and peripherals.

Server Sizing Considerations for VHD Deployments

Table 9.18 captures some relevant factors in assessing a VHD backend solution.

- Number of users (How many users are going to be supported via a virtualized client environment?)

- Type of user (Task, knowledge, or high performance workers) and corresponding workloads with each type of user

- Memory resources (Access to low cost memory and allocation of memory to client VM)

- Network sizing and latency (<150MS is standard applied by VMware and HP)

- Tolerance for risk (System level failure means downtime for a large number of users). Example: low tolerance means use multiple 2 socket systems, high tolerance means 4 socket systems.

Table 9.18 Sizing Consideration Details:

Number and Types of Users	Does your customer organize their user groups by business unit or by user type (task, knowledge, high performance)?
	A large number of data entry workers can work concurrently on a single system.
	Business unit organization may require more in depth testing to properly size loads.
	What percentage of time are users actually doing work?
	Call center workers may be working 90% of shift.
	General users may be on computer less than 10 minutes per hour.
Memory Resources	Over-commit memory.
	Matching up user type improves memory sharing (by OS and application use).
	If you organize by business unit, balance the cost of additional memory with the importance of work being done.
	High performance workers may require more memory; task workers may receive acceptable user experience with lower memory footprints.
Network Sizing and Latency	Remote Protocol Characteristics:
	150MS latency is generally acceptable maximum.
	Can be affected by device redirection, local printing, and streaming audio/video.
	RDP is okay for windowed applications.
	Software codec (HP RGP) or hardware codec (Teradici) is good for graphical and streaming video/applications).
	Remote protocols impact VDI CPU utilization and network traffic.
Tolerance for Risk	System level failure means downtime for a large number of users.
	The more sockets, the larger the risk.
	Include heavy users on each system to reduce absolute number of users per system.
	Know your risk tolerance when evaluating solutions.
	MP platforms support high tolerance for risk with reliability and scalability advantages.

To virtualize or not to virtualize on the desktop no longer represents the critical planning question. The new question that desktop managers are asking is, "What desktop environment strikes the balance between productive users and IT's need for increased manageability and security?" Emerging client virtualization technologies such as operating system streaming, remote operating system boot, application streaming, and virtual containers need to effectively answer the following question: How can we deliver a cost effective desktop solution tailored to each user scenario? This means that the traditional desktop model may become by comparison insecure, inflexible, and hard-to-manage, very much an anachronism in this context. Organizations will instead identify desktop users by criteria like task-based, knowledge, or power users and will deliver dynamic desktops accordingly. Client virtualization is not just an emerging trend; it's the future of the corporate PC.

Chapter 10

Increasing Data Center Efficiency with Server Power Measurements

Contributed by Ravi A. Giri

Intel IT defined methods for analyzing computing energy efficiency within our design computing environment, using measurements of actual server power consumption and utilization. We used these methods to identify trends and opportunities for improving data center efficiency, and to implement a pilot project that increased data center capacity.

Most efforts to measure and increase data center efficiency have been focused at the facilities level. However, we can also obtain significant benefits by employing server-level measurements to analyze and increase computing efficiency. Improvements at this level can enable us to expand data center capacity, reduce capital expenditure, and reduce operational power and cooling costs. We undertook several initiatives, including:

- Defining a computing energy efficiency metric that reflects server performance per watt in design computing production use.

- Using this metric, together with measurements of server power consumption and utilization, to analyze computing energy efficiency across all servers in an Intel data center.

- Identifying efficiency improvements due to server refresh.

- Identifying opportunities to reduce power and cooling costs without negatively impacting Intel product design workload throughput.

Our analysis of compute efficiency has already delivered benefits, enabling us to add capacity at a data center location that we previously thought was power-constrained. We plan to use these methods at other data centers, and we are continuing to build on our work with proof of concept projects that explore the energy efficiency opportunities we have identified.

Microprocessor design requires enormous computing capacity, and the requirements increase significantly with each processor generation. Because of this, silicon design workloads are the primary driver of compute capacity growth at Intel. This in turn results in rapid growth in data center power and cooling needs.

Today, our design computing environment includes about 65,000 servers, with very high compute utilization averaging around 85 percent.

We refresh these servers based on a four-year cadence; this enables us to take advantage of the substantial increases in performance and energy efficiency delivered by each new server generation. By replacing aging servers on a regularly scheduled cadence, Intel has realized operational cost savings, avoided incremental data center capital spending, and gained capacity. Our studies have shown that we can achieve 10:1 consolidation ratios on average when replacing single-core servers that had been in operation for four years.

However, newer server technologies such as blade servers are driving significant growth in rack power density and cooling needs. With the shift to blades, the number of servers per rack has increased 1.6 times from 40 to 64 over the past five years, while the rack power envelope has increased 3 times to 24 kilowatts. As a result:

■ Power and cooling costs can be a very large component of overall server total cost of ownership (TCO).

■ Power and cooling requirements constrain IT equipment capacity at some data centers. This can result in stranded rack capacity, racks that can't be filled because power and thermal limits have been reached.

The Role of Compute Energy Efficiency

Rising power and cooling costs have resulted in widespread efforts to analyze and increase data center efficiency within the industry and IT organizations. These efforts have mostly been focused at the facilities level. However, as shown in Figure 10.1, a holistic approach to energy efficiency is required to gain maximum benefits.

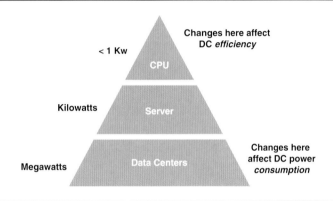

Figure 10.1 The Data Center Energy Efficiency Pyramid

For example, increases in computing energy efficiency (as indicated by performance per watt) can significantly improve overall data center efficiency and play a crucial role in countering the growth in power and cooling requirements. To achieve improvements in this area, we need to gain a better understanding of server power consumption and how it relates to server function and performance. Applied across many servers, improvements in compute efficiency can significantly reduce overall data center power consumption and Intel's carbon footprint. Potential benefits include:

■ Increased Data Center Capacity and Reduced Capital Expenditure. Data center power capacity includes a reserve intended to absorb spikes in power use caused by peaks in resource utilization. The reserve is typically based on either nameplate (nominal) server power consumption or on power consumption measured at peak utilization with specific workloads. Traditionally the reserve has been estimated using a static method from nameplate data. Intel Intelligent Power Node Manager technology in Intel® Xeon® processor 5500 series servers allows managing this reserve dynamically to actual power consumed in real time, thereby enabling the benefits mentioned.

If we can better understand trends in server power use and map them to server functions and performance, we can reduce the size of the reserve. This can substantially increase the effective capacity of existing data centers, thereby avoiding or deferring capital investment to retrofit data centers as well as reducing capital expenditure associated with provisioning power for new data centers.

■ Reduced Power and Cooling Costs with Power-aware Job Scheduling. Ideally, jobs should be allocated to the most energy efficient systems first. If we can adjust job-scheduling capabilities to preferentially direct jobs to the most energy-efficient servers available, we can reduce operational power costs and the corresponding cooling needs.

Measuring and Increasing Computing Energy Efficiency

At Intel IT we have undertaken several initiatives to analyze and improve computing energy efficiency within our design computing environment, including a long-term study and pilot project conducted at a data center in India. These efforts included:

■ Defining a computing energy efficiency metric that reflects design computing production use. There is a tradeoff here. Tighter measurement can be done only in a specific application domain; it can't be attained in general.

■ Using this measure, together with other data such as the number of servers, their compute utilization, and power utilization, to analyze computing energy efficiency across all servers in an Intel data center.

■ Identifying efficiency improvements due to server refresh.

■ Identifying opportunities to reduce power and cooling costs without negatively impacting design workload throughput. We took advantage of one of these opportunities to increase data center capacity by reducing the power reserve. Knowledge of actual power consumption allowed a much more precise equipment scheduling. Beyond that, in Chapter 12 we report results of research to operate servers in high ambient temperature as a method for reducing the energy that otherwise would be used for cooling the data center.

Computing Energy Efficiency Metric

Our first step toward improving computing energy efficiency was to define a useful measure based on actual Intel design workloads.

The most commonly used data energy efficiency metrics today are Power Usage Effectiveness (PUE) and its reciprocal, Data Center Infrastructure Efficiency (DCiE). These are defined by the Green Grid consortium, of which Intel is a member. PUE is defined as *total facility power/IT equipment power*. While PUE is very valuable for establishing facilities efficiency, it measures only the proportion of total power that goes to IT equipment, not the useful work that is done with that power.

EDA MIPS: A Measure of Design Computing Performance

We needed an energy-efficiency measure that reflected actual design computing server use within our environment. We decided to base our approach on measurements of performance per watt with design workloads. This is analogous to the Green Grid's recently proposed (but not finalized) Data Center Energy Productivity (DCeP) metric, which is defined as *useful work/energy consumed*.

To be realistic, our metric needed to be based on workloads representative of our actual design workloads. It needed to encompass both capacity and utilization, measure the performance of the entire server platform, and be applicable across different platforms. Because of these requirements, simplistic measures such as the number of cores or industry-standard CPU-specific metrics such as SPECint were not adequate.

As a basis, we selected EDA MIPS, an internal measure defined by Intel IT. It was originally created to compare the performance of different Intel server platforms for the purpose of calculating server refresh ratios. The Server Hardware Benchmarking team in Intel IT measures EDA MIPS by running a cross-section of real Intel EDA workloads on each platform. Figure 10.2 shows EDA MIPS ratings for several generations of Intel server platforms.

We defined computing energy efficiency as *utilized EDA MIPs/consumed watts*. To calculate this, we need to measure both system utilization and actual server power consumption.

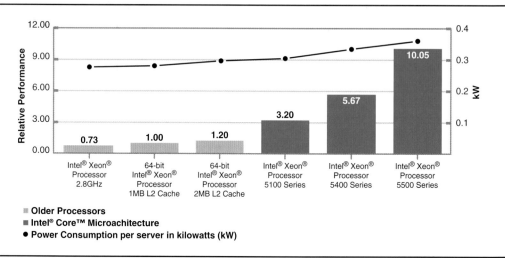

Figure 10.2   Relative Performance of Different Intel Server Platforms, in EDA MIPS.

Measuring Energy Consumption

To analyze and optimize computing energy efficiency, we need to measure server power consumption. However, at many organizations, data center power consumption is primarily measured at the facilities level; a lack of more detailed information about power consumption is available at the server, rack, or row level. This is mainly because there has been limited need to track this information, since the bill for energy consumption and the bill for server purchases are generally handled by different departments. Also, the cost of deploying additional instrumentation for measuring energy consumption can be significant.

A growing number of tools and technologies now enable us to gather more granular information about energy use, as shown in Figure 4.2. For example, we have already used row-level instrumentation to help us increase efficiency at one data center.

Methods for Measuring Server Energy Use

To measure server power consumption, several options exist:

■ Service Processor-based Power Sensors. Most recent generations of server platforms have service processors that include power monitoring sensors, accessible via an interface. The Intelligent Platform Management Interface (IPMI) is one the most common of these.

■ Estimating Power Use Based on Utilization and Server Function. Many data centers still include older systems lacking service processors or sensors. For these systems, two options exist:

- Assume that the systems constantly use power at their peak power rating. For these older machines, this provides a stop-gap approach that can be used until they reach their end of life. However, this method does not tell us how much energy the systems actually consumed.

- Estimate power usage based on server utilization and function. System utilization is correlated with power consumption; by taking a series of measurements, we can establish the relationship between system utilization and power consumption for a specific server model. This enables us to measure system utilization in our production environment and use it to estimate power consumption. Once we have established the correlation factor for each server model, we can use this method to estimate server power consumption across the data center.

■ Intel Intelligent Power Node Manager and Intel Data Center Manager. For recent Intel-based server platforms, such as the Intel Xeon processor 5500 series, Intel® Intelligent Power Node Manager and Intel® Data Center Manager allow very fine-grained monitoring and control of server power utilization. They enable us to view server power utilization in real time and implement power caps to ensure this power utilization stays within preset limits.

Intel Intelligent Power Node Manager provides power monitoring and policy-based power management for an individual server. Processors can regulate their power consumption through the manipulation of the P- and T-states. Node Manager works with the BIOS and OS power management to perform this manipulation and dynamically adjust platform power.

Intel Data Center Manager scales Intel Intelligent Power Node Manager functions to racks and groups of servers. It implements group level policies that aggregate data across the entire rack or data center to track metrics and historical data and provide alerts to IT managers.

■ Measurements from IP-based Intelligent PDUs that yield power readouts by branch circuit or by outlet.

Analyzing Data Center Computing Energy Efficiency

We applied our methods for measuring server performance and energy use to analyze computing energy efficiency trends across a data center containing four generations of Intel servers.

Computing Capacity and Power Consumption Baseline

We first needed to calculate the data center's total computing capacity and expected peak power draw. To do this, we summed up the EDA MIPS ratings and expected peak power consumption for all servers across the entire data center. This involved accurately mapping server hostnames to server models, then mapping the server models to their EDA MIPS ratings.

This provided the baseline for expected performance/watt based on the EDA MIPS ratings and expected peak power consumption of all servers, that is: available EDA MIPS/expected kilowatts.

Computing Energy Efficiency

We define computing energy efficiency as *utilized EDA MIPs/consumed kilowatts*. To calculate this, we:

■ Captured systems utilization data for all servers using in-house tools as well as open-source applications. We then multiplied the total data center EDA MIPS capacity by the percentage utilization to calculate utilized EDA MIPS.

■ Measured power consumption using the appropriate method for each server.

– For systems with service processor-based sensors, we were able to gather power consumption information using an IPMI-based tool.

– For models lacking these sensors, we correlated server utilization and function to power consumption.

– We augmented this data with power consumption data gathered from rack-level metered power distribution units and row-level external energy meters.

■ Using these measurements of utilized EDA MIPS and power consumption, we calculated the actual performance per watt achieved within the data center

Analyzing Trends

Our goal was to plot and analyze this data over time, in order to capture trends and identify opportunities to improve efficiency. We were able to do this because we had accurate data documenting the number of servers, when they were purchased, when they were retired, and their locations within the data center.

Figure 10.3 shows these statistics gathered over a 15-month period at a data center. This high-level view helped identify trends as well as opportunities for improving energy efficiency.

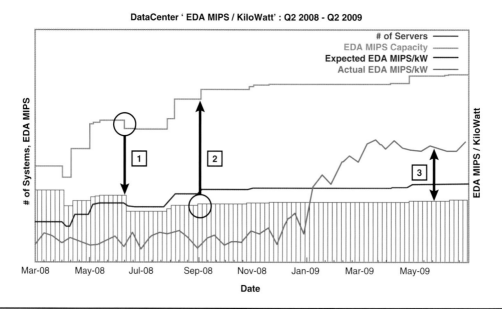

Figure 10.3   Compute Energy Efficiency Trends at an Intel Data Center

During this period, we periodically replaced older servers as part of our refresh strategy. The chart clearly shows the effects of this strategy as well as the impact of significantly improved server utilization and the initial efforts to improve energy efficiency. For points 1, 2 and 3 please refer to the respective numbers in Figure 10.3

1. A large decrease in the number of servers shows a corresponding but smaller drop in compute capacity. This is because we are removing the older, less-powerful servers from the environment.

2. Small increases in the number of servers result in a relatively large increase in compute capacity. This is because we are adding new servers that are much more powerful than previous generations.

3. The gap between the expected and actual EDA MIPS/kW (higher is better) shows a sustained improvement in the computing energy efficiency (the variations in the actual numbers are due to variation in percentage server utilization)

4. The data center compute capacity (EDA MIPS) increased significantly over time; however, the number of servers required to provide this capacity actually decreased.

5. The performance per watt (*utilized* EDA MIPS/kW) increased substantially during 2009 as the proportion of newer, more energy-efficient servers increases.

Energy Efficiency Improvements and Opportunities

Energy efficiency as measured by performance/watt can be improved by using one of two methods:

1. Increase the numerator:

   i. Increase available EDA MIPS by making it possible to add servers

   ii. Increase server utilization so that utilized EDA MIPS is closer to available EDA MIPS

2. Decrease the denominator:

   i. Reduce the power consumption of the servers even at high levels of utilization

   ii. Reduce the power needed to cool the servers at high levels of utilization

The data helped us identify opportunities in both these areas for improving energy efficiency in 2009 and beyond. We have already taken advantage of one of these opportunities in a pilot project to increase data center capacity.

Making More Computing Capacity Available by Managing Power Reserve

Data centers typically are able to use about 80 percent of the power capacity provided to the facility. The remainder acts as a reserve to absorb spikes in IT equipment power usage. We undertook a pilot project to determine whether, by analyzing actual power consumption, we could reduce the size of the reserve and increase the practical data center capacity as a result.

As seen from the graph in Figure 10.4, the actual energy efficiency in 2009 increased to above the expected levels. This is due to a combination of significantly improved server utilization (that is, the numerator or utilized EDA MIPS was close to available EDA MIPS) and also because the power drawn was lower than expected.

We have traditionally based data center capacity on measurements of peak server power consumption when running a wide range of real-world workloads. If we can better understand the trends of actual power consumption of servers mapped to specific functions and workloads and at different levels of utilization, we can take informed decisions to increase the compute capacity that can be landed in a given power footprint.

In our pilot project, our goal was to analyze power consumption and determine whether we could land additional servers in a data center row that we had previously considered to be power-constrained. To do this, we:

1. Analyzed trends in peak energy consumption and server utilization over a one-year period, as shown in Figure 10.4, and mapped this information to specific server models and functions.

2. Based on the analysis, identified reserve, and noted the area where actual peak utilization and power consumption was much lower than expected.

3. In the new scheme, we took advantage of the unused headroom by lowering the expected power usage thresholds of servers used for specific functions.

4. Quantified the additional capacity gained by lowering these thresholds, and established the feasibility of landing new servers based on other constraints such as physical space and network ports.

5. Added automated monitoring controls to ensure that, if the thresholds are breached or server functions change, the server processors are throttled down (reducing power consumption by changing the processor C- and P-states) and the datacenter and server operational teams are notified.

This project enabled us to significantly expand the row's compute capacity. We landed additional servers with power consumption equivalent to about 10 percent of the row's total power capacity.

We anticipate that leveraging such opportunities will become significantly easier with new technologies, such as Intel Intelligent Power Node Manager and Intel Data Center Manager, which provide the ability to cap power consumption at preset levels.

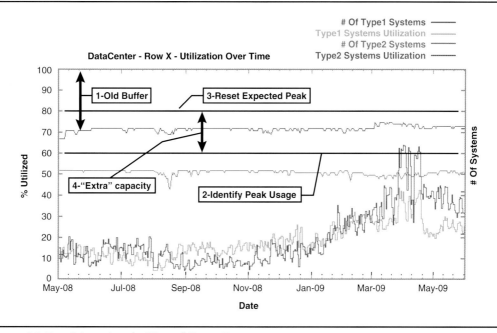

Figure 10.4   Managing the Unused Power Reserve.

Summary

Using performance per watt as the metric for energy efficiency is aligned to any IT shop charter, that is: improve utilization and reduce cost (power consumption).

Our analysis of compute energy efficiency has highlighted opportunities to enable both the work delivered and on the power consumed. It has already delivered benefits, enabling us to add data center capacity by managing the power reserve (we increase the numerator). We are planning to use this method in other data centers during the coming year.

Intel IT continues to build on this work through proofs of concept exploring energy efficiency opportunities previously identified identified such as power-aware job scheduling.

When determining where a job should run, the most power-efficient and higher-performance systems, usually the newer systems, in the data center, are to be scheduled first. However, current batch job scheduling algorithms and configurations are tuned only to optimize performance and ignore energy efficiency.

We will be studying methods for power-aware job scheduling, including automated actions such as resubmitting jobs to more energy-efficient systems (as indicated by their performance/watt metric), as well as reconfiguring less-energy-efficient systems for lower-priority work or moving them to low-power mode (CPU P and C states) when idle.

Such opportunities will be significantly easier to leverage with the use of Intel Intelligent Power Node Manager and Intel Data Center Manager, now available with server platforms based in servers provisioned with the Intel® Xeon® 5500 and 5600 series processors, which will enable more granular and accurate measurements as well as the capability to manage and set policies to govern the power consumption.

Chapter **11**

Platform Assisted Thermal Management of Data Centers

Advances in server technology have resulted in the inflation adjusted cost of acquiring server equipment trending down, while economies of scale in data centers have significantly reduced the cost of labor. This leaves the cost of the energy as the next target for optimization. Energy costs are used up in operating the IT equipment, the switchgear that provides uninterrupted power to the equipment, and in cooling the IT equipment.

In this chapter we explore a platform-assisted thermal management approach to add "smarts" to cooling solutions for data centers: assume it becomes possible for management applications to read temperature and possibly other data from instrumentation embedded in server platforms, assuming that the platform instrumentation becomes pervasive to the point that it becomes a check-off item for any platform vendor as a precondition to play in this space.

The presence of this instrumentation effectively constitutes a vast sensor network whose potential has not been tapped to date. One possible application is to build a real-time thermal map for the server grid to complement the real-time power monitoring and control capability covered in chapters 4 and 5.

This capability would complete the thermal part of the power and thermal (P/T) picture of the data center and hence it is highly synergistic to the power monitoring and control capability. The synergy extends to the application of innovative control mechanisms, including coordinated policies with facilities and workload migration to optimize thermal profiles and behaviors.

Role of Embedded Platform Instrumentation

As servers in data centers become more power efficient, attention is being given to another area of data center power consumption: the operational costs associated with data center infrastructure. Three important infrastructure considerations are

■ Availability of power to the data center consistent with target service levels

■ Given that there are no significant amounts of energy stored in server equipment, eventually all the power going into servers gets converted into heat. This heat needs to be promptly removed from the premises.

■ Reducing the heat emitted by IT equipment brings economic benefits not only from the energy saved directly, but also from the extra energy needed to cool the data center. An estimate for this extra energy can be derived from the data center PUE.

Thermal and other kinds of sensors in servers have been available in servers for some time. However, practices do not exist yet to harvest and use this data in a coordinated fashion to optimize data center operations.

There are a number of technical and administrative barriers that prevent the use of thermal information as part of an integrated data center operations practice.

■ From a technical perspective it would be helpful to be able to harness this information through standardized API layers. While single-vendor solutions are feasible, and such a solution could be architected to be self consistent, it would be expensive due to the need to recover research costs over a relatively small customer base, and at best it would result in an "island of manageability", a walled garden where only one vendor plays. Few data center operators would be willing to cast their destiny to the whims of a single vendor.

■ From an administrative perspective, harnessing thermal data requires the IT organization to take actions that do not necessarily improve the operational metrics of the organization such as specific QoS or service level goals, yet most of the monetization of the energy savings would accrue to the facilities organization. The way out of this conundrum is to take on a holistic approach with a mandate to the top to improve data center operations.

The focus of this research is more modest than trying to tackle the structural issues mentioned above: we report on a number usage models of monitoring and controlling thermals in the data center using platform thermal sensors and illustrate a number of techniques for rapid integration on the assumption that the success of this technology depends on making retrofits easy to implement. If a new data center becomes a precondition for deployment, adoption will be slow and might not happen at all. The processes and artifacts reported here come from experimental results from proofs of concept carried in several enterprise solution laboratories at Intel.

Data Center Thermal Management Considerations

The trend in data centers, especially in those dedicated to the delivery of cloud and internet portal services is toward larger sizes and power densities: advances in server technology keep increasing the amount of computing power that can be packed in a given form factor.

At the facilities level there are economies of scale to be had; at the platform level, while the performance yield per watt keeps increasing roughly at the same pace as Moore's Law, systems are shrinking even faster and hence the performance per unit volume is increasing. The average power consumed per rack has been trending up. At the same time, the cost of server equipment has not changed much or is slightly down if we factor in inflation.

These trends have altered the relationships in the TCO pie: operating expenses have become significant portion of the total cost of ownership. These costs are dominated by staffing and energy costs. One data point comes from an internal study done at Intel, shown in Figure 11.1. The results of study by Hewlett-Packard[1] are even more emphatic. The study claims that the 3-year energy cost of highly dense servers is roughly equivalent to their acquisition cost.

---

1   Christopher Malone, Christian Belady, *Metrics to Characterize Data Center and IT equipment Energy Use*, Digital Power Forum (2006)

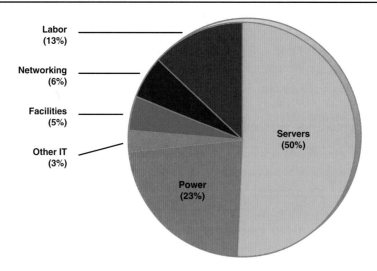

Figure 11.1 Data Center TCO Pie Chart

Going back for the moment to the trending in equipment energy density, racks populated with $3U^2$ and 4U servers four or five years ago with power consumption in the range of 2 to 4 kilowatts per server are now populated with 1U or 2U servers with per rack consumption in the order of 8 to 16 KW per rack. Blade form factors will push the power envelope to the 20–30 KW range.

Older data centers will reach their thermal limits before they will reach their physical capacity. Typically these centers, when operated at their limits of thermal capacity will still have racks half full. Deploying more servers beyond this limit will result in hot spots. Hosting environments will enforce an overall power quota per rack, with the same result: customers will hit the power ceiling before filling the rack. For instance, Beijing Telecom imposes a 2.2 kilowatts rack limit for servers leased to Baidu.[3]

---

2   The "U" term refers to a standardized pitch a server uses in a rack for rack server form factors. A 1U server is defined to fit in a 1.75 inch slot in a standard EIA 19-inch rack. Servers are manufactured in multiples of 1U. See http://en.wikipedia.org/wiki/19-inch_rack for additional information.

3   *Dynamic Power Optimization for Higher Server Density Racks* – A BTC Case Study with Intel® Dynamic Power Technology, an Intel White Paper. Also see Intelligent Power Optimization for Higher Server Density Racks, a joint Intel and Baidu white paper.

In a data center with average power per rack of less than 2 kilowatts and power densities smaller than 40 watts per square foot the temperature would rise slowly even in case of a massive cooling system failure to the point that operators would have time to shut down the equipment as needed. That is not possible even today. A study by Opengate Data Systems[4] reports that a typical data center running at 5 kilowatts per cabinet will experience a thermal shutdown within 3 minutes following a cooling outage.

With higher cabinet densities of 10 kilowatts and above the temperature rise is even faster; a thermal shutdown can happen in less than a minute. Under these circumstances it is not practical to have a human operator be part of a control loop; automated controls are necessary that can carry out pre-defined policies in short order in response to specific contingencies. In other words, the trend toward higher density data centers will create the need for automated controls to manage thermal contingencies.

Data centers today must be designed to prevent this scenario at all costs through N+1 or better redundancy or by mirroring at a remote site which can be an expensive proposition, or must prepare to sustain this kind of loss. These data centers would need to be designed to Uptime Institute Tier III or Tier IV specifications.

Thermal management control has been implemented at multiple logical levels, from the CPU cores to individual servers. For simplicity, most of the control loops operate autonomously: a lightly loaded processor will automatically switch to a lower power state thereby reducing server power consumption overall. Autonomous control loops, being independent, miss out on optimization opportunities across peers or up and down in levels of abstraction. For instance, Intel has demonstrated significant operational flexibility by having a higher level application switch CPUs to lower power states even when under load, and significant energy savings, again through application driven dynamic reconfiguration, by moving virtual machines across servers and shutting down idled servers. These optimizations have been focused on power and implemented mainly at the rack level by composing node-level power management capabilities.

---

4   Processor, January 11, 2008 • Vol.30 Issue 2, http://www.processor.com/editorial/article.asp?article=articles/ P3002/31p02/31p02.asp&guid=

An opportunity exists to increase the benefits of active thermal control if we can combine information from the server and the information from the cooling, electrical and mechanical systems in the data center into the control model. This work represents a first exploration into this approach.

Power and Thermal Control Loops in Data Centers

One metric for energy usage, is the Power Usage Effectiveness (PUE) as defined by the Green Grid consortium. Data centers spend substantial amount of power in the power and cooling infrastructures of their facility. A measure of how effectively power is utilized in data centers is called Power Usage Effectiveness (PUE). It is a ratio of total power spent by a data center to the power spent in IT equipment.

$$PUE = \frac{P_{IT}}{P_{IT} + P_{Infrastructure}}$$

The theoretical best PUE ratio is 1, which would mean that no power is diverted to infrastructure equipment, including cooling infrastructure. Best in class data centers operate at PUE of below 2.

Table 11.1   EPA Estimated PUE values in 2011[5]

Scenario	Estimated PUE
Current trends	1.9
Improved Operations	1.7
Best Operations	1.3
State of the Art	1.2

Table 11.1 captures some representative PUE values. The number for *current trends* represents the number from average industry practices. *Improved operations* represents the "low hanging fruit" that can be harvested through local process improvement without capital outlays. *Best operations* represent the application of integrated practices and are representative of the

---

5   EPA Report to Congress on Server and Data Center Energy Efficiency Public Law 109-431; http://www. google.com/corporate/green/datacenters/measuring.html.

best available facilities today. State of the art represents the achievable number with the best technology available today. This number usually requires new builds and can't be achieved with legacy data centers.

Reducing the power consumed by cooling system is one way to improve the PUE. Changes under improved operation might include the use of blanking panels to reduce hot/cold air mixing and raised metal floor grommets or seals to reduce cold air leakage. More sophisticated practices under best practices might include relocating server rows to define hot and cold aisles, air containment devices to minimize mixing and constructing plenums for hot air return and the use of economizer under integrated practices.

In many data centers, the cooling systems of data centers are usually designed at the time of planning of the data center. As equipment gets added and removed, the overall cooling system may become less efficient. This may result in overcooling or under cooling of IT equipment.

In today's data centers, the cooling systems control system typically does not interface with the IT equipment. Figure 11.2 is representative of the cooling approach in many data centers. A set point is determined based on initial planning as mentioned earlier. The airflow information (temperature and flow rate of hot air returning to the Computer Room Air Conditioning (CRAC) units is compared against the set point and the building or facilities management software is used to control the CRAC units.

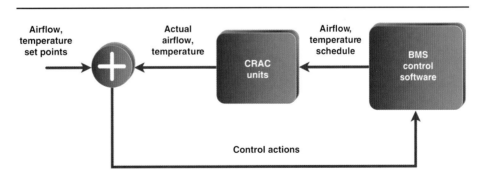

Figure 11.2 Fixed Set Point Used to Control Cooling IT Equipment in Data Centers

Today's servers typically have inlet air temperature sensors. It is possible to provision additional sensors without undue cost. These sensors would provide airflow readings as well as exhaust temperatures. These data can be aggregated at the rack, row, and zone level to provide airflow requirements in real time.

Likewise, the collection of temperature sensors can provide a real-time temperature map at a much higher resolution than the manual temperature maps taken during a static data center power and thermal analysis. These analyses are typically done for planning purposes, with measured temperature data points taken at floor level, three feet and six feet vertically, with readings spaced by five to ten feet. Data at higher spatial resolutions are computed quantities from running computational fluid dynamics (CFD) models.

With the server airflow data available, and assuming that the airflows in the perforated tiles are also measured, it is now possible to maintain a CFD model updated in real time. Although the initial solution is computationally heavy, once the system reaches steady state the parameters don't change much. Although this experiment has not been carried out, our experience indicates that this model can be updated for small perturbations in real time. The solved model provides the spatial isotherms and airflow velocity vectors for the zone in the data center where servers with embedded sensors are deployed. Temperatures are computed quantities, and hence the measured temperatures are used to verify and possibly correct the CFD model.

We can now use the set of temperatures and airflows in the model to compute a set of desired temperatures and airflow demand to be fed into the facilities control loop shown in Figure 11.2. Doing so would allow optimizing the thermal performance of the data center dynamically, based on real time data instead of static estimations. Hence we would have achieved a level of thermal monitoring and control similar to the one we were able to implement with Intel® Intelligent Power Node Manager Technology as described in chapters 4 and 5.

Figure 11.3 depicts relationship between the platform sensors, the aggregation function and the thermal mapping tool. Data centers running a virtualized cloud environment have another control mechanism: virtual machines can be migrated from one host to another to optimize thermal behaviors. For instance, servers running in a hot spot may experience over-temperature events that results in thermal throttling with a severe impact in performance. In severe instances, thermally induced shutdowns are possible.

The workload migration is carried out by a workload balancer application, also shown in Figure 11.3. It is likely that the control loop represented by the platform sensors, and the aggregation, thermal tool and workload balancing functions will be implemented separately, possibly by multiple vendors in a modular and interoperable fashion, interacting only with the facilities control loop through the temperature and airflow set points. Coordinated policies with the building management system (BMS), as suggested by the dotted line in Figure 11.3 may lead to incremental improvements.

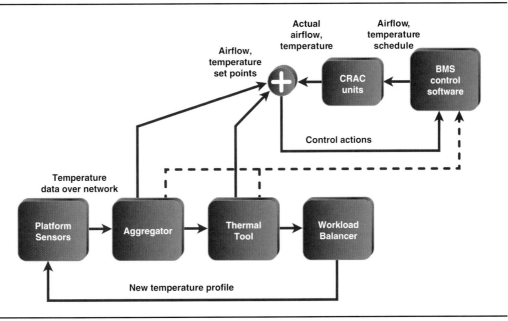

Figure 11.3   Integrated Data Center Thermal Control Loops

It is imperative that sensor information for thermal manager be available through published interfaces regardless of the equipment manufacturer because platforms deployed in a data center will need to coexist with equipment from different providers. The promise of integrated thermal management cannot be realized if equipment with these capabilities is segregated into vertically integrated islands from different manufacturers with little communication across.

Sensors can be placed anywhere: standalone, in PDUs, cabinets and in server equipment. It makes sense to fit these sensors in server equipment by default, with software drivers to access their information over the network, even if the sending information is overlaid over the data network for cost reasons. These sensors would represent a small cost adder to the platform, relatively insignificant to the value they bring, much in the same way that all present day laptops come fitted with wired and wireless networking. An alternative would be fitting a cabinet with networked sensors is likely a higher cost adder given that cabinets normally do not come fitted with networking components.

While thermal data coming from one server is intrinsically useful for managing that server, integrating the information from a grid of servers and other environmental sensors in the data center presents opportunities for optimization not possible by other means such as dynamic workload consolidation, operation under impaired conditions or even optimizing application performance across multiple data centers such as the execution of failover strategies, given that all the information is available over the network in real time. This is the promise for platform assisted thermal management of data centers.

This approach is not without its challenges. Today, building management applications controlling the infrastructure equipment like CRACs and the water chiller system do not communicate in real time or near real time with IT equipment. That is partly due to the way some data centers are set up organizationally. The approach we propose requires breaking down that barrier of communication between these two management domains (IT and facilities). The emerging trends in Cloud infrastructure with IT and facilities are under a common organization will help overcome this challenge.

Usage Models for Improving Data Center Cooling

As previously described, present day IT equipment cooling policies are likely suboptimal due to the administrative gulf between the data center facilities infrastructure equipment and the IT equipment. In a situation reminiscent of the suboptimal power management scenarios covered in Chapters 4 and 5, without knowledge of the actual cooling needs of the equipment the data center is quite often managed to provide the cooling required based on IT equipment nameplate estimations. Not surprisingly, the outcome is significant over-cooling in most cases. Unfortunately, the inaccurate estimates cannot preclude the possibility for severe under-cooling either, with potential performance and QoS consequences. To improve upon this model a number of use cases were considered with the goal of improving cooling delivery to the ITE but also identifying impending or present data center cooling problems.

Use Case 1: Cooling Balancer

This use case addresses the problem of delivering adequate airflow to all the systems within a rack or group or racks from both a monitoring and a control perspective.

From the monitoring perspective, under current practices, a data center operator can use the ASHRAE thermal report (if available) with its fixed airflow values to derive a rough estimation for the airflow requirements of a rack. In an existing data center, floor tiles are then located to deliver that flow based on the fixed value. Using the proposed thermal sensors exposed by the servers, the data center operator can determine whether airflow has been adequately sized based on the populated equipment but also whether recirculation as shown in Figure 11.4 is occurring within a rack or set of adjacent racks by evaluating inlet temperature conditions that deviate from the planned and expected variation within a rack.

From a control perspective, using real-time data from the servers and server inlet temperatures, optimal rack airflow can be calculated and provided to the DC operator. That data could be used to automatically adjust under floor airflow distribution, adjust CRAC operating points, adjust chilled water temperature or simply to enable the DC operator to move or reposition floor tiles to eliminate the imbalance.

Figure 11.4 merits an extended explanation to button up some concepts introduced in the last few sections. The figure depicts an isometric drawing of a solved CFD model in a small room. The room contains two rows of cabinets with the inlets facing each other. The room has a raised metal floor with two rows of perforated tiles in front of the servers. Cold air exits the CRAC unit under the floor, enters the room through the perforated tiles. Most of the cold air is sucked into the server inlets, exits through the back. We'll revisit this model further down in this chapter.

The server room has a ceiling plenum represented by the horizontal plane right above of the cabinets. The plenum has a grille opening behind the two rows of servers. Most of the air coming from the exhaust side of the server rows enters goes through the ceiling plenum grille and eventually returns to the CRAC, starting the cycle anew.

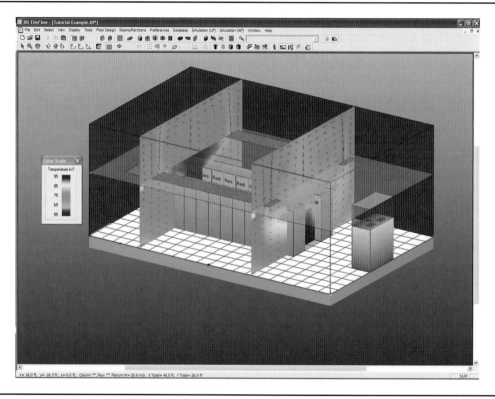

Figure 11.4   Example Airflow in a Raised Floor Environment with Recirculation from a CFD Model

The two green vertical planes are isotherms with the arrows representing airflow speed and direction along that plane. The model points to a trouble spot: because of the Bernouilli effect, airspeed under the floor is fastest near the CRAC unit and pressure is lowest. This means that the airflow of cold air out of the perforated tiles is smallest near the CRAC unit, and it stalls near the top of the cabinets. Because the cold air is not replenished, the inlet temperature is higher at the top. Exhaust temperature is also higher, topping at about 90 degrees Fahrenheit. In more severe cases, hot exhaust air blows over the cabinet tops, re-circulating into the inlets and compounding the problem.

Use Case 2: Data Center Thermal Map

To enable a data center operator to have an understanding of present and future problems in a data center it would be beneficial to have a characterization of power, utilization and thermal states of the IT equipment. By combining the sensors for these metrics, relationships between them can be quantified and understood. One could collect the power, thermal and usage conditions of the IT equipment and thereby comprehend how to better use the resources for the computing to be performed. Power metering of servers can be accomplished using appropriately instrumented servers, e.g. using either Intel® Intelligent Power Node Manager or by a DCMI-enabled system that reports system power. The thermal map would include airflow by system, rack, data center region and overall data center. This data could be used to better understand the overall air delivery requirements and implementation within the data center. Average exhaust temperatures for the same entities would also be available and could be linked with power consumption metrics to comprehend incongruous temperature vs. power distributions.

Use Case 3: Thermal Margin Evaluator

Well designed IT equipment enables full performance without constraint when demanded by the application based on the set policies. However, highly thermally stressed systems have an increased probability of processor or memory thermal throttling. Indications of this usage model are emerging where data centers are attempting to be operated at high ambient temperature, e.g. temperatures around 40°C, much higher than the ASHRAE recommended range. Some customers may want to address this thermal stress by shifting load to other systems. Additionally, for those components with no throttling function collected margin-to-critical data can be used to determine when to shift loads to less stressed systems to ensure data integrity and warn the data center operator that the system has little thermal margin. One could use the same information to compare across different servers under identical workloads.

A server-level agent would collect and collate the margin to non-critical and critical thermal limits for each component and assess whether throttling or data integrity loss is imminent and provide this assessment to a rack-level or data-center level agent to enable offloading of work thereby ensuring peak performance and data integrity.

Proposed Solution

In order to keep solution complexity manageable, it is useful to look at the process of architecting thermal management solutions as a layered approach. This approach allows for an efficient division of labor when building an integrated solution where any expert contributor need be concerned with only one layer and the interfaces with the layers above and below. The capabilities at any given layer depend on the foundation capabilities in the layer below. Each layer brings additional visibility to uncover opportunities for operational flexibility and energy savings.

Table 11.2 is organized with each row representing an implementation point in a layer of management and each column depicting a usage model. The lowest layer represents the hardware and silicon component layer. The next higher layer is for platform firmware typical of server out-of-band management solutions. Layered above are progressively higher levels of tasks: aggregation layer represented by group and rack level management software, workload management software that operates at a cluster level and allocates a set of workload to a server, and ultimately the facilities (or building) management software that control the cooling infrastructure of the data center as a whole.

The three usage models mentioned in this table, that is cooling balancer, data center thermal map, and thermal margin evaluator have been described earlier and this table shows the specific features that each layer of management has to provide to implement that usage model.

Table 11.2 Proposed Solutions for Platform Assisted Thermal Management

Abstraction Layer	Thermal Map	Cooling Balancing	Thermal Margin
Facilities Mgt	Display thermal, power, and utilization map	Perform airflow rebalancing (cooling corrective action	
Workload Mgt			Perform workload migration
Group & Rack Mgt	Read per server inlet & outlet temperatures	Server discovery per rack and workcell	Monitor server thermal margins
	Detect anomalies	Monitor server airflow	Issue alerts when thermal margins breached
		Aggregate server airflows to rack & row	
		Initiate airflow re-balancing	Initiate workload migration
OEM Platform BMC or Management Engine	Monitor real time inlet & outlet temperatures		Publish server thermal margins, including thermal throttling and shutdown for each sensor
	Expose inlet and outlet temperatures		
Platform Components: Processor, Memory, Chipsets			Expose server throttling margins for CPU, memory and chipsets

Reference Architecture

In order to take the framework described in Table 11.2 beyond a conceptual exercise, the team at Intel working in the platform-assisted thermal management project instantiated the framework with a number of readily available technology components and then built a working proof of concept with software and devices implementing the technologies.

The relationship between technology components constitutes reference architecture in the sense of Chapter 2, and the proof of concepts represents a physical embodiment of the reference architecture. See Figure 11.5.

The platform firmware running in a baseboard management controller (BMC) or Management Engine (ME) of a server gathers the silicon and chassis level thermal sensors and exposes them via a published external interface outside the platform.

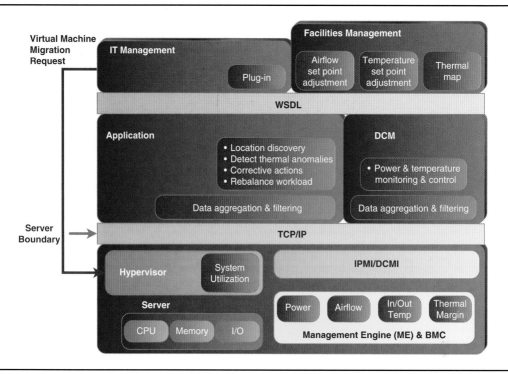

Figure 11.5   Reference Architecture of Platform Assisted Thermal Management

Intel® Data Center Manager (Intel® DCM) acts as the group level aggregation software and aggregates the platform sensors to implement group (rack and row) thermal monitoring and control. For example, based on a cluster or work cell defined by the data center to be thermally related to each other, it can determine the total airflow and average exhaust temperature, which cannot be determined by an individual server.

As a software development kit (SDK), Intel® DCM exposes an API described in Web Services Description Language (WSDL). IT management software can interact with this API to comprehend thermal information in the IT management capability. The workload placement software plug-in for a virtualized environment is an example of a control point performing workload migration between hypervisor hosts. Intel Data Center Manager can also be invoked by the facilities management application or building management system (BMS) to create a thermal map, and gather information to implement policies to regulate cooling set points. Examples of such control actions include airflow correction by regulating the fans that drive airflow through the lower plenum and changing the set point of the computer room air conditioners or handlers (CRAC/CRAH).

Challenges to Technology Adoption

Today the major roadblocks to the adoption of platform assisted thermal management are not technical but institutional. That is because the energy bill is paid by the "other person." From 600 IT practitioners in the Data Center Decisions 2008 Purchasing Intentions Survey, only 16 percent said power consumption in the data center was not a priority. However, for most of the other 84 percent it was difficult to put together a strategy to reduce power use, because most participants did not even know how much power was consumed by their data center: Less than 40 percent said that their business unit paid the electricity bill.

According to Ken Brill, founder of the Uptime Institute, "…our corporations are not organized to give full responsibility to IT departments. IT has been shielded from the inconvenient truth, namely that their utility bills are higher than they need to be."

One consequence of this state of affairs is lack of recognition of the need for communication between infrastructure management software and IT management software.

This issue is probably more prevalent with traditional data centers. Cloud and internet portal data centers are under greater pressure to improve on efficiency, and hence institutional alignment will likely be less of an issue. From the Data Center Decisions survey, the three most quoted power-saving strategies, namely power-down features in servers, improving air conditioning efficiency and server virtualization can benefit from platform assisted thermal management.

Data Centers may need to have certain improvements in infrastructure to take advantage of the mechanism we propose. They first need to follow recommended industry practice of hot and cold aisle containment, providing adequate unobstructed space in the plenum under floor and above the top of the racks for proper airflow. They need to take simple steps to minimize cold air leakage to hot areas of the data centers and to prevent recirculation of hot air from hot airs to cold areas. Such thermo-mechanical improvements are the initial steps in improving the PUE of a data center that have poor PUE to begin with, that is 2 to 3 or higher under the improved operations rubric described in Table 11.1.

At the other end, extensive use of sensors, especially those available in servers today will bring the efficiency gains a couple of notches, at least to those attainable under the best operations. The next step in improving the data center cooling efficiency is to use sensors already available to the fullest extent possible. Inlet temperature sensors are available in several servers today. However, they are often not used to take advantage in data center cooling decisions.

In this proof of concept, the team built demonstration of the benefits of using the inlet temperature sensors to dynamically optimize the data center cooling units has been documented that takes advantage of the knowledge of the inlet temperatures of servers and their spatial distribution to control proper temperature and airflow settings.

Another example of the implementation of the use of thermal sensors is Hewlett-Packard's Dynamic Smart Cooling system. It is a data center management application built as part of a thermal assessment service offering. The system integrates inlet and outlet temperature sensors embedded in blade servers and other sensors. This information is fed into control algorithms that include the use of computational fluid dynamics (CFD) modeling to understand the flow of air within the data center and route air to hot servers. The system is capable of controlling computer room air conditioning (CRAC) units for this purpose.

Building management systems that are capable of communicating with cooling system equipment using standardized interfaces (e.g. BACNet) constitute an increasingly important need for realizing the full benefit of the features we propose. Still a research subject, a working server location tracking strategy for identifying physical location of server in a data center (e.g. using signal reference grid or similar approach) is needed for the creation of spatial thermal maps.

CFD modeling is currently used only for static optimization, and its use as part of a dynamic control loop is still a research topic, primarily because of the heavy computational requirements. Given the enormous computational capability of cloud data centers, it would not be unreasonable to dedicate a few CPU cores to run a modeling application to make the data center operations self-optimizing on a real-time basis. The software implementation of the CFD model needs to be upgraded in two aspects: first the algorithms need to be modified to run in parallel, taking enough cores to run the simulation faster than real time, and second to take advantage of the solution available from the previous time step to incrementally calculate the solution for the next time step. Convergence to the solution of the underlying Navier Stokes equations will take place much faster than using initial conditions from the beginning of the simulation as it is done with the models used for static simulations.

Platform Level Sensors

The platforms used in the proof of concept were provisioning with the following new thermal sensors are defined for providing server level information:

- Total Airflow through the server.

- Average outlet temperature of the server.

Direct measurement of these quantities would require extra hardware, influence chassis or enclosure design and increase implementation cost. Thus, direct measurement of these physical quantities is infeasible or at least cost-prohibitive. For the purposes of the proof of concept the airflow and outlet temperature data were derived from other sensory data already available on the server. The values for the new sensors can be computed using new algorithms and mathematical formulas.

The sensors implemented can be queried in real-time by the other management agents like DCM software.

Sensor Accuracy

The accuracy of the derived sensor values depends on a number factors
- Limitation of the representation of a continuous type sensor value (0–255).
- Inaccuracy in the primary sensors; for example RPM values of all the fans have certain accuracy. Since the errors are independent, an estimated average error is a square-rooted sum of weighted squares of components.
- Model error, e.g. assumptions of linearity of relationships between the speed of fans (expressed in RPM) and air flow.

- Assumptions about physical properties. Air humidity is not factored in the model for simplicity. However, variations of the humidity can trigger small yet measurable changes in flow or outlet temperature.
- Unit-to-unit variation: chassis, ducting, cabling variations cause small variations in air-flow resistance.

Sensor External Interface

The sensory information from the new sensors is exposed via standard IPMI interface.

The agent running the code computing the values and instantiating the IPMI sensors is typically the system management controller, e.g. Baseboard Management Controller (BMC) or Management Engine (ME).

Airflow Sensor Computation

The airflow value is a function of multiple variables and constants. These include:

- RPM values of all the system/chassis fans

- Air inlet temperature

- The presence of devices in the baseboard altering air flow such as DIMM modules, expansion cards and processor heat sinks

- Pressure difference between front and back of the system/chassis.

Fans, ducts, internal components (flow obstacles) are a complex dynamic system with complex pressure, turbulences and other phenomena that influence air flow. Thus, analytically deducing the flow behavior from information about hardware may be infeasible.

We used an alternative method that uses an empirical determination of a model describing the general relationship with n fans. The model is parameterized with coefficients specific to the specific server (part number) with expectation that the coefficients yield good accuracy of the sensors for instances of that server (serial number). The coefficients need to be determined by the manufacturer for the type of chassis by performing thermal characterization using air-flow measuring test equipment like wind-tunnel.

The Intel® Data Center Manager SDK

Intel® Data Center Manager SDK provides power and thermal monitoring and management for servers, racks and groups of servers in data centers. Management Console Vendors (ISVs) and System Integrators (SIs) can integrate Intel DCM into their console or command-line applications and provide high value power management features to IT organizations.

For the purposes of this proof of concept, DCM

- Has built-in policy based intelligent heuristics engine that can maintain group power capping while dynamically adapting to changing server loads and minimizing performance impact of workloads
- Uses Intel® Intelligent Power Node Manager for node power and thermal management
- Designed as an SDK to integrate into existing management software products by means of a web service application programming interface (WSDL API)

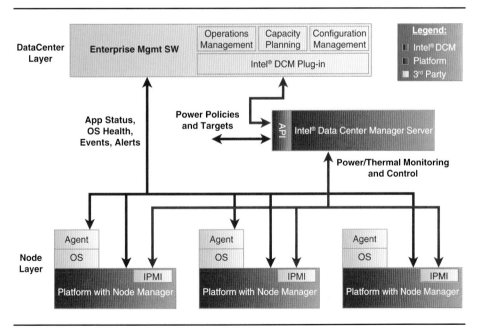

Figure 11.6 Intel® Data Center Interacting with Data Center Platforms

Figure 11.6 shows how Intel® DCM generally interacts with other parts in the datacenter.

For the purposes of thermal management, monitoring of server outlet temperature, server airflow, platform thermal margin, exhaust temperature, and exhaust energy for a group of servers are provided by a modified Intel® DCM version. Management console vendors and system integrators can expose the new usage models described earlier based on information collected by Intel® DCM.

Workload Migration

Data centers have been performing virtualization of servers for a variety of reasons. One of the benefits that come with virtualization is the flexibility in placing a workload running on a virtual machine (VM) on any one of several physical servers. This can happen during provisioning (while the workload is initially allocated) or during migration (when a virtual machine is moved from one server to another). Migration of workload is often based on utilization of the server. Recent advances enable using power data as criterion to migrate a workload and in deciding the source and destination of the workload.

The availability of the platform-based thermal sensors opens up another dimension to data center management. It allows workload migration for thermal reasons. At the simplest level, based on server inlet temperature, the workload migration manager can decide to move the VMs from hot servers to cold. The platform thermal margin and outlet temperature described in this document provide additional parameters that can be considered for the thermal-based migration of workload.

As mentioned in the reference architecture, a published API from the group level middleware would simplify the interface to the workload manager.

The Building Management System

Once the information from platform-embedded temperature and airflow sensors becomes available through published APIs, much integration work remains to attain the vision of a fully integrated platform assisted thermal management of data centers.

Fortunately, it is possible to start with a basic model built from the raw sensor network data, CRAC set temperatures, air flows, and data center topology to take advantage of the new information. This information at the very least will allow point management of servers, for instance to adjust workloads based on available power and inlet temperatures. This level of control represents an improvement over the autonomous approach used today where a CPU or server adjusts its power consumption purely on basis of the current workload.

Beyond the dynamic workload consolidation at the application level, additional control levels become available at the whole data center level, such as regulating CRAC set points and air flow rates and opening dampers in perforated tiles. The specific control actions depend on the actual data center architecture. For example, in data centers with total isolation between inlet and exhaust airflows, the placement of perforated tiles is not critical, and the focus should be on coordinating the CRACs, air handlers and economizers as needed. In data centers with alternating hot and cold aisles the placement and management of perforated tiles becomes important. In data centers without raised metal floors (RMF) or a return plenum management of vertical temperature gradients is critical and having a real-time CFD capability to calculate temperatures and air velocity vectors throughout the data center and beyond the vicinity of the sensors themselves.

To create a dynamic thermal map, a tool that combines the location information with real time thermal sensor information is required to create a spatial (2 or 3-dimensional) map. It can be augmented with the power and utilization information available from server sensors to create a consolidated power and thermal utilization map to provide comprehensive visual information of the operational state of the data center. This tool can be used to readily identify thermal anomalies and correlate that to power and utilization level.

The facilities management application is the critical component for controlling the cooling equipment and needs to play an important role in taking advantage of the additional sensors available for intelligent control.

The Proof of Concept

With the conceptual framework of the reference architecture in place, the research team proceeded to put together an instantiation of the reference architecture in the form of a proof of concept.

The goal of the proof of concept was to assess the technical feasibility of providing the platform level thermal sensors and in the process discover and document potential technical potholes.

We divided the proof of concept into two broad areas:

■ Implement and assess the new derived sensors on the server

■ Integrate usage of the new sensors into the data center management software

To this purpose, we created a specific architecture for the proof of concept based on the reference architecture mentioned before. This was created with the goal of using pieces of the reference software/firmware that are representative of real usage in data center currently or that we propose to be used as part of this solution. The proof of concept instantiation of the reference architecture in Figure 11.5 is shown in Figure 11.7.

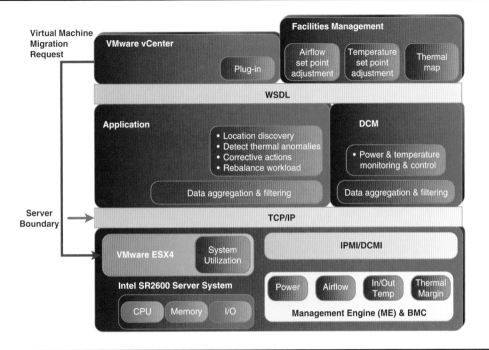

Figure 11.7   Proof-of-Concept Architecture

The proof of concept called for four SR2600UR Intel server systems code named Urbanna provisioned with dual Intel® Xeon® 5500 series CPUs running at 2.93GHz. The SR2600UR system is a 2U chassis with 3 thermal zones with non-redundant fans. The server was populated with 24GB of DDR3 memory using twelve 2-gigabyte 1066 megahertz memory DIMMs. This configuration is considered representative for this class of servers deployed in data centers. The server was also provisioned with customized BMC firmware implementing derived thermal sensors.

The team performed calibration runs to correlate estimated data against measured data as part of characterizing the server chassis. We also tested the system-to-system variation by determining the coefficients using one system and comparing the estimated and measured values on another system.

We repeated the correlation experiment on another 2U chassis with 3 zones but with redundant fans. This is a different chassis configuration from thermal point of view and provided another proof-point about the validity of our approach.

The proof of concept included the following software components

- VMware ESX 4 was installed in the servers, each running two or three virtual machines with the Microsoft* Windows Server 2008 operating system.

- A modified Intel Data Center Manager running in the management console to read the new IPMI sensors and expose the aggregated values via an enhanced API.

- VMware's VCenter and developed

- An in-house developed plug-in software module to VCenter that interfaces with both the VCenter SDK and the DCM SDK to obtain the server workload information and thermal information respectively. The plug-in is used to demonstrate triggering of workload migration using VMware's VMotion software.

We wanted to demonstrate the creation of thermal map using dynamic computation of airflow using CFD model and decision making using a facilities management application. However, since the scope of our proof of concept was limited to a cluster of servers located in a lab environment not subject to the data center thermals, we could not perform that part of the experiment, This effort is left to a future extension of the proof of concept where the reference stack is installed in a controlled data-center-like environment with interfaces to facilities management software representative of the ones used in industry.

Platform Level Sensors

The BMC firmware on the SR2600UR server was modified to read fan speed and derive the airflow values. Outlet temperature was calculated with the analytic formula described in the section on platform level sensors.

The platform thermal margin was taken as the worst case of the three margins for the CPU, memory and chipset. For experimental purposes, additional instrumentation was added on the BMC firmware to run the fans at a particular speed regardless of the temperature of the zone they are controlling. The firmware was also modified to provide ability to set the coefficients of the model while the firmware is running without having to modify the firmware that contains the model.

Overview of the Thermal Sensors

One of the goals of the proof of concept was to assess the linearity, stability and repeatability of the airflow model including the calibration of the derived sensors. The task involved measuring actual server airflows, and comparing these figures against with measured fan speed.

Fan speed readings are already available to the BMC firmware. To measure airflow, the server was encased in a thermally isolated ducting cage and the outlet air from the server was mixed and passed through a wind tunnel calibrated to measure airflow at the nominal airflow and temperature of the server air flow. Care was taken to minimize turbulence while mixing the outlet air of the server. We achieved this by making the volume of the mixing chamber large enough before the air entered the wind tunnel.

For the system with three thermal zones in the chassis and redundant fans, there were a total of 10 fans. Some of these fans were dual rotor fans. We noticed that for each pair of dual rotor fans, the speed of one fan did not match the other one even with the same pulse width modulation (PWM) signal. We took the higher of the two speeds as the input for the model. For zones with redundant fans, we took the average of the fan speed of each of those zones supplying airflow to that zone. We varied the fan speed of each zone over 4 possible values (corresponding to PWM signal values of 25, 35, 40, and 60). Since there were 3 such zones, we get $4^3 = 64$ distinct combinations of fan speed. We ran tests for each of this combination of fan speeds and measured the airflow.

This correlation experiment is an exercise with 3 variables resulting in 8 coefficients accounting for interference between zones. We solved for these variables with the method minimizing the sum of squares of errors. We obtained a coefficient of determination (R2) of 0.985 indicating very good correlation between airflow and the fan speeds.

The Management Solution Stack

The Intel® DCM software was enhanced to provide a node aggregation capability. The enhanced Intel® DCM software performed regular monitoring of server outlet temperature, air flow, and platform thermal margin. In addition, it also calculated the exhaust temperature and the exhaust energy for groups of servers in the proof of concept. Management console vendors and system integrators can retrieve these data via the enhanced WSDL API provided by Intel DCM.

Measurements of outlet temperature, airflow, and platform thermal margin were collected directly through corresponding sensors in the servers. The raw data of these sensors was retrieved with IPMI commands. To convert the data to meaningful values, sensor reading conversion formula in the server's sensor data records (SDR) was used.

DCM provided group level aggregation of exhaust temperature and exhaust energy for a set of servers (typically a rack or a row). For an individual server i, the exhaust energy, $Q_{exhaust,i}$ correlates with the inlet temperature, $T_{inlet,i}$, as well as the power consumption, P_i, of the server.

$$Q_{exhaust,i} = \rho f_i c_p T_{inlet,i} + P_i$$

where ρ denotes the air density, f_i denotes the airflow of the server and c_p denotes the specific heat of the air. The exhaust energy for a certain group of servers is the aggregated exhaust energy of the individual servers

$$Q_{exhaust} = \sum_i Q_{exhaust,i} = \rho c_p \sum_i f_i T_{inlet,i} + \sum_i P_i$$

Dividing both sides of the equation by

$$\rho c_p \sum_i f_i$$

yields the exhaust temperature of the group of servers

$$T_{exhaust} = \frac{\sum_i f_i T_{inlet,i}}{\sum_i f_i} + \frac{\sum_i P_i}{\rho c_p \sum_i f_i}$$

To simplify the calculation, we leverage the property of server's outlet temperature

$$T_{outlet,i} = T_{inlet,i} + \frac{P_i}{\rho c_p f_i}$$

Hence

$$T_{exhaust} = \frac{\sum_i f_i T_{outlet,i}}{\sum_i f_i}$$

and

$$Q_{exhaust} = \rho c_p \sum_i f_i T_{outlet,i}$$

Workload Migration Revisited

We developed a plug-in using VMware's vCenter management application. The plug-in architecture is shown in Figure 11.8 and essentially embodies the virtual machine migration policy in a single point of integration using the capabilities of DCM.

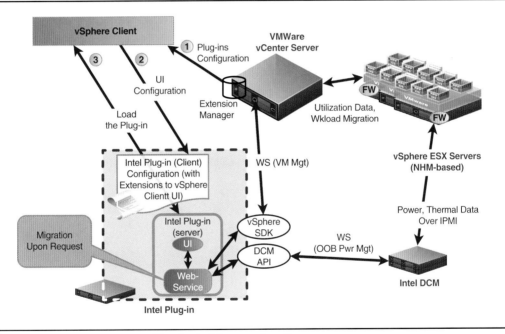

Figure 11.8   VM Migration Plug-in Architecture for vCenter

VMware's vCenter provides declaration of extension points describing the plug-ins, which are then discovered by vCenter and displayed on its console. The plug-in we developed is implemented as a Web service. It communicates with DCM SDK to obtain the thermal instrumentation data about airflow, outlet temperature and platform thermal margin. The plug-in also queries the vSphere SDK provided by VMware to discover which servers are hosting which VMs and their utilization levels. A consolidated display combining the information provided by VSphere and DCM is rendered by the plug-in as shown in Figure 11.9.

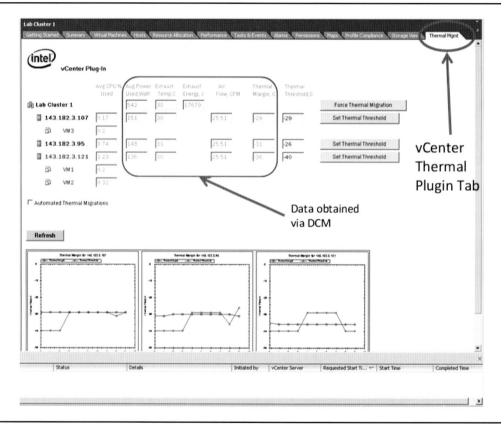

Figure 11.9   Example display from thermal plug-in

When a user-selectable threshold is reached for platform thermal margin, the plug-in selects a destination host for migrating workload to relieve the thermal stress. The algorithm for selection of VM and host is kept simple to focus on the feasibility to provide the necessary infrastructure for the migration. The plug-in invokes appropriate vSphere SDKs, which in turn invoke VMotion to migrate the virtual machines. The display then shows the new virtual machine hierarchy reflecting the state after the migration.

We chose to perform workload migration based on platform thermal margin; the decision could also be based on server outlet temperature just as well.

Building Management Software and CFD Model

Due to resource limitations the team did not perform any integration with building management software or CFD modeling tool for data center airflow in our proof of concept. However, a few thoughts may be appropriate to look at some of the potential benefits.

A real-time CFD model is an optional component in an integrated platform assisted data center thermal management application. It is useful in providing the "big picture" of the thermal profile for the whole data center beyond the data points provided by the sensors. Each simulation program has its particularities, in terms of the set variables and the derived variables. The set variables determine the initial and boundary conditions for the differential equations in the model. The solved model yields the derived variables. Where sensor data represents a derived variable, the variance from the computed value provides an indication of the accuracy of the model.

Each CFD model comes with a specific set of simplifying assumptions. These assumptions need to be incorporated into the control algorithms. Some of the accuracy requirements in static simulations can be relaxed. The goal is not necessarily to simulate the physics in minute detail, but to derive the appropriate control responses to current or anticipated conditions. Hence it would be a perfectly reasonable tradeoff to run the real time model with a coarser grid than the one used for static simulation to allow the computation of the model to keep up with real time changes in the physics.

As a specific example, let's bring the TileFlow* software into this context. TileFlow is a CFD tool for simulating cooling performance of data centers developed by Innovative Research Inc. (IRI.) Please note that this discussion is conceptual and hypothetical and does not reflect any product plans by IRI.

TileFlow carries out the numerical simulation of a CFD model in two major phases: the *under floor* and *above floor* simulations. The physics allow these computations to be carried out separately because in most cases there is little coupling between them.

The under floor computation establishes the pressure patterns under the RMF as well as the airflows coming out of the perforated tiles. The temperature under the floor is assumed to be uniform as defined by the temperature of the air coming out of the CRAC.

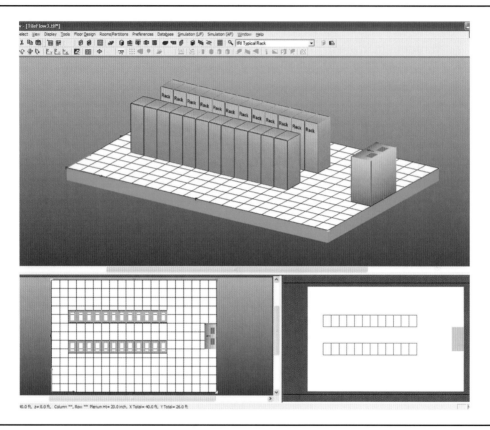

Figure 11.10   Model of a small data center room

The above floor computation starts with the airflows from perforated tiles and vents coming from the under floor computation. It takes into account the topology of server rows, power consumption and air flows in the installed servers to compute the temperature profile and air velocity vectors throughout the data center. The pressure above floor is assumed to be uniform across the room. Since temperatures are derived data in the CFD model, the temperatures read from the embedded platform sensors can be used to check the accuracy of the model.

Figure 11.10 shows a very simple TileFlow model of a data center room consisting of one CRAC unit and two server rows.

Figure 11.11 depicts the result of the under floor calculations. The color scheme in the floor surface represents the air pressure profile; the arrows are air velocity vectors. The plumes represent air flow out of the perforated tiles, coded by CFM. Note the Bernouilli effect: pressure is lowest in the perimeter of the CRAC where air speed is highest.

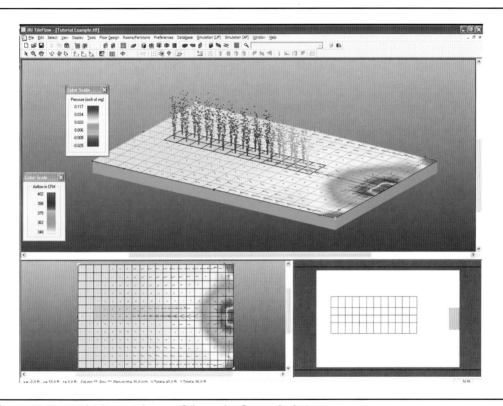

Figure 11.11   TileFlow rendering of the under floor calculation

Finally, Figure 11.12 shows the calculation results for the above floor model. The top picture shows three slices color coded for temperature; blue is coldest; green and yellow hottest. Air seeps out from perforated tiles in the middle, defining a cold aisle; there are two hot aisles between the cabinet rows and the walls where the hot air from the servers exhaust.

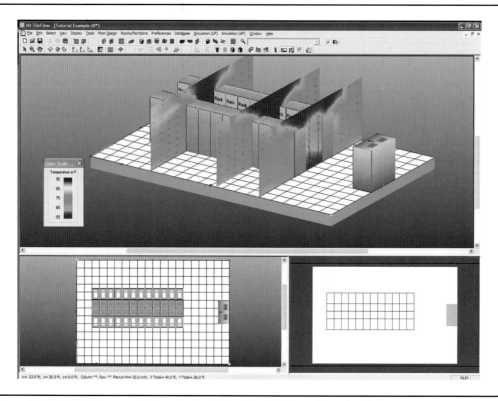

Figure 11.12   TileFlow rendering of calculations for the above floor simulation

Note that in the area nearest to the CRAC, where the under floor air pressure is the lowest, the column of cold air can't be maintained and some of the hot air from the hot aisles blows over the top of the cabinet, and mixes with the incoming cold air.

As a result, the inlet temperature for the servers near the top of the cabinet is higher than it should be. This is inefficient from two aspects: first, the air conditioning system needs to work harder to deliver inlet air at a certain temperature, and second, the set temperature for the CRAC needs to be lower to prevent servers at the top from overheating. Hence the air conditioning system is delivering colder air than necessary to servers near the bottom. The extra cooling requires more electricity consumption.

The control algorithm can compensate for this unevenness in temperature by opening under floor dampers to compensate for the reduced pressure near the CRACs.

With the more uniform inlet temperature profile enabled by the active control algorithm using the information provided by the CFD model it is now possible to raise the set temperature for the CRAC and adjust the air flow so inlet and outlet temperatures are closer to the manufacturer's specifications. Reducing the cooling requirements and the CRAC fan speeds will generally result in reduced power consumption by the cooling system. Additional power savings are also possible because the reduced cooling requirements may actually increase the number of hours in the year where economizer operation is possible, assuming that wet side or dry side economizers are installed.

The discussion above does not imply that the design of control algorithms is a trivial undertaking. For instance opening dampers near the CRAC may have the effect of moving the hot spots elsewhere because extra cold air is now consumed that would have gone to another place. If control actions are done too fast, undesirable oscillatory behaviors may ensue. Other observed phenomena may reappear, such as CRAC units fighting each other.

The integration of a near-real-time dynamic CFD model is possible only with improvements to the CFD modeling tools which operate in a static manner today. For example, they would have to take programmatic input via API from the group aggregating software layer like DCM about actual airflow and power consumption. In addition, they should solve the Navier-Stokes equation in an incremental fashion, starting from a solution arrived in a previous interval, assuming the perturbation in values of airflow observed in the next interval is small and not causing a solution from scratch.

Benefits and Discussion

Integrated platform assisted thermal management of data center is the current last rung in the thermal management hierarchy, and enables binding thermal management technical constructs to specific business metrics such as energy OpEx and increased uptime and availability due to the operational flexibility afforded by more precise thermal monitoring and control.

The solution discussed in this document helps to provide a monitoring capability that would enable a data center infrastructure administrator dynamically assess opportunities for improving the cooling solution. Thus it acts as a crucial step in aiding PUE improvement and consequently reducing the total cost of ownership (TCO). It is complementary to other technologies to improve the TCO. Additional infrastructure controls need to be in place to actually improve the PUE. The actual improvement depends on the maturity of the data structure and at what PUE value it was before these improvements are implemented. We believe it will help in those cases where it is neither too poor nor too good (i.e. about 1.7 to 1.3).

Summary and Next Steps

Integrated platform assisted thermal management of data centers will make it easier to logically connect activities related to data center power and thermal management to specific business goals. There is still significant work to be done in defining the logical layers and the APIs in between. Ideally these APIs should be public.

Original Equipment Manufacturers of servers need to perform thermal characterization of their server chassis and expose the additional thermal sensors. We have provided an approach to do that which can be extended to other types of chassis like blades and micro-servers. Data centers should begin taking advantage of these new sensors to implement new and improved IT management and building management solutions.

We'll know when this technology has come of age when a rich economic ecosystem is established enabling any data center operator to assemble best of breed solutions to particular needs. The application of real time CFD modeling is still under development and their potential benefit has not been fully assessed, even with proofs of concepts or pilots, let alone with full fledged deployments.

Control algorithms are still under research. It's likely that a one size fits all solution is not feasible and what we'll see are algorithms designed for specific application profiles and requirements.

Acknowledgements

As in any significant undertaking, this research represents the collaboration of many people from multiple organizations at Intel. The chapter authors include Murali Rajappa, David Filani, Enrique Castro-Leon, Andy Hoffman, Robin Steinbrecher, Dror Shenkar, Cong Li and Tianfei Zhu. The following people participated in the development of this technology: Chuck Rego, Bill Carter, Mike Patterson, John Leung, Chris Browning, Malay Trivedi, Jerry Kaliszewski, Onyegbule "AG" Agiriga, Jim Blakley, J Grady, Raj Ramaujan, Raghu Yeluri, Aswani Nerella, Sudhir Bangalore, Kamal Natesan, Nishi Ahuja, Sandeep Ahuja and Kanivenahalli "Gopi" Govindaraju.

Chapter 12

High Temperature Operation of Data Centers

Contributed by Chuck Rego, Gopi Govindaraju and Nishi Ahuja, Sandeep Ahuja, Trausch Terry

In today's data center environment, there is an increased pressure to reduce the total cost of ownership (TCO) for the data center. The main cost components comprise capital expenses and operational expenses. In turn, a major component of operational expenses is the cooling cost.

Cooling costs are approximately 40 to 60 percent of the total data center power[1]. One obvious way of reducing cooling costs is by applying less of it. Other factors being equal, this means allowing the ambient temperature inside the data center to rise. To the authors' knowledge, no prior research has been reported on data center power and performance implications of operating at higher temperatures, safe threshold temperature limits, and reliability assessments. In this chapter we look at power and performance implications for a number of standard workloads with known behavior profiles, examine the investigation results, and explore some of the potential benefits from the discoveries in these investigations.

---

1   See for instance J. Koomey in http://enterprise.amd.com/Downloads/svrpwrusecompletefinal.pdf or R. Cockrell in http://cleantech.com/news/5063/putting-heat-data-center-cooling-co.

Motivation for High Temperature Operation of Data Centers

A large number of data centers are being deployed worldwide to meet new business models such as the Internet portal data center, Web hosting, and high performance computing or HPC.

Power consumption at higher temperatures influences capacity planning.

Data center owners are trying to optimize the capital expenditures and operational expenditures. The use of commodity hardware can help moderate capital expenses. Options to reduce operational expenses include getting cheaper power and reducing the cooling costs. For instance, Google is publicly announcing their intention to operate their data centers at higher ambient temperatures. Microsoft is eliminating chilled water used to operate computer room air conditioners (CRACs) using free air cooling at 35°C and plan to operate their Gen 4 data center at 50°C. The European Union Code of Conduct (CoC) has set a target to operate data centers at 40°C by 2012. There is a significant interest with various customers to operate the data centers at higher temperatures as a means to reducing cooling costs. The first step in adopting high temperature operation as a default practice is to quantify the effect of operating in this mode. Here are some initial questions:

- What are the power and performance implications for servers at higher temperatures?

- What is the reliable thermal envelope the servers at which the data center can be operated?

- What is the optimum temperature control?

- How reliable are the server hardware components?

- How much power can be saved?

- Is throttling a better mechanism to save power? If yes, what are the guidelines?

The decision factors in data center design include:

- Data center location
- Network connectivity
- Cost control and compliance

- Utility rates
- Size
- Geographic considerations
- Cooling type architecture implemented

In this chapter we explore power and performance implications of servers in a data center when operated at high ambient temperatures under various workloads and benchmarks. We describe the experimental setup, analyze the results, and share our fundamental observations and recommendations. We hope these recommendations and guidelines will assist architects, data center operators, data center facilities engineers, capacity planning engineers, infrastructure, and hardware acquisition engineers to optimally select the type of servers and temperature ranges to optimize TCO.

Business Challenges

This section highlights some of the business challenges in high temperature operation of data centers.

The Data Center Story Yesterday

Traditionally, data centers were designed with a first priority to meet anticipated demand during the expected lifecycle. Power consumption and optimization were mostly an afterthought. Data centers are operated at 21 to 23°C range at 40 to 50 RH (relative humidity) and equipment inside cooled with external chillers. Design for future peak demand resulted in gross overprovisioning where power allocated was easily 3 to 4 times the actual power consumption. This approach results in overinvestment, that is, higher capital expenditures than actually needed and also higher operating costs from the unnecessarily larger equipment base.

Considerations for Today's Data Centers

Today TCO has become a primary concern for both the deployment and operation of data centers. With cooling being one of the major cost components of data center operation, conventional wisdom indicates that one way of reducing cooling expenses would be through having less of it.

One method is the increased use of cooling economizers using outside air or water to assist the data center chillers. On the same vein, an alternative is to allow the ambient temperature in a data center to rise.

However, there is scant research providing insight on how higher temperature can potentially impact the performance, reliability, and longevity of the equipment under these conditions. We believe this investigation is one of the first in the industry to shed light into these practices.

The Data Center of the Future

Leading data center operators have set a goal to reduce the Power Usage Effectiveness (PUE) from 3.0, a common figure today to the best in class number of 1.2. Thus 1.2 could become the "new normal."

Achieving this goal requires monitoring the power consumption for each component in the facility as shown in Figure 12.1 and defining controls to reduce energy consumption. Hence high ambient temperature operation may become commonplace once tradeoffs in power, performance, reliability, and SLA benefits are characterized.

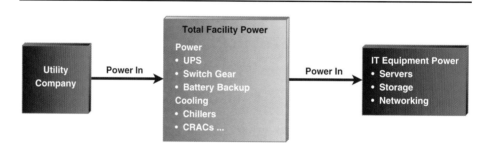

Figure 12.1 PUE Components

Research on High Ambient Temperature Operation

In this chapter we explore the following aspects of high ambient temperature operation in data centers:

■ Determine the power and performance characteristics and its implications when servers are operated at 25°C, 35°C and 40°C ambient temperatures

■ Characterize ambient temperature against server wall power and performance

■ Thermal profile of components

■ Trise over system ambient

■ System fan power characterized as function of fan controller pulse width modulation (PWM) setting

■ Power supply fan power characterized as function of fan speeds

■ CPU leakage sensitivity as a function case temperature

■ Estimate the benefits TCO when operating at higher temperatures.

Workload Selection

The research team picked a number of well known industry benchmarks and applications as the subject for this investigation, namely, SPECpower[†], SPECint[†] and Hadoop[†] workloads/benchmarks, Prime95[†] and Sandra[†] with the goal of generating meaningful and reproducible results. We noted server performance behaviors across specific subsystems: CPU, memory, I/O, and network during high ambient temperature operation. These applications are widely used in Internet portal data centers as well as Web server deployments, mainly search engines and in enterprise computing. The team added the Prime95 and Sandra stress tools following customer suggestions. Details for each of the workloads are outlined in Table 12.1.

Table 12.1 Workload Overview.

Workload/ Benchmark	Workload Description
SPECpower	Benchmark to measure performance and power of servers computers using graduated load levels
Hadoop/ GridMix	Open source software framework that dramatically simplifies writing distributed data intensive apps
	Provides distributed file system and map/reduce implementation that manages distributed computation
	A growing segment of data center workloads is managed with MapReduce-style frameworks (Yahoo, Google, Facebook, MySpace, Amazon, and so on.)
	Benchmark is large sorting program
	I/O-intensive workload
Prime95	Torture test imposing severe stress the CPU and RAM. If there is any problem with the CPU, RAM, or components on board, then Prime95 has a tendency to fail.
Sandra	Sandra is a memory-bandwidth intensive benchmark used to stress the memory sub-system
CPU2006/SPECint	CPU2006 is a set of benchmarks designed to test the CPU performance of a server

Platform Configuration

Two system types were used in this investigation based on the Intel® Server Board S5500WB, code named Willowbrook and the Intel® Server Board S5520UR, code named Urbanna. These servers feature the Intel® X58 Express Chipset code named Tylersburg supporting the Intel® Xeon® 5500 Series of processors, code named Nehalem. The S5500WB implements a power optimized platform specifically designed for the needs of Internet portal data centers. The S5520UR implements a dual socket performance system widely used in various business segments.

Table 12.2 outlines the hardware configuration.

Table 12.2 Hardware Configuration

Component	Description
Processor	2 x Intel® Xeon® Processor E5540
Power	80 Watt/processor
Frequency	2.53 GHz
Bus speed	6.4 GT/s Intel® QuickPath Interconnect (Intel QPI)
Chipset	Intel® X58 Express chipset
Memory Configuration	16 GB DDR3
Drive	2 SAS Drive (300GB) per node

The systems were instrumented with a total of 18 custom sensors are mounted on various subsystems as shown in Figures 12.2 and 12.3 for the SR5500WB and SR5520UR platforms: inlet, processors, chipset, BMC, voltage regulators, I/O Controller Hub (ICH), network interface controllers (NICs), hard disk drives (HDDs), power supply and fans in order to monitor the temperatures at various ambient temperature settings. In Figures 12.2 and 12.3 the label "TYB" refers to the Intel 5520 chipset code named Tylersburg. An overlay of the sensor locations is shown overlaid on a photograph of the machines as well as on a line diagram of the platform layout.

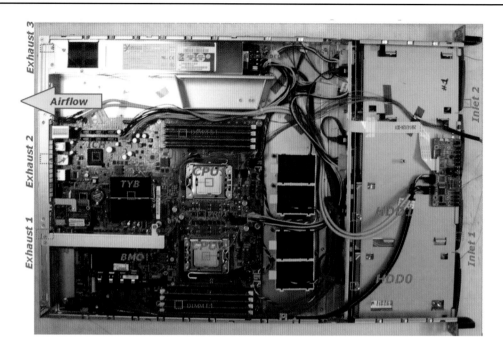

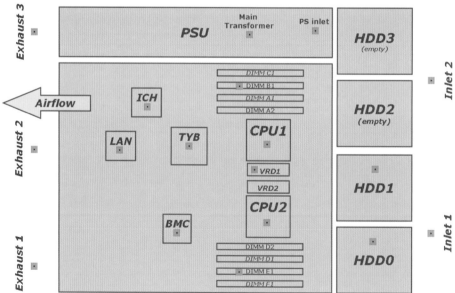

Figure 12.2 Custom Thermocouples on S5500WB Platforms.

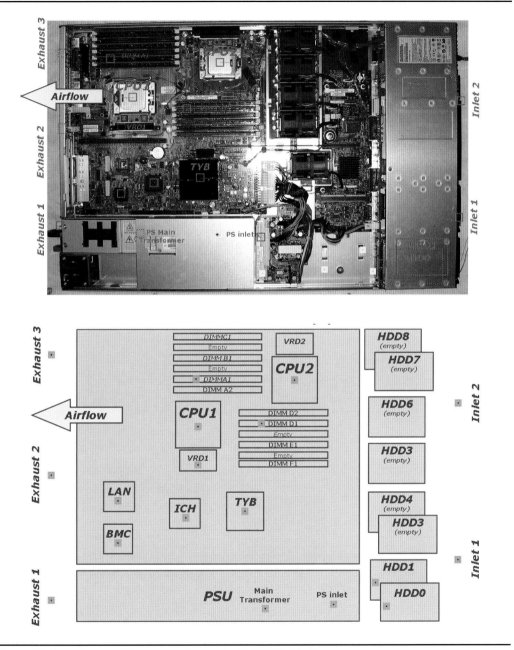

Figure 12.3 Custom Thermocouples on the S5520UR Platforms.

Assumptions Made in the Analysis

Following are some of the assumptions made in the analysis:

■ Constants: The Tcontrol value on the 80-watt CPUs is –10. The fan control adds a positive offset of +6, effectively making the T–control value a –4.

■ CPU leakage sensitivity are derived from the internal reliability models

Experimental Overview and Setup

The investigation was performed in three phases. Phase 1 includes running the servers in the lab environment using the complete solution end-to-end setup. Phase 2 includes running the pre-baseline and baseline testing performed in a thermally controlled environment chamber at 25°C, 35°C and 40°C.

A Yokogawa WT210 digital power meter and a MX100 data logger instruments were used for data acquisition as shown in Figure 12.4. A third phase of the investigation was performed at an actual data center, allowing for the observation of additional attributes such as airflow, humidity, and temperature at the entry to the data center, rack inlet and rack outlet.

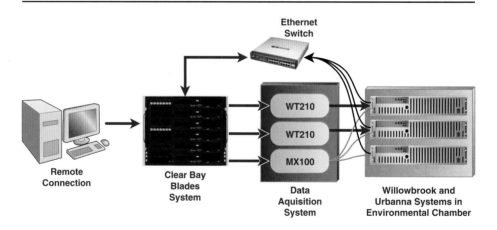

Figure 12.4 Experimental Setup

Data Acquisition Methodology

We collected data along six different tracks using hardware acquisition systems and the software stack as shown in Table 12.3.

Table 12.3 Data Collection Types

Type	Name	Description
Type 1	Server Application Utilization Data	Server application characterization
Type 2	Server Power Load	Total server power and energy drawn from the AC power plug
Type 3	Temperature Data	Thermocouple data from specified test points in the SUT
Type 4	Baseboard Management Controller (BMC) and BIOS Thermal State	Fan PWM, CPU Platform Embedded Controller Interface (PECI), Memory, voltage regulators (VR), and CPU temperature throttling, and hard disk drive temperatures
Type 5	BMC/BIOS Power State	DC current consumed by node from chassis AC-DC supply.
Type 6	System under test (SUT) Error State	Intel® QPI, Memory bus error states (CRC, and so on)

Table 12.4 describes the data management tools used during the experiments.

Table 12.4 Experiment Data Management Tools

Category	Description
Intel Data Collection Server	Clear Bay chassis with 6 blades are used. Monitoring software is installed on each blade which monitors the SUT
Performance Metrics Collection scripts	On the SUT, for SPECPower workload, 120+ Windows performance counters are monitored
	For Hadoop, Linux scripts continually monitor performance counters (*iostat, vmstat, sar* ...)
Yokogawa Power Meters	Power meters are installed in-line between the power source and the power supplies of the servers, and will provide power and energy consumption data via a USB connection back to the Intel Data Collection Server or Laptop
Custom Temperature Couples mounted on key components on SUT	MX-100 performs the data acquisition from the mounted sensors
IMPAC	Synchronize collected data into a master file for system analysis

The servers were placed in a rack, which in turn was placed inside a temperature controlled chamber. The temperature in the chamber is set 25°C (ramp-up time of 30 minutes and hold time for 30 minutes). Once the temperature in the chamber stabilizes, the workload or benchmark is started on the system under test (SUT.) Concurrently, the data acquisition software starts capturing server power data, server thermal data, performance metrics, BMC health, Intel QPI errors, and system error logs (SEL).

Data acquisition stops and log files are saved upon completion of the workload, as shown in Figure 12.5. The experiments are repeated for various workloads and temperature settings of 35 and 40°C settings. We use the IMPAC tool or manual methods to build a master file containing information from all log files against a common time base. The master makes it easier to examine events against a common timeline and facilitates performing detailed analysis. A degree of automation is essential to keep track over 150 counters generated by the data acquisition system.

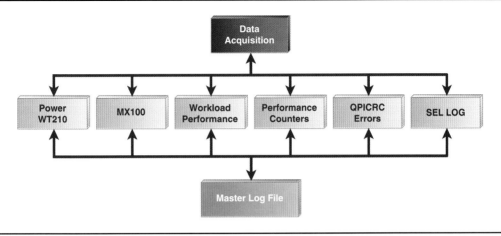

Figure 12.5   Data Acquisition Overview

Data Management

Data management is a critical step for performing data analysis. The process includes data collection, validation, transport, and storage. During the data collection process, a health check ensures the data acquisition software is collecting the data properly at specified polling intervals on the SUT and controller servers. Another check includes verifying there is no data missing before performing detailed analysis.

After the data has been collected and validated, log files are transported for analysis to the Intel Data Collection Server. Data will be retained permanently on the Intel Data Collection Server and archived on the cloud hardware shared server.

Workload Overview

Let's take a look at some of the essential characteristics for some of the workloads used during this investigation prior to discussing the detailed results.

SPECpower Workload

SPECpower_ssj2008 is a benchmark product developed by the Standard Performance Evaluation Corporation (SPEC). The benchmark provides a view of server system's power consumption running Java server applications. The following components work together to collect server power consumption and performance data by exercising the SUT with a predefined workload. The most basic SPECpower_ssj2008 test bed implementation consists of these four hardware devices:

1. Server Under Test (SUT) - SUT is the system that will be driven by the SSJ workload. The SUT's performance and power consumption characteristics will be captured and measured by the benchmark,

2. Power Analyzer - power analyzer is used to measure and record the power consumed by the SUT,

3. Temperature Sensor - temperature sensor is used to capture the temperature of the environment where the SUT is being benchmarked, and

4. Controller System - controller system is a separate system that runs the CCS and Power and Temperature Daemon (PTD) portions of the SPECpower_ssj2008 benchmark suite.

Hadoop[†] Workload

The Hadoop benchmark contains a Java program used to sort an input text data set. The program stores the sorted data set into a directory. Small, medium and large data sets are available. The Hadoop data sets are chopped up into blocks of a specified size, 64 MB by default, and the blocks distributed to data nodes. We use a small subset of the VARINFLTEXT data set blocks to run the small data size benchmark, a larger subset for the medium data size benchmark, and the full data set for the large execution mode. The goal of the benchmark is to exercise map/reduce APIs. The Hadoop cluster configuration is outlined in Table 12.5. The hardware configuration is described in Table 12.6 and the software configuration is described in Table 12.7.

Table 12.5 Hadoop Cluster Configuration

Type	Description
Cluster Architecture	Total 3 nodes
	1 Master and 2 Slaves
	Master is the workload generator
	1 of 2 Slaves is SUT
	All nodes connected to one Gigabit Ethernet switch
	GridMix Javasort Program
Workload	Data scaling :
	In this experiments scale field is 1, 6, 11, 16, 21, 26 that generates datasets with 512 MB, 3 GB, 5.5 GB, 8 GB, 10 GB, 13 GB
	Workload scaling: 1 instance of workload run
	Default block size is 64 MB
Performance	Time elapsed to finish the workload is used as indicator for performance

In a 3-node S5500WB and S5520UR cluster, one node runs *NameNode* and *JobTracker*, and each of the other two nodes runs the *DataNode* and *Task-Tracker*. All those nodes are connected through a gigabit Ethernet switch.

Table 12.6 Hardware Configuration for Hadoop

Component	Description
Processor	2 x Intel® Xeon® Processor E5540
Frequency	2.53 GHz
Bus speed	6.4 GT/s QPI
Chipset	Intel Chipset
Memory Configuration	16 GB
Drive	2 SAS Drive (300GB) per node
Processor	2 x Intel Xeon Processor E5540

Table 12.7 Software Configuration for Hadoop

Component	Description
Drive	2 SAS Drive (300GB) per node
OS	Windows 2003 SP2, Linux RH3 64-bit
BIOS	38
	Hardware prefetcher and adjacent cache-line prefetch enabled
	Both Enhanced Intel SpeedStep Technology and Turbo mode need enabled
	SMT (Simultaneous Multithreading) enabled
Firmware /FRUSDR	1.11
Hadoop	0.19.2

Prime95 Torture Test

Prime95 is a program for searching very large prime numbers. It has also gained a reputation for flushing out errors in marginally stable computers. A run will likely fail if the CPU, memory, or the logic connecting CPU and memory are in a less than perfect state. This process is useful for eliciting unspecified or intermittent faults. A system capable of running Prime95 for 24 hours without errors is likely to be healthy and stable. Prime95 imposes an intense workload on the CPU and carries finicky self-checking logic to halt the run even if the error is minor. Most practical applications are gentler on the CPU and will continue to limp along except for unrecoverable errors.

Experimental Results

In each of the following sections we look at summary data for each one of the benchmarks, applications, or workloads used during this investigation, namely SPECpower, SPECint, Hadoop, Sandra, and Prime95.

SPECpower Experimental Results

Experiments were conducted with Turbo mode ON and OFF setting in the BIOS. Tables 12.8 and 12.9 summarize the results for operation at 25°C, 35°C, and 40°C with Turbo ON and OFF and the benchmark set at 100 percent and 70 percent throttle. Tables 12.10 and 12.11 outline the results of the SPECpower complete results at 25°C, 35°C, and 40°C respectively. From the results it is clear that, there is no impact to the performance when the servers are operated at high ambient temperatures. For the S5500WB machines, the performance to power ratio at 100 percent load and 40°C is 1,373 and at 25°C is 1,357. Operating servers with turbo ON shows an expected increase in power consumption. With the SPECpower benchmark, variations of 2 percent up or down are within noise level.

Table 12.8 Baseline SPECpower, Full Workload

	S5500WB		S5520UR	
Temperature	ssj_ops	Power (Watts)	ssj_ops	Power (Watts)
25	411,228	303	393,796	296
35	411,438	300	389,643	307
40	416,152	303	367,221	304

Table 12.9 Baseline SPECpower, 70 Percent Throttle

	S5500WB		S5520UR	
Temperature	ssj_ops	Power (Watts)	ssj_ops	Power (Watts)
25	289,201	254	277,032	260
35	289,051	253	272,810	269
40	292,521	259	257,015	268

Table 12.10 Baseline SPECint S5500WB Component T-rise Over Ambient, C

Temp °C	CPU1 DIMM	CPU2 DIMM	CPU1 (80W)	CPU2 (80W)	CPU1 VRD	IOH	ICH
25	41.71	41.18	55.67	56.13	47.19	69.18	58.19
35	43.08	42.67	50.25	50.95	45.39	67.15	58.50
40	52.58	52.12	59.04	59.93	54.78	70.20	65.37

Temp °C	BMC	LAN IC	HDD0	HDD1	PS T1	PS Inlet
25	60.97	56.45	38.61	41.01	51.63	28.12
35	61.16	56.60	41.89	44.50	53.39	32.06
40	67.74	63.20	49.70	51.62	64.24	42.58

Temp °C	Inlet 1 (L)	Inlet 2 (R)	Exhaust 1 (L)	Exhaust 2 (M)	Exhaust 3 (R)	SAS Heat sink
25	25.36	25.27	44.20	41.63	39.20	82.97
35	29.58	29.54	46.37	42.43	42.30	81.11
40	40.13	40.15	57.04	51.14	52.40	82.97

Table 12.11 Baseline SPECint S5520UR Component T-rise Over Ambient, °C

Temp °C	CPU1 DIMM	CPU2 DIMM	CPU1 (80W)	CPU2 (80W)	CPU1 VRD	IOH	ICH
25	41.30	36.87	43.90	42.76	44.85	43.51	52.14
35	48.15	44.81	50.08	49.00	52.29	50.87	59.40
40	53.85	50.63	56.20	55.58	57.99	55.85	64.39

Temp °C	BMC	LAN IC	HDD0	HDD1	PS T1	PS Inlet
25	58.39	50.76	33.72	34.25	51.99	29.27
35	65.25	57.90	42.73	43.21	61.45	38.84
40	70.40	62.98	47.61	48.09	66.52	43.72

Temp °C	Inlet 1 (L)	Inlet 2 (R)	Exhaust 1 (L)	Exhaust 2 (M)	Exhaust 3 (R)	SAS Heat sink
25	25.58	25.42	38.77	31.38	37.16	37.64
35	35.33	35.23	48.24	39.94	44.82	45.88
40	40.26	40.16	53.38	45.04	50.71	50.80

Tables 12.12 and 12.13 outline the fan and CPU power consumption, T_{case} and leakage. For the S5500WB platform at 25°C, the fans operate at 28 percent PWM and 32 percent at 40°C. However, for the S5520UR platform the fans operate at 35 percent and 40 percent at 25°C and 40°C, respectively. Higher fan rotation assists in keeping the CPUs at lower temperatures.

Table 12.12 Baseline SPECpower Power Increase Drivers, S5500WB 100 percent

Sys Am-bient (°C)	AC power (W)	PWM	Fan Power (W)	PS Fan Power, (W)	Total Fan Power, (W)	Fan Power Incr (W)	CPU 1 Tcase, °C	CPU 2 Tcase, °C	CPU Lkg Incr (W)	Fan+ lkg pwr incr(W)	Actual pwr incr (W)
25	303	28	6.5	3.2	9.2	-	82.4	81.7	0	0	0.0
35	300	32	11.5	4.2	15.7	5.0	72.7	74.4	-3.3	1.72	-3.0
40	303	32	11.5	4.8	16.3	5.0	71.3	64.4	-5.4	-0.4	0.0

Table 12.13 Baseline SPECpower Power Increase Drivers, S5520UR 100 percent

Sys Am-bient (°C)	AC power (W)	PWM	Fan Power (W)	PS Fan Power, (W)	Total Fan Power, (W)	Fan Power Incr (W)	CPU 1 Tcase, °C	CPU 2 Tcase, °C	CPU Lkg Incr (W)	Fan+ lkg pwr incr(W)	Actual pwr incr (W)
25	296	35	15.8	3.8	19.6	0	43.9	42.8	0	0	0.0
35	307	40	23.8	3.95	27.8	8	50.1	49.0	2.4	10.4	11
40	304	40	23.8	4.03	27.8	8.2	56.2	55.6	4.9	13.2	8

For the S5500WB platform, there was no increase in the total power increase from 25°C to 40°C temperature setting. However, for S5520UR servers there was a total increase of 8 watts when the system was operated at 40°C and 11 Watts at 35°C.

For the S5520UR platform, when servers are operated at 35°C and 40°C, there is an increase in the system power utilization. The following factors explain the difference:

■ System fans are operating at higher PWM

■ Power supply fans are consuming more power

■ Leakage current due to fans and CPUs.

It is well known that the CPU leakage power is a function of temperature. For the CPUs used in the experiment leakage power sensitivity data was obtained from an Intel physical model predicting a leakage power increase of 0.19 watts/°C (case temperature). The leakage increase is accounted for both CPUs in the system. From the results it is clear that the system power increase closely matches with the sum of the systems fans, power supply fans, and CPU leakage.

Table 12.14 shows thermal margin in Celsius for the lowest margin components. CPU margins are lower than in Hadoop because the SPECpower workload imposes a larger workload on the CPU. Note that the hard disk drive has a low margin against its sustained temperature thermal specification; this low margin could have an impact in failure rates.

Table 12.14 Baseline SPECint Thermal Margin1 Select Components, °C

Component	Ambient, WB			Ambient, UR		
	25	35	40	25	35	40
CPU PECI[2]	2.0	8.0	9.0	30.0	24.0	20.0
CPU T_{case} [2]	-9.5	-2.2	-0.4	22.3	16.4	11.4
DIMM T_{case}	45.0	35.2	36.9	47.6	40.8	36.6
IOH PECI[3]	11.0	16.0	15.0	46.0	38.0	33.0
IOH T_{case} [3]	4.3	18.8	10.3	40.9	23.7	28.9
BMC T_{case}	15.4	13.6	13.1	24.9	18.3	13.5
HDD T_{case}, excursion	18.9	10.6	7.8	15.6	16.6	11.7
HDD T_{case}, sustained[4]	8.9	0.6	-2.2	5.6	6.6	1.7
SAS IC[5]	11.2	15.0	16.8	30.0	24.0	20.0

Notes:

1. Monitored components not listed in this chart had > 15° C thermal margin, and are therefore not reported.

2. Margin to both CPU PECI and CPU T_{case} (thermal profile) are reported for clarity; negative margin to CPU T_{case} is acceptable provided CPU PECI < $T_{control}$. Refer to the CPU's governing electrical, mechanical, and thermal specifications (EMTS) for further details, or to the Thermal and Mechanical Design Guide (TMDG) for applicable $T_{control}$ values.

3. Margin to both IOH PECI and IOH T_{case} (thermal profile) are reported for clarity; negative margin to IOH T_{case} is acceptable provided IOH PECI < 0. Refer to the IOH's governing EMTS for further details, or to the IOH TMDG. Also, note that the IOH is preheated by CPU/DIMMs in the S5500WB system, but not in S5520UR.

4. The hard disk drives used for this testing have a sustained maximum temperature of 50° C, with allowable excursions up to 60° C.

5. The SAS interface controller is on a ROMB optional add-in card. A PCIe-RAID card can be used instead.

| ▨▨▨ ### SPECint Experimental Results

Table 12.15 illustrates the SPECint benchmark results on S5500WB and S5520UR servers at 25°C, 35°C, and 40°C temperature settings. When the ambient temperature was increased from 25°C to 40°C, there was no impact to the *SPECint_rate_base* and *SPECint_rate_peak* scores. However, there was an increase of 16 watts on S5520UR and a 3-watt increase observed on S5500WB platform. This is due to the fact that processors were operating at higher temperatures and fan was spinning at higher speeds which consumed additional power.

Table 12.15 Baseline SPECint Results for S5500WB and S5520UR Servers

Platform	Temp (°C)	SPECint rate base	SPECint rate peak	PWM	Average Power (watts)
S5500WB	25	185	197	28	293
	35	185	197	31	293
	40	185	197	34	296
S5520UR	25	185	197	35	302
	35	185	196	40	314
	40	185	197	40	318

Table 12.16 depicts the SPECint power increase analysis. The dynamics involved are very similar to the ones observed for SPECpower.

Table 12.16 Baseline SPECint Power Increase Analysis

Platform	Temp (°C)	AC power (W)	PWM	Fan Power (W)	PS Fan Power, (W)	Total Fan Power (W)	Fan Power Increase (W)
	25	293	28	6.48	4.1	10.48	0.0
S5500WB	35	293	31	8.69	4.2	12.89	2.41
	40	296	34	13.4	5.7	19.10	8.62
	25	302	35	15.8	4.2	20.00	0.0
S5520UR	35	314	40	23.8	4.4	28.20	8.2
	40	318	40	23.8	4.6	28.40	8.4

Platform	Temp (°C)	CPU 1 T_{case} (°C)	CPU 2 T_{case} (°C)	CPU Leakage Increase (W)	Fan + Leakage pwr incr (W)	Actual power increase, (W)
	25	76.43	76.11	0.0	0.0	0.0
S5500WB	35	70.18	71.95	-1.97	0.44	0.0
	40	68.75	70.84	-2.46	-6.16	3.0
	25	53.76	51.29	0.0	0.0	0.0
S5520UR	35	58.91	56.46	1.96	10.16	12.0
	40	64.07	61.59	3.92	12.32	16.0

Tables 12.17 and 12.18 show T_{rise} is lower at higher temperature indicating higher fan speeds.

Table 12.17 Baseline SPECint S5500WB Component T-rise Over Ambient, C

Temp (°C)	CPU1 DIMM	CPU2 DIMM	CPU1 (80W)	CPU2 (80W)	CPU1 VRD	IOH	ICH
25	47.71	46.36	71.91	71.93	59.56	74.69	72.36
35	49.85	49.05	57.07	58.84	52.90	70.19	71.70
40	55.95	54.45	68.75	70.84	62.95	73.99	76.51

Temp (°C)	BMC	LAN IC	HDD0	HDD1	PS T1	PS Inlet
25	66.90	63.25	39.95	42.47	60.11	31.30
35	66.53	62.53	46.75	49.01	61.59	38.94
40	71.22	66.76	49.11	51.44	72.37	43.10

Temp (°C)	Inlet 1 (L)	Inlet 2 (R)	Exhaust 1 (L)	Exhaust 2 (M)	Exhaust 3 (R)	SAS Heatsink
25	27.77	27.75	49.10	46.63	42.97	88.54
35	36.28	36.28	53.75	47.90	48.56	84.09
40	40.05	40.09	62.88	54.94	55.08	87.17

Table 12.18 Baseline SPECint S5520UR Component T-rise Over Ambient, C

Temp (°C)	CPU1 DIMM	CPU2 DIMM	CPU1 (80W)	CPU2 (80W)	CPU1 VRD	IOH	ICH
25	41.09	36.77	44.05	42.33	47.01	42.17	55.98
35	46.71	43.65	48.60	47.02	51.76	50.57	64.01
40	59.95	51.29	64.07	61.59	65.17	56.28	72.25

Temp (°C)	BMC	LAN IC	HDD0	HDD1	PS T1	PS Inlet
25	55.31	49.95	34.54	34.69	59.50	32.98
35	63.27	57.46	42.89	43.01	64.44	40.61
40	71.51	64.98	47.97	47.77	68.22	44.05

Temp (°C)	Inlet 1 (L)	Inlet 2 (R)	Exhaust 1 (L)	Exhaust 2 (M)	Exhaust 3 (R)	SAS Heatsink
25	27.85	27.79	43.18	33.58	36.21	37.58
35	36.41	36.33	50.04	41.22	43.06	45.92
40	40.20	40.08	54.98	46.09	54.65	50.82

Table 12.19 shows the thermal margin (°C) for the lowest margin components. CPU margins are lower than Hadoop because the SPECpower workload is stressing the CPU. Note that hard disk drives carry a generally low thermal margin.

Table 12.19 Baseline SPECint Thermal Margin1 Select Components, °C

Component	Ambient, S5500WB			Ambient, S5520UR		
	25	35	40	25	35	40
CPU PECI[2]	1.0	3.0	5.0	24.0	18.0	13.0
CPU T_{case}[2]	-9.4	-5.3	-2.3	17.0	11.5	6.1
DIMM T_{case}	41.9	36.2	23.3	40.9	34.6	29.5
IOH PECI[3]	11.0	13.0	15.0	44.0	38.0	33.0
IOH T_{case}[3]	4.1	6.5	8.6	40.0	33.3	28.2
BMC T_{case}	14.3	12.3	11.3	23.3	16.5	11.7
HDD T_{case}, excursion	16.4	11.5	7.1	24.1	16.9	8.9
HDD T_{case}, sustained[4]	6.4	1.5	-2.9	14.1	6.9	-1.1
SAS IC[5]	11.6	13.1	20.3			

Notes:

1. Monitored components not listed in this chart had > 15° C thermal margin, and are therefore not reported.

2. Margin to both CPU PECI and CPU T_{case} (thermal profile) are reported for clarity; negative margin to CPU T_{case} is acceptable provided CPU PECI < $T_{control}$. Refer to the CPU's governing EMTS for further details, or to the TMDG for applicable $T_{control}$ values.

3. Margin to both IOH PECI and IOH T_{case} (thermal profile) are reported for clarity; negative margin to IOH T_{case} is acceptable provided IOH PECI < 0. Refer to the IOH's governing EMTS for further details, or to the IOH TMDG. Also, note that the IOH is preheated by CPU/DIMMs in the S5500WB system, but not in S5520UR.

4. Hard disk drives used for this testing have a sustained maximum temperature of 50° C, with allowable excursions up to 60° C.

5. The SAS interface controller is on a ROMB optional add-in card. A PCIe-RAID card can be used instead.

Hadoop Experimental Results

The Hadoop workload results on the servers are outlined in Table 12.20. From the results it is clear that, there is an increasing power trend at higher temperatures. The server power (S5500WB) increases by 3.3 percent at 35°C and 5.2 percent at 40°C. Most of the power increase is the net result of increase fan power and CPU leakage. The workload shows no performance degradation at higher temperatures. Performance does not degrade at 35°C and it degrades 0.9 percent at 40°C that is within run-to-run variation. The S5520UR server power increases by 5.5 percent at 35°C and 6.5 percent at 40°C. The performance does not degrade at 35°C (it is actually better than at 25°C) and performance degrades 0.8 percent at 40°C, both within run-to-run variation.

Table 12.20 Baseline Hadoop Performance

Platform	Chamber Set Point (°C)	Workload Completion Time (s)	Performance Loss
S5500WB	25	217	0.0%
	35	217	0.0%
	40	219	0.9%
S5520UR	25	246	0.0%
	35	245	-0.4%
	40	248	0.8%

Performance versus Ambient Temperature

There was no impact to server performance with increasing ambient temperature. The CPU utilization was low as the workload is predominantly disk I/O intensive. Disk utilization increases with an increase in data set size. The performance degradation seen is within the run-to-run variation. The Hadoop job is a distributed application and its execution can be somewhat nondeterministic. Hadoop offers the service to assign all workers into the different physical nodes dynamically among clusters. After the job has been submitted, it will be initialized into many tasks, and all of these tasks will be distributed to all the Hadoop task tracker nodes, but there is no fixed sequence and rule for the tasks distribution. For example, if there are 50 tasks totally, the first task can occur on Node A during Test I, but next time this task might be found on Node B in Test II.

Furthermore, there are some caches in the memory for HDFS. If the related test is run for the second time without restarting the Hadoop, all these metadata will be stored in the memory. This rerun test benefits from the previous test. Because of this, we recommend running the test job once, restarting Hadoop, and running another round of tests again. This can help to reduce the run-to-run variation.

It was also observed that performance was better on the S5500WB as compared to the S5520UR by 13 percent. This is attributed to S5500WB hard disk drives running at 138 Mb/s average while the S5520UR hard disk drives running at 103 Mb/s average.

Power versus Ambient temperature

Total wall power for the server was measured during the workload. Table 12.21 shows average power consumption during the Hadoop workload at different chamber temperature settings. It was observed that the server power for S5500WB increases by 3.3 percent when the chamber temperature is increased from 25°C to 35°C and by 5.2 percent when the chamber temperature is increased from 25°C to 40°C. It is also observed that the server power for the S5520UR increases by 5.5 percent when the chamber temperature is increased from 25°C to 35°C and by 6.5 percent when the chamber temperature is increased from 25°C to 40°C.

Table 12.21 Baseline Hadoop Power versus Ambient

Platform	Chamber Set Point (°C)	Wall Power (W)	Percent Power Increase
S5500WB	25	177.9	0.0%
	35	183.8	3.3%
	40	187.1	5.2%
S5520UR	25	199	0.0%
	35	210	5.5%
	40	212	6.5%

Drivers Contributing Power Increase

Further analysis was performed to determine the factors contributing to the server power increase. System fans and power supply fan operate at higher speed at higher ambient settings. This was evident from the PWM settings recorded for system fans and RPM data collected for power supply fan. System fan power was characterized as a function of PWM and power supply fan power was characterized as a function of RPM as summarized in Figure 12.6. In addition, CPU T_{case} values showed an increase when system ambient is increased from 25°C to 35°C or 40°C.

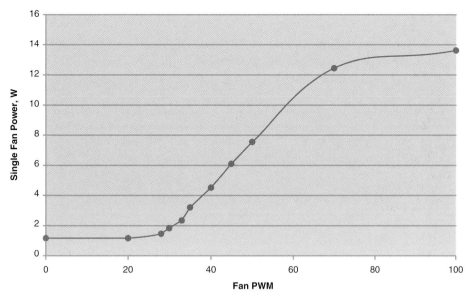

Notes:

1. Monitored components not listed in this chart had > 15° C thermal margin, and are therefore not reported.

2. Prime95 is an industry standard benchmark that stresses both CPU and memory. "Torture test" mode was used for the proof of concept.

3. A value of "worst-case" indicates that the highest measured temperature during testing was used to compute margin. A value of "average" indicates that average temperature during the duration of testing was used to compute margin. Margin against both worst-case and average component temperature was reported only for workloads that resulted in dynamic stress / temperature profiles over the duration of testing.

4. Margin to both CPU PECI and CPU T_{case} (thermal profile) are reported for clarity; negative margin to CPU T_{case} is acceptable provided CPU PECI < $T_{control}$. Refer to the CPU's governing EMTS for further details, or to the TMDG for applicable $T_{control}$ values.

5. Internal PSU components were measured in addition to PSU inlet temperature; significant component thermal margin was observed for all ambient temperatures and workloads with the tested HW configuration. Therefore, low (or negative) thermal margins to PSU inlet temperature are considered acceptable.

6. Hard disk drives used for this testing have a sustained maximum temperature of 50° C, with allowable excursions up to 60° C.

7. ROMB is an optional add-in card. A PCI-mounted RAID card can be used instead.

8. IOH is preheated by CPU/DIMMs in systems with Chenbro chassis, but not with SR1550 chassis code named Petrof Bay. The SR1550 chassis supports a higher Wattage CPU/DIMM envelope than the Chenbro system. Neither system is CPU-aware; both cool to an envelope.

Figure 12.6   Fan PWM versus Power Variation.

The considerations for leakage analysis are similar to those in the SPECint analysis. Table 12.22 and Table 12.23 show PWM settings at various ambient settings for the system fans. The Tables also list power supply fan RPM. The associated total fan power corresponding to the PWM values and RPM values is listed. In totality, the sum of leakage power increase and fan power increase are the two contributing factor for the power increase seen at the higher temperature settings.

Table 12.22 Baseline Hadoop Power Increase Drivers, S5500WB

Sys Am- bient (°C)	AC power (W)	PWM	Fan Power (W)	PS Fan Power, (W)	Total Fan Power, (W)	Fan Power Incr (W)	CPU 1 Tcase, °C	CPU 2 Tcase, °C	CPU Lkg Incr (W)	Fan+ lkg pwr incr(W)	Actual pwr incr (W)
25	177.9	28	6.48	3.0	9.5	0.0	49.7	49.6	0.0	0.0	0.0
35	183.8	30	8.69	4.2	12.8	3.4	55.3	54.6	2.0	5.4	5.9
40	187.1	33	13.42	5.5	18.9	9.4	55.9	56.3	2.4	11.9	9.2

Table 12.23 Baseline Hadoop Power Increase Drivers, S5520UR

Sys Am- bient (°C)	AC power (W)	PWM	Fan Power (W)	PS Fan Power, (W)	Total Fan Power, (W)	Fan Power Incr (W)	CPU 1 Tcase, °C	CPU 2 Tcase, °C	CPU Lkg Incr (W)	Fan+ lkg pwr incr(W)	Actual pwr incr (W)
25	199	35	15.8	3.85	19.7	0.0	38.9	36.0	0.0	0.0	0.0
35	210	40	23.8	3.90	27.7	8.1	46.8	44.9	3.2	11.3	11.0
40	212	40	23.8	3.92	27.7	8.1	52.2	49.4	5.1	13.2	13.0

Table 12.24 lists the component temperatures at various ambient temperatures. All the component temperatures are well within the specifications and no issues were observed.

Table 12.24 Baseline SPECint S5500WB Component T-rise Over Ambient, C

Temp (°C)	CPU1 DIMM	CPU2 DIMM	CPU1 (80W)	CPU2 (80W)	CPU1 VRD	IOH	ICH
25	40.3	39.8	49.7	49.6	43.0	66.6	64.4
35	48.4	47.8	55.3	54.6	49.9	70.9	71.2
40	51.6	51.2	55.9	56.3	52.0	70.6	72.6

Temp (°C)	BMC	LAN IC	HDD0	HDD1	PS T1	PS Inlet
25	60.3	56.0	39.7	42.5	49.7	28.2
35	66.5	62.5	47.8	50.5	57.0	37.8
40	68.1	63.7	51.1	53.5	60.6	42.5

Temp (°C)	Inlet 1 (L)	Inlet 2 (R)	Exhaust 1 (L)	Exhaust 2 (M)	Exhaust 3 (R)	SAS Heat sink
25	25.4	25.4	39.2	38.7	38.2	81.8
35	35.2	35.2	49.4	46.5	46.9	85.0
40	40.2	40.2	54.6	49.7	51.0	83.4

Table 12.25 shows T-rise is lower at higher temperature indicating higher fan speeds.

Table 12.25 Baseline Hadoop S5500WB Component Trise over Ambient, C

Temp (°C)	CPU1 DIMM	CPU2 DIMM	CPU1 (80W)	CPU2 (80W)	CPU1 VRD	IOH	ICH
25	15.3	14.8	24.7	24.6	18.0	41.6	39.4
35	13.4	12.8	20.3	19.6	14.9	35.9	36.2
40	11.6	11.2	15.9	16.3	12.0	30.6	32.6

Temp (°C)	BMC	LAN IC	HDD0	HDD1	PS T1	PS Inlet
25	35.3	31.0	14.7	17.5	24.7	3.2
35	31.5	27.5	12.8	15.5	22.0	2.8
40	28.1	23.7	11.1	13.5	20.6	2.5

Temp (°C)	Inlet 1 (L)	Inlet 2 (R)	Exhaust 1 (L)	Exhaust 2 (M)	Exhaust 3 (R)	SAS Heat sink
25	0.4	0.4	14.2	13.7	13.2	56.8
35	0.2	0.2	14.4	11.5	11.9	50.0
40	0.2	0.2	14.6	9.7	11.0	43.4

Table 12.26 shows thermal margin in Celsius for the lowest margin components within the high ambient temperature proof of concept S5500WB systems using a chassis manufactured by Chenbro Micom Co. Ltd. CPU margins are higher for S5500WB/Hadoop because the Hadoop workload is not stressing the CPU. The Hadoop workload is a very disk I/O intensive workload and it was observed that the hard disk drive has low margin against its sustained temperature (applies to MTBF).

Table 12.26 Baseline Hadoop Thermal Margins1 Select Components, C

	Ambient, WB (°C)			Ambient, UR (°C)		
Component	33	27	27	43	37	32
CPU PECI[2]	26	21	20	35	26	22
CPU T_{case}[2]	45	37	34	37	38	33
DIMM T_{case}	25	21	21	47	39	34
IOH PECI[3]	18	14	14	42	34	29
IOH T_{case}[3]	25	19	17	27	20	15
BMC T_{case}	19	11	8	24	25	10
HDD T_{case}, excursion	9	1	(-2)	14	5	0
HDD T_{case}, sustained[4]	19	15	17			
SAS IC[5]	33	27	27	43	37	32

Notes:

1. Monitored components not listed in this chart had more than 15° C thermal margin, and are therefore not reported.

2. Margin to both CPU PECI and CPU T_{case} (thermal profile) are reported for clarity; negative margin to CPU T_{case} is acceptable provided CPU PECI < $T_{control}$. Refer to the CPU's governing EMTS for further details, or to the TMDG for applicable $T_{control}$ values.

3. Margin to both IOH PECI and IOH T_{case} (thermal profile) are reported for clarity; negative margin to IOH T_{case} is acceptable provided IOH PECI < 0. Refer to the IOH's governing EMTS for further details, or to the IOH TMDG. Also, note that the IOH is preheated by CPU/DIMMs in the S5500WB system, but not in S5520UR system.

4. Hard disk drives used for this testing have a sustained maximum temperature of 50° C, with allowable excursions up to 60° C.

5. The SAS IC is on a ROMB optional add-in card. A PCIe-RAID card can be used instead.

Experimental Sandra Results

Sandra ran for 4 hours without error on both systems. The baseline results are shown in Table 12.27.

Table 12.27 Baseline Sandra Results

Platform	Temp (°C)	Test Results
S5500WB	25	Pass
	35	Pass
	40	Pass
S5520UR	25	Pass
	35	Pass
	40	Pass

Power versus Ambient temperature

Total wall power for the server was measured during the workload. Due to the nature of workload, power changes based on which component of the server is being stressed at that time. Table 12.28 shows power is varying significantly during the test, so no comparison is made for power values at various ambient conditions.

Table 12.28 Baseline Sandra Power Variation

Temp (°C)	Method	S5500WB Power, W	W5500UR Power, W
25	Average	172.9	195
	Minimum	152.9	179
	Maximum	300.0	311
35	Average	170.7	205
	Minimum	152.7	188
	Maximum	298.9	323
40	Average	183.6	210
	Minimum	157.2	192
	Maximum	303.4	342

Table 12.29 shows average power consumption during Sandra workload at different chamber temperature settings. The server power for the S5500WB platform increases by 6.2 percent when the chamber temperature is increased from 25°C to 40°C. Furthermore, the server power for the S5520UR platform increases by 5.1 percent when the chamber temperature is increased from 25°C to 35°C and by 7.7 percent when the chamber temperature is increased from 25°C to 40°C.

Table 12.29 Baseline Sandra Average Power Consumption

Platform	Chamber, (°C)	Average power, W	Power Increase, percent
	25	172.9	0.0
S5500WB	35	170.7	-1.3
	40	183.6	6.2
	25	195	0.0
S5520UR	35	205	5.1
	40	210	7.7

Thermal Margin

Table 12.30 lists the component temperatures at various ambient temperatures. Most of the component temperatures are well within the specifications and no issues were observed. The worst-case temperature is reported here, the highest measured temperature during testing.

Table 12.30 Baseline Sandra S5520UR Component Temperatures, C

Temp (°C)	CPU1 DIMM	CPU2 DIMM	CPU1 (80W)	CPU2 (80W)	CPU1 VRD	IOH	ICH
25	50.4	44.1	56.7	54.1	55.5	43.9	52.4
35	57.3	52	62.7	59.7	63.9	51.4	60.2
40	62.4	56.9	68	64.7	69.1	56.3	65

Temp (°C)	BMC	LAN IC	HDD0	HDD1	PS T1	PS Inlet
25	58.6	51.6	34.6	37.2	53.9	30.4
35	66.6	59.5	45.7	46.1	63.9	39.7
40	71.1	64.2	50.9	51.1	68.1	44.8

Temp (°C)	Inlet 1 (L)	Inlet 2 (R)	Exhaust 1 (L)	Exhaust 2 (M)	Exhaust 3 (R)	SAS Heatsink
25	25.9	25.7	40.7	32.9	43.6	37.9
35	36	35.9	51	41.7	51	46.3
40	41	41	55.3	46.5	56	51.3

Table 12.31 shows T-rise is lower at higher temperature indicating higher fan speeds.

Table 12.31 Baseline Sandra S5500WB Component T_{rise} over Ambient, C

Temp (°C)	CPU1 DIMM	CPU2 DIMM	CPU1 (80W)	CPU2 (80W)	CPU1 VRD	IOH	ICH
25	48	52.5	82.8	82.1	65.9	75.7	63.7
35	55.8	58.3	77.8	80	67.8	77	68.5
40	58.7	60.9	74.8	77.1	68.3	75.2	69.7

Temp (°C)	BMC	LAN IC	HDD0	HDD1	PS T1	PS Inlet
25	66.2	62.2	40	42.9	60.9	28.9
35	71.9	66.2	47.6	50	70.1	38.4
40	71.9	67.2	50.9	53.3	73.3	43.3

Temp (°C)	Inlet 1 (L)	Inlet 2 (R)	Exhaust 1 (L)	Exhaust 2 (M)	Exhaust 3 (R)	SAS Heatsink
25	25.7	25.7	59.8	48.8	41.1	89.1
35	35.9	35.9	64.9	54.4	50.6	90.8
40	40.9	40.9	65.3	56.4	54.4	88.6

Table 12.32 shows the thermal margin in Celsius for the lowest margin components within the high ambient temperature proof of concept systems, S5500WB with Chenbro chassis and S5520UR systems with SR1550 chassis. CPU and Memory margins are lower for SR5500WB because the Prime95 is stressing the CPU and memory subsystem.

Table 12.32 Baseline Sandra Thermal Margins1 Select Components, C

Component	Ambient, WB (°C)			Ambient, UR (°C)		
	1	3	6	26	20	14
CPU PECI[2]	-10	-4	-1	19	13	8
CPU T$_{case}$ [2]	33	27	24	35	28	23
DIMM T$_{case}$	25	22	22	46	38	34
IOH PECI[3]	7	8	10	41	34	29
IOH T$_{case}$ [3]	19	13	13	26	18	14
BMC T$_{case}$	17	10	7	23	14	9
HDD T$_{case}$, excursion	7	0	-3	13	4	-1
HDD T$_{case}$, sustained[4]	16	14	16			
SAS IC[5]	1	3	6	26	20	14

Notes:

1. Monitored components not listed in this chart had > 15° C thermal margin, and are therefore not reported.

2. Margin to both CPU PECI and CPU T$_{case}$ (thermal profile) are reported for clarity; negative margin to CPU Tcase is acceptable provided CPU PECI < Tcontrol. Refer to the CPU's governing EMTS for further details, or to the TMDG for applicable T$_{control}$ values.

3. Margin to both IOH PECI and IOH T$_{case}$ (thermal profile) are reported for clarity; negative margin to IOH Tcase is acceptable provided IOH PECI < 0. Refer to the IOH's governing EMTS for further details, or to the IOH TMDG. Also, note that the IOH is preheated by CPU/DIMMs in the S5500WB system, but not in S5520UR system.

4. Hard disk drives used for this testing have a sustained maximum temperature of 50° C, with allowable excursions up to 60° C.

5. The SAS IC is on a ROMB optional add-in card. A PCIe-RAID card can be used instead.

Prime95 Experimental Results

Prime95 testing places stress on the CPU and memory subsystems of the systems under test. The torture test profile of Prime95 is nonstatic, meaning the power consumption varies rapidly—it is not at all a uniform consumer of power. Because of this, it is only meaningful to analyze and discuss the average power consumption over the duration of the test.

Performance versus Ambient Temperature

The test passed in all cases on both the SR5500WB and SR5500UR systems. In this case, passing means that there were no hangs, resets, memory, or Intel QPI errors over the duration of the test. Based on this, it is safe to say that the CPU and parts involved with the CPU-RAM interface are stable and working well for both systems at all ambient temperatures.

Table 12.33 shows average power consumption during Prime95 workload at different chamber temperature settings. The server power for the SR5500WB increases by 1.2 percent when the chamber temperature is increased from 25°C to 35°C and by 1.8 percent when the chamber temperature is increased from 25°C to 40°C. It is also observed that the server power for the S5520UR systems increases by 3.1 percent when the chamber temperature is increased from 25°C to 35°C and by 3.7 percent when the chamber temperature is increased from 25°C to 40°C.

Table 12.33 Baseline Prime95 Results, PWM, and Average Power

Platform	Temp (°C)	Test Results	PWM Avg	Max power (W)	Min power (W)	Avg power (W)	Power Incr (%)
S5500WB	25	Pass	30	333.2	299.0	319	
	35	Pass	33	335.0	323.0	323	1.2%
	40	Pass	35	340.0	325.0	325	1.8%
S5520UR	25	Pass	36	349.2	318.2	336	
	35	Pass	40	362.5	190.3	347	3.1%
	40	Pass	40	362.9	332.1	349	3.7%

The average power consumption changed by 5 watts and 13 watts from 25°C to 40°C for S5500WB and S5520UR systems, respectively. Further, the difference between the S5500WB and the S5520UR power consumption is 17 watts at 25°C and 24 watts at 35°C and 40°C.

Drivers Contributing to Power Increase

Tables 12.34 and 12.35 present the analysis for how this increase can be accounted for between fan and CPU leakage power changes for the S5500WB and S5520UR systems.

Table 12.34 Baseline Prime95 Average Power Increase Analysis, S5500WB

Sys Am-bient (°C)	AC power (W)	PWM	Fan Power (W)	PS Fan Power, (W)	Fan Power Incr (W)	CPU 1 Tcase, °C	CPU 2 Tcase, °C	CPU Lkg Incr (W)	Fan+ lkg pwr incr(W)	Actual pwr incr (W)
25	319.5	30	8.69	4.2	0.0	79*	80*	0.0	0.0	0.0
35	323.2	33	13.42	5.4	5.9	77*	78*	-0.8	5.2	3.7
40	325.4	35	15.65	5.8	8.6	77*	79*	-0.6	8.0	5.9

Table 12.35 Baseline Prime95 Average Power Increase Analysis, S5520UR

Sys Am-bient (°C)	AC power (W)	PWM	Fan Power (W)	PS Fan Power, (W)	Fan Power Incr (W)	CPU 1 Tcase, °C	CPU 2 Tcase, °C	CPU Lkg Incr (W)	Fan+ lkg pwr incr(W)	Actual pwr incr (W)
25	336.5	36	17.4	3.9	0.0	57	59	0.0	0.0	0.0
35	346.9	40	23.8	4.6	7.1	68	62	1.7	8.8	10.4
40	349.1	40	23.8	4.8	7.3	67	72	3.4	10.7	12.6

* This value exceeds T_{case} specification, but the PECI value is less than -1.

Thermal Margin

A presentation of the thermal margin (in degrees Celsius) for the lowest margin components within the high ambient temperature proof of concept S5500WB and S5520UR systems in Table 12.36 shows that the only components of concern when moving to 40°C ambient are the hard disk drives. Note that the negative margin on the CPU for the S5500WB is acceptable only because the PECI margin is also positive.

Table 12.36 Baseline Prime95 Thermal Margin1 Select Components, °C

	Ambient, S5500WB			Ambient, S5520UR		
Component	2	4	3	15	14	10
CPU PECI[2]	-8	-8	-4	8	7	3
CPU T_{case}[2]	32	27	27	27	23	18
DIMM T_{case}	14	15	13	44	36	32
IOH PECI[3]	6	6	7	39	32.0	27.3
IOH T_{case}[3]	12	13	10	16	16	11
BMC T_{case}	13	10	7	16	13	8
HDD T_{case}, excursion	3	0	-3	6	3	-2
HDD T_{case}, sustained[4]	24	18	16	*	*	*
SAS heat sink[5]	2	4	3	15	14	10

LINPACK Workload Results

LINPACK (linear equation package) benchmarks are a measure of a system's floating point computing power. LINPACK workload measures how fast a computer solves a dense N by N system of linear equations $Ax = b$, which is a common task in engineering. The solution is obtained by Gaussian elimination with partial pivoting, with $2/3 \cdot N^3 + 2 \cdot N^2$ floating point operations. Results are reported in millions of floating point operations per second (MFLOP/s, sometimes simply called MFLOPS). The problem size varied from 1,000 to 42,000 and number of times the test were repeated. Table 12.37 outlines the results obtained on S5500WB platform with problem size of 42,000 and number of tests set to 4. For the S5520UR platform, results are with problem size of 21,000 and number of tests set to 4. For the S5500WB and the S5520UR platforms performance was not impacted with the variation in chamber temperature settings.

Table 12.37 LINPACK Power and Performance Results

Platform	Chamber Temp, (°C)	Performance (GFLOPS)	Power (Watts)
S5500WB	25	76.08	309
	35	75.88	311
	40	76.17	315
S5520UR	25	75.20	321
	35	75.24	327
	40	75.20	306

Hmmer Workload Results

Hmmer is part of the CPU2006 SPECint benchmark. When the SPECint benchmark is executed, the results score is geometric mean of all the modules in the SPECint benchmark. SPECint benchmarks were updated to run the Hmmer benchmark alone. Profile Hidden Markov Models (profile HMMs) are statistical models of multiple sequence alignments, which are used in computational biology to search for patterns in DNA sequences. Table 12.38 outlines the results obtained on S5500WB and S5520UR platforms. For S5500WB and S5520UR platform there was degradation in performance when the chamber temperature was varied from 25°C to 40°C. However, at higher ambient temperature settings, servers consumed higher power. Tests were repeated for 6 times and results were reproducible for each and every run. The performance data matches with the data published with other teams as well.

Table 12.38 Hmmer Power and Performance Results

Platform	Chamber Temp, (°C)	Performance (GFLOPS)	Power (Watts)
S5500WB	25	153	309
	35	153	311
	40	153	315
US5520URrbanna	25	152	321
	35	150	325
	40	149	320

Summary

Within Intel and the IT industry there exist a number of concerns, not necessarily proven related to IT equipment operation in high ambient temperature environment including loss of performance, processor throttling, increased software error rates, reduced mean time between failures (MTBF) of Intel silicon, increased hardware failure, system overcooling, and increased power consumption and its sources. The results from the high ambient temperature proof of concept allay many of these concerns.

The high ambient temperature proof of concept results obtained in pre-baseline and baseline testing are in close agreement with previously developed Intel models and correlated data. Some caution needs to be applied due to the small sample, and for certain, all conclusions are for workloads that operate up to, but not beyond total design power or TDP.

In general, the proof of concept servers were found to operate flawlessly and to meet component thermal limits in a 40°C thermal chamber environment with a relatively modest increase in server fan power. Diligent fan management and system layout is required to meet full MTBF rating of mechanical hard disk drives at 40°C and to minimize server system power consumption. Overall, system optimization is critical to minimizing system power increase as ambient temperature increases.

Performance

■ The results demonstrate there is no degradation of performance or increase in error rates due to running these servers in higher ambient temperature environments up to 40°C.

■ Both the S5500WB and S5520UR systems were capable of meeting thermal specifications even at 40°C. As long as the thermal specifications are met, there was no degradation of performance or increase in error rates at higher ambient operation. The S5500WB system performance is better than the S5520UR's under some workloads due to difference in I/O components as hard speed in S5500WB was higher compared to S5520UR platform. The difference was due to the hard drive speed.

■ Proof of concept systems are designed to operate in a 35°C ambient environment, and are designed to meet Intel Rotational Vibration Interference (Intel RVI) requirements up to 35°C. Because these systems were capable of meeting a 40° C operating environment with no modification to existing fan speed, risk for RVI issues at 40° C is considered low.

Power

■ Running the S5500WB server at 40°C resulted in a general increase of 0 to 6.4 percent across all workloads when compared to the same workload at 25° C. Running the S5520UR server at 40°C resulted in a general increase of 2.7 to 7.7 percent across all workloads when compared to the same workload at 25°C. This differences are well accounted for by the changes in fan power and CPU silicon leakage. As such, this refutes the controversy raised about power consumption increasing significantly when operating a system in higher ambient temperatures.

■ The S5500WB-based servers have been power-optimized both in terms of fan speed control and layout, resulting in a lower overall power consumption and variance. Thermal test data revealed, however, that as configured for the proof of concept, fan speeds could be reduced in the S5520UR-based servers even when subjected to power-intensive workloads. Based on measured fan power and margin analysis, a fan power reduction of about three watts could be realized at all ambient temperatures. Sustained operation at 40°C in conjunction with this power savings could lead to degraded mechanical hard disk drives reliability unless solid state drives (SSDs) are used. Use of SSDs would allow a total of approximately ten watt savings in fan power.

■ Clever use of fan speed control allows beneficial tradeoffs between CPU and fan power. This tradeoff may create a net reduction in server level power at a specific ambient temperature between 25°C and 40°C. This phenomenon was observed when running the Sandra benchmark where optimal server power occurred at 35°C on S5500WB and the SPECpower benchmark at 35°C. Optimum system operating temperature (in terms of server level power only) varies from system to system and workload to workload. The method used to optimize the fan speed control for power consumption on S5500WB appeared to be effective in this range.

Thermal

Both S5500WB and S5520UR system designs and configurations under test were capable of maintaining positive margin to specs for CPU and chipsets under all ambient conditions (25°C, 35°C and 40°C).

■ For some workloads such as Hadoop and SPECPower, Intel silicon has margin available at higher ambient temperatures in a S5500WB with Chenbro chassis configuration due to fan speed control implementation. Because these systems do not violate the guidance given by the Intel TMDG or EMTS, Intel silicon reliability is not impacted by running proof of concept systems at higher ambient temperatures.

■ For the S5500WB and S5520UR systems, the hard disk drive components operate with minimal or negative sustained operating margin at high ambient temperatures. However, there were no hard disk drive failures during the testing as a result of elevated temperatures. According to the manufacturer, sustained operation in this temperature range could lead to degraded MTBF. For these systems, all hard disk drive temperatures were below the absolute maximum rated temperature for all workloads and for all ambient temperatures.

System Design

■ There are a number of differences between the two systems included in these proof of concept experiments: The S5500WB-based system includes four 40 mm fans, while the S5520UR system includes five 40 mm fans. Fan model number is different for each system.

– The S5500WB layout is "un-shadowed", meaning DIMMs and CPUs are arranged in parallel, and not preheated by other upstream DIMMs or CPUs. The S5520UR layout is shadowed, so some of its DIMMs and one of its CPUs are preheated.

– The S5500WB-based system includes a fan speed control algorithm that is optimized for minimal power consumption, while the S5520UR-based system includes a fan speed control algorithm that provides higher, more conservative airflow levels.

- The two proof of concept systems were conducted with two different hardware configurations as shown in Table 12.39.

- Accounting for these differences, it is estimated that the fan power penalty for the S5520UR's shadowed layout vs. the S5500WB un-shadowed layout is approximately 2 to 3 percent of total system power.

Table 12.39 Hardware configuration

Platform	Number of DIMMs	Hard Disk Drives	PCI Cards
S5500WB	8	3.5 inch, 4 bays, 2 used for running the proof of concept	One, short, none used for running the proof of concept
S5520UR	12	2.5 inch, 8 bays, 2 used for running the proof of concept	One, full length, none used for running the proof of concept

■ The work done with modeling during the pre-baseline phase confirmed the belief that access to a very accurate, responsive inlet temperature sensor for all systems is vital to being able to generate a power-saving fan speed control algorithm in a system. For the S5520UR system, the type and location of its ambient air sensor leads to a loss of granularity and linearity due to the workload. To develop good fan speed control, accurate measurements are required. Develop a robust platform design guide; supplement to the existing design guide. This should be part of a best known procedure. Include this in a separate document.

Recommendations

Following are key recommendations:

■ Perform the experiments by running servers in an actual data centers: Running the same workloads in a data center environment will produce results meaningful to customers. This allows a correlation between thermal chamber data and real world data. Importantly, it also allows for the characterization of data center level parameters not comprehended by thermal chamber testing. Finally, it allows customers the ability to analyze results from their own workloads and to fully characterize the positive impact associated with operating at higher ambient temperatures.

End-user's and OEMs need to pay attention to thermal margins associated with sustained operation of hard disk drives in high ambient temperatures. Customers operating in high ambient temperatures should investigate tradeoffs associated with the use of Intel solid state drives.

■ Raise Silicon Operating Temperatures: CPU design must comprehend required design and process margins while optimizing for the end-user need to reduce system power. Meeting current Intel Xeon 5500 series processors EMTS and TMDG thermal guidance may cause unnecessary power consumption as compared to parts capable of operating at higher case and junction temperatures. Small increases in case or junction temperature can lead to significant fan power savings depending on system layout, thermal solution, and other factors.

■ Minimize Airflow: Optimize fan speed control settings across the entire operating range to minimize power consumption while still adequately cooling all components. Make the fan speed control content aware (CPU, memory, HDD components) so that it is does not over-cool.

■ Run Hadoop Workload with SSDs, JBOD, NAS: Validate lower power consumption and higher ambient temperature capability by running Hadoop with a JBOD or NAS configuration. This will also allow a test of larger data set sizes.

Using servers provisioned with Intel® Xeon® 5500 Series processors in data centers at high ambient temperatures provides a significant TCO benefit when compared to older data centers with high PUE. This will be more fully characterized in phase III data center testing. Because of the significant TCO savings possible, update the Intel silicon reliability model to bring it up to 27°C, the ASHRAE 2008 standard. Further, consider a model change that allows a change of ambient that comprehends a change in fan speed.Likewise, here are a number of related topics under consideration for future research proposals.

■ Locating a data center in frigid areas can lower cooling costs significantly. Microsoft announced a data center in Siberia primarily because of its cheap and readily available power, but the ability to use free cooling for a substantial amount of the year was also a factor.

■ Cost control and compliance: It is hard to forecast TCO savings until measurements are captured by running various workloads in real data center environments. Performing high temperature operation experiments is of a strategic value to the industry because they yield

- Hints for establishing hardware quality standards

- Insight into platform reliability under high ambient temperature operation

- Potential lower cost of operation

Chapter **13**

Pluggable Policy Engines in Virtualized Cloud Environments

Contributed by Sudhir Bangalore, Kamal Natesan, Raghu Yeluri

In today's virtualized cloud environments, resource optimization decisions are based on only the CPU and memory usage of the workload. In particular, for power management decisions, these two parameters constitute at best indirect indicators for system power usage. Recent technology developments allow actual, real-time power measurements to be factored into power management decisions.

This proof of concept of pluggable policy engines extends the ability of the resource management engines for virtualized cloud environments to provide a highly optimized resource distribution mechanism in an independent and modular fashion through existing software APIs and without the need to re-engineer the software environment or to request additional capabilities from software vendors.

The fast-paced adoption of virtualized clouds by the industry brings a number of security concerns to operators and architects alike. In this chapter we illustrate the use of the Intel® Trusted Execution Technology (Intel® TXT), part of Intel's Safer Computing Initiative[1] to address some of these concerns.

---

1   For additional detail on Intel's Safer Computing Initiative please refer to David Grawrock's book *The Intel Safer Computing Initiative*, Intel Press, ISBN 978-0976483267.

To illustrate these concepts, we extend the VMware vSphere† management console to include power-based and thermal-based resource distribution within a cluster of trusted VMWare ESX† servers. This can easily be extended to any quality-of-service–based metric, readily incorporating information from counters and sensors in the CPU, chipset, server platforms, and the network to architect and implement specific system management strategies.

Policy Engine Overview

As previously mentioned, in current virtualized environments, resource optimization decisions are based only on CPU and memory usage patterns for a particular workload. There are advanced features in Intel platforms with potential to yield improved decision algorithms and also provide a safer environment for workloads to run. A traditional approach for Intel to make the benefits of these features available to customers has been enabling independent software vendors (ISVs) and independent hardware vendors (IHVs) to assist in integrating new features into their offerings. This is a long drawn and time-consuming effort for all parties involved. The plug-in approach described in this chapter helps in shortening the process.

Shortening the deployment lifecycle also encourages experimentation and rapid prototyping, quickening the pace for technology innovation, not just for Intel but for industry participants that include Intel technology into their products.

Policy engines provide a generic plug-in architecture for cloud and virtualization resource management engines using their native APIs and extension mechanisms. This mechanism allows composing features typically embedded in a platform into global capabilities applicable to resource pools more typical of cloud computing. For example, the plug-in model allows for extending the resource management applications to provide power-based, thermal-based, QoS-based distribution and migration of workloads within a VMware cluster, taking advantage of information derived from CPU, chipset and network entities.

Furthermore, when we add Intel® Virtualization Technology and the Intel Trusted Execution Technology root of trust, we can ensure a trusted boot of the hypervisor and the virtual machines running on that hypervisor.

The approach is not limited to a specific cloud and virtualization management vendor. The design concept can easily be extended and adopted by any management vendor allowing additional capabilities through published APIs.

Purpose of Policy Engine

In sum, pluggable policy engines for virtualized cloud environments

- Allow quick prototyping of new usages and usage models for advanced technologies.

- Provide proof of existence for advanced technologies where Intel leads by example as an incentive to ecosystem players to build even more powerful capabilities.

- Allows quick integration of emerging technologies to quickly percolate through the ecosystem to the eventual benefit of end user customers.

Architecture

Figure 13.1 captures the high level architecture for the virtualization and cloud resource manager plug-in. The left side components are of the resource manager. It comprises both the client and console and the server components.

The middle section comprises of the plug-ins, Web applications implemented as required by the resource management application for extending functionality. The plug-ins are registered with the management console using the extension API. The functionality of Web applications is implemented using the APIs of the resource management server, which in turn carries out the tasks on the virtualized platforms.

The right side section uses a server with Intel® Data Center Manager (Intel DCM) installed. Intel Data Center Manager implements group-level power management abstractions by composing Intel® Intelligent Power Node Manager single-server power management capabilities.

The bottom section represents the cluster of the virtualized servers managed by the resource management application. These servers require Intel Intelligent Power Node Manager to be included in the group management scheme supported by Intel Data Center Manager.

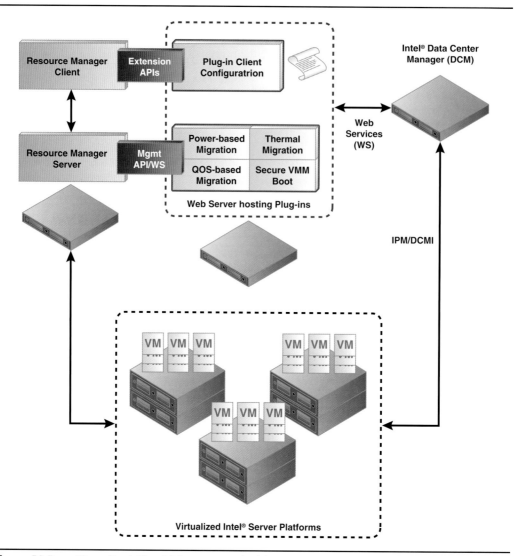

Figure 13.1   Virtualized Cloud Management Architecture

Proof of Concept Implementation

To illustrate the general applicability of the plug-in approach, we developed three distinct plug-ins for this proof of concept, each bringing a new, unique capability.

The proof of concept uses VMWare vSphere[†] 4.0 as the virtualization platform along with Virtual Center[†] Server and its supported software development kit (SDK) and VMware vSphere client for management. We also used Intel Data Center Manager SDK to integrate the single-node power management capabilities provided by Intel Intelligent Power Node Manager.

We choose the VMWare platform considering its wide adoption. With some minor changes, the plug-ins would interface with other hypervisor vendors as well.

Virtual Center SDK Overview

Figure 13.2 shows the VMware VirtualCenter[†] SDK integration stack. Software vendors can use this SDK to integrate virtualization management capabilities into their applications. The SDK also allows for extending the capability of VMware vSphere through plug-ins.

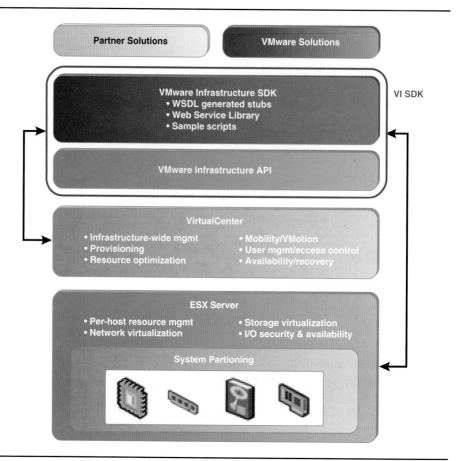

Figure 13.2 VMware VirtualCenter† Integration Stack

VirtualCenter† Plug-in Overview

As previously mentioned, VMware allows extending the functionality of VMware VirtualCenter through plug-ins. Plug-ins are implemented as Web applications. A plug-in gets registered with VMware VirtualCenter through an XML configuration file. When the vSphere client connects to the VirtualCenter server, the content of the plug-in is displayed according to the configuration settings.

Figure 13.3 shows how the plug-in is integrated and the corresponding data appears in the console:

1. The user connects to VMware vCenter via VMware vSphere client. VMware VirtualCenter gets the list of plug-ins registered, redirects VMware vSphere to the configuration file location.

2. VMware vSphere gets configuration file from the Web server and populates user interface information such as menus, icons and tabs.

3. When user selects the appropriate menu or tab, VMware vSphere connects to the Web server mentioned in the configuration file and retrieves the data.

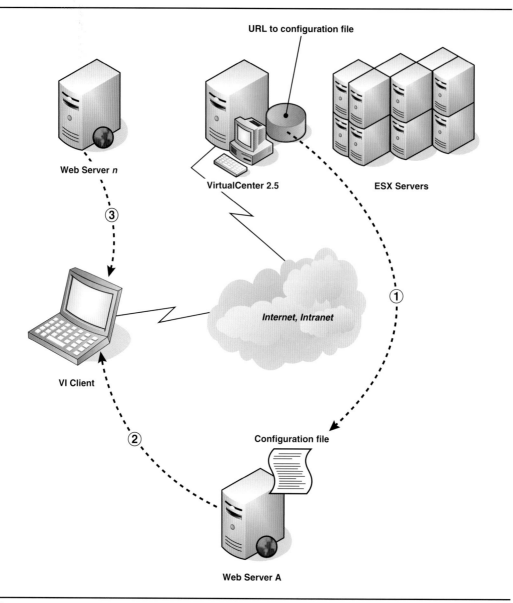

Figure 13.3   Cloud Plug-in Integration Process

Hardware and Software Used in the Proof of Concept

Table 13.1 describes the server equipment used for this particular power and thermal management proof of concept. For reasons of equipment economy, plug-ins, the Intel Data Center Management SDK and the virtualization management software run installed on the same systems. An architect can designate running these component anywhere it's convenient as long as these components are accessible through the network.

Table 13.1 Proof of Concept Equipment

Equipment Type	Description
Intel® Xeon® 5500 Series Processor-based Server	Minimum of 2 servers to showcase resource distribution with virtualized clouds
	Server SKU enabled with Intel® Intelligent Node manager
	Board Management Controller card
	PMBus† and ACPI enabled power supply
	16GB/32GB RAM, Min 20GB Hard disk
	Minimum : 2 x 1 gigabit Ethernet Ports. 3 is optimum
	Shared Storage : SAN/NFS
	VMWare ESX 4.0
Intel® Xeon® 5300 Series Processor-based Server	Minimum 16GB RAM and 80GB hard disk.
	1 gigabit Ethernet port
	Microsoft Windows† 2003 Server R2 (SP2), IIS, .NET 2.0
	VMware VirtualCenter 4.0, vSphere Client 4.0
	VMware vSphere SDK 4.0
	Intel plug-ins
	Intel® Data Center Manager 1.0 SDK

Power-based Resource Management

The idea behind this plug-in is to showcase using actual server power consumption as criteria for power-aware virtual machine distribution and migration decisions instead of the more traditional CPU and memory utilization metrics. None of the existing resource management tools consider power as a parameter in their algorithm for resource distribution, mainly because platform power readings had not been available before, let alone available from an API.

This plug-in demonstrates power-based virtual machine migrations using VMware VirtualCenter and Intel Data Center Manager. The migrations happen from a power constrained host to less power constrained host if a target host available in the cluster. The plug-in allows for setting up the power policies on the server using Intel Data Center Manager instead of having to implement this capability from scratch. Power policies are set up either at a node level or at a group level.

Table 13.2 vCenter API Calls Implemented in Plug-ins

vCenter API call	Purpose
addEntity	To add either a node or a group
associateEntity	To associate a node to a group
findEntities	To get details of either a node or group.
getQueryData	To get the details of the power consumed by node or group/ retrieve historical data
enumeratePolicies	To get the details of the policies for a node or group
setPolicyState	To enable or disable a policy
setPolicy	Add a new power policy to a group or a node
removePolicy	Removes an existing policy
updatePolicy	Updates an existing policy
getPolicyData	Gets the details of an existing policy

Table 13.3 vCenter API Calls Implemented in Plug-ins

vCenter API call	Purpose
Login/Logout	For logging into web service
RetrieveProperties	For retrieving the hierarchy information or properties of specific objects. The details of what needs to be retrieved should be specified in the propertyFilterSpecs object
QueryAvailablePerfMetric	Queries all the performance metrics that an entity (Host or cluster or VM) supports
QueryPerf	For querying a particular performance counter for an entity. Ex: cpu.usage.avg
MigrateVM_Task	Initiates the migration of the VM
WaitForUpdates	To check for updates on the Migration task that was initiated

Figure 13.4 shows the initial screenshot of the plug-in. The plug-in is configured to be shown at the cluster level of the hierarchy. The hierarchical information including cluster, hosts, virtual machines, and the corresponding CPU utilization is obtained through the VMware vSphere Web services SDK shown in Tables 13.2 and 13.3. The indicators *Average Power Used*, *Average Power Cap*, and *Requested Power Cap* are provided by the underlying Intel Data Center Manager and retrieved through its Web services API.

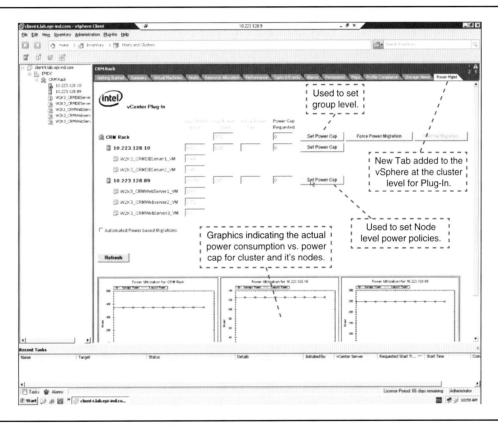

Figure 13.4   Initial Plug-in Display

Once we set a power policy on a node or host, Intel Intelligent Power Node Manager brings down the p-state of the system to align actual power to target power consumption policy. In this case, the system that was consuming about ~250 watts is now brought down to 200 watts. The P-state mechanism defines preset voltage and frequency scaling settings for the CPU. Lowering the voltage and frequency reduces power consumption. Generally, there is a tradeoff between performance and voltage and frequency scaling.

As shown in Figure 13.5, at some point the indicated *Actual Power Cap* reaches the value specified by *Requested Power Cap*. When a power cap is requested at the Node/Host level, these two values will be honored. If a power cap is requested at the Group/Cluster level, then based on the historical power usage of the system, Intel Data Center Manager prioritizes achieving global power targets first.

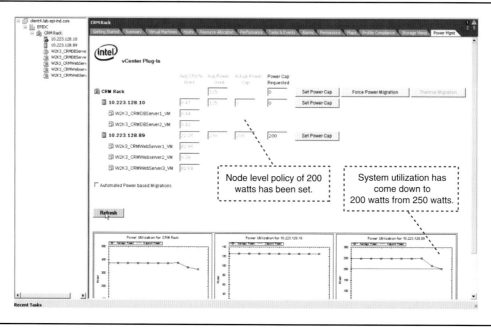

Figure 13.5   System Reaches Power Capping Target.

A power cap so low that's beyond the Intel Intelligent Node Manager control authority is entirely possible. Under this condition it is not possible to bring down the actual power consumption to match the policy request. In the plug-in we treat this event as a triggering point for either manual or automated virtual machine migration.

As shown in Figure 13.6, let's assign a cap of 190 watts to the 10.223.128.89 host. This cap can't be reached under the current workload; that is, the requested policy can't be fulfilled.

One method to restore order and ensure that the host or node meets the requested power policy, is to rebalance workloads across the cluster, migrating virtual machines running in power constrained hosts to less constrained hosts.

There are several possible motivations for this policy: perhaps the host is running in a power constrained rack, or power consumption needs to be reduced because of thermal constraints in the data center.

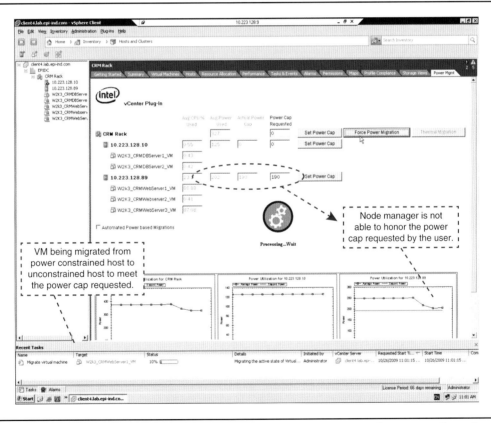

Figure 13.6   Setting a Power Cap beyond the Intel® Intelligent Power Node Manager Control Authority.

To address the power constraint issue, the user clicked on the "Force Power Migration" button shown in Figure 13.6, and Figure 13.7 shows the outcome: The plug-in identifies the highest CPU utilization running on the power constrained node, then migrates the virtual machine to the server in the cluster with lowest utilization. Checking the *Automated Power based Migration* allows this transition to happen automatically on a specific threshold.

Chain reactions are possible, where the target host exceeds its power quota upon accepting the virtual machine. This case was not considered for simplicity in the proof of concept.

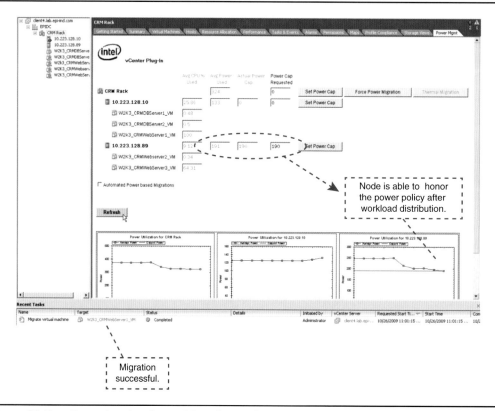

Figure 13.7   Post-migration Status. Note the Machine Now Meets its Power Quota

Thermal-based Resource Management

Due to technical and organizational reasons, in today's data centers cooling configurations are determined statically and cooling usage is not matched to the real-time demand. Airflows into racks and CRAC set points are optimized for the peak usage, determined by trial and error or by static optimization. Set points and airflows are not adjusted for workload cycles or even for the inevitable equipment changes that occur over time.

With Intel's platforms exposing new thermal sensors and events, data center cooling opens the possibility of dynamic optimization. Using real-time data from the group of servers about airflow, server inlet, and exhaust temperatures, optimal rack airflow and temperature can be provided for those servers.

Along with optimizing cooling, using the new sensor values, we can avoid platform hot spots by distributing the workloads to cooler systems. This improves availability of servers by preventing thermal tripping. The indicator for hot spots used for the purposes of the thermal plug-in is the server *thermal margin*, normally a negative number indicating the number of degrees Fahrenheit below the maximum inlet operating temperature specified by the manufacturer. We usually don't want to wait until a temperature rise takes a server over the specified temperature. Hence the plug-in supports the notion of a user-defined thermal threshold. The plug-in initiates a corrective action if the inlet temperature exceeds the threshold.

As in the power management plug-in, the thermal management plug-in uses VMware vSphere Web Services SDK 4.0 to retrieve cluster, host and virtual machine information and the corresponding CPU utilizations. Intel® Data Center manager provides power and thermal information.

When a machine's temperature crosses the predefined thermal threshold for that machine, the plug-in takes action by lowering the machine's workload. The plug in identifies a migration target with more thermal headroom and initiates a VMotion to the target. If the plug-in can't find another system in the cluster that is cool enough to take on the additional workload, it alerts the console with an error message.

As with the power management plug-in, this prototype does not evaluate the aftereffects of a Virtual Machine moving on to a host. There is a potential cascading effect whereby the target host machine exceeds its thermal threshold after receiving the additional workload.

In the example captured in Figure 13.8, the first host, 143.182.3.90, is operating with a margin of -29 degrees, below the -20 user-designated threshold margin. The second host, 143.182.2.121, has a more aggressive threshold margin of -40 degrees, and is operating with a margin of -37 degrees.

When the user clicks on the *Force Migration* button, an error is displayed saying that *all the hosts are within the thermal limit or there are no VMs to be migrated*. Even though the second system is technically operating in a hotspot, there is nothing that can be done to reduce the temperature since there is no workload running on the system to be moved out. These kinds of scenarios usually happen because of incorrect configuration settings.

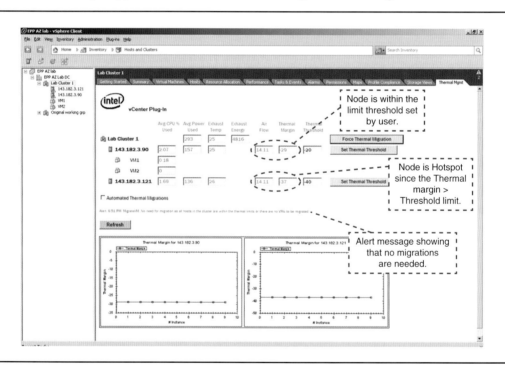

Figure 13.8　Initial Conditions Reported by the Thermal Management Plug-in

Now let's reset the thermal threshold margins to -30 degrees across the two machines. With the new settings, the first host is operating beyond its threshold value, where as the second host is well below the threshold value.

When the user initiates a migration, whether manual or automatic, work-loads (that is, virtual machines) in the machine operating beyond threshold are moved to a cooler system. See Figure 13.9.

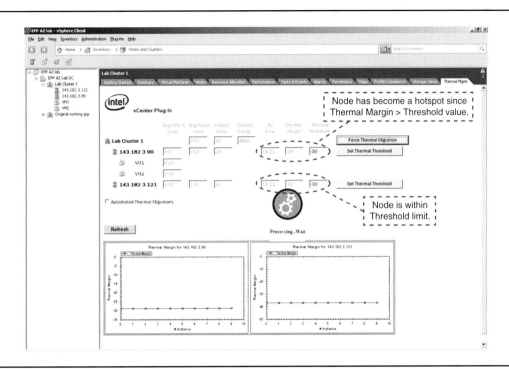

Figure 13.9   Under the New Profile, Machine .90 Is Now Operating Beyond Threshold.

The cooler system, as measured by thermal margin, happens to be node .121. The outcome is shown in Figure 13.10.

Note that the temperatures do not change immediately after the workload migration. It takes a few minutes for machines to reach the new operating temperature.

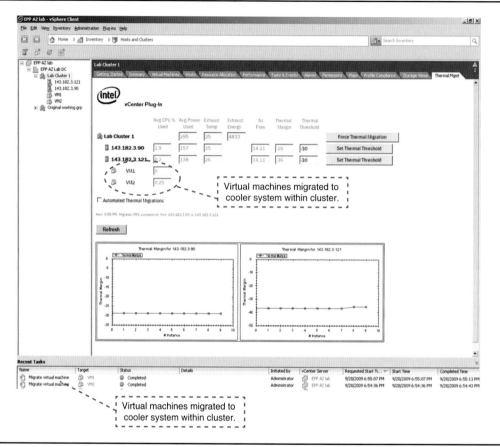

Figure 13.10   Status after a Thermal Migration.

Secure Hypervisor Boot

In today's environment with stringent security requirements, an OS cannot blindly trust its execution environment in the presence of malicious rootkit, reset, and hyperjacking attacks. Intel platforms starting with the Intel® Xeon® 5600 Series processor codenamed Westmere, provide a feature known as Intel® Trusted Execution Technology (Intel® TXT) for addressing such kind of software based attacks. This feature has been available on the desktop platforms for some time and is being integrated into the server platforms to address some of the security concerns. The main purpose of Intel Trusted

Execution Technology is to provide a trusted way for loading and executing system software, such as the operating system kernel or virtualization machine monitor.

Intel® Trusted Execution Technology Overview

Intel® Trusted Execution Technology (Intel® TXT) is a set of enhanced hardware components designed to help protect sensitive information from software-based attacks. Trusted execution features include capabilities in the microprocessor, chipset, I/O subsystems, and other platform components. When coupled with an enabled operating system and enabled applications, Intel® TXT can help protect the confidentiality and integrity of data in the face of these increasingly hostile security environments.

Intel® TXT capabilities include:

- *Protected execution:* Provides applications with the ability to run in isolated environments so that no other unauthorized software on the platform can observer or tamper with the information being operated upon. Each of these isolated environments have dedicated resources that are managed by the platform.

- *Sealed Storage:* Provides the ability to encrypt and store keys, data and other sensitive information within the hardware. This can be decrypted by only the same environment that encrypted it.

- *Protected Input:* Protects communication between keyboard/mouse and the execution environment so that no one can observe the communication.

- *Protected Graphics:* Provides mechanism which enables applications running within the protected execution environment to send display information to the graphic frame buffer without being observed or compromised by any other unauthorized software running on the platform.

- *Attestation:* Enables a system to provide assurance that the Intel® TXT's protected environment was correctly invoked. It also provides the ability to provide a measurement of the software running in the protected space. The information exchanged during attestation is called Attestation Identity Key credential and is used to establish mutual trust between parties.

- *Protected Launch:* Provides for the controlled launch and registration of the critical OS and system software components in a protected execution environment.

Intel® TXT Components

Intel® TXT relies on a set of enhanced hardware, software, and firmware components designed to protect sensitive information from software-based attacks. Intel® TXT platform requirements:

1. *Intel® TXT capable CPU (Intel® Xeon® 5600 Series processor)*
2. *Intel® TXT capable chipset (BXB-C0, ICH9/10)*
3. *Intel® TXT compliant BIOS*
4. *TPM, which must be provisioned by OEM (v1.2 command compliant)*

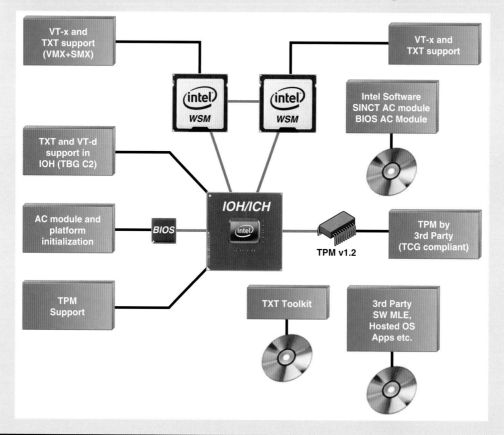

Figure 13.11 Technology Components for Intel® Trusted Execution Technology

The plug-in in this proof of concept allows creating a secure pool of servers by ensuring a secure launch of the VMware vSphere 4.0 (ESX 4.0) hypervisor. The plug-in uses the VMware vSphere Web Services 4.0 SDK. The SDK provides an interface to get the measurement/signature of the hypervisor from the Trusted Platform Module (TPM), and verifies the same against the known value stored in the database.

Figure 13.12 shows a host within a cluster, which has a secure boot. A virtual machine running can be sure that the underlying hypervisor has not been tampered with. The plug-in also shows that the platform does support Trusted Platform Module (TPM), which is a prerequisite for using Intel® TXT. All the measurements/signature are stored in the TPM.

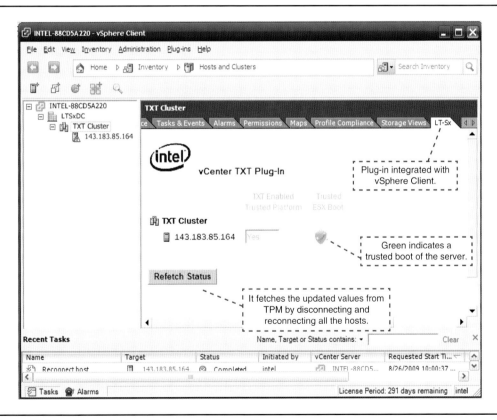

Figure 13.12   Host within a Cluster, with Secure Boot.

The TPM register values are cached in the VMware VirtualCenter database when the host is initially added to the cluster for management. These values are not refreshed on subsequent restart of the host, as shown in Figure 13.13. To enable complete refresh of the PCR register values, the host need to disconnected and reconnected back. The plug-in has implemented this functionality in the "Re-fetch Status" button.

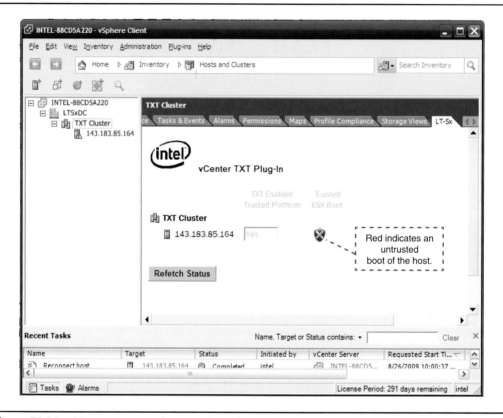

Figure 13.13   TPM Register Values Need a Refresh Upon Restart

Summary

The successful implementations of the power management, thermal management, and secure boot plug-ins prove that the concept of the pluggable policy engine provides the flexibility to expose its new platform capabilities, enabling newer usage models directly while minimizing ecosystem dependencies and integration costs and providing significant value to our customers.

The plug-ins were developed under the VMware vSphere 4.0 environment, but could have been done under a different environment just as easily.

Chapter 14

Power-Aware Management in Cloud Data Centers

Contributed by Milan Milenkovic, Naveen Mellempudi,
Sailaja Parthasarathy, and Vidya Srinivas.

Power efficiency is a major concern in operating cloud data centers, one that impacts operational costs and return on investment as well as significantly affecting the environment. Power consumption in a data center is driven by the operation of the IT equipment, including servers, networking, and storage, directly and indirectly through coupling with cooling. Current data center operating practices through cloud control software stacks and commercial management consoles tend to optimize performance and service level agreements (SLAs), largely ignoring power implications when evaluating workload scheduling decisions.

The research reported in this chapter points to the value of elevating power consumption to a first-class consideration in data center resource allocation and workload scheduling. The underlying hypothesis, supported by experimental evidence, is that power-aware placement, management, and balancing of workload can reduce power consumption in a data center yet have negligible impact on performance. Additional savings are possible through power capping policies that manage power-performance tradeoffs in accordance with business objectives and allow occasional execution of low-priority and latency-tolerant workloads with reduced performance in exchange for predictable power savings.

A few fundamental design principles for power efficiency seem to work well both at the component, subsystem, and at multisystem, data center levels:

■ Dynamically activate only the processing capacity necessary to execute the offered workload.

■ Operate active components at their optimal power-performance points.

■ Put the unused capacity to sleep. In general, deeper sleep states result in increased power savings, but have longer wakeup latency.

Contemporary servers tend to achieve peak power-performance ratios at high processor utilization and are inefficient when doing nothing, often exceeding 50 percent of their maximum power consumption when idling. Thus, application of the above design principles to servers implies that workload should be consolidated on a subset of machines necessary to run it, operating at high utilization, and the remainder of the capacity should be put to sleep, or *parked.*

Key power management techniques include consolidation and migration of workloads to keep active machines at optimal operating points, creation of pools of standby machines with different wakeup latencies (and proportionally reduced power consumption) to accommodate dynamic up and down capacity scaling in response to load variations, matching workload characteristics to individual machine power-performance profiles, and placement and balancing of workload to minimize thermal variance in the data center and thus reducing cooling inefficiencies. A case study on this approach is presented in Chapter 22.

The long term vision for this work is one of a heavily instrumented data center resulting in a fine-grained "weather map" of power consumption and thermal measurements acquired in real time and used for judicious placement of workload so as to maximize energy efficiency while meeting performance and other business constraints.

The first step towards comprehensive, whole data center power and thermal management is to instrument the data center. Fortunately, much of this infrastructure is already available in data centers in the form of sensors built into the servers. Specifically, most servers shipping today include several software-accessible thermal sensors, typically one for inlet temperature and one or more per processor package. In addition, power usage sensors embedded in instrumented power supplies are becoming the norm on newer servers and will likely become pervasive in the future since they are a prerequisite for the more advanced forms of platform power management that are under development. Sensors built into the servers are machine readable, using standard interfaces such as IPMI and the more recent Data Center Management Interface, DCMI.

Cloud management software can scan sensor information in real time and enforce appropriate policies for resource allocation decisions. For example, information from thermal sensors may be used to dynamically direct new workloads into cooler parts of the data center, thus reducing temperature variance and resulting in increased overall efficiency by reducing cooling costs that often represent one third or more of the overall data center power costs. Significant additional savings are possible by using the fine grained, location-correlated thermal measurements from individual servers to drive operation of the cooling equipment. In principle, this capability is implementable through a direct API between the data center control software and the cooling control infrastructure.

For the rest of the chapter, we'll focus primarily on power sensing to support power-aware workload placement. Common data center power usage modes include:

■ Real-time power usage monitoring. The primary goal is to provide measurements and insights into power consumption to customers and operators as well as management automation. Measurements and derived data include recording of peak usage, trending, and logging of thermals and power consumption data at individual server, and rack, and power distribution unit (PDU) levels. The primary use of this data is for manual and automatic power-performance correlation of commonly run workloads and for accurate capacity dimensioning, that is, determining how many servers to place in a rack without exceeding the data center power and thermal limits, based on measured as opposed to estimated power usage. The latter tends to be conservative and often results in underutilization of rack space.

■ Power-limit enforcement. Control is applied to limit, or cap, the power consumption of servers in a rack, and the objective is to maximize performance possible within the specified power budget limit. Usages and policies in this category allow enforcement of a consumption cap on rack power when the measured usage exceeds the quota specified by the operator, automation policy, or the default assumed by the capacity planning tools when populating the rack. These usage scenarios cover situations such as intentional over-provisioning of rack capacity for improved packing density (and counting on not all servers reaching maximum power consumption at the same time), fault and contingency management such as loss of cooling or power delivery problems, or smoothing out sporadic utilization spikes to conserve power, say when running a low priority job or light workloads.

■ Power-aware load placement and management. The primary objective here is to meet a specified performance target, such as SLA, and the goal is to optimize power savings after the performance target is met. There are several variants applicable to different stages of a deployment the life cycle. In systems with static binding of applications to servers, only the initial workload can be optimized in terms of projected resulting power impact. In virtualized systems where binding of applications to virtual machines or servers can be performed at runtime (dynamic), the additional available control is rebalancing of workload to handle power and thermal imbalances or suboptimal allocations as they develop due to variations in load and application life-cycle changes. This can be performed through virtual machine migration.

The three examples above are data points in a much larger continuum of usage models covered in Chapter 18.

Virtual Machine Migration to Save Power

Group-Enabled Management System, or GEMS, is a prototype for autonomic management of collections of server nodes.

A variant of GEMS developed for virtualization with power management, GEMS-VPM, specifically implements rebalancing of workload in collections of virtualized systems in order to save power by

- Proactively consolidating the active workload on a subset of machines that can run it at optimal power-performance settings.

- Shutting off unused capacity.

GEMS-VPM provides a vehicle to explore the components, policies, behavior, and power savings made possible in virtualized environments by power-aware rebalancing of the workload.

The specific implementation of GEMS-VPM described in this document uses Xen[†] for virtualization, Virtual Iron[†] as a commercial virtualization manager, and a collection of Intel prototype components for grouping and group management described in detail in subsequent sections.

The system consists of a collection of physical servers hosting a virtualized environment, which in turn defines a pool of virtual machines executing user workloads in response to incoming requests, as illustrated in Figure 14.1. This is a common setting for cloud operators that provide Infrastructure as a Service (IaaS) offerings, essentially running customer workloads, packaged and managed as virtual machines as a revenue activity.

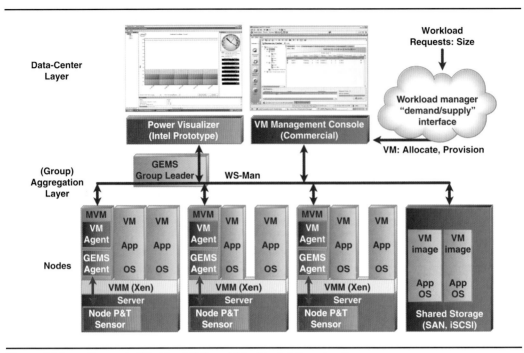

Figure 14.1   Dynamic Workload (Virtual Machine) Allocation System

In a typical usage, work requests arrive at the workload, which in turn is linked with virtualization manager (whose console screen shot is shown above the Virtual Machine Management Console server in Figure 14.1) to create, provision and place virtual machines on a suitable physical machine for execution. The life cycle of individual virtual machines is dictated externally by workload requests; they are created, activated, suspended, or terminated as appropriate.

GEMS adds power and thermal awareness to the process of allocating workloads and binding workloads to physical servers. In particular, instead of random allocation of virtual machines to suitable nodes, a common practice with today's cluster and cloud schedulers, GEMS carries out power-aware placement and balancing of workloads. This process optimizes optimal placement of workload among a collection of eligible physical machines based on power projections.

The GEMS-VPM prototype implements workload rebalancing to mini-mize global power consumption. It operates as a policy-driven automation mechanism, proactively seeking opportunities to migrate virtual machines away from lightly loaded nodes and to save system power by shutting down vacated nodes.

All nodes contain built-in power and thermal sensors, referred as *Node P&T sensors* in Figure 14.1, already available in shipping server platforms. The GEMS group leader described below and Intel® Data Center Manager, provide real-time individual server and aggregated cluster power readings. These are valuable data center operator tools yielding insight in how workloads correlate with power usage and therefore enable a capability to measure power savings from virtual machine migrations.

The prototype system, depicted in Figure 14.1 consists of

■ Three virtualized servers hosting a pool of virtual machines running workloads.

■ Two management servers: one management server handles virtu-alization management. The second management server aggregates and displays system power usage.

■ A shared storage device that facilitates provisioning and speeds-up migration of virtual machines.

Each virtualized server is equipped with a power sensor for real-time measurement of server power consumption. Each server node is shown as having a dedicated management virtual machine, labeled as MVM, hosting a management agent for virtualization (labeled as VI agent) and management agent for power management and group operations, labeled as GEMS agent. These components are described in detail below.

Savings resulting from shutting down unused nodes are significant due to the fact that current server platforms consume in the order of 50 percent of their maximum power consumption when idle, as noted above. Thus, the resulting savings are on the order of 50 percent of maximum per-node power for each server we can shut down in the course of implementing a virtual machine migration power-management policy.

Figure 14.2 depicts system configuration right after shutting down the third node. In this particular scenario, this condition occurs after one of virtual machines on node 3 is terminated due to a user request, and our power management triggers the out-migration of the only remaining virtual machine, to node 2 in Figure 14.2, allowing node 3 to be shut down. The corresponding power savings, in the order of 280 watts in this case, is shown in the aggregate power-consumption display on the left server running Intel Data Center Manager.

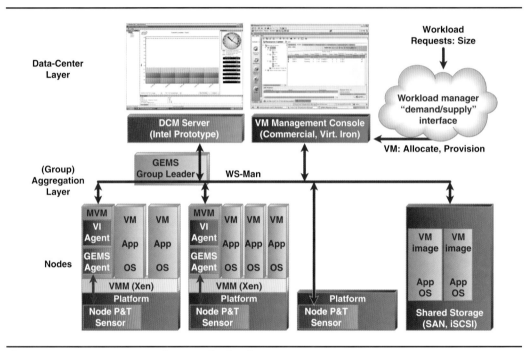

Figure 14.2. System State After a Node Shutdown

A shut down server keeps its baseboard management controller (BMC) active to allow external control systems to restart a server when needed.

Hence, GEMS-VPM allows operating the system with a minimal subset of equipment necessary to meet the committed SLA. The rest of the equipment is maintained in a low power state to conserve energy.

GEMS-VPM Implementation

Figure 14.3 summarizes system components and the logical flows of the GEMS-VPM implementation. The diagram depicts the management console and two managed nodes, the GEMS leader, the other a typical group member or managed node. In implementations with more than two managed nodes, additional instances of member nodes are present.

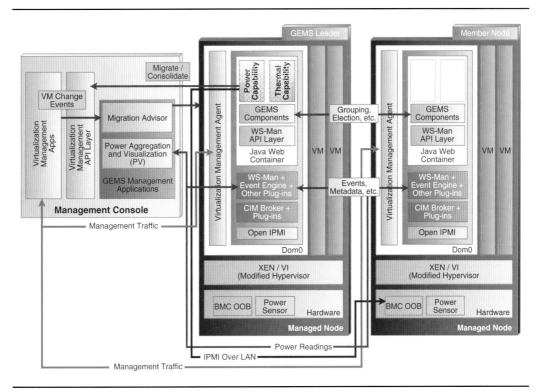

Figure 14.3   System Components and Flows

On the left, the diagram depicts a management console, which is usually a server that runs virtualization management software for the group or cluster of managed nodes that implement the prototype in our example. The management console encompasses virtualization management applications, commercially available products from virtualization management vendors including Virtual Iron, Xensource, and VMware. Typical features include a GUI and an API for managing the life cycle of virtual machines on managed nodes, such as virtual machine creation, suspension, migration, and termination. These functions can be invoked from the management GUI of the console, and also programmatically through public interfaces in the virtualization management API Layer shown in Figure 14.3.

Virtualization management systems comprise a console server node communicating with dedicated virtualization management agents on each of the managed nodes. A common practice in Xen-based systems is to install those agents in domain 0, hereafter referred to as *dom0*. A virtualization management client agent is shown in dom0 of each of the managed nodes. A virtualization management agent operates on each node linked to the control API of the virtual machine monitor to query status, including virtual machine states and performance metrics, and to exercise local control, such as virtual machine life-cycle management mentioned earlier. Virtualization management systems operate through interactions between the central management console and virtualization management agents on individual nodes. In our GEMS-VPM prototype, all of these components are provided by a commercial offering from Virtual Iron.

On the right, Figure 14.3 shows two managed nodes, one of which acts as a leader. Both managed nodes contain identical components that implement GEMS-VPM management stack, including major components:

■ Web Services Management (WS-MAN) protocol stack.

■ Group-Enabled Management System (GEMS) components.

■ [GEMS leader node only] Power and Thermal capabilities.

GEMS-VPM requires real-time power consumption sensing for its operation. This is depicted by the *power sensor* block in the hardware section of each managed node. Practical implementation of power sensing may be accomplished by using instrumented power supplies that provide power consumption readings through an industry-standard protocol, such as PMbus, or via some OEM-proprietary mechanism. In either case, power readings should be made available to management software—and to the GEMS-VPM stack in particular—through public interfaces, such as IPMI. These features are available with Intel® Intelligent Power Node Manager-enabled platforms.

System Flows

Figure 14.3 also depicts principal system flows that accomplish its functionality. Two primary functions of the prototype are

■ Real-time display of aggregate power consumption.

■ Policy-based virtual machine migration to save power. The two corresponding flows are described in subsequent sections.

Power Consumption: Aggregation and Visualization

Each of the production nodes in the system is equipped with instrumented power supplies enabling management applications to query platform power consumption (wall power) in real time. These readings are aggregated across all nodes in a group and displayed to the system operator. Power consumption data can be useful in a variety of usage modes, including power-aware workload placement and correlation of frequently-run workloads with power usage. In the prototype, power information is used primarily to indicate power savings resulting from execution of virtual machine migrations and node shutdowns.

The GEMS-VPM prototype performs power data aggregation in two places using two independent flows:

■ In the power aggregation and visualization (PV) application running on the management console server.

■ In the power management application running on the GEMS leader node (dom0 of one of the production nodes).

This duplication of function supports two different architectural approaches, one that favors aggregation of group readings at a group "super node," GEMS leader in our case, and another approach that favors aggregation at a centralized point in the system, such as the management-console server. In any case, power visualization function is performed only by the PV function since it is running on the node that runs all human interface functions.

■ The first flow uses the PV application to aggregate and display power usage data for all production nodes executing workloads by running corresponding virtual machines. This flow operates through the PV periodically issuing WS-MAN formatted requests for power readings from individual nodes, indicated by the line labeled Power Readings in Figure 14.3. The PV application aggregates and stores individual nodes in its database for subsequent visualization and processing, such as logging, averaging, and trending.

■ The second power aggregation flow is provided by power management application running the power aggregation function. It uses the same WS-MAN interface access point described above to query and obtain power readings from individual nodes, including self. Power readings are cached and logged by the power management. They are available for external use, say by the visualization function, via public interfaces exported by GEMS power management (Power Capability box at the top of the stack in Figure 14.3.)

Policy-Based Virtual Machine Migration

The virtual machine migration flow consists of the following elements:

■ State assessment, monitoring virtual machine state changes

■ Policy evaluation, the execution of virtual machine migration analysis in response to each state change

■ User dialog, informing the operator of migration feasibility and projected power savings, and requesting a go/no go decision

■ Policy execution, the actual execution of a virtual machine migration and shutting down of vacated node as appropriate.

The state assessment is executed by migration advisor component listening to virtual machine state change notifications furnished by virtualization management API, Virtual Iron for the prototype. The migration advisor evaluates each state change by invoking a power policy Web service call to the GEMS leader node for policy evaluation, to assess whether a virtual machine migration away from a lightly loaded node would allow vacating and shutting down a physical server leading in turn to energy savings. If GEMS policy manager, a component of GEMS power management, determines that a migration is advisable, it returns its recommendation to the migration advisor. The migration advisor tags the virtual machine to be migrated, source and target nodes, and projected power savings based on the most recent cached power reading of the candidate source node. Upon receiving this response, the migration advisor constructs and displays a dialog to the system operator, asking for a yes/no decision.

The operator dialog and user involvement in the control loop are not strictly necessary, as the operation of policy decision could be executed in fully automated fashion by the system. There are, however, two reasons for this interaction,

- Early user feedback on autonomic operation indicates that system operators are not comfortable with completely automated resource reallocation due to possible unintended effects. Hence the system deliberately presents a visible notification to the operator, at least during early assessment.

- The dialog helps underscore system behavior, pinpointing to the presence of a policy-driven change at the moment it takes place and the associated energy savings.

If the operator opts for advised migration, system proceeds to policy execution through the appropriate virtualization management public API.

After GEMS policy manager gets notified that migration is complete, if no other application virtual machines are running in that node, the policy manager shuts down the vacated node by sending IPMI commands to it over the LAN.

The WS-MAN Stack Processor

The WS-Man stack is depicted in Figure 14.4. Web Services Management GEMS components communicate with each other through industry standard, nonproprietary protocols. Constituent components define their external interfaces as extensions for WS-Man and use *WS-Eventing* for asynchronous communication. The power and thermal sensor interfaces have also been abstracted to standard *WS-Transfer* requests.

We took an open implementation of WS-Man, *openwsman* providing a minimalist Web server and a protocol parser and extended it for our use. The design was modular and easily extensible through plug-ins for expressing new functionality.

Figure 14.4 shows a detailed view of the various components in the WS-Man stack processor. The stack shows a Web server and an addressing schema defined by WS-Addressing for accessing the plug-ins implemented as loadable modules. Subsequent subsections describe the three major categories of interfaces implemented by the plug-ins.

As shown in Figure 14.4, GEMS components use the WS-Man Java API layer to interact with WS-Man stack to send or receive events, get instrumentation data and read or modify metadata.

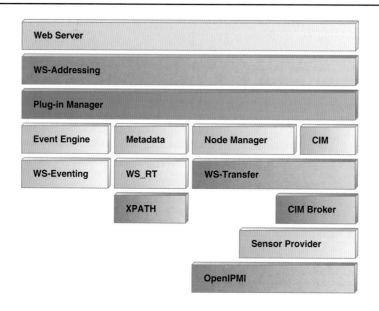

Figure 14.4 WS-MAN Protocol Stack

Eventing Interface

GEMS components depend on events for tracking nodes, managing node groups and electing group leader. These operations require a more generic eventing interface for the components to define custom events and a notification mechanism for sharing the event occurrences.

Event Engine plug-in implements these interfaces as extensions to WS-Eventing for the components to:

■ Publish custom defined events (Extended)

■ Enumerate and list published events (WS-Enumeration)

■ Subscribe to published events (WS-Eventing)

■ Notify event occurrences (Extended)

Event definitions must be unique within and across node boundaries. For this reason, we have defined the following XML data type for defining events.

The WS-MAN API layer in Figure 14.4 implements the function interfaces for the GEMS components to interact with Event Engine to publish, subscribe and notify the events. The API layer also implements a mechanism to receive all the incoming events for the node in the form of an *aggregated event listener* and then dispatches them to the respective components.

Power and Thermal Data Interface

Having a common public interface for collecting platform instrumentation is crucial for managing a group of heterogeneous nodes, each exposing a different low level interface for interacting with the power and thermal sensors such as those in PMBus-enabled power supplies and those provided by Intel Intelligent Power Node Manager. Our implementation abstracts these different layers to a standard WS-Transfer (*Get/Put*) interface.

Figure 14.4 shows plug-ins for CIM, and Intel Intelligent Node Power Manager abstracting thermal and power sensors respectively to a standard WS-Transfer *Get* interface. The power aggregation and visualization tool from the management console requests the power numbers from each node though WS-Man requests. The power and thermal functions also interact with WS-Man though the API layer to collect and aggregate power and thermal readings.

Metadata Interface

As part of GEMS operation the leader/nodes need to keep track and update certain metadata that describes one or more of the following:

■ Node description and list of capabilities (all nodes)

■ List of nodes in a group and leader information (all nodes)

■ Tracking data for all the active nodes in the group (leader node only)

It is also important that this information is available for other nodes in the group on a standard publics interface. Metadata plug-in organizes the data in XML files and exposes a standard WS-ResourceTransfer (WS-RT) for querying and modifying this data.

The Java API Layer (refer to Figure 14.3) exposes the WS-RT Get/Put interfaces, for the GEMS components to interact with metadata plug-in.

GEMS Power Management

Group-Enabled Management System (GEMS) is a set of mechanisms, protocols, and APIs enabling group-level management of Intel platforms. GEMS takes advantage of group level usage and utilization information to ensure power economy and hence achieve energy efficiency.

GEMS power management (Power Capability) is the GEMS component that runs on a group leader. It monitors power consumption of the collection of nodes belonging to a group and allocate power budget for each node based on the group power budget. In a virtualized environment, GEMS power management gains additional significance: it performs server parking. Server parking yields a significant reduction in power consumption relative to power capping alone. Policy manager, a component of GEMS power management, is the module that determines the kind of balancing to be done.

Tasks carried out by GEMS power management are

■ Monitor managed nodes, retrieving instantaneous and average power consumption.

■ Allocate power budget for nodes based on the group budget in conjunction with the specified power policy. Power budget per node is the maximum power that a node can consume.

- Determine potential load balancing scenarios to yield power savings in a virtualized environment.

- Perform the identified migration and shut down vacated nodes to realize power savings.

Main GEMS Components

GEMS power management comprises the following components, the aggregator, allocator, and policy manager proper.

- Aggregator. The aggregator polls each of the nodes that comprise the group and maintains a table of instantaneous, average power consumption, and the maximum power budget allocated for each node in the group. The aggregator caches the information. The data collection interval is adjustable. Caching can be overridden if required. The power information obtained by the aggregator is through WS-Man interfaces communicating with the power sensors.

- Allocator. GEMS power management enables setting a power budget per rack. The allocator doles out individual power quotas for each node. The communication between the power sensors for setting the individual power budget limits takes place through WS-Man.

- Policy Manager. The GEMS policy manager implements the mechanisms for power-aware virtual machine relocation across nodes.

Implementation of GEMS Power Management

One instance of GEMS power management runs in the group's leader node, interacting with other GEMS services, such as the *registrar, discovery,* and *identification.*

Similarly to other GEMS Services, GEMS power management is deployed as an Apache Axis 1.3 Service over Apache Tomcat[†]. Apache Tomcat 5.5 is the Web container used for development of GEMS and Axis is the SOAP engine and framework used for developing SOAP based Web services.

Public Interfaces

GEMS power management supports a collection of interfaces to obtain the aggregated power information from the managed nodes and to perform virtual machine migrations. This section describes the interfaces applicable to a virtualized environment. The following capabilities are supported:

■ CanMigrate: This interface determines if in the current scenario, a migration, can be performed for power savings.

■ Output: Identifies the candidate virtual machine for migration as well as the source and destination nodes for migration.

Logic for determination:

– A node on which a virtual machine has been suspended is the potential candidate.

– Determine the node with the least number of active or running virtual machines (other than the source node.)

– The migration advice involves the above two nodes and target power reduction, using cached power data.

■ PerformMigrate: Carries out the virtual machine migration. Once the migration is completed, it powers off the machine using IPMI.

■ Input: Virtual machine to be migrated, source and destination nodes

■ Output: Boolean indicating success or failure of the migration operation.

In the current implementation of GEMS-VPM, the above interfaces are used by GEMS Migration Advisor. These interfaces are available to higher level management applications.

Virtual Iron[†] Interfaces

GEMS power management uses Virtual Iron interfaces to achieve its functionality. The main Virtual Iron interfaces used are listed below.

■ VirtualizationManager.dynamicConnect. Connect to Virtual-ization Manager.

■ ConfigurationManager.getObjects. Retrieve handle to managed nodes.

- Node.getVirtualServer. Retrieve handle to virtual machines in a managed node.

- EventLog.listenForEvents. Listen for Virtual Server Stopped, that is, virtual machine Stopped Events.

- Job.begin. Start job.

- VirtualserverToMigrate.migrate (nodeToMigrateTo). Perform migration operation.

- Job.commitAll. Commit operation.

More details regarding the API can be obtained from the Virtual Iron 4.2 SDK documentation.

Management Console Modules

The main GEMS management functions running in the console are the migration advisor and the power aggregation and visualization modules, described below.

GEMS Migration Advisor

The GEMS migration advisor is a client component of GEMS. This is the user interface for performing migration in situations when conducive. The migration advisor listens for Virtual Iron's virtual machine stopped events. On receiving a virtual machine stopped event, it connects to GEMS power management running on the leader and assesses the potential for power reduction. GEMS power management returns with a potential migration advice displayed by the user interface. The migration is carried out depending on the user response.

The GEMS migration advisor is a standalone Java application built using J2SE 5. It communicates with GEMS through GEMS power management and listens to Virtual Iron Events by using the Virtual Iron API.

Power Aggregation and Visualization

GEMS power aggregation and visualization (PV) is a standalone application that visualizes the amount of power consumed by the group of managed nodes in terms of a graph. PV retrieves group information from the GEMS leader. For each node in the group, it communicates with WS-Man running on the node and displays the power consumption. PV also calculates the aggregated group power consumption and power saved from rebalancing virtual machines.

Summary

In this chapter we have described how power-aware policies, running in GEMS leader node, are evaluated in response to significant system events, such as creation and deletion of virtual machines whose life cycle is dictated by workload requests that are external to the system.

The GEMS policy manager activates live virtual machine migration by issuing the necessary API calls to the virtual machine management console. Nodes shut down to save power due to comparatively low overall utilization of the virtual machine execution pool, can be programmatically brought back into operation later when needed in response to workload demand fluctuations.

It should be noted that wakeup latency of servers is quite considerable. In order for a server to become eligible to execute user payload, it has to power up, execute the BIOS boot sequence, boot the hypervisor, activate management virtual machine if any, activate virtualization and power-management agents shown in Figure 14.1, and have them successfully register with their respective management consoles. In our experimental setup, this process took on the order of 4 minutes to complete after issuance of the power-up command. Practical workload allocators in data centers with rapidly changing workloads must factor in server wakeup latency by keeping a reserve pool of nodes in a quick to dispatch state, such as provisioned but idle. Future system designs need to address this issue by introducing new power-efficient sleep states with shorter recovery times. For a variety of reasons, most contemporary servers and server operating systems do not support the S3 ACPI state, which is commonly used in laptops and often referred to as the "standby" mode.

Savings resulting from shutting down unused nodes are significant due to the fact that contemporary server platforms tend to consume on the order of 50 percent of their maximum power consumption when idle. Actual power saving depend on characteristics and variations of the specific workload. As in illustration of the potential, consider a cluster of 200 physical servers that consume 300 watts each at full load and 150 watts at idle. At 100-percent total aggregate load, the server pool consumes 60 kilowatts. At 50-percent aggregate load, the unbalanced pool would consume somewhat in excess of 45 kilowatts, depending on load distribution. With virtual migration to save power described here, the system could use as little as 30 kilowatts while executing the same workload by consolidating it on 100 active servers and shutting off the remaining ones, thus yielding power savings on the order of 30 percent. Similar calculations indicate power savings on the order of 60 percent with aggregate utilization at 25 percent, and 14 percent savings at 75 percent utilization. Even though in practice operators tend to set a limit below 100 percent for maximum server utilization, power-aware VM migration results in significant power savings often in double digit percentages.

Chapter **15**

The Intel Cloud Builder Test Bed

Intel as a company is motivated to ensure that the latest servers and computers with x86 processors and networking products constitute a good fit for building the industry's cloud computing infrastructure. At the time of writing there were few proof points, at least within public knowledge, of clouds built with servers featuring the Intel® Xeon® 5500 series processors and advanced 10 gigabit networking. These servers are built with the Intel® Quickpath Interconnect (QPI) architecture for high memory bandwidth and low latency and advanced power monitoring and control capabilities with Intel® Intelligent Power Node Manager and extended power proportional computing dynamic range.

The Intel® Cloud Builder program seeks to increase industry process knowledge in the deployment of cloud solutions. Developed with cloud independent software vendors (ISVs), the program provides an initial proof point to set up, deploy and manage a cloud infrastructure. The Intel Cloud Builder program produces materials, including documented reference architectures and best known methods on how to build and operate a cloud by running the ISV software stack on a test bed hosted by Intel.

The primary goal is to build the collective knowledge on integrating and deploying cloud-based solutions for service providers, hosting service providers and enterprise customers looking to use cloud architectures. The program provides tools and best practices for cloud service providers to create a cloud environment based on a defined software and hardware stack.

Intel® Cloud Builder solutions provide an easy starting point to build a cloud environment based on a basic hardware blueprint and using available cloud software management solutions to manage the resource pools. These solutions provide a defined starting point and over time will take advantage of future Intel technologies and industry software solutions to address ISV's needs such as trusted multi-tenancy and power management.

Service providers and hosting infrastructure providers want to innovate where they will get the greatest return. Work under Intel Cloud builder facilitates this process through early experience and proof points with advanced infrastructure technology providing documented solutions to reduce technical barriers for cloud deployments by service providers and hosting solution providers. Based on the test bed methodology, the program provides design specifications, APIs, and best practice information for the industry at large.

Industry leading ISVs have joined the Intel® Cloud Builder program, including Canonical, Citrix, Microsoft, Parallels, Red Hat, Univa UD, VMware, Novell, and Enomaly.

Cloud Builder Test Bed Infrastructure Overview

In order to meet goals for automation and cost effective operation of Cloud data centers, we provisioned the test-bed with a virtualized environment, flat layer two-network, direct and network attached storage and Intel Xeon 5500 and 5600 series servers.

For services to be responsive to transient demands with acceptable costs, Cloud workloads must either directly leverage distributed computing capabilities in the cloud (using tools such as Apache Hadoop or exploit the flexibility that virtualization provides within cloud environments to optimize resource utilization and improve resiliency to hardware failures.

The ever present risk of hardware failures means that either the application or the cloud management software needs to be able to perform the necessary recovery actions.

The application may be responsible for retry/recovery or the state of each compute element must be maintained in shared storage if recovery is initiated by cloud management function. For a typical enterprise workload, the application is usually wrapped into a virtual machine and that virtual machine and all application data are in shared storage. If a server fails, the cloud management software can simply restart the same virtual machine on another physical server.

These basic principles were used in designing the Intel Cloud Builder Test Bed. The diagram in Figure 15.1 represents the physical test bed.

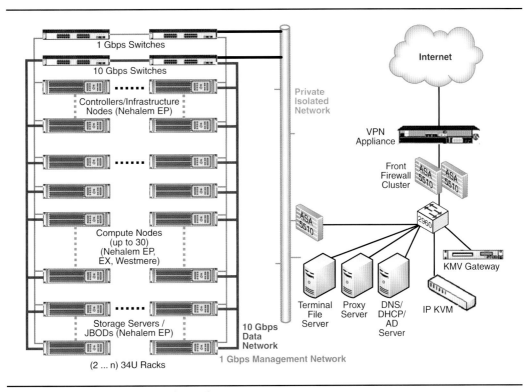

Figure 15.1   Test Bed Physical Topology

Intel® Xeon® Processor 5500 Series servers, code named Nehalem and 5600 Series servers, code named Westmere, are connected using a 1G network and 10G network with "top of rack" switches. The switches were configured to achieve the logical architecture shown in figure 15.1. In this configuration, there are no dedicated function servers and no especially distinguished connections: all servers are configured the same. This uniformity allows for simple replacement, or reassignment of workloads.

Server Architecture

The Intel Cloud Builder uses Intel's most advanced processor technology available, providing a foundation for architecting new cloud data centers and increase performance with the goal of using less energy and space, and reducing operating costs, with significant improvement over the previous generation.

The Intel Xeon processor 5500 and 5600 series offer the following high performance features:

■ Built-in mechanisms and algorithms to adjust the processor frequency to meet the business and application performance requirements.

■ Automated energy efficiency to scale power usage to workload demand to achieve optimal performance/watt and reduce operating costs.

■ Intel® Virtualization Technology (Intel® VT) and Intel® VT Flex-Migration offer best-in-class performance and manageability in virtualized environments to strengthen the infrastructure and reduce costs.

■ Intel® Hyper-Threading Technology, with eight or twelve cores and 16 or 24 threads per 2-socket platform, speeds up the execution of multi-threaded software applications to execute threads in parallel within each processor core.

The first two features constitute an excellent base to implement dynamic platform power monitoring and control that provides significant linearity of power consumption to workload.

In the remainder of the chapters we present three cloud software industry leaders, Eucalyptus and Canonical, Enomaly, and Univa UD present the results of hosting their offerings on the Intel Cloud Builder infrastructure. The mapping to solution in each of the case studies should prove an insightful exercise for decision makers contemplating private cloud deployments or integrating hosted offerings into an organization's application strategy.

The Eucalyptus/Canonical Case Study

The operation of IT using the ideas and principles of the cloud are of great interest because of the benefits of agility and cost savings. For those workloads that need to remain under close control of IT, using an IaaS structure is often the best choice. When the IaaS (Infrastructure as a Service) is hosted internal to the IT (a Private Cloud) the next question is how to build this cloud. Given the bewildering array of choices, tradeoffs, in the technology decisions involved, each with potentially profound cost consequences, previously documented solutions provide a useful starting point. As a first example, in this section we recount the experience with Ubuntu[†] Enterprise Cloud (UEC) software from Canonical powered by Eucalyptus Systems Inc.

The Ubuntu Enterprise Cloud implementation is a straightforward, small, but conceptually nontrivial cloud encompassing twelve servers and 1.4 terabytes of storage exposed as a compute service and a storage service. The interface is similar to the interface presented by Amazon Web Services[†] and as implemented by Eucalyptus[†].

The architects optimized the architecture for hosting virtual machines (VMs) for a number of logical customers, supporting multi-tenancy, with the associated isolation of compute, storage and network entities.

Other design requirements included self-contained storage and the ability to delegate management of the logical customer's computation and storage resources to the customer in the spirit of a cloud implementing the notion of a self service portal.

The Ubuntu Enterprise Cloud Intel Cloud Builder design, shown in Figure 15.2, is a simple Eucalyptus setup with two computing clusters and a single storage pool. This setup supports up to 128 virtual machines with associated storage. This design supports the implementation of multi-tenancy through the use of the KVM hypervisor for isolating application execution and virtual dynamic VLAN to isolate network traffic.

This configuration allows starting and stopping virtual machines with command line tools and connecting to any virtual machine via a secure shell (SSH). Access keys allow cloud customers to create, start, stop or terminate virtual machine instances independently from other tenants in the same cloud.

Virtual machine instances are stored in the Walrus Storage Service. Walrus is implemented as iSCSI volumes hosted on the Storage Server.

The Cluster Controller capability provides a routing function to allowing hosted virtual machines to access the Internet and the Walrus Storage System, where as the Node Controllers hosting the cloud virtual machines run on Intel Xeon processor 5500 series-based servers.

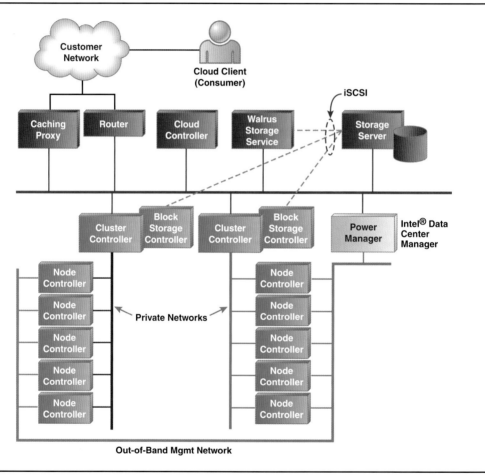

Figure 15.2   Reference Cloud Design Using Eucalyptus

Consistent with the design principles described in the infrastructure overview, and to achieve lowest operational costs for the infrastructure, a homogeneous pool of compute and storage with uniform connectivity is the simplest to manage, easiest to troubleshoot, and is the easiest for adding/removing capacity.

This is not to say that a cloud contains only one kind of server or storage elements. The goal is to create pools of uniform computing storage, and networking resources to allow new pools to be added over time, as new generations of server technology becomes available. This design approach allows for the automation of the placement of workloads, the connection to external networks and storage, and for the delegation of the management of the workloads in the cloud. Because bare-metal access is not required, operating system-based methods for access can be used uniformly.

A set of twelve Intel Xeon processor 5500 series-based servers are connected using a 1-gigabit network to a 1-gigabit top-of-rack switch. The switch was configured to implement the logical architecture shown in Figure 15.3. The configuration is consistent with the goal of not having special purpose servers and no special connections. All servers are configured the same. This uniformity allows for simple replacement, or reassignment of workloads. There were some additional considerations as follows:

■ The *use of the Cluster Controllers* to manage the network traffic is a key component of the multi-tenant design. While the KVM hypervisor provides isolation for the workloads on the servers, the network traffic isolation between virtual machines is implemented by network packet tagging and routing by the Cluster Controllers.

■ The *use of standard Intel® server building blocks* means that any server in the rack can be used for any purpose (Cluster Controller, Walrus Storage Service, etc.).

■ As discussed in the infrastructure overview, the UEC implementation uses a *flat layer 2 network* for reduced cost and to retain the flexibility to assign any workload to any server. This approach is flexible at the cluster level but may create bottlenecks as this design is aggregated at the data center level. Under this consideration, Cloud Controller assigns workloads keeping related workloads together and close to the data.

■ *Walrus* uses local DASD (Direct-Attached Storage Devices) as a convenient and low-cost way to get a large quantity of storage capacity accessible to the clusters. Other implementations could connect the Walrus server to a SAN (Storage Area Network) or NAS (Network Attached Storage) device without using DAS storage.

This implementation provided provisioning, monitoring, virtual machine management capabilities to deliver the required IaaS functionality. The remaining Ubuntu Enterprise Cloud sections provide details on the software implementation, the hardware test bed and observations about cloud service design.

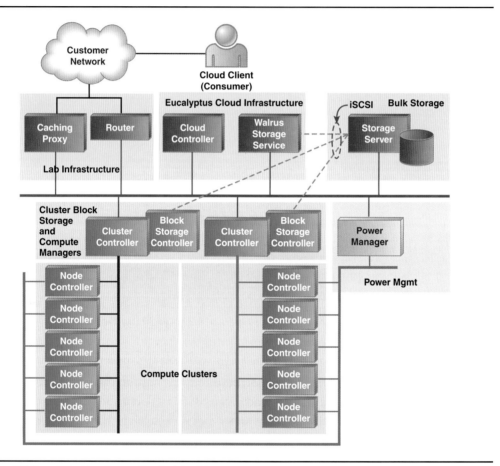

Figure 15.3   The Eucalyptus Logical Architecture

UEC Implementation Overview

Ubuntu Enterprise Cloud is an Open Source software stack complementary to Eucalyptus, allowing for the implementation of a private cloud infrastructure using a combination of Canonical and Eucalyptus Systems technologies. The Ubuntu choice of Eucalyptus was made after a careful study of the cloud market, identifying the Elastic Compute Cloud (EC2), Elastic Block Storage (EBS) and Simple Storage Service (S3) API access to the Amazon Web Services[†] (AWS) as a widely used industry interface, and selecting the best open source component replicating the API.

Eucalyptus Systems provides and supports an Open Source cloud platform under the same AWS API, but in a way that automatically translates the Amazon AMI image format to the image format required by the local hypervisor. Thus, a Eucalyptus cloud is API compatible with AWS regardless of the underlying virtualization technology, providing a functionally equivalent capability.

With Ubuntu 9.04 Server Edition[†], Canonical delivered its first integration of Eucalyptus with its own installation and image repository enhancements for Ubuntu and known as the UEC. This technology preview allowed deployment of an internal cloud supporting the Amazon AWS API uses and with an image format supporting interoperability with AWS.

Ubuntu 9.10 Server Edition was the first release to include Ubuntu Enterprise Cloud and Eucalyptus as a fully supported and maintained option, with a very simple mechanism to deploy it from the installer.

The UEC Cloud Builder design comprises the following elements:

■ The general lab infrastructure including the caching proxy, a router, and power management (Intel® Data Center Manager). The Linux Squid caching proxy was used to accelerate the update process for each of the Ubuntu server instances.

■ The Cloud Controller provides the primary interface point for interacting with the cloud. Commands to create or terminate virtual machines are initiated through the API interface at the Cloud Controller.

■ The Walrus storage service exposes the object store. The object store is used to hold the virtual machine images prior to instantiation and to hold user data.

■ The storage server hosts the actual bulk storage (a 1.4 TB JBOD in this case). Storage is exposed to the Block Storage Controllers and the Walrus Controller as a set of iSCSI volumes.

■ Cluster Controllers managing a collection of Node Controllers and provide the traffic isolation.

■ Block Storage Controllers (SCs) manage dynamic block devices such as EBS to support persistent storage for virtual machines

■ Node Controllers (NCs), servers in the pools that comprise the compute elements of the cloud.

Together, these elements implement the cloud for the purposes of this case study.

Cluster Design Overview

In this design, we have chosen to use a Class C address space for each cluster for simplicity. Therefore, each cluster is limited to 254 machine instances, at one IP address per VM instance. Eucalyptus allows the administrator to configure the degree of multi-tenancy (i.e., the number of VMs hosted per machine) that the cloud should implement. The Eucalyptus installation is set to allocate no more than 16 "small" machine instances per server. Most likely, this configuration will result in underutilization of the server, but it conforms to the published AWS API specification and simplifies the design.

The number of virtual instances allowed per server should be a function of

■ The memory in the system given that memory is partitioned among instances,

■ The performance capability of the system

■ The load generated by the VM instances

To allow for multi-tenancy network security, Eucalyptus supports a Managed VLAN networking mode. This mode transforms Cluster Controller into a router for all virtual machines running in the cluster under it, also known as the availability zone. This allows Cluster Controller to dynamically create tagged VLANs on its private network. This requires each cluster with a dedicated physical switch or segment of a switch to ensure adequate performance.

Additional scaling is possible through the addition of additional 10 cluster nodes on a separate Cluster Controller.

Storage Design Overview

Ubuntu Enterprise Cloud uses two components for storage:

1. Walrus, a functional equivalent of the Amazon S3

2. Block Storage Controller, a functional equivalent of Amazon Elastic Block Storage (EBS).

The Cloud Builder storage design used a single large store for cloud storage. In a commercial implementation this would provide a convenient place for backup and replication. For our purposes, the Storage Server exposed a set of block devices via iSCSI mounted as volumes in the Walrus or Block Storage Controllers.

Each Node Controller uses a local storage device. Local storage is used to hold the virtual machine image at run time and for caching virtual machine instances. When a virtual machine instance is terminated, the storage on the Node Controller local storage is released and is, therefore, not persistent. Therefore, in order to maintain persistent data, either a volume from the Block Storage Manager must be used or the application must be designed to use the Walrus object store.

Managing Images and Instances

Each user of the infrastructure prepares machine images and instantiates as many times as the infrastructure permits. Since the infrastructure is multi-tenant, multiple machine images from multiple users can be running on the same infrastructure within their own virtual environment with the KVM hypervisor, the storage controllers, and the network providing the isolation. Once a user is approved to use the infrastructure, instances can be started or stopped at the request of the user without the need for the operator of the cloud to get involved.

This infrastructure uses the same API as Amazon EC2. From the point of view of the user, this API implements semantics that surprise first-time users:

■ Instances are not persistent across a server hardware reboot

■ Machine images are the only persistent form of a machine

■ Administrators define base architectures for machine image allocation (32 or 64 bits, memory, and so on), and users decide which architecture they need

■ Persistent storage is available through other mechanisms such as Walrus Storage Service or the Block Storage Controller

The usage model requires users to prepare templates of virtual machines, or machine images, to be instantiated as many times as needed. A machine image is a template while a machine instance is an actual instantiation of the template.

The state of a virtual machine instance is lost unless saved to disk. The semantics are similar to switching off a physical server.

Users can instantiate a machine image, modify the running server configuration, and then save the result as a new machine image. This operation is called re-bundling. When an image is instantiated, it is possible to pass it a block of data, which the instance can then use during initialization.

Table 15.1 Eucalyptus Cloud Test Bed System Configuration

System	Processor Configuration	Specifications
Cloud Controller [CLC] Cluster Controller(CC) and Block Storage Controller [CCa and CCb]	Intel® Xeon® Processor X5570	Form Factor: 2U Rack Mount Server
		Processor: Intel® Xeon® processor 5500-based series 2.93 GHz; 2-way x 4 cores = 8 cores
		Memory: 24 GB RAM
		Storage: 300 GB HDD
Node Controller [NC1a-5a and NC1b-NC5b]	Intel Xeon Processor X5570	Form Factor: 1U Rack Mount Server
		Processor: Intel Xeon processor 5500-based series 2.93 GHz; 2-way x 4 cores = 8 cores
		Memory: 24 GB RAM
		Storage: 136 GB HDD
Walrus Storage Service	Intel Xeon Processor X5570	Form Factor: 2U Rack Mount Server
		Processor: Intel Xeon processor 5500-based series 2.93 GHz; 2-way x 4 cores = 8 cores
		Memory: 48 GB RAM
		Storage: 300 GB HDD
Storage Server	Intel Xeon Processor X5570	Form Factor: 5U Tower
		Processor: Intel Xeon processor 5500-based series 2.93 GHz; 2-way x 4 cores = 8 cores
		Memory: 24 GB RAM
		Storage: 6x300 GB HDD (1.4 TB RAID)
Proxy Server	Intel® Xeon® Processor 5140	Form Factor: 1U Rack Mount Server
		Processor: Intel® Xeon® processor 5100-based series 2.33 GHz Xeon; 2-way
		Memory: 4 GB RAM
		Storage: 4x68 GB HDD

A common practice is to create a base operating system image template, such as the freely available yet maintained Ubuntu Server Edition, and to invoke a script customizing instance based on the data passed to it. Since re-bundling can be time consuming, it is common practice to use the capability of Eucalyptus to pass scripts and data to an instance at startup to allow for run time customization of an instance and avoid the need to continually re-bundle.

It should also be noted that Eucalyptus automatically converts Amazon's AMI format to one that is compatible with KVM. This means that the same image can be moved from UEC's private cloud to Amazon's public one without any modifications, thus allowing hybrid cloud designs where instances from one cloud can also be started in Amazon's cloud.

Table 15.1 summarizes the UEC hardware configuration along with UEC roles.

UEC System Design

The UEC design comprises three functional blocks:

- Cloud Controller and infrastructure control
- Storage elements, namely Walrus Storage Service and Block Storage Controllers
- Compute elements, that is, Cluster Controllers and Node Controllers

For this purpose, servers with JBODs are assigned to storage elements with the balance of servers dedicated to the other functions as needed. The network is partitioned into five sub-networks:

- One network for the customer network, the network by which the customer accesses the cloud
- One network internal to the cloud, the network over which all command and control functions occur from the Cloud Controller to the Cluster Controllers
- Two networks, one for each of the clusters
- One network for out of band management access to the servers, this network is used for power on/off control and to implement power management.

For network configuration, we used three Cisco 3750G 1 gigabit switches.

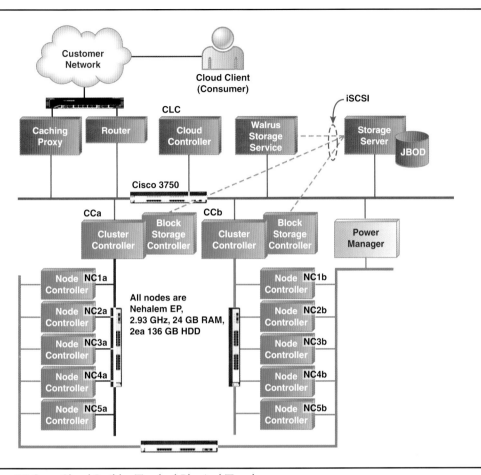

Figure 15.4   Cloud Builder Test bed Physical Topology

All switches were "out of the box;" that is, no VPN configuration with all 48 ports configured onto a single subnet, with a total of three subnets. We used 1-gigabit switches in this design. However, for scalability and bandwidth considerations, 10-gigabit is recommended. This is due to the fact that all data traffic is concentrated in the cloud network due to the high density of virtual machines.

The design reserves static IP addresses for specific nodes: Cloud Controller and Cluster Controllers and the servers in the lab infrastructure.

Node Controllers and virtual machine instances use IP addresses obtained from their respective Cluster Controller.

In the lab infrastructure, we configured a server using Squid to act as a caching proxy server. This was done specifically to speed the process by which the servers were able to get up and running. Since each server is installed with a clean copy of Ubuntu Enterprise Server, each server will need to get updates and packages from the Internet. The Caching Proxy (Squid) server is configured to cache these packages to speed up the process.

Figure 15.4 shows the mapping from UEC logical constructs to the Cloud Builder infrastructure.

User Account Considerations

In Linux[†] (and UNIX[†] in general), there is a superuser named root. The Windows equivalent of root is Administrator.

The superuser can do anything and everything, and hence doing daily work as the superuser can be dangerous. It is possible to inadvertently type an erroneous command and destroy the system. Ideally, a user would carry only the privileges needed for the task at hand. In some cases, this is necessarily root, but most of the time it is a regular user.

By default, the root account password is locked in Ubuntu. This means that you cannot log in as root directly or use the *su* command to become the root user. However, since the root account physically exists it is still possible to run programs with root-level privileges. This is where *sudo* comes in; it allows authorized users to run certain programs as root without having to know the root password.

Power Footprint

Power optimization is an important consideration in cloud implementations. Not only because of the higher density but also because reducing the power footprint of a data center reduces the overall operation cost. One of the simplest forms of power management is to put servers into a lower power mode when idle. UEC implements a simple form of this power management using the Canonical tool *PowerNap*. PowerNap transitions a server into sleep mode when it determines that the server is no longer being utilized.

Conversely, when UEC needs the server, UEC uses Wake-on-LAN to wake up the server so that workloads can subsequently be placed on the server. One of the factors is the time to put the server to sleep and to wake the server. Below are the measurements we made on the servers in our clusters. The time to hibernate and resume will vary depending on CPU, the amount of memory, and disk performance.

Table 15.2 Wakeup Time

Scenario	Time
Time to hibernate the node	1:00 (1 minute)
Time to resume a node from hibernate	3:08
Time to power-on the node using wake-up command (boot OS without hibernation)	2:40

Performance Considerations

The choice of a storage server with DASD versus a SAN was arbitrary, driven by the available Cloud Builder capabilities.

A more fundamental requirement is for the Node Controllers to have access to a shared storage device with sufficient capacity and performance. An NAS device connected to a SAN would have worked just as well. The choice is really driven by design factors such as the back-up strategy, performance, and cost.

Scalability

Consider the case where a service needs to grow over an initial baseline. Below are considerations when increasing the capacity of the cloud. If the reason to increase the size of the cloud is to get more compute power, then adding servers to the existing clusters will suffice. If the need is for improved availability, then more clusters are needed, which in turn, creates new availability zones. With the additional availability zones, applications can be spread out so that the failure of a Cluster Controller or a switch will not impact the application.

Increasing the scale of the cloud may have other side effects as well. Below are some factors to consider as the size of the cloud is increased.

Network Capacity

When scaling network capacity,

■ As additional applications are added, the network traffic will increase. The increase will come not only from the application traffic but also for any storage activities.

■ Network traffic will increase if there is a higher load from the applications carrying out administrative and housekeeping functions such as disaster recovery and data replication.

Cloud Topology

Consider how the cluster and node topology will influence robustness and performance of the cloud solution. Also consider how network faults will impact the user-perceived performance of the cloud. Note that the failure of a switch not only breaks the network connections but can create islands, leaving a segment of the network isolated for a period of time.

■ Storage topology is also a key consideration as a separate data network and storage solution can limit scale benefits. It is important to look at the performance demands placed on Block Storage Controllers and the networks that connect to them.

■ Consider the case of needing to add support for 1,000 virtual machines to the cloud. Eucalyptus supports up to eight clusters in a single cloud. Based on analysis of workloads, one might come to a design point where we average 16 "small" VM instances per server. Note that many servers will have more VM instances based on server performance and workload demands. Using the above average, this would mean that we need:

  – 1000/16 = 63 Node Controllers (that is, servers) total in the cloud to support the incremental 1,000 virtual machines.

  – Assuming we have the maximum number of clusters (eight) then we have eight Node Controllers per cluster.

  – Alternatively, assuming we stay with the Class C IP address space, we are limited to 10 Node Controllers per cluster, we would need seven clusters.

Would the Use of SSD Drives Improve Performance?

Using SSDs as hard disk replacements can improve performance in a cloud. However, to get the best use of the SSDs, there are two locations in the cloud that can especially benefit.

■ The Node Controllers use the local disk to cache virtual machine images. Therefore, if many copies of the same instance will be run on the same node, using an SSD as the storage device for a Node Controller can greatly speed up the loading of VMs.

■ The Walrus Storage Service is an object store. This means that for each request for an object, the location of the object must be determined from the provided key. This lookup operation is done frequently from a metadata store. Using SSDs to hold this metadata store can greatly improve the performance for the process of locating the object.

The Enomaly Case Study

From the Enomaly perspective, the ideas and principles of the cloud are of great interest in the industry because of its agility benefits and cost savings. In recent years, many companies have set up cloud infrastructures accessible over the public Internet and are now offering services that customers can utilize to host their applications. Typical cloud services can be classified as Infrastructure-as-a-Service (IaaS), Platform-as-a-Service (PaaS) and Software-as-a-Service (SaaS).

For preexisting workloads, for workloads unique to an organization, and those workloads that need to remain under close control of an organization, using an IaaS structure provides the best choice. To support and host an IaaS cloud service, whether as a revenue-producing customer facing service (a public cloud) or internal to an organization behind corporate firewall (a private cloud), the natural question would be what are the steps to build this cloud.

Given the many choices, tradeoffs, and decisions, it is clear that being able to build on a known and understood starting point is key. In this section we describe the experience of building a cloud with Enomaly's Elastic Computing Platform[†] (ECP), Service Provider Edition (SPE) on top of the Intel Cloud Builder infrastructure.

Design Principles

The Enomaly cloud implementation shares design principles similar to those covered under the UEC implementation, including using servers as fungible resources, a flat layer-2 network architecture and virtualization for logical isolation.

Regarding networking, Enomaly ECP SPE supports much more sophisticated network topologies not deployed for the purpose of this test bed.

For the purposes of this exercise, the Xen Hypervisor was used to provide isolation for the workloads on the servers, and network traffic was segregated by Enomaly ECP SPE using network packet tagging (VLAN) and routing. Xen is one of several hypervisors supported by Enomaly ECP SPE, in addition to KVM and VMware.

An NFS (Network File Server) server was used in combination with Direct Attached Storage Devices as a convenient and low cost way to provide storage accessible to the clusters. Enomaly ECP SPE also supports the use of sophisticated storage architectures such as cluster file systems and SAN, and can avoid the use of node-local storage.

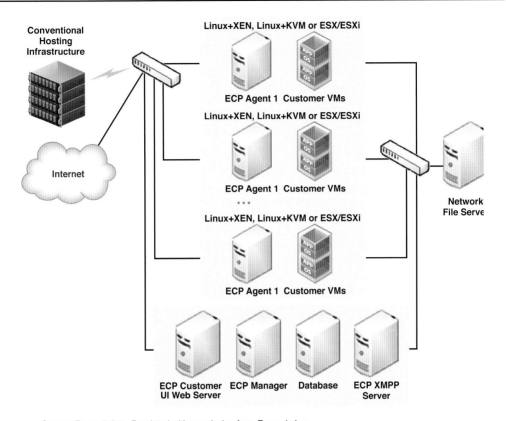

Source: Enomaly Inc . Reprinted with permission from Enomaly Inc .

Figure 15.5 Basic Architecture Deployment for Enomaly ECP† SPE.

ECP Logical Architecture Configuration

Figure 15.5 shows the logical architecture of the Enomaly ECP SPE deployment for the case study. This is a basic architecture for Enomaly ECP SPE deployment, suitable for small-scale test beds. The approach used was to create a compute pool with access to a common storage pool and access point.

Figure 15.6 shows more sophisticated logical architectures also supported by Enomaly ECP SPE. This is provided for reference only, and was not employed in our test bed.

Enomaly's SPE offering represents a complete *Cloud in a Box* solution, designed to meet the requirements of carriers, service providers and hosting providers offering revenue-generating Infrastructure-on-demand (IaaS) cloud computing services to their customers quickly and easily, with a compelling and highly differentiated feature set.

ECP/SPE features include

■ Fully multi-tenant, carrier-class cloud service platform

■ Detailed resource metering and accounting

■ Simple but powerful customer self-service portal with provisions for customer branding and internationalization

■ High availability (HA) capability for customer workloads

■ Strong security capabilities (plus an additional High Assurance feature set available in Enomaly ECP, High Assurance Edition)

■ Scale-up as well as scale-out capability

■ Instant startup of hot spare servers

■ Public and private (per-customer) VLAN security

■ Integrated Application Store

■ Powerful automation APIs comprising both customer-facing APIs and administrative APIs

■ Intelligent and dynamic workload provisioning and orchestration

■ Flexible integration with billing, provisioning, and operational monitoring systems

■ Ability to leverage Enomaly's robust provisioning and orchestration engines, the earlier open source versions of which are already deployed by 15,000 organizations around the world.

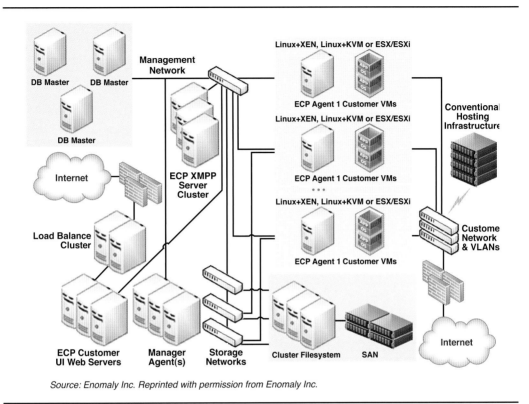

Source: Enomaly Inc. Reprinted with permission from Enomaly Inc.

Figure 15.6 Carrier-Grade Deployment Architecture for Enomaly ECP†, Service Provider Edition.

ECP Architectural Principles and Design Philosophy

The Enomaly Elastic Computing Platform is a complete end-to-end platform enabling a telecommunications company or a service provider such as a hosting company to deliver an IaaS offering to its customers. Enomaly ECP is based on a robust distributed architecture. ECP applies the key attributes of the Internet cloud to the service provider datacenter; like the Internet, Enomaly ECP uses a decentralized command and control structure model and can therefore continue to operate in the event of critical failures. The ECP system architecture provides an optimal degree of fault-tolerance, backward and forward application compatibility, extensibility, reliability, maintainability, availability, serviceability, usability, and security.

Modular and Composable Scalable Design

ECP comprises a large number of modular and composable components. Once a user designs a virtual architecture for a specific application, that virtual architecture can be put in place by running and interconnecting the modules requested by the application. This enables ECP to operate efficiently in a wide range of application deployments.

Decentralization

ECP achieves high levels of reliability and reaches massive scale through an architecture patterned on that of the Internet itself, in which multiple redundant components interoperate without a single central point of coordination.

In order to build scalable cloud platforms, capable of operating effectively at 1,000-node and even 100,000-node and million-node scale, it is essential to leverage loosely-coupled and decentralized architectures.

The cloud must run like a decentralized organism, without a single person or organization managing it. Like the Internet, it should allow 99 percent of its day-to-day operations to be coordinated without a central authority. Applications deployed on a cloud managed in this fashion are more adaptive and fault tolerant because single points of failure are reduced or eliminated.

Over-Subscription

To be cost-effective, a carrier-class IaaS platform must be capable of efficiently provisioning resources for both peak and low-volume usage periods while providing an agreed upon minimum service standard.

Enomaly's ECP approach to this challenge is based on two essential principles: oversubscription and class-of-service-based resource quota management, which together enable powerful capacity control.

In a public cloud infrastructure, an oversubscription model depends on the ratio of allocated resources to the maximum peak usage levels, the frequency and volume of peak usage, and the minimum service level agreement. The key is to manage resources around the standard deviation from the normal usage benchmarks while simultaneously guaranteeing a particular quality-of-service for each customer. Enomaly's ECP quota system manages predetermined levels of deviation across a specified resource pool serving a population of customers. Service providers can oversubscribe their environments, while remaining protected from intentional or inadvertent overuse and misuse, and while allowing for a variety of pricing and costing schemes to be implemented using a model that incorporates usage tiers, quality-of service tiers, and the ability to provision additional resources dynamically as desired.

Unified Access to Heterogeneous Resources

Enomaly ECP provides unified access mechanisms with common management points for heterogeneous collections of resources, including multiple virtual server platforms, multiple hypervisors and large numbers of compute nodes potentially spanning multiple data centers. All of ECP's interfaces, namely, the administrative user interface, the fully brandable customer self-service interface, and the end-user and administrative REST APIs, can simultaneously manage diverse resources distributed across multiple geographic locations.

Command and Control Architecture of Enomaly ECP

ECP provides a lightweight publish/subscribe messaging bus for command and control operations between the ECP Agent software controlling each compute node and the ECP Manager cluster. This scalable message bus is based on the Extensible Messaging and Presence Protocol (XMPP). XMPP is an open technology for real-time communication which is well-suited to the lightweight middleware role. XMPP runs on standard HTTP (TCP port 80) and HTTPS (TCP port 443) ports allowing connections across most firewalls.

Our implementation supports all Enomaly ECP SPE features including provisioning, monitoring, virtual machine management and high availability required to deliver IaaS functionality. The following sections will provide details on the software implementation, the hardware test bed, the test cases executed, and things to consider when designing a cloud.

Hardware Description

The physical architecture for the Intel Cloud Builder instantiation of Enomaly ECP is shown in Figure 15.7.

The cloud implementation consists of five Intel Xeon processor 5500 series-based servers exposed as a compute service. Enomaly ECP SPE does not differentiate between compute and storage pools and offers a very simple mechanism to build and manage the cloud. Enomaly ECP SPE supports multi-tenancy, enabling our infrastructure to host virtual machines belonging to different customers, along with isolation of storage and network. Enomaly ECP SPE provides a very powerful yet simple portal interface through which we demonstrate the ease of establishing an IaaS with connected storage.

The Cloud Builder design consists of one cluster of compute capacity and a single storage pool. There is no specific upper limit on the number of virtual machines that can be provisioned using Enomaly ECP SPE, enabling the support very large clouds with many thousands of servers in more complex architectures than the one implemented here.

Depending on the end user resource requirements, the number of virtual machines allowed per server can be allocated as needed. The cloud setup has a total of 160 gigabyte RAM across five nodes. Since the hypervisors or virtual machine monitors occupy approximately 500 megabytes, the test bed can support up to $5 - 31 = 155$ virtual machines with the five server nodes in the Cloud Builder environment with 1 gigabyte of RAM provided to each virtual machine. When designing cloud configurations for lighter weight computing resources, each virtual machine can be assigned less than 1 gigabyte of RAM, and the specific allotment can be customized.

The Enomaly ECP SPE's portal interface, accessible through any modern browser, allows for the provisioning of virtual machines for multiple customers. It also allows connecting to these machines using remote connection protocols such as Remote Desktop Protocol (RDP) and Virtual Network Computing (VNC). Traffic for each customer is isolated from all of the other customers using VLAN packet tagging.

The Cloud Builder storage for the virtual image repository was provided using the Network File System (NFS) and the virtual machine instances reside on the local disk of the node on which the virtual machine was running. NFS was chosen because of ease of use and quick deployment.

For production purposes and in parallel or cluster configurations, we recommend more robust storage architecture be used. Some options to consider include Cluster File System solutions such as GFS, available with major Linux distributions, and supported by Red Hat Inc., which may be combined with iSCSI or Fibre Channel SAN storage from any of a large number of vendors.

Simpler solutions based on NAS technologies, as well as simpler server-based storage solutions supplemented with high performance or bonded network links are also feasible, depending on the scale of the cloud deployment.

Network traffic is managed by a virtualized Enomaly ECP SPE node.

A common cause of system bottlenecks is the sheer network traffic itself. In our test bed, we used 10-gigabit Ethernet to help address the growing bandwidth needs of a cloud computing environment.

Enomaly ECP Manager Agents and Enomaly ECP Node Agents were implemented on Intel Xeon processor 5500 series-based servers.

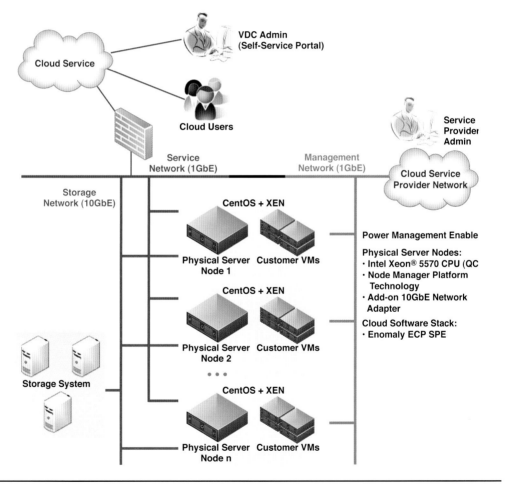

Figure 15.7 Tested Physical Architecture

The Cloud Builder network design is partitioned into four functional blocks: Infrastructure control for managing the cloud, storage, network and compute elements for hosting cloud based services. Table 15.3 describes in detail on how we distributed the servers to handle the various functional blocks.

Furthermore, the network was partitioned for isolation, security and QoS requirements:

■ An external customer network for end customer accessing the cloud via a self service portal

■ An internal management network over which all command and control functions are managed

■ An internal private network for managing data from the virtual machines hosted on the compute nodes

The implementation uses two Cisco 3750G[†] 1-gigabit switches and one Extreme Networks Summit[†] X650-24t 10-gigabit switch for the storage network. All switches were had all the 48 ports configured onto a single subnet, with no VPN and a total of three subnets.

The Cloud Builder design reserves static IP addresses for nodes that participate in hosting compute and storage: ECP-master, ECP01, ECP02, ECP03, ECP04, and ECPstorage.

Table 15.3 User Cloud Test Bed System Configuration

System	Processor Configuration	Other Info
1 ECP* Master and 4 ECP Agent Nodes	Intel® Xeon® Processor X5570	Form Factor: 1U Rack Mount Server
		Processor: Intel® Xeon® processor 5500-based series 2.93 GHz; 2-way x 4 cores = 8 cores
		Memory: 32 GB RAM
		Storage: 4 x 500 GB HDD SATA2
1 Storage server	Intel® Xeon® Processor E5345	Form Factor: 2U Tower Server
		Processor: Intel® Xeon® processor 5300-based series 2.33 GHz; 2-way x 4 cores = 8 cores
		Memory: 16 GB RAM
		local Storage: 1x160 GB HDD SATA
		Expansion storage: 10 x 160GB SDD
1 Proxy server	Intel® Xeon® Processor	Form Factor: 1U Rack Mount Server
		Processor: Intel® Xeon® processor based
		Memory: 2 GB RAM
		Storage: 2x160 GB HDD SATA
Network	Summit* X650-24t	Ports: 24x 10GBASE-T ports (port 1# ~ 24#); 4x 1000BASE-X (SFP) ports (port 25# ~
		28#); 2x SummitStack ports (shared with last 2x 10GBASE-T ports/dedicated 10 Gbps
		without auto-negotiation)
		VLAN: 802.1Q; Port-based and tag-based VLAN

An additional server was configured to act as a caching proxy server. This was done specifically to speed the process by which the servers were able to get up and running. Since each server is installed with a clean copy of Enomaly ECP SPE, each server will need to get updates and packages from the Internet. The Caching Proxy server is configured to cache these packages to speed up the process.

Planning Considerations

Here are a number of planning considerations. Their priority depends on the circumstances of a particular deployment.

- The scalability of the solution is heavily impacted by:
  - Network technology such as the use of 10-gigabit switches and network architecture
  - Selected storage architecture
  - Choice of server hardware for compute nodes and management nodes
- Another consideration is the use of solid-state drives (SSDs) as hard disk replacements, since SSDs can significantly improve the performance in a cloud.
- Network Technology Architecture. Enomaly ECP SPE supports several network technology architectures.
- For this test bed we selected a very simple network topology. The selection made for this test bed performed well for our purposes, but more advanced technologies and architectures, such as 10-gigabit Ethernet, channel bonding technologies, and highly segmented network architectures will be more suitable for production deployments.
- Storage Architecture. Enomaly ECP SPE supports several storage architectures. For this test bed we selected the simplest option, a single NFS. This performed acceptably for our purposes, but more advanced architectures are recommended for production deployments.
- Hardware Considerations. A full discussion of processor and overall server performance considerations is beyond the scope of this paper. However, it is important to note that the performance of virtual machines running on the cloud platform is heavily influenced by factors of processor architecture, and specific feature sets available in the processor such as Intel® VT-d. The use of high-performance server processors equipped with virtualization and I/O support feature sets, such as the Intel® Xeon® processor 5500 series, and the Intel Xeon processor 5600 series, is strongly recommended. For more details on Intel® Virtualization technologies please refer to [11]. Solid-State Drives

- The performance of storage nodes (and compute nodes when local storage is utilized), as well as the overall power consumption of the cloud, may be favorably impacted by the use of SSDs. This was not specifically tested within our exercise.

- Security Considerations. Security is a key consideration in the selection and management of IaaS. Regarding security, a complete discussion of best practices for cloud security, from the perspective of both the Service Provider and the end-user organization, is beyond the scope of this document. However, the following points should be considered:

  - Established best practices for host security in a conventional physical host context (such as password management, patch management, server hardening, and anti-malware) should be applied equally to virtual hosts operating on an IaaS platform.

  - IaaS platforms such as Enomaly ECP provide full isolation between virtual servers, by employing full hardware-assisted virtualization. This provides each virtual server with its virtual hardware, its own private operating system instance, and so on. This contrasts with cloud platforms based on "domains" or "containers," in which some virtual hardware and some operating system components are shared between virtual hosts, which creates additional avenues of attack.

  - Enomaly ECP can further segregate the virtual hosts belonging to different customers at the level of the network, isolating the network traffic of each customer into one or more private VLANs.

  - Additionally, to meet the highest security requirements, Enomaly provides a High Assurance Edition (HAE) of the Enomaly ECP platform. Enomaly ECP High Assurance Edition leverages the Intel® Trusted Execution Technology (Intel® TXT) capabilities of selected Intel processors to deliver an IaaS environment that is strongly protected against hacking, tampering, and unauthorized administrative changes.

The Univa UD Case Study

In this section we describe architectural and implementation details of a Private Multi-Cloud (PMC), a prototype built jointly by Intel and Univa to demonstrate an internal cloud environment consisting of multiple Virtual Data Centers (VDCs). In addition to standard functionality expected from any cloud system, such as provisioning and destroying virtual machines as needed, the Univa Cloud Builder prototype offers its users a complete set of tools to automate management of their VDCs, including workload management software, monitoring capabilities, and a policy engine.

The discussion in this section illustrates the cloud functionality with several real-world use cases, such as policy-based application scale-out/scale-in and automated VDC reconfiguration based on type of user workload running in the cloud.

Typical Infrastructure as a Service (IaaS) providers like Amazon, EC2, or Rackspace offer their clients on-demand network access to a shared pool of configurable computing and storage resources. Likewise, IT organizations for large enterprises are cloud-enabling their internal infrastructure to create an on-demand resource pool to serve the computing needs of multiple departments or divisions. The most obvious benefits in each case are flexibility and cost savings, as users can quickly gain access to precisely the resources they need without having to worry about the physical infrastructure. In addition, IT organizations can maximize their investments in expensive computing and storage resources.

Even though cloud compute resources can usually be provisioned and released with only minimal effort, users still need to install, configure and manage their own software applications. Depending on the infrastructure complexity and number of machines needed, software and application management can represent a significant burden. In addition, cloud users whose compute resource requirements frequently change are faced with having to make a decision on whether to constantly monitor usage of their servers and make the necessary adjustments manually, or to try to anticipate and plan for peak server usage periods.

Neither option is ideal, as each involves tradeoffs between higher cloud resource costs versus increased effort associated with configuration and monitoring of cloud servers.

Ideally, IaaS providers and internal IT organizations would not only provide their end users with easy access to bare compute and storage resources, but would also provide them with software tools to simplify and automate management of those resources to the greatest extent possible. This is our primary motivation for building a Private Multi-Cloud prototype that can manage an environment of multiple clouds by serving as a Virtual Data Center management system. Since each VDC itself is a private cloud, the PMC prototype can be viewed as meta-cloud or "cloud of clouds."

Given the fact that we placed emphasis on being able to host VDCs for a number of logical customers or end user groups, multi-tenancy (the isolation of compute, storage and network resources) was one of our primary requirements. Other design requirements included self-contained storage and the ability to provide VDC resource management functionality via the self-service portal, command line tools, and APIs.

The Private Multi-Cloud prototype software components include Univa's UniPortal[†], Reliance[†] and UniCloud[†1].

- *UniPortal* is a self-service Web-based portal for submitting and monitoring cloud management requests and user workload. It is based on NICE's EnginFrame application portal.

- *Reliance* provides infrastructure and application governance services. It plugs into an existing infrastructure and leverages monitoring and management systems to analyze performance issues, and then automatically provisions physical and virtual resources as needed to satisfy performance requirements or service level agreements (SLAs). Reliance can also proactively provision resources based on anticipated issues weighed against customer expectations to ensure SLA violations are avoided and not just reacted to.

- *UniCloud* is a cloud management software product that delivers unique capabilities for enabling private, public and hybrid cloud computing environments. With UniCloud, companies can build their own internal private cloud, or can use public cloud services to supplement internal processing demand via a hybrid or fully outsourced cloud.

---

1   Univa product documentation:
     http://www.univaud.com/hpc/products/uniportal.php
     http://www.univaud.com/hpc/products/reliance.php
     http://www.univaud.com/hpc/products/unicloud.php

The system, as shown in Figure 15.8, supports two VDCs, each having a pool of physical servers on their own VLAN. The administrator of an individual VDC will be a data center owner for a specific department or division in the case of an internal IT organization's private cloud, or a single end customer in the case of a service provider cloud.

The PMC self-service portal offers VDC administrators the ability to bootstrap their VDCs (that is, start VDC head node) with a touch of a button. Also, VDC administrators have a choice of provisioning physical servers from bare metal either as compute nodes or as hypervisors.

Hypervisor nodes are used for instantiating and running virtual machines as VDC compute nodes. This setup provides users with maximum flexibility with respect to configuring their VDCs in the manner most appropriate for running their applications and user workload.

In addition, each VDC head node comes with a fully functional UniCloud installation, which provides cloud management tools, workload management software, simple policy engine, and other important features.

In the following sections we present the Private Multi-Cloud architecture and implementation details. We outline various use cases including policy-based application scale-out/scale-in and automatic VDC reconfiguration based on the type of workload running in the cloud. We also discuss possible future work and vision for the Univa software products.

Multi-Cloud Usage Scenarios

As described above, there are two primary scenarios for using a private multi-cloud:

■ A cloud service provider, such as a managed service provider, a telecom or company. In this case, the PMC owner is the service provider and their customers or end user groups who access the Virtual Data Centers (VDCs) contained in the PMC are the service provider's client companies.

■ An IT organization for a single, large enterprise or business. In this case the PMC owner is the IT organization and their customers or end user groups who access the Virtual Data Centers (VDCs) contained in the PMC are logical groups of users such as divisions or departments.

In both cases, the computing environment must be separated into distinct environments for each customer yet must be able to be managed at a high level, across each environment, by a single entity. Thus, a "cloud of clouds" must be created where each sub-cloud functions distinctly but can be managed at a meta-cloud layer.

PMC Implementation Overview

As illustrated in Figure 15.8, the Private Multi-Cloud (PMC) prototype relies on several infrastructure services, each running on its own machine. UniPortal (self-service portal) sends VDC management requests to Reliance (infrastructure and application service governor), which routes those requests to appropriate VDC head nodes running UniCloud software.

Note that there are three types of user roles in the PMC prototype:

■ The PMC administrator has the ability to create or delete VDC administrator accounts via UniPortal.

■ The VDC administrator has the ability to manage the VDC using UniPortal (bootstrap/shutdown VDC, provision/delete VDC nodes) or by logging into the VDC head node as root.

■ The VDC user can utilize VDC resources by logging into the VDC head node.

Microsoft[†] Active Directory keeps track of both PMC/VDC administrator accounts, while UniCloud manages VDC user accounts.

VDC head nodes are virtual machines hosted on the main PMC hypervisor (VMware ESX Server) and serve as both VDC management and login nodes. They have two network interfaces: the public interface allows administrator and user login via SSH, while the private interface is connected to the VDC network and is used for provisioning other VDC nodes. Each Virtual Data Center managed by the Private Multi-Cloud is assigned its own VLAN. This provides support for isolation of compute, storage and network resources that belong to a given VDC.

Head nodes have a "clean-state" snapshot that is used for bootstrapping the corresponding VDCs. Once the head node is up, VDC administrators can request provisioning of their (bare metal) physical servers either as compute nodes or as hypervisors. Provisioning requests trigger powering on bare metal servers via IPMI interfaces as well as invoking UniCloud command that controls the provisioning process. Note that machines must be configured to boot via PXE in order to be discovered and configured by UniCloud.

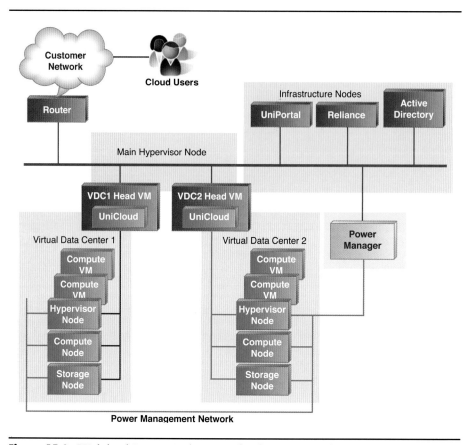

Figure 15.8. High level System Architecture for the Private Multi-Cloud prototype.

Provided that they already have at least one hypervisor node in their VDC, administrators can also request adding new virtual machines as VDC compute nodes. Similar to the provisioning of physical servers from bare metal, virtual machines are provisioned by installing the operating system into an empty image. All virtual machine images are stored on a VDC NFS-based storage server, which enables virtual machine recovery in case of hypervisor hardware failures. Note that although our prototype portal implementation offers no choices for virtual machine configuration, administrators can nevertheless modify virtual machine characteristics such as memory and number of virtual CPUs, by editing UniCloud configuration files.

Operating System Choices

We selected 64-bit Oracle Enterprise Linux (OEL) 5.4 for running both UniPortal and Reliance infrastructure machines. For simplicity, the same operating system was also used for provisioning VDC storage and physical/ virtual compute nodes, even though UniCloud supports a number of other Red Hat Enterprise Linux (RHEL) distributions. The remaining two infrastructure nodes, those used for Active Directory and VMware vCenter Server, were provisioned with 64-bit Microsoft Windows Server 2003.

VDC hypervisors used Oracle VM Server 2.2. On the other hand, the main PMC hypervisor node was running VMware ESX Server 4.0.1. These selections were driven by the current hypervisor support in UniCloud and Reliance, respectively.

System Functionality

The PMC prototype provides the following capabilities:

- ■ VDCs isolated in the same physical LAN for both performance and user access.

- ■ VDC head nodes accessible from outside via SSH.

- ■ Administrator portal (UniPortal) delivers self-contained compute and storage resource pools.

- ■ Reliance provides PMC infrastructure management, as well as VDC application governance services

- ■ UniCloud provides internal VDC management.

UniPortal offers the following capabilities:

- ■ Administrator account management by utilizing PMC Active Directory (PMC administrators can create/delete VDC administrator accounts)

- ■ VDC administrators can bootstrap their VDC by installing and configuring virtual machine (VM) that serves as UniCloud head node

- ■ Allows VDC administrators to add physical machines (bare metal servers) to their VDC by provisioning them either as compute nodes, or as storage nodes, or as VDC hypervisors

- VDC administrators can provision additional compute virtual machines on their hypervisors
- VDC administrators can remove (physical or virtual) machines from their VDC
- VDC administrators can shut down their VDC by shutting down their UniCloud head node

Reliance provides the following capabilities:

- PMC resource management (keeps track of machine availability and responds to node management requests made by VDC administrators on UniPortal)
- Executes workflows responsible for VDC head node installation (VDC bootstrapping)
- Executes workflows for adding (removing) physical or virtual machines to (from) VDC
- Executes workflows responsible for VDC shutdown and freeing up of its resources (for example, shutting down all physical machines that were used by the VDC)
- Provides support for VDC application scale-out using its rule management framework (each VDC has its own application rules)

Finally, UniCloud provides the following capabilities:

- VDC administrators have access to a full set of command line tools and Python APIs to configure and manage their VDC.
- Virtual/physical machine provisioning, including hypervisor provisioning (Oracle VM Server is used as VDC hypervisor)
- Node management
- VDC user account management
- Application configuration
- Package management
- Cluster configuration
- Cluster updates

- Network management (VDC firewall, IP management, DNS)
- Software kits (including workload management, monitoring, HPC tools, and so on)
- Imaging tools
- Simple Policy Engine (can be used, for example, for automated migration of VMs to vacate selected hypervisor in case hypervisor machine needs to be re-provisioned as compute node)

All of the functionality listed above was exercised during the Cloud Builder prototype testing.

Hardware Mapping

Here are some considerations for mapping the physical infrastructure described at the beginning of the chapter to Univa software capabilities:

Some of the other design considerations are given below:

- The 1-gigabit network was used for power management of the physical VDC nodes. The cloud management functions power-down or power-up servers using Intelligent Platform Management Interface (IPMI) commands over this network.

- The 10-gigabit network was used for cloud management (provisioning or de-provisioning) of cloud resources and carries all the cloud user (administrative and application) traffic.

- Similar to the other case studies, the Univa Cloud Builder instance uses a flat layer-2 network to reduce the implementation cost and to retain the flexibility to assign any workload to any server. This approach is flexible at the VDC level but may create bottlenecks as this design is aggregated at the data center level. Paying attention to compute and data locality can help in alleviating these bottlenecks.

- VDC resources (servers and storage) are assigned statically.

- Network traffic isolation between VDCs is implemented by segmented VLANs and routing traffic through the VDC head node which implements a user-configured firewall.

■ The use of Intel server building blocks means that any server in the rack can be used for any purpose.

■ We chose to implement local direct-attached storage (DAS). This was merely a convenient and low cost way to get a large quantity of storage capacity accessible to the VDCs. Other implementations could connect the VDC to a SAN (Storage Area Network) or NAS (Network Attached Storage) device and not require local DAS storage.

The above considerations are typical of a cloud data center design: highly efficient servers, flat layer 2 networks, consolidated storage, and highly virtualized. These attributes provide for the cost effective operation and support a highly automated infrastructure.

Table 15.4 captures the roles assigned to servers in the mix.

Table 15.4 Server Roles

System	Processor Configuration	Specifications
Infrastructure Nodes Main Hypervisor nodes	Intel ®Xeon® Processor X5570 on Intel ® Server Board S5520UR	OEM: Intel server codename Urbanna
		Form Factor: 2U Rack Mount Server
		Processor: Nehalem EP; 2.93GHz; 2-way x 4 cores = 8 cores
		Memory: 24GB RAM
		Storage: 300GB HDD
		Nehalem-EP Product Information …
		http://ark.intel.com/ProductCollection.aspx?codeName=33163
		Intel® Xeon® Processor 5000 Series product support
		http://www.intel.com/support/processors/xeon5k/
8 Compute nodes	Intel ®Xeon® Processor X5570 on Intel ® Server Board S5500WBV	OEM: Intel server codename Willowbrook
		Form Factor: 1U Rack Mount Server
		Processor: Nehalem EP; 2.93GHz; 2-way x 4 cores = 8 cores
		Memory: 24GB RAM
		Storage: 136GB HDD
2 Compute Nodes	Intel ®Xeon® Processor X5667 on Intel ® Server Board S5500WBV	OEM: Intel server codename Willowbrook
		Form Factor: 1U Rack Mount Server
		Processor: Westmere EP; 3.06GHz; 2-way x 6 cores = 12 cores
		Memory: 24GB RAM
		Storage: 136GB HDD
Storage Servers	Intel ®Xeon® Processor X5570 on intel ® Server Board S5520HC	Form Factor: 5U Tower
		Processor: 2.93GHz Nehalem EP; 2-way x 4 cores = 8 cores
		Memory: 24GB RAM
		Storage: JBOD 6x300GB HDD configured as 1.4 TB RAID

The test bed was configured to support two Virtual Data Centers: VDC 1 and VDC 2. We partitioned the system into three functional blocks as shown in Figure 15.9.

3. Infrastructure management functions (UniPortal, Reliance, Active directory)
4. Main Hypervisor node (UniCloud, vCenter Server)
5. Virtual Data Centers (compute nodes, hypervisor nodes, storage elements).

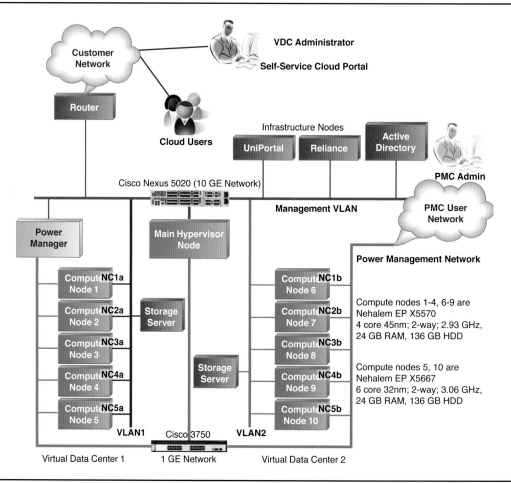

Figure 15.9   Mapping Univa software to the Cloud Builder infrastructure.

As in the other case studies, the server types listed above were allocated such that the servers with JBODs were used in the storage elements, and all other servers were used as needed.

We partitioned network in the following way:

■ 10-gigabit network using Cisco† Nexus 5020 10-gigabit switches segmented into 3 port based VLANs with accompanying subnets:

  – Management VLAN connecting Infrastructure nodes, main hypervisor node. This is also the means by which the customer accesses their VDC through the head node.

  – VLAN for VDC1

  – VLAN for VDC2

■ The 1-gigabit power management network was implemented using Cisco 3750G 1-gigabit switch. This network is internal to the Cloud and only accessible by the PMC customer (the Cloud service provider or internal IT department). This is the network over which all server power control functions occur (power on/off control and power management). The switch was "out of the box" (no VLAN configuration).

To address scalability and bandwidth considerations, 10-gigabit is recommended to support the expected high traffic in the cloud network.

Additional Infrastructure Considerations

Regarding storage, as mentioned earlier, for simplicity and cost effectiveness our prototype uses DASD for storing virtual machine images. The PMC software components do not impose any restrictions with respect to using any particular storage technology. When designing production deployment, the choice to use a SAN (Storage Area Network) or NAS (Network Attached Storage) device would be driven by factors like desired performance, cost, anticipated customer usage, and so on.

Scalability is one of the prime motivations for deploying clouds. The solution as presented in this paper can scale both horizontally (adding new Virtual Data Centers) and vertically (increasing the size of a VDC). The limits in both directions are primarily the limits on network and storage capability.

Scaling a VDC vertically will allow the VDC administrator to add new physical and virtual compute nodes to support increased customer demand. Without taking into account any application storage requirements, the VDC storage needs are directly related to the number of virtual nodes, so that a flexible and powerful storage infrastructure is critical.

Fast read and write access to the storage network is equally critical. As the number of virtual nodes being provisioned, started or stopped simultaneously grows, so too grows the maximum bandwidth required to access the storage in order to provide provisioning, startup, or shutdown times that are acceptable from the end user viewpoint.

Support for larger number of VDCs as part of a strategy for horizontal scalability creates additional challenges. Isolation of customers in the PMC prototype solution is done by isolation of network and VLAN configuration. With theoretical limit of 4096 VLANs on a single trunk, it is obvious that scaling VDCs beyond this number requires physical segmentation to keep network security strong in a production deployment.

Furthermore, the prototype infrastructure metadata (customer configuration and operational parameters) uses some artificial naming conventions to keep things simple for demonstration purposes. Real production deployment would not rely on those conventions and would require additional customer metadata derived from the service provide or enterprise CRM systems or other external data sources.

Acknowledgments

The work recounted in this chapter represents the collaborative contributions from many teams across a number of companies. We have made an effort to identify contributors. Unfortunately, in spite of our effort, the list may not be all-inclusive. In alphabetic order by company: Canonical: Dustin Kirkland, Nicolas Barcet. Enomaly: Pat Wendorf, Reuven Cohen, Richard Reiner. Eucalyptus Systems: Daniel Nurmi, Rich Wolski. Intel: Aamir Yunus, Billy Cox, Enrique Castro-Leon, Kamal Natesan, Paul Guermonprez, Rekha Raghu, Trevor Cooper. Univa: Mary Bass, Sinisa Veseli.

Chapter 16

Virtual Machine Live Migration across Heterogeneous Systems

Contributed by Sudhir Bangalore and Kamal Natesan

Cloud computing offers the promise of much greater efficiency, flexibility and more simplified data centers, but realization of these benefits will require interoperable, multi-vendor solutions that embrace standards and seamlessly support servers (hosts) based on different generations of processors for a key usage model called live migration. A highly available private cloud enables the live migration of running virtual servers from one physical server to another with zero downtime, continuous service availability, and complete transaction integrity. In today's virtualized data centers, live migration is a required technology for building an agile and dynamic data center based on server virtualization. It has not been possible, however, to perform successful live migration between servers based on different generations of processors, each with different instruction sets. This limited the ability to implement large resource pools, creating islands of servers and hindering the implementation of advanced data center capabilities.

Intel® Virtualization Technology (Intel® VT) FlexMigration and VMware's† Enhanced VMotion† are designed to overcome this limitation by enabling all servers to expose the same instruction set to applications, even if they are based on different processor generations from a single CPU supplier. This case study showcases how these technologies allow enterprises to reuse and scale their existing resource pools by adding higher performing power efficient servers into the pool.

In this proof of concept, we created an enterprise reporting application workload representative of IT workloads. We then tested a variety of manual live migrations between host servers based on three generations of Intel® Core™ microarchitecture with different instruction sets (Merom: SSE3, Penryn: SSE4.1, and Nehalem: SSE4.2). All migrations completed successfully without any failures in the workload.

Proof of Concept Overview

This proof of concept was conceived to showcase how Intel's VT FlexMigration[1] supports customer's hardware investment and future proofing resource pools in a virtualized environment.

In this of concept, we created an enterprise reporting application workload representative of IT workloads. We then tested a variety of manual live migrations between host servers based on three generations of Intel Core microarchitecture with different instruction sets:

- A two-socket server based on Intel® Xeon® processor 5148 with SSE3

- A two-socket server based on Intel Xeon processor X5365 with SSE3

- A four-socket server based on Intel Xeon processor X7350 with SSE3

- A two-socket server based on Intel Xeon processor X5450 with SSE4.1

- A four-socket server based on Intel Xeon processor X7460 with SSE4.1

- A two-socket server based on Intel Xeon processor X5570 with SSE4.2

---

1   For additional information on Intel® VT FlexMigration, please refer to http://smcr.intel.com/SMCRDocs/
    Intel_VT_FlexMigration.zip

IT Business Reporting Overview

The IT Business Reporting Application is a representative of a highly utilized set of enterprise reports served to a large number of users: financial reports, customer data, and so on. This workload has multiple aspects to not only provide compute workload, but also network workload. All Web servers in this configuration are load balanced via Microsoft network load balancing (NLB) with all requests generated and results recorded by an external physical test client. The workload also requires users to be authenticated and validated against a standard domain controller. This combination of Web traffic, computational workload authentication, and network load balancing provide an example of an Intel IT business reporting application based on Intel standard server builds and configurations.

Workload scalability is achieved via a variable number of concurrent users able to be generated via the test client. The primary metric of interest for this workload is requests/second and these are recorded for each individual test run undertaken. The workload that is generated is synthetic with no time delays between each request generated and sent to the workload.

The architecture and configuration of each component of the workload is described in Table 16.1 and Figure 16.1. The virtual machines in the proof of concept used the Virtual Machine 7 format that is supported starting with ESX build 148592.

Table 16.1 Workload Configuration

Server	vCPUs	Memory (GB)	Operating System	Application
flexmigDC	1	1	Microsoft[†] Windows Server[†] 2003, 64-bit	Domain Controller
flexsql1	4	4	Microsoft Windows Server 2003, 64-bit	SQL Server 2005, Reporting Server
flexweb1	2	2	Microsoft Windows Server 2003, 32-bit	NLB and SSRS controller
flexweb2	2	2	Microsoft Windows Server 2003, 32-bit	Web Server
flexweb3	2	2	Microsoft Windows Server 2003, 32-bit	Web Server
flexweb4	2	2	Microsoft Windows Server 2003, 32-bit	Web Server

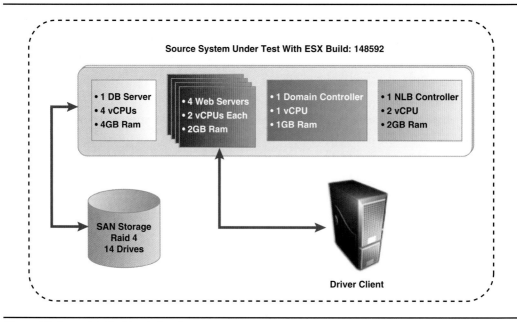

Figure 16.1   IT Workload Configuration

vConsolidate Workload Overview

The vConsolidate benchmark is a virtualization performance benchmark that simulates real server performance in a typical environment. The vConsolidate benchmark consolidates four separate benchmarks that run simultaneously, one each for database, Web, Java, and e-mail. As this is targeted for a virtual environment, each component runs in its own separate virtual machine (VM), each with its own operating system. In addition to the four benchmark components there is a fifth VM not running any benchmark, which simulates an idle VM. These five virtual machines comprise a consolidation stack unit (CSU). To determine the full capabilities of a given system, more than one CSU may need to be added. Figure 16.2 and Table 16.2 capture a high level architecture of the workload and the specific configurations of each of the virtual machines.

All the following virtual machines in the vConsolidate workload used the Virtual Machine 4 format. Even though starting with ESX build 148592, there is a support for the new Virtual Machine 7 format. ESX build 148592 still supports the older version. VMs with Virtual Machine 7 format cannot be migrated to ESX 3.x hosts. If you need backward compatibility with versions of ESX prior to VMware vSphere[†] 4.0, keep the VMs in Virtual Machine 4 format.

Table 16.2 vConsolidate Components

Server	vCPUs	Memory (GB)	Operating System	Application
Web Server	2	1.5	Windows Server 2003, 32 bit	IIS
Mail Server	1	1.5	Windows Server 2003, 32 bit	Exchange
Database Server	2	1.5	Windows Server 2003, 64 bit	MS SQL
Java Application Server	2	2	Windows Server 2003, 64 bit	BEA JVM
Idle Server	1	0.4	Windows Server 2003, 32 bit	Web Server

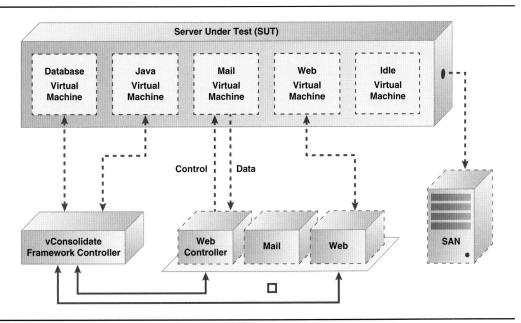

Figure 16.2 vConsolidate workload Architecture

Proof of Concept Hardware

Table 16.3 describes the server hardware used for testing the FlexMigration feature.

Table 16.3 Hardware Description for the Intel® VT FlexMigration Proof of Concept

Server	Operating System	Configuration
Intel® Xeon® 5148 [wdc1.lab.epi-ind.com]	ESX Build: 148592	2S, dual-core 2.33 GHz, 16 GB RAM, 1.33-GHz FSB, 4-MB L2 cache [65nm Intel core, Merom]
Intel® Xeon® X5365 [cltn1.lab.epi-ind.com]	ESX Build: 148592	2S, quad-core 3.0 GHz, 16 GB RAM, 1.33-GHz FSB, 8-MB L2 cache [65nm Intel core, Merom]
Intel® Xeon® X7350 [tgtn1.lab.epi-ind.com]	ESX Build: 148592	4S, quad-core, 2.93 GHz, 32 GB RAM, 1.06-GHz FSB, 8-MB L2 cache [65nm Intel core, Merom]
Intel® Xeon® X5450 [hptn1.lab.epi-ind.com]	ESX Build: 148592	2S, quad-core, 3.0 GHz, 32 GB RAM, 1.33-GHz FSB, 12-MB L2 cache [45nm Intel core, Penryn]
Intel® Xeon® X7460 [dntn1.lab.epi-ind.com]	ESX Build: 148592	4S, hex-core, 2.67 GHz, 32 GB RAM, 1.06-GHz FSB, 16-MB L2 cache [45nm Intel core, Penryn]
Intel® Xeon® X5570 [nhm1.lab.epi-ind.com]	ESX Build: 148592	2S, quad-core, 2.93 GHz, 32 GB RAM, 1.33-GHz FSB, 12-MB L2 cache [45nm Intel core, Nehalem]
Intel® Xeon® X5365	Windows Server 2003 R2, SP2 vCenter Build: 140742 vSphere Build: 140742	2S, quad-core 3.0 GHz, 16 GB RAM, 1.33-GHz FSB, 8-MB L2 cache [65nm Intel core, Merom]

Proof of Concept Setup and Configuration

This section describes the steps that are need to be followed to create a cluster and enable the Enhanced VMotion, using Intel® VT FlexMigration technology.

The cluster is EVMotion enabled. Hosts need their BIOS settings as follows:

■ Execute Disable bit in the BIOS should be enabled

■ Intel's VT bit in the BIOS should be enabled and an AC power cycle has to be done.

Creating and Configuring the Cluster

Here are the steps for the creation and configuration of the cluster.

1. After logging into the vSphere client, create the high level Data Center Node as shown in Figure 16.3.

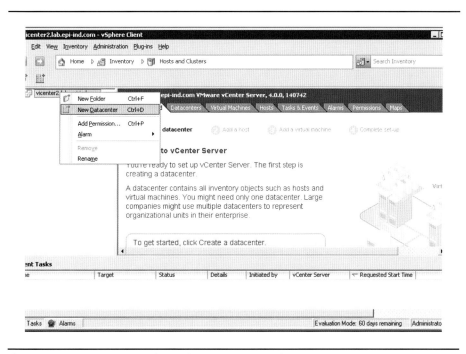

Figure 16.3 Creating a High Level Data Center Node

2. Now create the cluster, as shown in Figure 16.4.

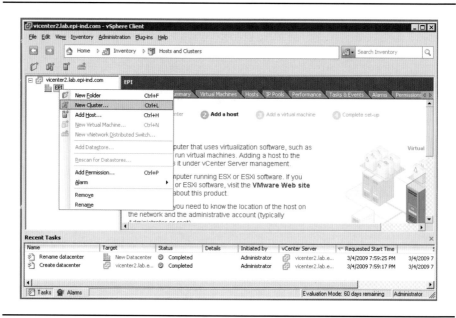

Figure 16.4 Creating a New Cluster

3. Depending on the requirement, appropriate flags need to be enabled for VMware high availability and DRS. This setting can be changed at any point of time later by editing the settings of the cluster. For this proof of concept we will enable the DRS feature as shown in Figure 16.5.

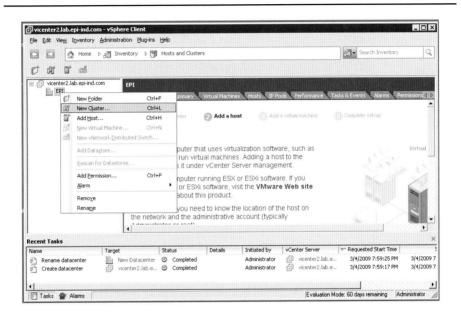

Figure 16.5 Enabling the VMware* DRS feature.

4. With the DRS feature enabled, additional settings for the DRS are needed, as illustrated in figure 16.6 and figure 16.7. Note that the number of live migrations depends on this setting. For example, if the mode is set to "Fully Automated" and "Aggressive" (figure 16.6), then depending on the workload and if there were much variation, you would see many migrations happening to balance the cluster.

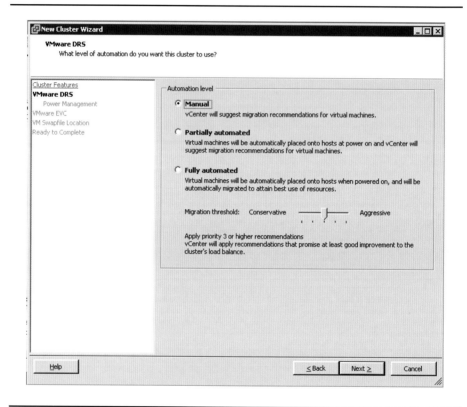

Figure 16.6 Selecting the VMware DRS Automation Level

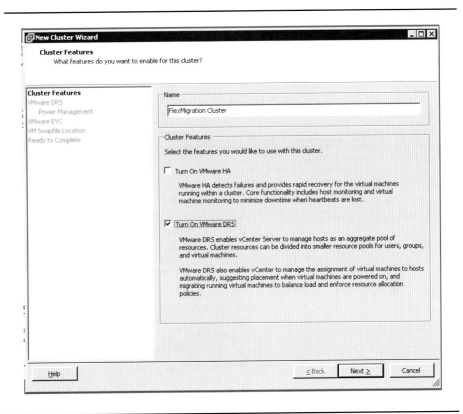

Figure 16.7 Turning on VMware DRS for the cluster.

5. Dynamic Power Management [DPM] is a new feature in ESX build 148592. This was introduced earlier in ESX 3.5 as a test feature. Depending on the requirement, enable or disable this option. Note that there is additional hardware required to enable this option, which is specified in Figure 16.8.

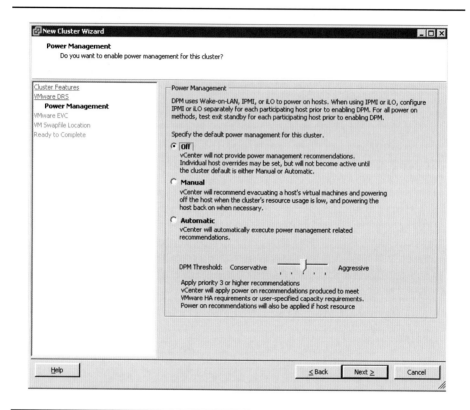

Figure 16.8 Specifying Power Management for VMotion

The Enhanced VMotion Compatibility [EVC] configuration setting depends on the different kinds of hardware the ESX hosts have that need to be added into the cluster. Table 16.4 summarizes the settings based on the hardware of the ESX hosts present in the cluster.

Table 16.4 Intel® Microarchitecture Settings for VMware EVC

Intel® Microarchitecture	EVC Setting	Example
Merom + Penryn + Nehalem	Intel® Xeon® Core 2	X5365, X5450, and X5570
Penryn + Nehalem	Intel® Xeon® 45nm Core 2	X5450, X7460, and X5570
Nehalem	Intel® Xeon® Core i7	X5570

Note: If in case all the servers in the cluster belong to the Nehalem family, and the EVC setting is set to Intel® Xeon® Core 2, then the applications running on the server with in the virtual machines will not be able to utilize the new instructions present in the Nehalem processors. See Figure 16.9.

Table 16.5 shows a high level summary of the instructions present in these families of processors.

Table 16.5 Instruction Set Architecture Summary

Intel® microarchitecture	Instruction Set
Merom	Baseline that includes x87, SSE, SSE2, SSE3, SSSE3, MMX, etc.
Penryn	Baseline + SSE4.1 [40+ media/video instructions]
Nehalem	Baseline + SSE4.2 [7 instructions (POPCNT, CRC32, PCMPGTQ, STTNI)

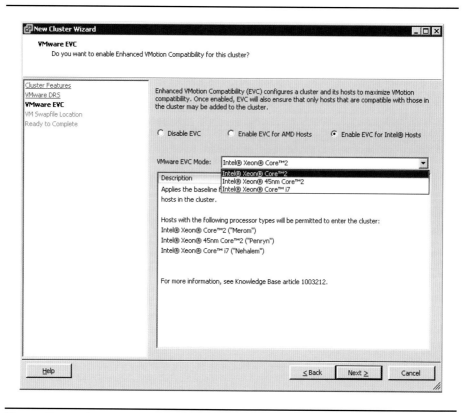

Figure 16.9 Selecting the EVC settings

6. For optimal performance keep the recommended option of storing the swap file in the same directory as the virtual machine, as shown in Figure 16.10.

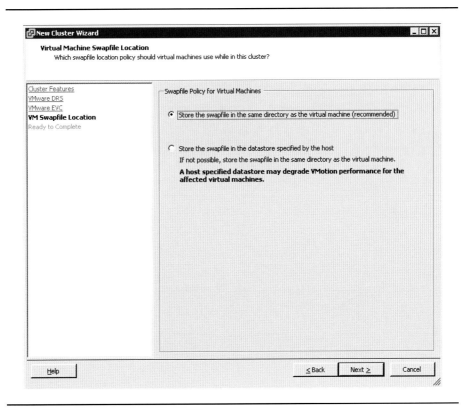

Figure 16.10 Settings for the Swap File

7. Ensure all the settings are correct and complete the creation of the cluster as depicted in Figure 16.11.

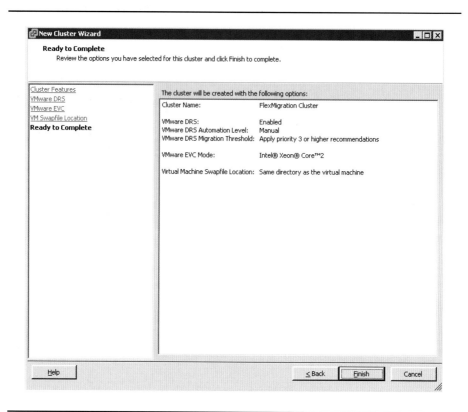

Figure 16.11 Checking Cluster Parameters and Creating the Cluster

8. After the cluster has been created, we can start adding hosts into the cluster. If the hosts have already been added to the data center directly, they need to be moved into the cluster. But make sure all the VMs in the hosts are shut down and the BIOS settings mentioned at the start of the section are enabled. See Figure 16.12.

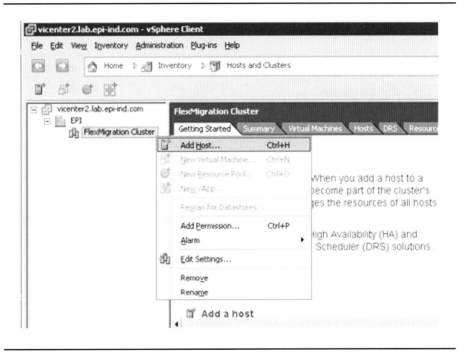

Figure 16.12 Adding Hosts to the Cluster

9. Specify the connection string for the host as in Figure 16.13, which can either be an IP address or a fully qualified domain name (FQDN.) If any conditions are not met, like BIOS changes, appropriate errors/warnings would be generated.

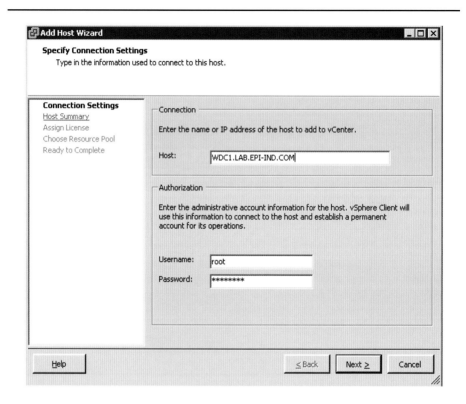

Figure 16.13 Specifying Host Connection Settings

Hosts being added to the cluster for the first time will prompt an alert to confirm the authenticity of the server, shown in Figure 16.14.

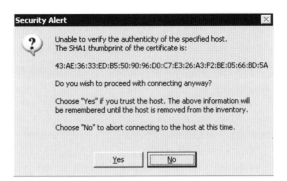

Figure 16.14 The Operator gets to Attest the Authenticity of the HostConfirm the host creation settings and go the next screen, depicted in Figure 16.15.

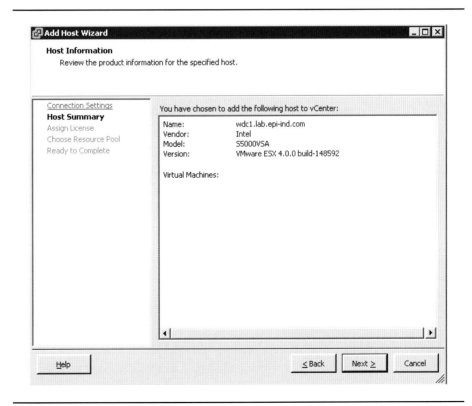

Figure 16.15 Confirmation Screen for Host

10. Enter the license information if you have it or continue with the next step for using the host under the evaluation mode as shown in Figure 16.16.

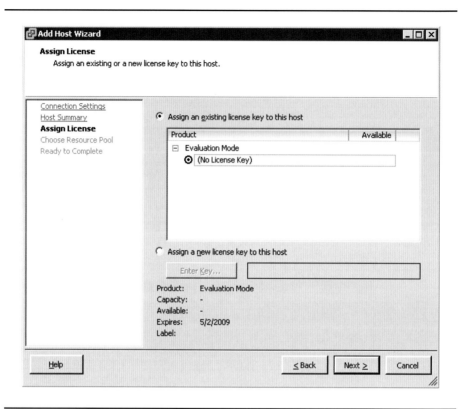

Figure 16.16 License Key Sheet.

11. Based on the requirements, choose the Resource Pool configuration as shown in Figure 16.17 and complete the final step of the host creation. Repeat the steps for adding additional hosts into the cluster.

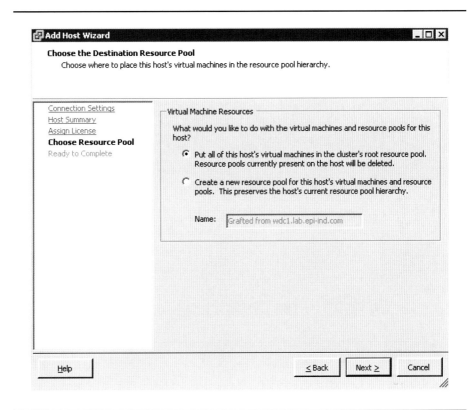

Figure 16.17 Resource Pool Sheet.

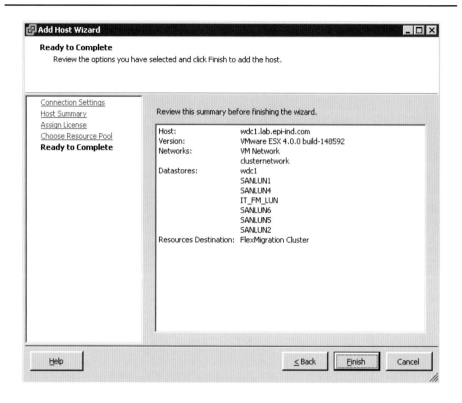

Figure 16.18 Completion of the Resource Pool.

Results

This section describes experimental results for three test cases:

■ Manual migration of virtual machines between dual processor systems

■ A migration using DRS from an Intel Xeon processor X5550 system

■ A migration using DRS to an Intel Xeon processor X5550 system

Case Study 1: Manual Migration of VMs between Dual Processor Systems

For this case study, we started the IT business reporting workload (7 VMs) on an Intel Xeon 5148 processor system. The test starts with a load of 14 concurrent users generated using the Microsoft[+] Application Center Test.

As shown in the Figure 16.19, we started the workload on the Intel Xeon 5148 processor system. The workload ran on the system for three to four minutes before being migrated manually to the next server. All the migrations completed successfully without any errors in the workload.

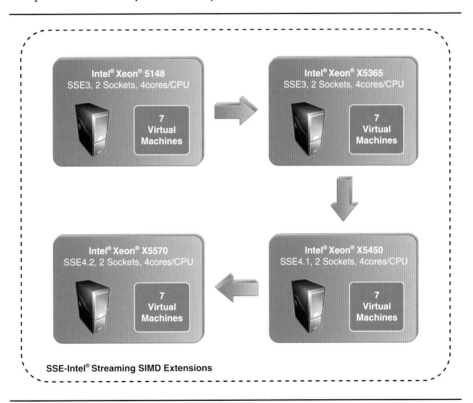

Figure 16.19 Manual Virtual Machine Migrations

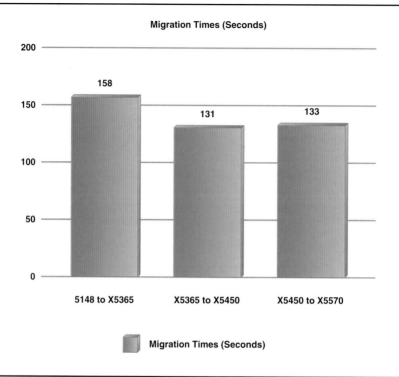

Figure 16.20 Times for Manual Virtual Machine Migrations

The Microsoft Application Center Test screen shown in Figure 16.21 captures the performance of the workload as we manually move the VMs from older generation servers to the later generation ones. The tool plots requests/second that was processed by each of the servers. [2]

---

[2] Note that even though there are drops in the requests that were processed during the actual migrations, no errors were generated.

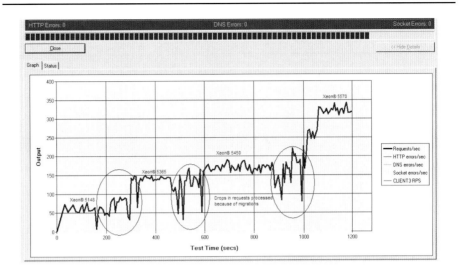

Figure 16.21 Workload Performance under Virtual Machine Migrations

Case Study 2: Migrations using DRS from an Intel ® Xeon® Processor X5550 System

For this case study, we added the multi-socket Intel Xeon X7350 and Intel Xeon X7460 into the cluster to showcase that FlexMigration works across 2-socket (DP) and 4-socket (MP) systems. Along with the IT business reporting workload, we added additional workload of vConsolidate benchmark consisting of 10 VMs.

The focus of this test is to showcase that virtual machines could be migrated from an Intel Xeon X5550 system to various other DP/MP systems across generations. Also this test showcases how the DRS feature of ESX handles the migrations depending on the configuration.[3]

The diagrams in Figures 16.22 through 16.25 indicate the VM migrations for the various different DRS settings of the cluster. As we move to more aggressive settings, the distribution of VMs across the various DP/ MP hosts is more uniform.

---

3   A higher DRS setting is not indicative of a better performance. Rather it tries to create a more load-balanced cluster. The optimal setting of DRS has to be evaluated for the individual workloads.

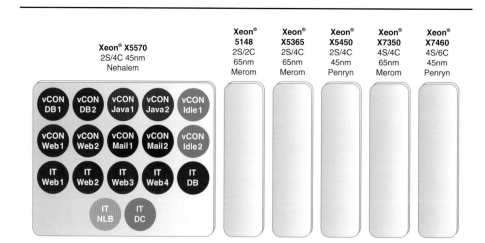

Figure 16.22 Virtual Machine Layout before Enhanced VMotion.

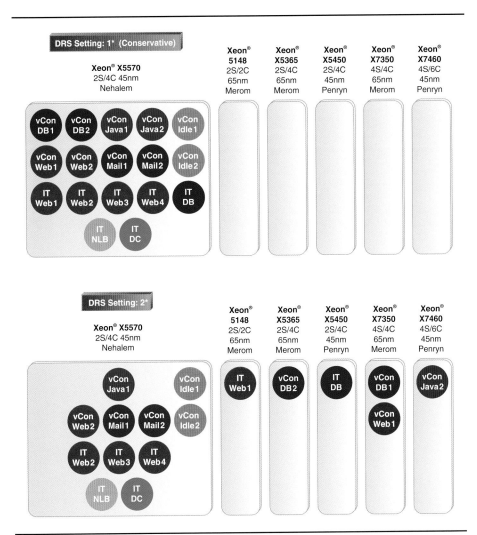

Figure 16.23 Virtual Machine Layout after Enhanced VMotion, DRS Settings 1 and 2.

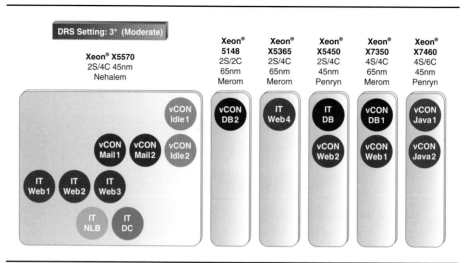

Figure 16.24 Virtual Machine Layout after Enhanced VMotion, DRS Setting 3

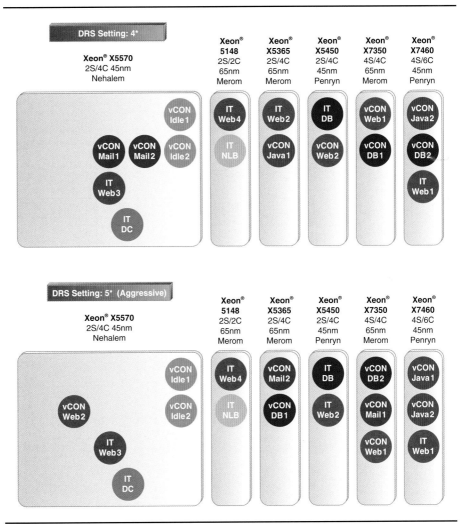

Figure 16.25 Virtual Machine Layout after Enhanced VMotion, DRS Settings 4 and 5.

In this case we tested the DRS functionality with various different settings of the "Full Automation" level. Figure 16.26 shows the number of migrations based on the settings of DRS. For all the cases both the IT workload and vConsolidate workload were started on the Intel Xeon X5570 server. The workloads executed successfully without any error.

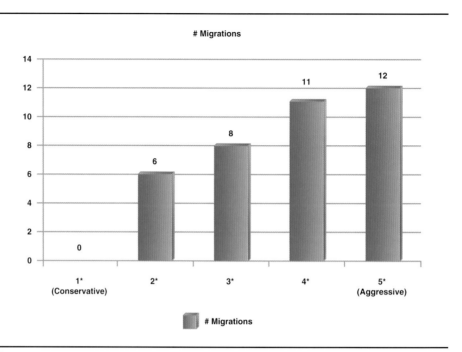

Figure 16.26 Virtual Machine Migration Times for Test Case 2.

Case Study 3: Migrations Using DRS to an Intel® Xeon® X5550 System

This case study demonstrates virtual machine migrations from older generation DP/MP systems to the newer generation Intel Xeon processor X5550 system. In this scenario, all seven virtual machines running the IT workload were started on the 2-socket Intel Xeon X5450 server and the vConsolidate benchmark workload was started on the 4-socket Intel Xeon 7460 server.[4]

Figure 16.27 depicts the virtual machine layout before the enhanced VMotion.

---

4   As mentioned earlier, a more aggressive DRS setting is not indicative of a better performance. Rather it tries to create a more load-balanced cluster. Optimal setting of DRS has to be evaluated for the individual workloads. In this test case the aggressive setting (5*) was used to showcase higher numbers of VM movement to all the different hosts in the cluster.

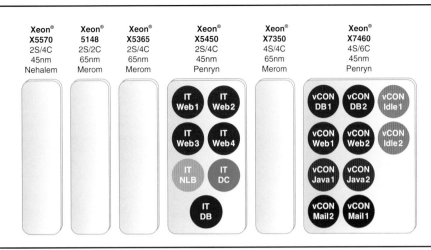

Figure 16.27 Virtual Machine Layout before Enhanced VMotion.

Figure 16.28 shows the layout after enhanced VMotion has taken place.

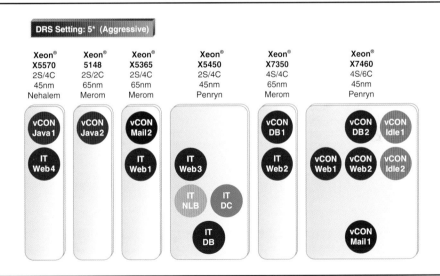

Figure 16.28 Virtual Machine Layout after Enhanced VMotion.

Proof of Concept Conclusions

The Intel® VT FlexMigration technology along with VMware Enhanced VMotion worked flawlessly in the cluster consisting of three different generations of Intel's dual processor and multiprocessor systems. The multifaceted IT business reporting workload and the virtualization benchmarking vConsolidate workload executed successfully without any errors providing scalable and consistent performance.

The above technologies allow enterprises to reuse and scale their existing resource pools by adding higher performing, power-efficient, latest generation servers into the pool. Intel® VT FlexMigration provides investment protection and future proofing of resource pools.

Additional Notes on the Proof of Concept

Here are some additional details about the technologies involved in the proof of concept.

Differences in Instruction Sets from Merom to Penryn to Nehalem

Table 16.6 summarizes the instruction support in the above micro-architectures.

Table 16.6 Instruction Sets per Processor Generation

Intel® microarchitecture	Instruction Set
Merom	Baseline that includes x87, SSE, SSE2, SSE3, SSSE3, MMX, etc.
Penryn	Baseline + SSE4.1 [40+ media/video instructions]
Nehalem	Baseline + SSE4.2 [7 instructions (POPCNT, CRC32, PCMPGTQ, STTNI)

Requirements to Enable FlexMigration and Enhanced VMotion

There are two main requirements:

- ■ Hosts should have virtualization-supported Intel Xeon processors.
- ■ "Intel® Virtualization Technology" and "Execute Disable Bit" should be enabled in the BIOS.

Requirements for Mixed Hosts in the Same Cluster

Hosts with ESX 3.5 U2 or higher and ESX Build 148592 can coexist in the same cluster and support live migration. An important consideration is that VMs built using Virtual Machine 7, supported only by ESX Build 148592, cannot be migrated to earlier versions of ESX. This will limit the VMs ability to migrate to any host in the cluster, which in turn might unbalance the cluster.[5]

Adding a New Host into an EVC-enabled Cluster

An ESX host can be added into an enabled cluster. A constraint is that either the VMs should be migrated out of the host or shut down before it is added. Also, ensure that the proper BIOS settings are updated as mentioned earlier.

Retiring the Last Merom Machine from an EVC Pool

No reboot is required to use the Penryn instruction set. All you need to do is update the cluster settings for it to use the Penryn instruction set as the base line. Having said that it really depends on the application as to whether it can see this change dynamically or not even though ESX allows it.

Conversely, adding an ESX host that belongs to the Merom generation when all the existing ESX hosts belong to the Penryn family requires lowering the cluster settings to use Merom instruction set. It is necessary to reboot the virtual machines to accomplish this transition. VMware displays a warning, as depicted in Figure 16.29.

---

5   Hosts with ESX 3.5 U1 or below do not support FlexMigration.

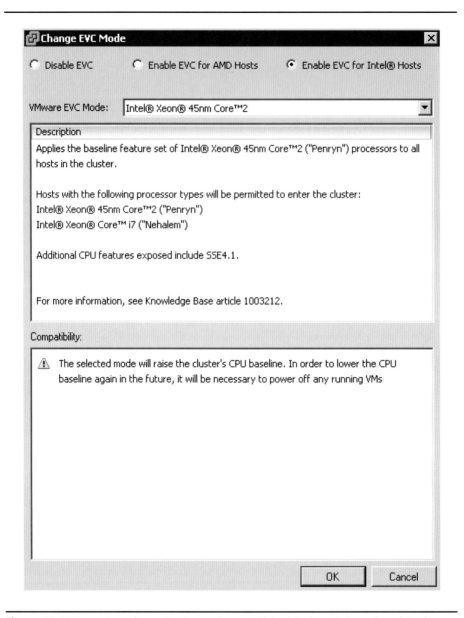

Figure 16.29 Lowering Cluster Settings when an Older Machine is Introduced in the Cluster.

Summary

Private Clouds are an extremely practical way for Enterprises to enable flexible, efficient and highly available Data Centers. Enterprises can streamline the execution of IT management processes such as provisioning, capacity management, availability management, continuity management and service level management, and also improve the utilization of their current hardware and system investments.

Enterprises can ensure very high availability and eliminate planned downtime for server and storage maintenance with live migration of virtual machines across physical servers and storage arrays. Intel VT FlexMigration is designed to enable seamless migrations among current and future Intel processor-based servers, even though newer systems may include enhanced instruction sets.

With this technology, hypervisors can establish a consistent set of instructions across all servers in the migration pool, enabling seamless migration of workloads. The result is a more flexible and unified pool of server resources that functions seamlessly across multiple hardware generations. This provides for more flexibility in dynamically allocating resources to meet business needs and facilitates the addition of new server technology without creating islands of compute resources.

This proof of concept experiments have showcased that live migration of VMs using Intel VT FlexMigration and VMware's Enhanced VMotion works successfully and can be used as a key enabling technology to utilize the heterogenous systems that are typical of an Enteprise datacenter, and also future proofing it for seamless migrations across multi-generations of Intel-based servers.

Chapter 17

Managing Power in Cloud Storage Appliances

Contributed by Enrique Castro-Leon

Recent advances in networking technology are making it practical to deliver software and IT infrastructure as a set of distributed services. This network of services is collectively known as the cloud. The technological impact of the cloud to customers and IT providers is significant, but perhaps of more consequence will be on the business side in the way IT is delivered and in changes of patterns of the ownership of data, applications and infrastructure and the services wrapped around them.

For instance, one way end-users will utilize cloud computing is to access their applications and information from a third-party provider such as a large telecommunications company with the resources and clout to build a global cloud infrastructure. That cloud infrastructure will make massive amounts of unstructured information available on the Web, and will require a policy-based approach to efficiently disperse the information worldwide.

Existing storage technologies, however, were not designed to deliver cloud services, and so cloud service providers require a new category of storage that can address their requirements, namely:

- *Massive scalability.* Providers must assemble applications and information from multiple sources to create unique experiences for the consumer.

■ *Global distribution.* An information policy is necessary to enable the applications and information to move closer to the consumer.

■ *Efficiency at scale.* Providers need an easy, cost-effective way to operate and manage massive amounts of unstructured information.

This new category of storage is defined as Cloud Optimized Storage (COS). COS complements and optimizes the cost of traditional storage categories. COS brings resources, tools and processes for delivering IT services to customers more efficiently.

As part of EMC's COS offering, EMC Atmos[†] implements a multi-petabyte information storage and distribution capability. It combines massive scalability with service level-driven automated data placement to efficiently deliver content and information services anywhere in the world. EMC Atmos allows managing the geographic dispersion of data to attain any desired level of reliability. EMC Atmos supports the policy-based approach mentioned above, providing a solid foundation from which to build cloud storage.

EMC Atmos operates logically as a single entity, yet its use of meta-data and sophisticated policy engine facilitates easy mapping to business policy and helps support service level agreements (SLAs) transparently to users. These qualities combine to increase operational efficiency, reduce management complexity and cost of operations.

Cloud technologies represent an emerging IT architecture: one with greater scalability, elasticity, and lower costs. An effective cloud strategy begins with establishing a solid cloud infrastructure from which to build, virtualize, and deploy services and applications. The storage component is no exception to an effective cloud strategy.

The Atmos Appliance

EMC Atmos software runs on low-cost, high-density hardware delivered in an industry standard form factor. The hardware is customer-installable, serviceable, and configurable based on capacity and/or compute requirements. See Figure 17.1.

Figure 17.1 EMC Atmos Appliance.

EMC Atmos is housed in a modular appliance consisting of an EIA standard 40U or 44U cabinet deployed with six to sixteen Intel® Xeon® 5500 Series processor-based servers. Each server is connected to direct-attached storage devices (DASD) housed in disk array enclosures (DAEs). Each DAE can house up to fifteen SATA drives. Each server is connected to one to three DAEs depending on system configuration with SAS wide port (4 lanes) cable connections.

Connectivity from an EMC Atmos appliance to the customer's network is through Gigabit or 10-Gigabit Ethernet.

Need for Power Management in Cloud Storage

EMC Atmos is currently supported with three appliance configurations: the WS1-120, WS1-240 and WS1-360 with 120, 240, and 360 hard drives respectively. The appliances have a nominal maximum power consumption of 4.9, 10.0, and 10.3 kW. Each appliance is designed with redundant power through standard NEMA L6-30, 220 V plugs providing at least 1+1 redundancy at the cabinet level as well as at the chassis (server, DAE, switch) sub-power supply level.

Power efficiency represents a valuable feature to EMC Atmos customers from the standpoint of minimizing operating expenses. Even though cloud storage represents an evolution from traditional data center-based, custom-designed storage, the need for power efficiency remains.

In fact, the ROI from making EMC Atmos appliances power efficient is very high because benefits from this effort are multiplied over all the units deployed, whereas efforts to optimize an in-house data center are by their very nature one-of-a-kind. This added efficiency is attained on top of the inherent efficiency from cloud resource pooling: multi-tenancy implies that the power consumed is shared over the users of a cloud device with lower power consumption compared to dedicated devices.

From a power consumption perspective, the servers use Intel® Xeon® 5500 Series processors representing the state of the art in power efficiency. Some of the power efficient features require no particular action from the user to be elicited, for instance low idle power consumption under Enhanced Intel® SpeedStep® technology.

Cloud Plug-in Approach for Rapid Integration

The power management technologies available in Intel-based servers would be of little use if they were difficult to integrate. These technologies were architected with a modular approach in mind allowing system integrators to pick the optimal tradeoff between level of abstraction and the granularity of control.

The implementation of power policies at the IPMI level allows very fine grained control down to the individual machine. This approach is useful under particular circumstances, but not as a general method for application power control due to the labor involved. The situation is similar to using assembly language in software development projects.

Intel® Data Center Manager as a software development kit (SDK) can be used as a ready-made module that has a number of power management capabilities already built in such as the support of server groups, eventing, and historical records. Hence this SDK can be incorporated as a power management module in a pre-existing application. The API is supported through a Web services interface, with the technology's inherent advantages of late binding and rapid integration.

The application implements the desired power management strategy and makes the appropriate calls to the Intel Data Center Manager to carry out that strategy. Intel Data Center Manager also provides a small-scale reference user interface that allows implementing, testing and debugging power management capabilities with incremental development enabling progressive refinement of the control policies while minimizing the risk of large scale rework from deferring testing toward the end of the project.

EMC and Intel undertook a proof of concept project to endow the EMC Atmos application with a power management capability in a resource-constrained exercise. This project is still in progress at the time of writing.

In Figure 17.2 we have integrated all the technology components discussed so far into an abstract cloud storage power management architecture. This architecture supports the use cases mentioned above as well. The numbered paragraphs below correspond to the numbered tags in Figure 17.2.

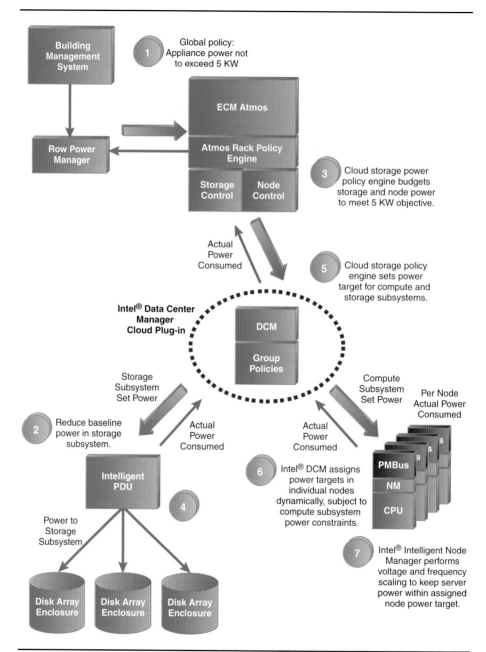

Figure 17.2 Power Management Cloud Plug-in Architecture Applied to EMC Atmos.

1. The cloud storage application may be implemented with multiple physical Atmos appliances arranged in a row. We postulate a management application regulating the power behaviors of the appliances in that particular row, the row power manager. The row power manager may be connected to the building management system (BMS) application, whose role, among others, is to oversee power management across the whole data center.

   The row power manager implements a number of policies that get mapped into specific directives to each storage appliance. For instance, the row power manager may instruct the EMC Atmos appliances under its command to operate in a power constrained mode imposing a guard rail in power consumption not to be exceeded by the appliance. Without this guard rail, the circuit feed for the row of appliance would have to be provisioned for the worst case assuming concurrent peak consumption in all the appliances in the row. This condition is rarely reached, if ever. Because this power needs to be allocated, but rarely, if ever reached, it effectively represents stranded capacity. The stranded capacity increases data center capital expenses, avoidable through improved management practices. This application of power control technology is an instance of usage model 2 described in Table 18.1, using Intel® Intelligent Power Node Manager as a power guard rail. We call it *branch circuit optimization*.

2. In addition to the application of power management-specific technologies, there are emerging technologies that bring reduced power consumption. A case in point is the replacement of hard drives with solid state drives (SSDs). SSDs consume less than 1 watt at idle and less than 5 watts versus 10 to 15 watts typical of mechanical hard drives. Hence using SSDs will yield a lower $P_{baseline}$.

3. The rack policy engine in the storage appliance oversees its power consumption by monitoring the power draw from the power distribution unit (PDU) feeding the hard drives and the power consumption by the server subsystem as reported by the instance of Intel Data Center Manager running in the appliance.

4. The implementation of the storage appliance may provide a monitor-only capability for the storage subsystem, in which case the appliance policy engine needs to meet the power quota for the appliance by regulating the power consumed by the servers in the appliance.

5. The rack policy engine in the storage application assigns a power target to Intel Data Center Manager. This power target can change dynamically depending on workload conditions and the policies set at the higher levels.

6. Intel Data Center Manager takes the overall power quota for the server subsystem and divides it across the servers in the appliance.

7. Intel Intelligent Power Node Manager instances adjust CPU frequency and voltage scaling accordingly to meet the quota imposed by Intel Data Center Manager.

In our experience, interfacing an application to the Intel Data Center Manager usually takes less than a weeks' time even with implementation team not previously exposed to the API; all it takes is a few Web services calls. Most of the effort goes into validating the new capabilities. Because of the small effort involved in the interfacing, Intel Data Center Manager, for practical purposes, functions as a *plug-in* module to quickly add a power management capability to a cloud-based application; in this case, a cloud storage application. This capability is added without need of re-architecting the original application in any fundamental way.

One of the goals for this proof of concept is to use Intel Data Center Manager as an archetype or conceptual proof point for using SDKs that expose APIs as technology building blocks to rapidly equip a cloud application with specific management capabilities. In the rest of this section we examine some of the Intel Data Center Manager capabilities we found useful for power enabling EMC Atmos.

■ Intel Data Center Manager implements sophisticated control algorithms. A group policy in effect may be conceptually simple, for instance, maintaining a preset power target for the server group. Internally, Intel Data Center Manager sets power targets for the individual nodes in real time to account for disturbances introduced by time varying workloads and the need to stay within each node's control range. Intel Data Center Manager carries power monitoring and control activities while concurrently updating the history database, performing thermal monitoring, monitoring event thresholds and delivering events. The complexity involved does not make it practical to implement these housekeeping activities for every deployment except when there is a need for extremely fine-grained control and implementation cost is not an issue.

■ Conceptual simplicity does not negate scalability. Intel Data Center Manager can potentially manage the nodes in multiple appliances should that capability be necessary in the future. In fact the software can handle tens of thousands of servers without overwhelming the system with network traffic or hitting database bottlenecks.

■ Intel Data Center Manager handles the IPMI low level protocol, whose grammar is not too far from assembly language. Intel Data Center Manager also handles TCP/IP sockets and sessions and concurrency across as many nodes as an installation comprises.

■ Intel Data Center Manager exposes a high level Web services-based API that makes it easy to implement specific use cases for a given application.

■ Intel Data Center Manager provides the benefit of platform abstraction provided by Web services, reducing the hurdles for equipment upgrades and migration.

A Power Management Proof of Concept

A joint EMC/Intel team put together a demonstration system shown at the one of the Intel Developer Forum technology showcase conferences. This occasion presented the first opportunity to assemble working end-to-end system within the context of an Atmos proof of concept. We report on experiments related to the branch circuit optimization use case using the plug-in architecture described above.

One of the goals for operating a set of appliances under a power constrained regime is to prevent breaker outages. Breaker outage prevention would be a last resort measure. A more common situation will be the use of power constraints to meet SLAs, consistent with the design goals of EMC Atmos. Meeting the SLA may require the use of N+1 redundancy, for instance feeding a group of appliances with three branch circuits of the same rating, with only two needed for normal operation.

Hence, if we impose a power cap to the power available from two of the three branch circuits, the group of appliances can continue with normal operation even if one of the branch circuits fails. If a failure occurs, redundancy is lost. In this case the imposed power cap prevents the appliances from drawing more power than the amount possible with two branch circuits and triggering a breaker outage.

In Figure 17.3 we start with an unconstrained system at idle up to T0. Workload ramps up until the power draw exceeds Pmax. Most of the time the system will operate under the power ceiling such as the interval between T2 and T3, with only occasional excursions (T1 to T2, T3 to T4).

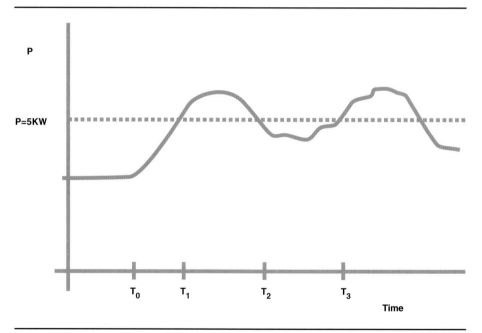

Figure 17.3 Unconstrained Power Consumption.

Figure 17.4 depicts operation under a power-capped regime where Intel Intelligent Power Node Manager is used as a guard rail mechanism to keep power consumption at or below the P_{max} boundary to maintain N + 1 power supply redundancy, allowing the system to operate without exceeding the P_{max} envelope at all times.

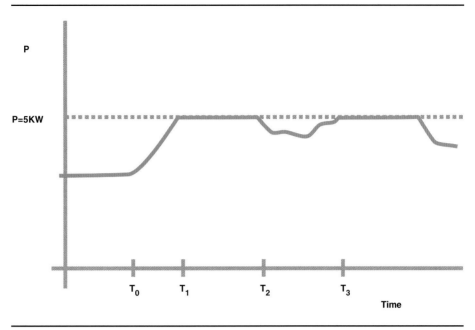

Figure 17.4 Operation Under a Capped Power Regime.

Unlike what Figure 17.4 suggests, the system will likely operate under the P_{max} cap most of the time, hitting the ceiling infrequently, if ever. Operation under a power constrained regime may have an effect on CPU performance. Since capping events are infrequent, users will not experience performance degradation, if at all.

Even if a second branch circuit fails, this event does not necessarily translate into catastrophic failure. It may be possible to bring the power cap to a maximum level, perhaps with selective shutdown of nonessential node to the point that the system can continue operations with a single branch circuit, albeit with degraded performance.

Actual power plots from the Intel Data Center Manager reference GUI are shown in the next figures based on the conceptual view just described.

System Description

Because of the limited time and engineering resources available for the demo, it was implemented to run on top of VMware VSphere† 4 and hosted on the smallest hardware footprint as shown in Figure 17.5. For DASD storage, instead of the usual SAS disk array enclosures we used only hard drives in the drive bays in two Intel® Xeon® 5500 Series servers. Also it was not practical to integrate an adjustable I/O workload in the short time available, and hence a synthetic workload was used to simulate the ups and downs of server workload.

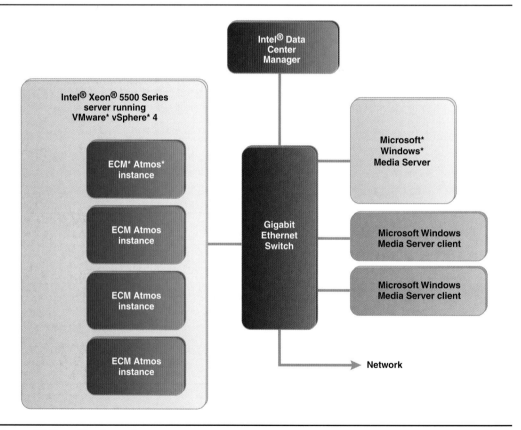

Figure 17.5   Hardware Setup.

One of the two servers hosted the EMC Atmos software, running in four virtual machines. A fifth virtual machine was loaded with Microsoft Windows Server 2008 running the Intel® MaxPwr synthetic workload used to impose a background workload on the system.

The second server ran Microsoft Windows Media Server. EMC Atmos was presented to Windows as a single CIFS file containing a number of videos to be streamed.

The implementation efforts were focused in delivering a functionally correct demo without an attempt to optimize performance. Even then, the system was able to support the delivery of seven HD video streams without hiccups. Power capping did not have any appreciable effect on the video frame rate.

The hardware diagram actually obscures the logical simplicity of the test rig, whose logical diagram is shown in Figure 17.6. Even though there are multiple instances of EMC Atmos, it operates as a single logical entity as mentioned in the beginning, functioning as a cloud-based data source for Microsoft Windows Media Server. Also note that the Intel Data Center Manager SDK becomes an entity embedded within Atmos, acting as the single proxy for Intel Intelligent Power Node Manager to carry the EMC Atmos power policies.

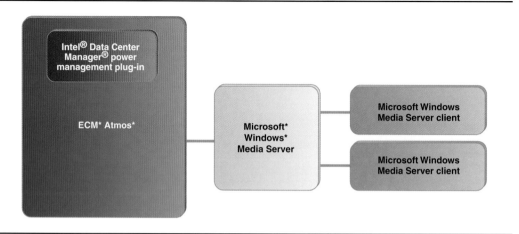

Figure 17.6 EMC Atmos Microsoft Windows Media Server Application Logical Setup.

Power Management Experiments

Figure 17.7 shows the actual power consumption trace starting with the host powered up and idle. The power consumption numbers correspond to the single physical host running EMC Atmos using the hard drive bays in the server itself. Hence power consumption numbers are considerably lower than those in a full size appliance.

We ran the server for few minutes until it stabilized before booting the virtual machines and starting Atmos, and give it a few more minutes until it stabilizes again. Note that the booting the VMs and starting Atmos induces a significant power bump. This behavior suggest another potential use case in data centers with large numbers of servers whereby servers are started in staggered groups to manage power draw during startup.

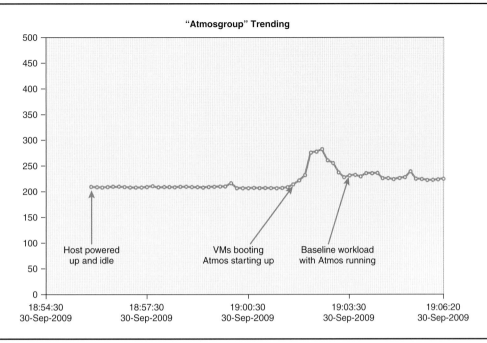

Figure 17.7   Virtual Machine System Initialization.

As shown in Figure 17.7, idle power is about 210 watts. With the virtual machines and EMC Atmos operating, power consumption increases to about 220 watts. Power consumption is somewhat unsettled, probably due to interactions between virtual machines, EMC Atmos, and the application server.

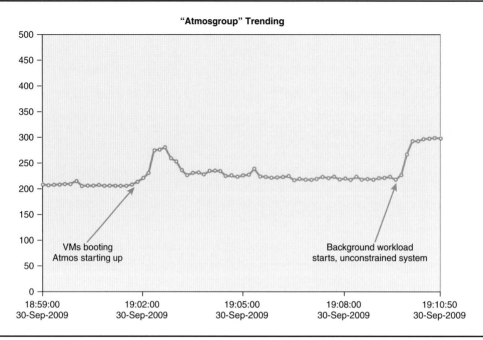

Figure 17.8   Unconstrained Workload.

Figure 17.8 shows one run throttling the background workload to 100 percent to test the power capping range. The run is started after the system reaches steady state with EMC Atmos. The graph shows an appreciable power proportional computing range from about 220 watts to 310 watts also shown in Figure 17.8.

As shown in Figure 17.9, we remove the workload a couple of minutes later and as expected, the system settles back to the previous baseline.

In Figure 17.9, toward the right we impose an aggressive cap of 250 watts and throttle once more to 100 percent. The system complies, somewhat reluctantly as the presence overshoot indicates.

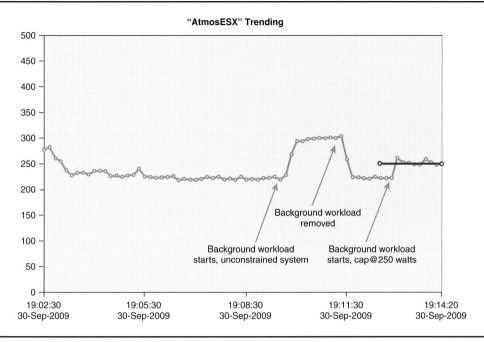

Figure 17.9   Unconstrained Operation and Start of Power Capped Regime.

In Figure 17.10 toward the right edge we repeat the same process with a more generous cap of 270 watts. Note that this time Intel Data Center Manager maintains a smoother capping action with less overshoot.

Once more, we remove the workload and the system returns to baseline EMC Atmos power consumption.

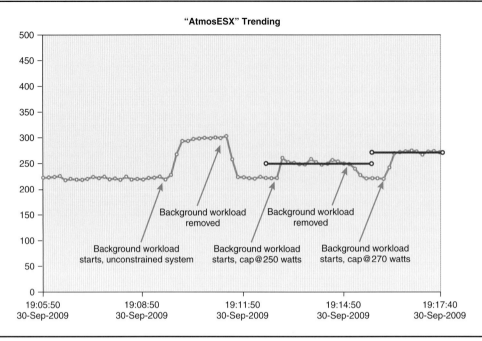

Figure 17.10   Power Caps Set at 250 and 270 Watts.

In the next experiment, shown in Figure 17.11, we simulate a variable workload using 25 percent increments. This time we use a 280-watt cap. Note that this ceiling is reached at the 75 percent level. Pushing for full throttle barely budges the power consumption as Intel Data Center Manager clamps it down.

At this point we throttle back to 75 percent and then remove the cap. Note how power consumption, now unconstrained, spills over to 280 watts. Increasing the workload to 100 percent increases consumption to 310 watts, the limit we saw before and well beyond the 280 watt boundary. This behavior illustrates the role Intel Intelligent Power Node Manager and Intel Data Center Manager play in keeping power consumption clamped at a pre-determined boundary and the spillover that takes place if for some reason the cap is removed.

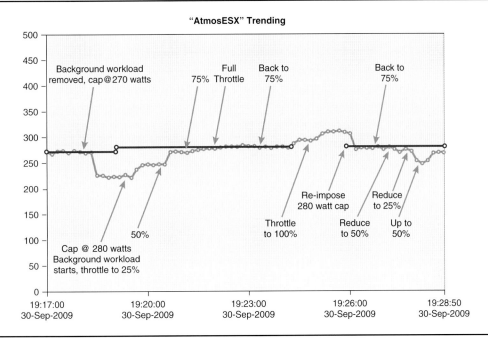

Figure 17.11   Power "Spills" Over the Gap When the Power Cap Is Removed.

Summary

The experiments described in this test report were performed with a human observing the system behavior through the Intel Data Center Manager reference GUI and setting power policies manually. A next logical step will be to integrate power policies with the EMC Atmos application with EMC Atmos driving the policies through calls to the Intel Data Center Manager API.

The experiments with the full appliance would include A/B testing, that is, demonstrating that with power capping on the power consumption of an Atmos appliance stays within the preset limit, and to demonstrate the existence of significant power excursions when power capping is off. A number of methods can be used to inject a disturbance. One method would be through a synthetic workload as in this experiment. Results will be more realistic if we apply disturbances associated with the operation of EMC Atmos, for instance by imposing workloads associated with the encryption or decryption of data streams, XML processing, and data compression and decompression, preferably using the Grinder workload generator.

This rig would allow testing the feasibility of regulating the power consumption of an appliance by regulating the power consumption of the nodes within. Beyond the verification of the branch circuit optimization use case the additional experiments will smooth the path of for more complex use cases that implement extreme power/workload scalability. These test cases would include server parking and hard disk drive spin-downs.

A desirable target to attain is to bring idle power consumption from the 50 percent attainable with a single Intel® Xeon® 5500 Series server down to 15 percent for the whole appliance. Ideally power scalability should enable bringing down power consumption close to the expected load average.

Chapter 18

Policy-Based Virtualized Data Center Cloud Usages

Contributed by Enrique Castro-Leon

As discussed in Chapter 4, power management represents a collection of IT processes and supporting technologies geared toward optimizing data center performance against cost and structural constraints, for instance increasing the deployable number of servers per rack when racks are subject to a power or thermal limits and making power consumption more predictable and easier to plan for.

Server equipment represents the most energy-intensive portion in a data center and the server infrastructure constitutes a logical starting point for any comprehensive data center power monitoring and control strategy. Furthermore, because of the data center PUE, opportunities for synergy exist between improvements in server efficiency and reduced data center cooling requirements. For static power management, the relationship is implicit. More sophisticated dynamic schemes call for inserting data center cooling into the control loop for additional gains.

State-of-the-art servers carry embedded sensors that enable the monitoring of power consumption of that server in physical units, namely watts, and in real time. The next jump in capability is to have servers fitted with controllers allowing the setting target power consumption limits for the server platform, also in real time. This capability is called *power capping*. Higher level software entities can aggregate data across multiple servers to set up and enforce server group policies. The range of power capping attainable is a function of the server architecture. For current generation servers the range is in the order of 20 to 30 percent of a server's peak power consumption.

The payback for the adoption of power management practices can be substantial. However it can only happen in the context of a strategy, institutional learning, and process maturity. A strategy would assume an evolution toward the deployment of increasingly sophisticated management schemes.

The first opportunities at the early stages come from the adoption of monitoring technologies, simply from gaining this level of visibility. Beyond the monitoring stage, a minimalist approach consists of using a power capping capability as a guard rail to enable a more tightly controlled utilization of the available power.

The effect of these practices on application performance would be invisible to applications yet would allow data center operators to schedule power consumption to actual power instead of less accurate estimates.

A more aggressive application of power capping includes the enforcement of power quotas and workload prioritization. At this point more gains become possible through further optimizations that include time-varying power caps and power-aware server shutdowns. The highly variable nature of cloud computing brings opportunities for the application of dynamic policies not practical in traditional data centers.

The integration of server power monitoring and control technology with sophisticated IT processes allows for the setting of goals for reduction in data center energy consumption, not just instantaneous power reduction. It is important that this integration be interoperable across equipment providers to accommodate the diversity of equipment in the data center.

Usage Models for Virtualized Cloud Data Centers

In the remainder of the chapter we present a number of usage models in a logical sequence from simple to complex usage models.

A *usage model* for a system is formally defined as a collection of data describing the system's usage within a stated context. The usage model data describe the interactions between the user and the system at a level that identifies the system's benefits to the user[1]. The context for all usage models in this chapter is their application to virtualized cloud data centers.

The focus of the usages is on policy-based usages. A *policy* refers to a course or method for action chosen from a number of alternatives and applicable to specific conditions.

Policies are preferably defined in terms meaningful to the user, not in some obscure platform-specific entities such as P-states. For instance, power monitoring is to be defined in terms of server platform consumption, measured in watts, and the policy is to be in effect based on time of day. A policy mechanism that provides only CPU watts or is defined in terms of the processor internal P-states would not be very useful because it requires the user to map these artifacts to units meaningful to the workload. And even if the user is willing to do this work upfront, the translation would not necessarily be consistent across implementations, leading to equally inconsistent outcomes.

Table 18.1 captures a series of six usage models applicable to virtualized cloud data centers. The list is not exhaustive by any measure. The usage models are ordered by increasing complexity and integration requirements as well as by the increasing number of Intel® Intelligent Power Node Manager Technology features put to work. The virtualized cloud data center represents the most general application context.

---

1   Erik Simmons, "The Usage Model; Describing Product Usage during Design and Development," *IEEE Software,* May/June 2006 (vol. 23 no. 3).

Table 18.1   Virtualized Cloud Data Center Power Management Usage Models

Usage Model	Benefits	Use Cases
Perform real-time server power monitoring	Reduce stranded power by scheduling available data center power to actual server power consumption	Real-time monitoring of power consumption Manage data center hot spots Power and thermal scheduling Power use trending and forecasting
Power guard rail: impose power guard to prevent server power consumption from straying beyond a preset limit	Deterministic power limit and guaranteed server power consumption ceiling	Maximize server count per rack and therefore CapEx ROI per available rack power when rack is under power budget with negligible per server performance impact
Static power capping: operate servers under a permanent power capped regime	Operation under impaired power availability conditions	Maximize per rack performance yield when rack under power budget Application power optimization Application performance compensation Business continuity: continued operation in the presence of power outages
Time-varying power capping: adjust server performance profile to workload demand	Optimize infrastructure for QoS to match SLA exactly	Match capping set points to workload Support for multiple service classes
Manage data center energy consumption for time-varying workloads	Cut electricity costs	Dynamic reconfiguration to achieve extreme power proportional computing
Carry out integrated data center power	Realize power optimization across server, communications, storage	Use server sensor data to optimize cooling equipment set points

For each scenario there are one or more use cases. The following sections cover each of the usage scenarios in Table 18.1. Each of the tables starting at Table 18.2 picks on one of the use cases in the left column of Table 18.1. Not all the use cases are highlighted for brevity. All use cases below assume deployed server equipment with a power and thermal monitoring capability.

Static Capping Usage Models

The first three usage models also apply to nonvirtualized environments where the operating system runs on bare metal. These use cases assume static capping where the capping level is set once and does not get changed during normal operations.

Real Time Server Power Monitoring

Collecting real-time power consumption figures constitutes an essential capability for power monitoring. Without this data, the best approximation for server power usage comes from the manufacturer's specifications. Using nameplate numbers as a guidepost requires leaving a hefty safety margin. Honoring the safety margin in turn leads to data center power overprovisioning and stranded power, infrastructure power that needs to be allocated in case is needed, but very unlikely to be used.

Table 18.2   Real Time Power Consumption Monitoring

Description	Servers provisioned with Intel® Intelligent Power Node Manager (Intel® Node Manager) carry embedded sensors that enable the monitoring of power consumption of that server in physical units, namely watts, and in real time.
Actor(s)	Application and solution architects designing applications for maximum power efficiency
	Data center operators and facilities managers optimizing the use of available data center power infrastructure
Event Flow	Assign group power consumption targets. The definition of group is application-specific: it can be a rack, a row, servers assigned to a PDU, or any logical grouping.
	Monitor the historical power consumption over the expected range of operating conditions.
	Note the maximum power consumption number.
	Two options are possible at this point:
	Add more servers to increase the application throughput on the basis of the measurements performed while staying within the power envelope
	Reduce the group power quota to the actual power used.
	Option 1 increases the application performance or throughput for a given power quota. Option 2 releases data center power capacity that otherwise would be stranded, that is, assigned to a group of servers but never used.
	Repeat the measurement process to verify that the actual power consumption is matched to the actual available power.
	The system needs to be recalibrated or recertified over time to accommodate for workload growth or events that would change the group power consumption. This can be done prescheduled maintenance milestones, or monitored continuously. The operator gets an alarm when a server group is about to exceed the assigned power quota.
Exceptions	Only systems with Intel Node Manager technology will benefit from the usage model described above. Legacy systems and systems that do not support IPMI or DCMI need to be measured with external instrumentation. This process can be expensive in terms of equipment and labor costs.
Benefits	Data center power availability is scheduled to actual server power consumption. Minimizes over-provisioning and stranded power.

The availability of power monitoring data allows management by numbers, tightly matching servers by power consumption to available data center power. The use case is useful in older data centers underprovisioned for power and in hosting settings with power quotas in effect.

Table 18.2 expands on the "Real Time Power Consumption Monitoring" use case in the rightmost column in Table 18.1. The rest of the tables in the chapter follow a similar pattern.

If we go back 10 to 15 years, power used to be an afterthought for servers deployed in data centers. Even today, some of the old practices still persist. For this particular use case, in many facilities today the power bill still comes bundled with the facilities charge and is managed by a different group from the IT infrastructure.

Furthermore, a large number of established data centers were not originally architected to factor in increased power densities, and are quickly reaching their load-bearing limits, both in terms of available infrastructure to power more servers and to keep the physical infrastructure from exceeding thermal limits. Yet, due to lack of visibility, data center planners need to significantly overprovision power to provide enough of a cushion because the falling short is not an option. This is not efficient use of infrastructure and capital resources.

Table 18.3 briefly captures the use case for managing data center hot spots.

Table 18.3 Manage Data Center Hot Spots, Power, and Thermal Scheduling

Description	Shift virtual machines around in a server pool to optimize power and thermal behaviors. In a server pool operating under a power budget, optimize operating equipment to available power
Actor(s)	Data center operators, solution architects
Event Flow	Relocate workload virtual machines to optimize and rebalance power and thermal margins based on measurements.
	Optimize number of servers across pools while monitoring temperature and power consumption to check for excursions.
Exceptions	Adjust number of servers in pool to limit power excursions
Benefits	Number of servers deployed optimal for a given power budget across server pools

The Intel® Data Center Manager aggregation software also keeps a log of all the power readings taken in the managed system. The data establishes a useful track record for the purposes of trending and forecasting in power scheduling and data center planning, as shown in Table 18.4.

Table 18.4 Data Center Power Use Trending and Forecasting

Description	Use historical power consumption data to develop forecasting models for data center planning
Actor(s)	Data center operators, solution architects
Event Flow	Develop statistical models, such as time series analysis autoregression and moving average (ARMA) models to map future power and energy use against available data center power to plan for data center remodels, expansion and migrations.
Exceptions	None
Benefits	Power consumption forecast models are now based on actual power demand data.

Using a Power Capping Capability as a Power Guard Rail

In a highway setting guard rails are placed at critical places to prevent vehicles from accidentally exiting the roadway. This usage model functions in exactly the same way: in spite of careful planning, power excursions are still possible under the monitoring-only usage model described above. One alternative is to apply a conservative policy that leaves enough available power margin for these excursions. Unfortunately this margin means some degree of overprovisioning and stranded power. Perhaps a better alternative is to impose a power cap that kicks in only when these excursions occur, as described in Table 18.5. Since the power cap is not active during normal operation, the system behaviors don't change, and yet we deterministically prevent excursions from occurring.

The process for deploying a power guard rail is similar to the monitoring use case except that a power consumption ceiling is imposed on a server group. Whenever the group consumption would exceed this ceiling, Intel Node Manager power capping kicks in, effectively preventing group power consumption to go beyond the ceiling.

Power capping can potentially impact performance. Two additional conditions need to be satisfied on top of the monitoring tuning process:

1. That the system performance stays within the SLA even when capped

2. The capping level stays within the capping range for the target platform.

Table 18.5 Power Capping as a Guard Rail

Description	Limit excursions by imposing a power capping guard rail
Actor(s)	Application and solution architects
Event Flow	Learning phase: determine a safe operational limit that matches number of servers deployed to available power budget. Set a power cap above the normal operational envelope.
	Operational phase: The power cap in effect does not kick in during normal operations; it does however if there is an extraordinary surge in demand, keeping power consumption inside a preset envelope to prevent thermal throttling or shutdowns, or worse, to prevent breaker tripping events.
Exceptions	Readjust capping levels for changes in workload and system configuration.
	Servers without Intel Node Manager can't be capped. When these servers are included in a power managed group, two undesirable scenarios are possible: servers with Intel Node Manager become the "swing" servers. If the servers without Intel Node Manager go through a peak, the power cap on the Intel Node Manager servers needs to be set low enough to compensate. When this happens, the severe cap impacts performance beyond the SLA or the cap target exceeds the server power control range causing the group server consumption to go over the limit.
Benefits	Equipment can now be tightly and deterministically scheduled.

Static Power Capping

Static power capping is a stricter version of the guard rail usage model. The system is now expected to operate under a permanent, always in effect power cap.

The goal for rack performance yield optimization, shown in Table 18.6, is to place as many servers in a rack as the power limit allows maximizing MIPS yield. The number of machines will be so large that all machines will likely need to operate under a permanent cap. However, the overall MIPS yield for the collection of machines will be larger than otherwise possible than any combination of machines running uncapped, but whose aggregate power consumption is still subject to the rack power quota.

Power optimization, shown in Table 18.7 requires building a table with various workload profiles and a performance loss target not to be exceeded. A series of experiments is performed to characterize how much capping can be applied without straying away from committed performance targets. Afterwards, during normal operations, the applications engineer sets power capping targets based on the prior measurements. The system is now said to be "optimized," because the impact of applying these caps is now known.

Table 18.6 Maximize per Rack Performance Yield

Description	Operation under permanent power cap
Actor(s)	Application and solution architects
Event Flow	Learning phase: When operating under a preset rack power budget, provision as many servers as possible. Impose a cap to stay within the budget. There will be some performance loss due to capping, but the performance yield overall increases as more servers are added.
	Operational phase: operate the rack at the present power cap.
Exceptions	Readjust number of servers in rack if cap can't be maintained.
Benefits	Allows equipment to be tightly and deterministically scheduled.

The main benefit of this approach is to match actual QoS against service level requirements. Exceeding the SLA generally does not give the provider extra points and indicates unnecessary extra spending. On the other hand, under-delivering on the SLA may result in a noncompliance action by the customer.

Table 18.7 Application Power Optimization

Description	Power cap tailored to workload profile that minimizes performance impact when imposed
Actor(s)	Application and solution architects
Event Flow	Learning phase: set power impact target. Characterize how much capping is possible without exceeding the impact targets.
	Operational phase: operate the rack at under power caps defined at learning phase
Exceptions	Makes it possible to match application yield and QoS to SLA requirements.
Benefits	Allows equipment to be tightly and deterministically scheduled.

Performance compensation, shown in Table 18.8, requires the workload to be re-prioritized or throttled up after capping to restore the uncapped performance. How much to re-prioritize depends again on the workload profile, and the assessment is done on basis of prior measurement. Not all loads have knobs that allow re-prioritization. Also, performance compensation reduces performance headroom, that is, the ability of a server to respond to demand upticks. In the extreme case, if the workload has been re-prioritized to the point that the server is near 100-percent utilization, any uptick in demand will likely result in an SLA violation.

Table 18.8 Application Performance Optimization

Description	Apply a power cap to a workload while throttling up or re-prioritizing the workload to compensate for workload yield loss.
Actor(s)	Application and solution architects
Event Flow	Learning phase: For a given workload and capping level, re-prioritize workload until the original performance yield is restored. Increase capping level until the uncapped performance can't be restored. Operational phase: operate the rack under permanent power cap, reprioritize workload to restore uncapped yield.
Exceptions	Apply capping, but not at the limit where the original performance can't be restored. Reduce capping if capping level turns out to be too aggressive.
Benefits	Lower server power consumption with no application performance impact.

The business continuity use case, shown in Table 18.9, brings operational flexibility by allowing continued data center operation under impaired power conditions.

Table 18.9 Support for Business Continuity

Description	Continued operation under impaired power
Actor(s)	Application and solution architects
Event Flow	Restore N +1 and 2N redundancy level for Uptime Institute Tier III and Tier IV facilities by applying capping when power consumption exceeds a certain threshold or a power outage occurs in a redundant feed. Maximize the equipment operating under emergency power by applying a cap to minimum power policy. Support graceful shutdown of equipment after an outage.
Exceptions	If the requesting capping level is below the equipment capping range, the requested redundancy level won't be maintained. The operator needs to understand the extra risk involved should available power be further impaired, or must preemptively shut down equipment to maintained the target redundancy.
Benefits	Lower server power consumption with no application performance impact.

Dynamic Capping Usage Models

The opportunities for reducing energy consumption using power capping technology alone are limited. If energy reduction is to be significant, power cuts need to be deep and sustained over time. For instance, if the policy in effect is capping as a guard rail, capping seldom kicks in, if at all. Furthermore, some energy savings are possible under a permanently capped regime, but these are limited by the capping range, or by the need to remove the capping policy to optimize performance yield.

Policies under dynamic power management take advantage of additional degrees of freedom inherent in virtualized cloud data centers as well as the dynamic behaviors supported by advanced platform power management technologies. Power capping levels are allowed to vary over time and become control variables by themselves. Selective equipment shutdowns enable reductions in energy consumption, not just power management. These shutdowns alter the profile and topology of the equipment, and hence we call this scheme *dynamic reconfiguration*. The action of shutting down servers specifically is called *server parking*.

The tradeoff for dynamic policies is additional complexity: if the capping level becomes a control variable, this means a mechanism to exert this control needs to be implemented. The applicability for the more complex cases discussed below may be narrower requiring long term planning and a transformation strategy. However, for applications amenable to this kind of treatment the improvement can be radical as shown in the examples in Chapter 5.

Virtualized cloud data center environments introduce a number of operational degrees of freedom not possible in traditional data centers. First, applications hosted in virtualized cloud data centers run on virtualized operating systems, that is, the operating system does not run on the bare metal, but it is mediated through a virtualization hypervisor. The practical effect is that applications are no longer bound to a physical host and can be moved around within a pool of servers to optimize the overall power and thermal performance of the pool. Second, the loose binding between applications and hosts allows treating a group of hosts as a pooled resources, allowing optimizations as a group that were not possible with individual machines, such as powering down some equipment during low demand.

In the remainder of the chapter we'll continue walking through the remaining three usages in Table 18.1.

Time-Varying Power Capping

Under this usage model a management application adjusts power caps in a server pool as it watches the performance yield of the pool and available reserve performance needed to overcome workload spikes. To the extent extra reserve exists, it applies a more aggressive power cap until the performance yields are aligned with target performance levels as dictated by contracted service level agreements.

As explained in Chapter 4, the effect of power limitation or power capping with Intel Intelligent Power Node Manager (Intel Node Manager) is attained through manipulation of processor dynamic voltage and frequency scaling (DVFS). Power capping is attained by the slowing the applied voltage and operating frequency of the processor in discrete steps defined by the ACPI P-states.

Power capping reduces processor performance. The degree of this effect is a function of capping intensity and the application type. A key operational consideration is that the maximum performance is not always needed, especially when utilization factors are low. A more relevant consideration is the application service SLA or service guarantee. Ideally a service provider would deliver quality of service or QoS to meet the SLA and no more. Unless there are specific incentives, exceeding the SLA means unnecessary cost, whereas under-delivering may lead to customer complaints.

A number of applications, for instance in cloud and telecommunications space where SLA is a prime consideration, are already wired to monitor key performance indicators or KPIs for QoS. Under this situation it is practical to insert power capping as part of a control loop driven by an application KPI. If the application performance starts degrading, the power cap is relaxed to coax additional performance from a server. On the other hand, if the SLA is being exceeded, the cap increased allowing a reduction in power consumption. This mode of operation is called *flex capping,* where the power capping objectives for a server can vary over time. See Table 18.10 for details.

Table 18.10 Capping as Function of Workload

Description	Operation under permanent power cap. Power cap adjusted to match workload demand while maintaining contracted SLAs.
Actor(s)	Application and solution architects
Event Flow	Learning phase: Define power capping targets as function of workload utilization. Determine the feasibility of the allocation algorithms.
	Operational phase: Monitoring application adjusts power caps as function of workload level.
Exceptions	Power demand excursions beyond scheduled power are charged at penalty rates.
Benefits	Makes possible hour-by-hour power consumption forecast. This level of predictability makes it feasible to negotiate favorable power rates with the utility company.
	Improved data center power utilization over the monitoring use case.

Picture three service classes for workloads: representing high, medium, and low priority workloads. The high priority workloads run on unconstrained servers; they can take all the power they need to run as fast as they can.

Medium priority workloads are assigned to power capped servers. These will run slower but they will still run. A server running a low priority workload may be put to sleep if the power it would use needs to be reallocated elsewhere.

Table 18.11 Power-Aware Support for Multiple Service Classes

Description	Operation under permanent power cap. Global power quota allocated to sub-groups of servers operating under own service level targets
Actor(s)	Application and solution architects
Event Flow	Learning phase: A server pool is partitioned into sub-pools by service class. Set Intel® Node Manager to enforce a global quota while assigning individual quotas for each sub-pool, and individual power quotas for each of the nodes in the pool.
	Operational phase: Monitoring application adjusts power caps as function of workload level.
Benefits	Ability to enforce multiple SLAs across different populations of users

The benefit of this use case, shown in Table 18.11, is that it is possible to operate a pool of servers to a defined global power consumption quota for the collection of servers. This degree of predictability allows operating servers under pre-scheduled power consumption targets at pre-negotiated rates with the power utility company.

Adjusting Power Capping to Time Varying Workloads

The power cap level imposed in the previous section is adjusted by time of day. This usage model assumes the presence of a higher level management or monitoring function capable of translating workload environmental conditions to capping levels.

A main goal for this usage model is to achieve power proportional computing over an extended workload demand range as explained below.

As in time-varying power capping, policies designed to track time varying workloads take advantage of additional degrees of freedom inherent in virtualized cloud data centers as well as the dynamic behaviors supported by advanced platform power management technologies. Power capping levels are allowed to vary over time and become control variables by themselves. Selective equipment shutdowns enable reductions in energy consumption, not just power management. The tradeoff for dynamic policies is additional complexity: if the capping level becomes a control variable, this means an orchestration mechanism to exert this control needs to be present.

Cloud service workloads may exhibit a more or less predictable pattern, with demand peaks during office hours and deep valleys in the small hours of the morning. In fact, it is not uncommon for demand to vary as much as 10:1 through the day. For the purposes of an example, let's use the stylized load curve shown in Figure 18.1. This workload takes seven servers to fulfill at the period of highest demand. During the small hours of the morning it can take as few as one server to maintain the contracted SLA.

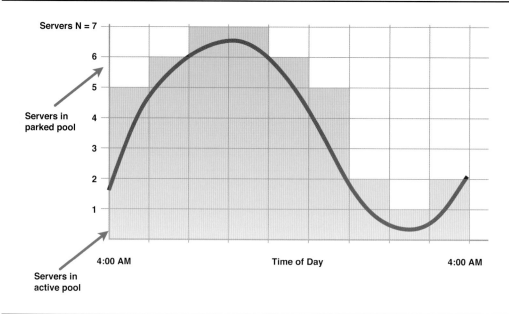

Figure 18.1   Time-varying workload serviced by a pool of servers.

If the seven servers are running 24 by 7 as it is the norm in most data centers today, even if we apply power capping to the lowest possible policy, the best we will do with current technology is to bring power consumption down to 50 to 60 percent of peak power consumption. This mode of operation is very inefficient during demand valleys considering that the workload demand might be less than 10 percent of peak. This is why most traditional data centers end up being run at an abysmal 10 to 20 percent utilization.

Ideally, if the power consumption per unit of workload demand remained constant, if workload demand goes down to 10 percent of peak, so would the power consumption. This concept is known as *power proportional computing*. There is a bottom for power proportional computing for every known technology. For the present generation of servers, the bottom for an idling server lies at around 50 percent of peak. This means a server that's powered up but doing no work consumes 50 percent of its peak power. This is the "price to play," the power needed to keep a server running even if it's doing zero work.

Fortunately, there are additional server states we can exploit under these circumstances. If we know that a server won't be used for a period of time, we can put it to sleep. To be precise, we can put it into ACPI S5 (soft off) or even ACPI S4 (hibernation). A management application can put a server to sleep when not in use and restart it as needed. A sleeping server makes it possible to reduce power consumption by more than 90 percent of peak.

In a common real life analogy, when we leave a room, we turn off the lights. If this is the sensible thing to do, why do we see servers blazing 24 by 7 in most data centers? This is because most legacy applications will break. However this is no longer true in virtualized environments that allow dynamically consolidating virtual machines into fewer physical hosts during demand valleys and spread them out during high demand.

Placing servers in a low energy state essentially changes the configuration of a pool of servers servicing a cloud workload, and hence we name this approach dynamic reconfiguration.

Table 18.12 captures all the elements described in this section into a specific use case for dynamic reconfiguration.

Table 18.12 Dynamic Reconfiguration for Extended Power Proportional Computing

Description	Operation under permanent power cap. Power cap adjusted to follow daily workload cycles
Actor(s)	Application and solution architects
Event Flow	This use case is the flex cap use case where the number of active hosts varies over time depending on workload demand. This process is called dynamic reconfiguration. Learning and tuning phase Run the application through a few daily cycles with no power management mechanisms to establish the baseline power consumption. This means running the machines 24 x 7 with no power capping. Note the baseline energy consumption in this operating mode. Establish the allocation schedule for parked and active server sub-pools. Re-run the workload to establish that there is no gross over- or under-allocation. The allocation can be done by time-of-day or in more sophisticated schemes as a control feedback loop using KPI monitoring. Overlay the power capping schedule to establish the different service classes and perform power consumption curve shaping. Re-run the system for a few days to ensure there are no gross mismatches between the power allocation algorithms and workload demand. Execution phase Deploy the system previously tuned and monitor the KPIs for a few weeks to ensure there were no corner cases left behind. At this point the system can be released for production. Calibration or learning runs may be necessary to ascertain the feasibility of the allocation algorithms.
Exceptions	This algorithm represents a tradeoff between operational flexibility and complexity. Careful monitoring will be needed initially to ensure that all corner cases are managed. For instance, it takes time to shut down and resume a server. If the workload picks up faster than the time it takes to bring a server back on line, it may be necessary to allocate extra active servers to manage a possible QoS degradation.
Benefits	Extreme power proportional computing range, as much as 90 percent, well beyond what is attainable with servers running 24 x 7. This use case also yields significant energy savings, in the order of 25 to 50 percent depending on the workload and pool size.

Integrated Data Center Power Management

Integrated data center power management use cases comprehend the use cases described in Chapter 11. A platform-assisted thermal management approach adds "smarts" to cooling solutions for data centers. Assume we enable management applications to read temperature and possibly other data from instrumentation embedded in server platforms. The presence of this instrumentation effectively constitutes a vast sensor network whose potential has not been tapped to date. One possible application is to build a real-time thermal map for the server grid to complement the real-time power monitoring and control capability enabled by Intel Intelligent Power Node Manager, as summarized in Tables 18.13 and 18.14.

Table 18.13 Building Data Center Thermal Maps

Description	Build real-time spatial temperature profile using server sensors
Actor(s)	Application and solution architects
Event Flow	Learning phase: set up management application with database containing server (x, y, z) coordinates in data center and to read the server inlet temperature sensors. Operational phase: Perform regular scan of server inlet temperatures; record and plot.
Exceptions	Management application enforces policies when hot regions are detected.
Benefits	Enables real-time temperature readouts in the zone where a pool of servers is located.

Table 18.14 Set CRAC Temperature Set Points

Description	Coordinated management of ICT and data center cooling equipment
Actor(s)	Application and solution architects; data center operators
Event Flow	Facilities management application aggregates server power consumption data and temperature inlet information across a pool of servers and adjusts CRAC set points optimally.
Exceptions	Distributed control and modeling algorithms still under research.
Benefits	Matches server cooling demand to building cooling supply, increasing data center efficiency.

Summary

The payback for the adoption of power management practices can be substantial. However it can only happen in the context of a strategy, institutional learning and process maturity. A strategy would assume an evolution toward the deployment if increasingly sophisticated management schemes. The first opportunities at the early stages come from the adoption of monitoring technologies. A number of come up just from gaining this level of visibility.

Beyond the monitoring stage, a minimalist approach consists in using a power capping capability as a guard rail to enable a more tightly controlled utilization of the available power. The effect of these practices on application performance would be invisible to applications yet would allow data center operators to schedule power consumption to actual power instead of less accurate estimates.

A more aggressive application of power capping includes the enforcement of power quotas and workload prioritization. At this point more gains become possible through further optimizations that include time-varying power caps and power-aware server shutdowns. The highly variable nature of cloud computing brings opportunities for the application of dynamic policies not practical in traditional data centers.

Chapter 19

A Data Center Efficiency Maturity Model

Contributed by Enrique Castro-Leon, Charles G. Sheridan, Jim Kenneally, William Carter, and Murali Rajappa

Implicit in the continuum of the six usage models discussed in Chapter 18 is also an evolution in time. A case in point is a data center with explicit operational practices in effect for server power management. The steps for any organization in this situation will always be the same: first in-lab proofs of concept, followed by small pilot projects, and eventually institutionalized, general practice. For instance, it would not be feasible for an organization with no institutional history on power practices to immediately start deploying infrastructures that take advantage of dynamic reconfiguration.

Actually, the same dynamic applies to equipment manufacturers, system integrators, and solution providers, with offerings that start with power monitoring, which eventually evolve into more sophisticated forms of power management and control.

A maturity model captures this evolution as a series of transitions an organization goes through over time in terms of technical capability, process sophistication that eventually gets linked to specific, desirable business outcomes. This process, once understood, is not a passive process. The maturity model allows architects, planners, and executive staff to assess where an organization lies within an evolutionary sequence and deliberately define roadmaps and allocate investment to accelerate this process and optimize business outcomes.

Given the initial motivation for this chapter as an abstraction exercise overlaid on the power management usage continuum, we will follow a bottom up path in this chapter,

- Mapping the server power management continuum to an evolutionary model for server power technology adoption

- Recasting this evolution as an instance of the Innovation Value Institute IT Capability Framework or IVI IT-CMF, and

- Generalizing server power management to data center efficiency,

- Concluding the chapter with a summary description of the IVI IT-CMF and the IVI itself.

A Data Center Server Power Management Evolutionary Model

Data centers can be over 40 times as energy intensive as conventional office buildings[1] to the extent that they represent a measurable portion of the national energy consumption in developed economies at about one percent as well as contributors of greenhouse gases[2]. Industry concerns provide a motivation for a number of initiatives such as the European Union Code of Conduct, the US Government Energy Star program and global industry forums such as the Green Grid.

Within the backdrop of energy as a limited resource and consistent with many organizations' stated strategy for increased energy efficiency and the reduction of the carbon footprint from data center operation, an evolutionary model for data center power management practices would be extremely useful to understand the transformation dynamics.

1   S. Greenberg, et al. (2006), *Best Practices for Data Centers: Lessons Learned from Benchmarking 22 Data Centers.* Proceedings of the ACEEE Summer Study on Energy Efficiency in Buildings in Asilomar, CA. ACEEE, August. Vol. 3, pp. 76–87. http://eetd.lbl.gov/emills/PUBS/PDF/ACEEE-datacenters.pdf.

2   J. Koomey, *Worldwide Electricity Used in Data Centers*, Environ. Res. Lett. 3 (2008) 034008, IOP Publishing

Such an evolution model facilitates planning and would allow those involved in the planning to

- ■ Establish roadmaps for technology adoption and quantify the benefits and business ROI from technology investments.

- ■ Establish continuous improvement practices and more sophisticated processes to realize the benefits of improved technologies.

- ■ Factor in and find out when energy becomes a first consideration for data center capital investment and the outsourcing of services.

For this purpose we propose the Data Center Power Management Capability Maturity Framework. Researchers at the Software Engineering Institute (SEI) at Carnegie Mellon University developed the idea of a capability maturity model as a part of their overall thinking about how to improve the software development process. Stripped of its software development content, the maturity level concept provides a useful framework for thinking about the improvement roadmap of nearly any process or capability, in our case data center power management.

The IT-Capability Maturity Framework™ (IT-CMF™) developed by the Innovation Value Institute (IVI) uses a similar maturity concept but deviates from the traditional CMM models in that each step in the IT CMF represents an increased level of sophistication for both processes/practices used and the output delivered, rather than the degree of control and institutionalization across a particular key process area.

The IT-CMF has five maturity levels (initial, basic, intermediate, advanced, and optimizing).

- ■ Maturity Level 1: There is no formal process and processes are executed in an ad-hoc manner.

- ■ Maturity Level 2: There is basic process functionality to deliver a basic service or function.

- ■ Maturity Level 3: There is an intermediate level of process sophistication and functionality to deliver an intermediate level of service or process output.

- Maturity Level 4: There is an advanced level of process sophistication and functionality to deliver an advanced level of service or process output.

- Maturity Level 5: The process optimized both within the process area and in the context of other related processes.

Using this framework which can provide a way to help manage and solve complex and competing pressures, providing a roadmap of maturity paths for value provisioning - IT organizations can move from being perceived like a utility provider to become a core competency of the firm. Ultimately the goal is to create conditions of sustainability, controllability and predictability of the IT Capability in support of continuous value creation and use of the IT-CMF can support this goal.

Our instantiation of the framework for data center power management practices follows a similar line of reasoning.

- Level 1: Unmanaged/ Ad hoc. No explicit power management in place. Applicable to established data centers that have grown organically. The existing equipment layout, a result of this organic growth, tends to be haphazard. Equipment may have been placed by different departments with no specific power coordination other than staying within the power envelope defined by facilities management. The data center may be supporting a hosted environment, with no coordination on power management or established power management practices across tenants in effect. This environment is the baseline for measuring data center power and energy savings.

   In this environment a significant number of "zombies" may be present. These are deployed servers no longer performing useful work. These servers may be leftovers from applications that evolved over time, or the owner may have moved on without dismantling it or perhaps the server was left behind from a finished project. These servers consume power, space, network ports and IP addresses. Without active monitoring it is very difficult to identify and root out these servers, and even with a server and owner identified, following due process and decommissioning the machine is a drawn-out and labor-intensive process; it may take weeks to complete the approvals and releases needed to un-rack the machine. For instance, once power monitoring is instituted (a Level 3 capability), processes can be implemented to flag always-idle servers for possible decommissioning.

A Level 1 shop may be running a mix of legacy and newer servers. With the newer servers there are no specific practices to take advantage of any of the power saving features they bring. In the absence of specific processes to take advantage of these features, the features may be turned off to prevent interference. For instance, eliciting the new features may require firmware updates. Even though the updates may be free from the equipment manufacturer, budget may not be allocated to perform these tasks.

■ Level 2: Passive/Static Power Management. At this stage individual projects of departments take on first steps toward power management practices. The practices involve local actions without the use of specific active power monitoring and control or the overhead of invoking cross-departmental coordination. Strong bureaucratic barriers and disincentives for experimentation exist. Without established practices in effect, requests for exceptions will likely be denied.

The mechanisms applied are usually of the "fire and forget" type applied to servers individually. Examples of these mechanisms include Intel® Demand-Based Switching Technology (DBS), Enhanced Intel SpeedStep® Technology (EIST) and Intel Hyper-Threading Technology (Intel HT Technology).

While these mechanisms have a significant potential in reducing server power consumption, they can't be enabled or turned off or controlled while the system is running, and the benefits are accrued under specific operating conditions.

For instance, EIST works best when servers are idling or under light load. This won't help much in an environment where servers are optimally loaded. In an optimally loaded virtualized cloud data center where servers are continually run at 60 to 80 percent utilization factors and hence the capability to lower idle power consumption is never realized.

If for some reason the mechanism needs to be turned off, a reboot and application re-initialization is usually necessary, a major inconvenience in many cases.

For historical reasons, without standardized instrumentation that provides real-time power consumption to application, applications working in this environment need to rely on proxy power metrics such as CPU and memory utilization to make power-based decisions. Actual metrics in watts are not available except when external devices are attached, such as lab watt meters or IP-based PDUs and power strips, which are expensive or unwieldy to deploy.

■ Level 3: Active/Dynamic Power Management. This stage is characterized by the application of standardized platform instrumentation and APIs for power management. Applications can perform real-time platform power monitoring and control is possible, measured in watts.

The first action under this stage is instituting real-time server power measurement as part of system operations. Intel provides Intel Node Manager to support this environment, accessible through the industry standard IPMI protocol.

Practices under Level 3 bring operational flexibility to the data center from a power perspective, allowing application performance optimization under power-constrained conditions and a significant reduction in stranded infrastructure. End users can build a power management environment out of best-of-breed, interoperable components across product and service providers. Another opportunity for improved power management at this level is optimized server rack loading.

■ Level 4: Dynamic Reconfiguration. At this stage practices have been developed to be able to adjust an application's platform profile and network topology to match workload demands.

In addition to Level 3 benefits from infrastructure optimization, Level 4 brings a potential reduction in energy consumption. The main mechanism to implement dynamic reconfiguration is *server parking*, that is, placing servers in a low energy state. The most likely candidates for low energy states available today are ACPI sleep states S5 (soft off) and S3 (standby to memory). Server parking can be used to achieve power consumption linearity for a cluster of servers. Please refer to the section on power proportional computing for a more detailed look.

Dynamic reconfiguration requires loosening the binding between an application and the underlying hardware host. A practical mechanism today is virtualization supporting virtual machine migration to implement dynamic reconfiguration. A side effect that needs to be managed is the recovery cycle, the time to shut down and bring a server back on line. This ranges between 5 and 15 minutes. S3 reduces the time to about one third. S0 can reduce it by at least one or two orders of magnitude. Perhaps a lesser consideration, but still a consideration, is the latency from virtual machine migration switchover.

More complex schemes can use multiple parked states in such a way that power consumption approximates the lowest energy state, but recovery time approximates the scheme with the fastest recovery time by dividing a group of servers into platoons backing each other, hence the term *platooning*.

An initial data point from the Telefónica proof of concept covered in Chapter 22 indicates a potential of 27-percent energy consumption reduction with a pool of only two servers for one of their applications.

There are no obvious technical impediments to bring a Level 3 environment to Level 4 after retrofitting and process improvement. The retrofitting needed may be significant, for instance to make sure there are well-defined hot and cold aisles and perhaps through the installation of a hot air return ceiling plenum.

Level 4 data centers present a good match for virtualization and supporting multi-tenant server pools without requiring hard binding between applications, virtual machines, and physical hosts.

■ Level 5: Integrated Power Monitoring and Control/Optimizing. Computing, networking, and data center cooling equipment are coordinated and managed to specific global power consumption targets and SLAs.

Fine-grained power monitoring becomes possible, enabling individualized power billing for cloud data center tenants and per-VM power metering.

Integrated power monitoring and control will likely require a data center redesign, or a purpose-built data center.

The five levels just described are summarized in Figure 19.1.

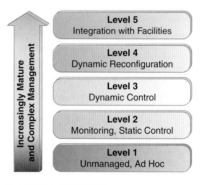

Figure 19.1 Data Center Power Management Maturity Model

In Table 19.1 we present some approximate calculations about the potential benefits from the adoption of power management practices for each stage. The numbers are to be taken with a grain of salt. They represent our knowledge gained from performing lab experiments, proofs of concept, and some extrapolations. The authors have no knowledge of large scale Level 3, 4, or 5 deployments, and while the technologies to support Level 2 have been available for a while, without platform instrumentation it's difficult to measure actual power savings, let alone energy savings.

Table 19.1 Benefits from Advanced Data Center Practices

Power Management Maturity Level	Power Saving Potential	Energy Saving Potential	Yearly Utility Bill Reduction per MW at USD 0.12/kWh
Level 5	No data	No Data	Depends on PUE
Level 4	80% for N=4[1]	27% for N=2[2]	USD 270,000
Level 3	30%[3]	0– 5% est.5	USD 0 to 50,000
Level 2	10%4	Negligible	N/A
Level 1	Baseline	Baseline	Basis: USD 1 million to power 3,000 servers for 1 year

[1] Kamal Natesan and Sudhir Bangalore, Intel EPI Solution Center, Bangalore
[2] Miguel Gómez et al., Telefónica Investigación y Desarrollo.
[3] Intel EPI Solution Center, Oregon

Here are some capabilities possible with advanced data center power management practices. Some are reachable for Level 3 shops. All of them are reasonable goals for Level 4 and 5 shops. A first step in managing power in the servers in a data center is having a fairly accurate monitoring capability for power consumption. The second step is to have a number of levers that allow using the monitoring data to carry out an effective power management policy.

■ Implement a power consumption peak shaving capability. The data center power infrastructure needs to be sized to meet the demands of peak power. Reducing peaks effectively increase the utilization of the existing power infrastructure.

Become smart about shifting power consumption peaks. All watts are not created equal. The incremental cost of generating an extra watt of power during peak consumption hours is much higher than the same watt generated in the wee hours of the morning. For most consumer and the smaller commercial accounts flat rate pricing still prevails. Real time pricing (RTP) and negotiated SLAs will become more common to put the appropriate economic incentives in place.

The incentive of real time pricing is a lower energy bill overall, although the outcome is not guaranteed. In pilot programs residential consumers have complained that RTP results in higher electricity costs. With negotiated SLAs the customer can designate a workload to be subject to lower reliability; for instance, instead of three nines, 99.9 percent uptime, or outages amounting to about 10 hours per year, the low reliability workload can be designated as only 90 percent reliable, and can be out on the average of two hours per day at a lower price per KWh.

■ Match the electric power infrastructure in the data center to server workloads to minimize overprovisioning. This approach assumes the existence of an accurate power consumption monitoring capability.

Upgrading the electrical power *infrastructure to accommodate additional servers is not an option in most data centers today.* Landing additional servers at a facility that's working at the limit of thermal capacity leads to the formation of hot spots, this assuming that electrical capacity limits are not reached first with no room left in certain branch circuits. Hence measures that allow the deployment of additional equipment under the existing power infrastructure are to be preferred over alternatives that require additional infrastructure.

For the purposes of data center strategic planning, it may make economic sense to grow large data centers in a modular fashion. If the organization manages a number of data centers, consider making effective use of the existing data centers, and when new construction is justified, redistribute the workloads to the new data center to maximize the use of the new electrical supply infrastructure.

Data Center Server Power Management as an Instance of IVI IT-CMF

The Innovation Value Institute (IVI) has developed a capability maturity framework for managing Sustainable Information and Communication Technology, or SICT. This framework is part of the IT-Capability Maturity Framework™ (IT-CMF™) developed by the IVI consortium, under evaluation within leading organizations around the world. The framework leverages existing approaches and complements them with a comprehensive value-based model for organizing, evaluating, planning, and managing SICT capabilities. The framework organizes SICT around nine Capability Building Blocks (CBBs) grouped under four main categories and execution of four key actions to increase the business value delivered by SICT to an organization.

The four key actions are:

1. Define the scope and goal of SICT

2. Understand the current SICT capability maturity level

3. Systematically develop and manage the nine SICT capability building blocks

4. Assess and manage SICT progress over time

The IVI IT-CMF tracks a number of critical processes, key activities, and procedures to be defined and mastered within IT organizations to plan and deliver IT solutions and to measure the business value consequences of IT initiatives and daily activities. A sustainable ICT (information and communications technology) lens underlies the design of these processes with the goal of instituting sustainable practices, outcomes, and metrics. The data center server power evolutionary model fits naturally into a SICT category.

The IVI IT-CMF starts with a summary page describing the scope of the particular CMF as shown in Figure 19.2. The scope page contains a high level summary of the capabilities attained through the data center server power management evolutionary mode.

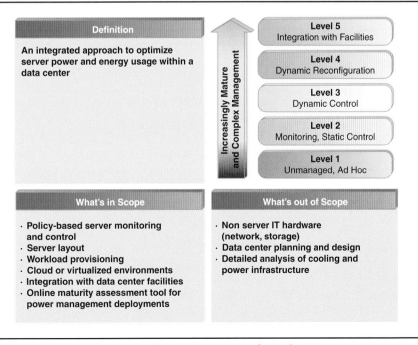

Figure 19.2 Data Center Server Power Management Scope Page

Data center power management represents a category or major area of focus under SICT. The strategic goals for each category are attained through specific capability building blocks or CBBs. The set of CBBs need to be necessary and sufficient with respect to the category: the tracking of the CBBs also presents a complete picture for tracking data server power management as a whole.

Three CBBs are essential for data center server power management comprising integration, scalability, and interoperability, shown in Figure 19.3.

Integration comprises capabilities that will work across the physical plant, lifecycle planning, and business processes. A technology capability won't be useful for instance if it can't eventually be integrated into specific business processes with metrics to assess business value.

Scalability refers to a capability to aggregate a capability across collections of entities. For instance, a power capping capability, initially an attribute of a single server, eventually needs to be mapped to a capping capability applicable to arbitrarily large groups of servers.

Finally, interoperability refers to a capability to transparently mix and match offerings from different vendors.

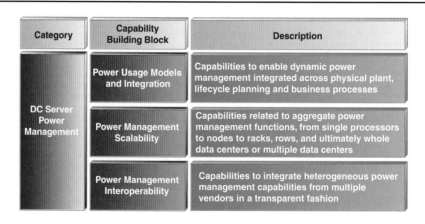

Figure 19.3 Categories and Capability Building Blocks for the Data Center Server Power Management IT-CMF

Figure 19.4 summarizes the essential characteristics for data center server power management by level. Level 3 is the breakthrough level, the lowest level at which an organization is able to demonstrate significant linkages between power management and business. The five levels essentially replicate the capabilities in the evolutionary model in the previous section, so there is no need to revisit them at this point.

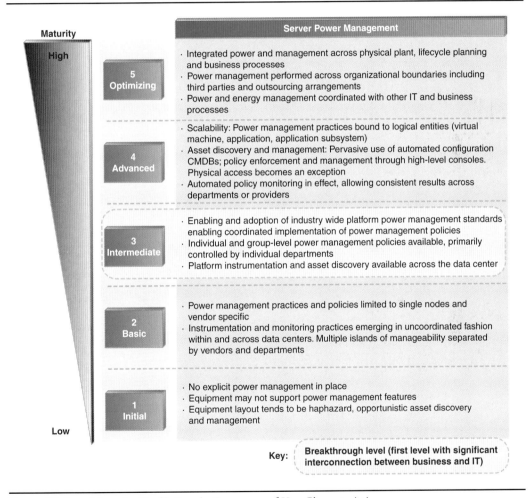

Figure 19.4   Maturity Profile Levels: Summary of Key Characteristics

Figure 19.5 captures a view of the five levels described in Figure 19.4 with detail by capability building block. The details for each level are aligned with the evolutionary model covered in the previous section.

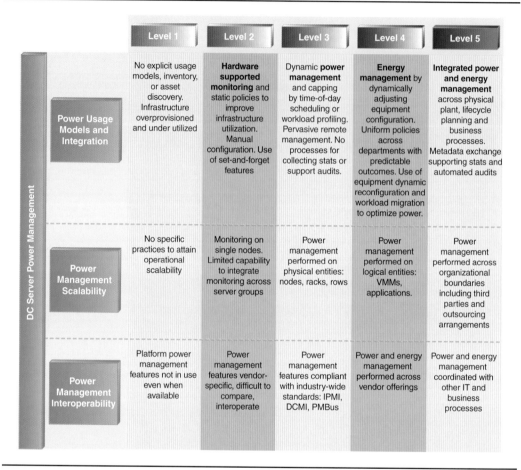

Figure 19.5 Summary Maturity Curve for Capability Building Blocks

Figure 19.6 provides a perspective by key practices, the expected outcomes from the practices, and recommended metrics to measure progress.

	Key Practices	Outcome	Key Metrics
5 Optimizing (High)	· Integrated management across physical plant, lifecycle planning, business processes and organizational boundaries	· Power and energy implications of power usage understood within business processes · Lifecycle management · Supporting stats and automated audits	· Percent facilities with audit and compliance capability · Percent of business process with integrated power management · Percent of improvement in PUE
4 Advanced	· Dynamic reconfiguration and workload migration · Workload profiling performed on logical entities · Uniform policies across departments · Cross-vendor integration	· Equipment profile is dynamically adjusted to minimize energy usage · Clarity of power management policies with predictable outcomes	· Number of uniform policies · Percent of equipment within integrated cross-vendor power management · Percent equipment supporting regulatory compliance
3 Intermediate	· Workload profiling performed on physical entities · Power management features compliant with industry standards	· Improve understanding of power implications across entities · Pervasive remote management · Integration of some power features where compatible	· Percent of workloads profiled · Percentage of equipment with industry-compliant features
2 Basic	· Hardware power monitoring is vendor-specific · Single node monitoring with manual configuration	· Basic node level power management · Static power management policies are in place	· Percent of hardware-based power saving features use · Percent of applications with static power management policies
1 Initial (Low)	· Power management is by individual owner of champion	· Basic knowledge of power consumption at individual processor level	· Power consumption of some individual processors

Figure 19.6   Summary of Key Practices, Outcomes, and Key Metrics

For an organization operating at any given level, Figure 19.7 captures some general actions necessary to move the organization to the next level. More specific actions are likely needed depending on the mission objectives of the organization.

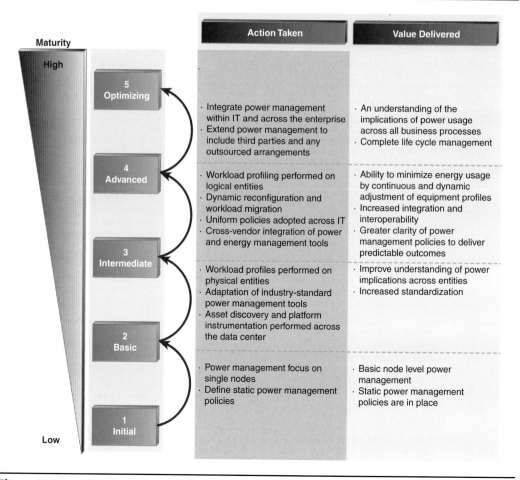

Figure 19.7 Transition Steps to Move across Maturity Levels

Before deciding what to do probably a more meaningful task is to determine precisely the maturity level of an organization. The assessment is done through a survey of relevant technical contributors and decision makers in the organization. The model is situational and includes two assessment questions per capability building block. The questions are captured in Table 19.2 along with the justification or goal for each one of the questions. Tables 19.3, 19.4, and 19.5, one per capability building block, capture answers to help the assessor determine the maturity level of the organization.

When the answers are tabulated, there will be a maturity range depending on each participant and also across the questions. The assessor will look at the answers and come up with a general determination of the organization's maturity level. Differences in averages of less than a unit are not likely to be significant. Hence two organizations scoring 3.3 and 3.7 are at about the same maturity level, and the organization receiving the 3.3 score is not necessarily less advanced than the one that received the 3.7.

Table 19.2 Data Center Server Power Management Assessment Questions

Capability Building Block	Assessment Question	Justification
Power Usage Models and Integration	Assess and understand the approaches taken by the organization to managing server power consumption	Assess and understand the approaches taken by the organization to managing server power consumption
	Describe the scope of integration for server power management at your facility.	Scope of integration refers to the number of artifacts under a formal, policy-based server power management practice, starting with monitoring of single servers to integrated power management practices encompassing the whole facility at the other end of the spectrum. Increasing scope brings new opportunities to optimize power usage, but also brings operational complexity.
Power Management Scalability	What approach has been taken to scale power management across physical, virtual and organizational entities?	What approach has been taken to scale power management across physical, virtual and organizational entities.
	What capability does the organization have to deploy power management solutions across servers, applications and departments?	Understand an organization's execution capability to architect and build power management solutions to attain necessary goals.
Power Management Interoperability	What server power management tools are in place in your organization, what functionality do they have and how do they conform to industry standards? (This can cover the monitoring of single servers to integrated power management practices encompassing the whole facility).	Understand what tools are currently being used in the organization: who are the suppliers, what functionality and interoperability do they provide and how do they conform to industry standards.
	To what extent has the IT organization normalized data center server power management practices?	Normalized practices facilitate coordination across teams making it easier to set up and execute on coordinated sustainable computing strategies.

Table 19.3 Answers to Data Center Server Power Integration Assessment

Maturity Level Characterization	Answers to Question 1	Answers to Question 2
Optimizing	Ability to dynamically optimize power and energy consumption across the enterprise enables meaningful discussion with the business on managing server loads. Holistic enterprise wide policy delivers the ability to predict power impact of new business services.	Power and energy management is integrated across the physical plant, and takes full account of all the life cycle planning and Business processes.
Advanced	Energy management and power optimization is achieved by dynamic equipment configuration. There are uniform policies across departments with predictable outcomes.	Integration at the software level: applications, OS, hypervisor. Practices allow reconfiguring the physical infrastructure to optimize application behavior, for instance powering down equipment when not needed, or dynamically consolidating virtual machines.
Intermediate	Power management is now dynamic and uses time-of-day scheduling and workload profiling. Remote management is pervasive in the organisation.	" Integration at the server pool, hardware level, with an ability to set up predictable power consumption targets to optimize electricity purchase pricing. Time-varying, dynamic power capping supported."
Basic	Hardware supported monitoring, and static policies to improve infrastructure utilization, have been introduced. Configuration management is manual and uses set-and-forget functionality.	Integration at the single server level. Server power monitoring allows the enforcement of policies based on actual power consumption at the point of consumption, rather than proxy metrics such as CPU or memory utilization. Advanced Level 2 may include static power capping.
Initial	No coordinated use of tools or model at this level.	No formal integration at this level.

Table 19.4 Answers to Data Center Server Power Scalability Assessment

Maturity Level Characterization	Answers to Question 3	Answers to Question 4
Optimizing	Power management is performed across organizational boundaries including third parties and covers any outsourcing arrangements	Most entities in a data center can be integrated into a power management deployment as part of normalized, system-wide IT processes
Advanced	Power management is performed across logical entities; VMMs, applications.	Deployments support power management at the application, OS and VMM level.
Intermediate	Power management is performed across physical entities: nodes, racks and rows.	Dynamic power management enables the tailoring of policies to the physical entities: nodes, racks and rows.
Basic	There is monitoring of single nodes with a limited capability to monitor across server groups	Power management deployments emerging across a few servers within a rack. There still is a significant presence of static policies which impedes larger deployments
Initial	Power management scalability does not yet register as an issue	Dominance of static policies make power management deployments difficult.

Table 19.5 Answers to Data Center Server Power Interoperability Assessment

Maturity Level Characterization	Answers to Question 5	Answers to Question 6
Optimizing	Power and energy management within IT is coordinated and integrated with power and energy management across the enterprise. This is a central management and control function ensuring interoperability of systems and conformance to industry best practice	Power and energy management is standardized and coordinated across the enterprise.
Advanced	Power and energy management is interoperable across all vendor offerings	Centralized policy and control embedded across IT, ensures all tools are interoperable and conform to industry standards.
Intermediate	The power management features are compliant with industry-wide standards e.g. IPMI, DCMI, PMBus. There is some interoperability between vendors	There is a consistent policy emerging across the IT organization to ensure conformance to industry standards. The purchase of all power management tools is centrally controlled, to ensure interoperability and conformance to policy.
Basic	Power management has limited functionality from a small set of vendors. There is no attempt at interoperability between tools.	Local policies in place ensuring consistency across similar hardware platforms, there is little if any interoperability between tools.
Initial	There is no insight available into what platform power management tools are in use	There is no formal process in place; any effort is confined to local champions working on their own initiative with single servers.

The model was still under construction at the time of writing. For a more up-to-date version, please refer to the IVI Web site, http://ivi.nuim.ie/. In particular, data center server power management is only one of many possible categories under the more general rubric of a data center efficiency maturity model. Additional categories are under consideration, including data center design and data center quality of service management.

From Server Power Management to Data Center Efficiency

We envision the Data Center Server Power Management Maturity Model, illustrated in Figure 19.8, as the first of a number of categories that collectively would comprise an IT-CMF instantiation for data center efficiency integrated with the SICT model. A second category in the works is the Data Center Design for Efficiency Maturity Model, which we will sketch in this section. The number of categories is potentially unbounded and determined by industry needs.

Research is in process to add additional categories. A capture of practices for high ambient temperature operation of data centers is under consideration. Allowing the ambient temperature in data centers to rise would in principle yield energy savings from reduced cooling requirements. The model would provide a framework to manage potential side effects, such as the impact on equipment manufacturer warranties, and environmental and labor regulation considerations.

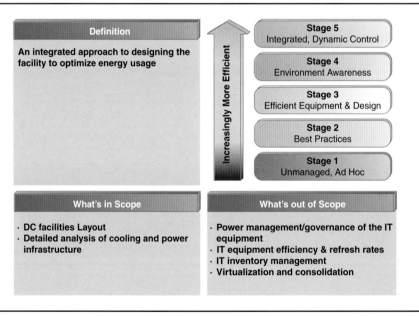

Figure 19.8 Data Center Design for Efficiency Maturity Model Scope Page

Essential characteristics by level are as follows:

■ Level 1: Unmanaged, Ad Hoc. Captures the default initial stage with an organization with no history in deploying data centers for which efficiency is a primary consideration.

■ Level 2: Best Practices. This stage captures the efficiency gains possible through process improvement possible without significant infrastructure changes.

■ Level 3: Efficient Equipment and Design. Captures improvements possible by upgrading equipment. Improvements through equipment and infrastructure coordination are still limited.

■ Level 4: Environment Awareness. Factors in environmental considerations into data center design for efficiency, including site considerations. For instance organizations may choose a primarily cool and dry place to maximize the use of economizers.

■ Level 5: Integrated, Dynamic control. Optimizing stage where all elements in levels 2, 3, and 4 have been integrated synergistically.

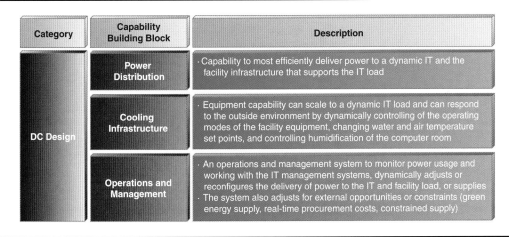

Figure 19.9   Data Center Design for Efficiency Maturity Model Capability Building Blocks

Figure 19.9 provides an initial selection for capability building blocks. An organization with a strategic goal of introducing improvements along the three capability building blocks mentioned can also advance in terms of maturity levels. Figure 19.10 describes key characteristics for organizations at each of the five levels.

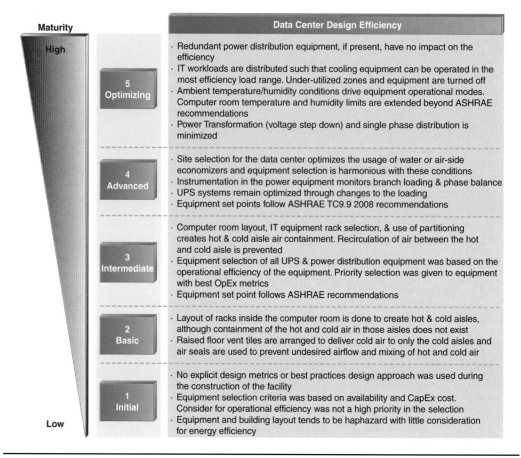

Figure 19.10   Data Center Design for Efficiency: Summary of Key Characteristics

Figure 19.11 synthesizes the information in Figures 19.9 and 19.10 as a single, two-dimensional matrix comprising the capability building blocks and the characteristics of each CBB for each stage of development. It is very much a work in progress at this point, included for example purposes only. The data is tentative, and most of the information on operations is yet to be determined and filled in.

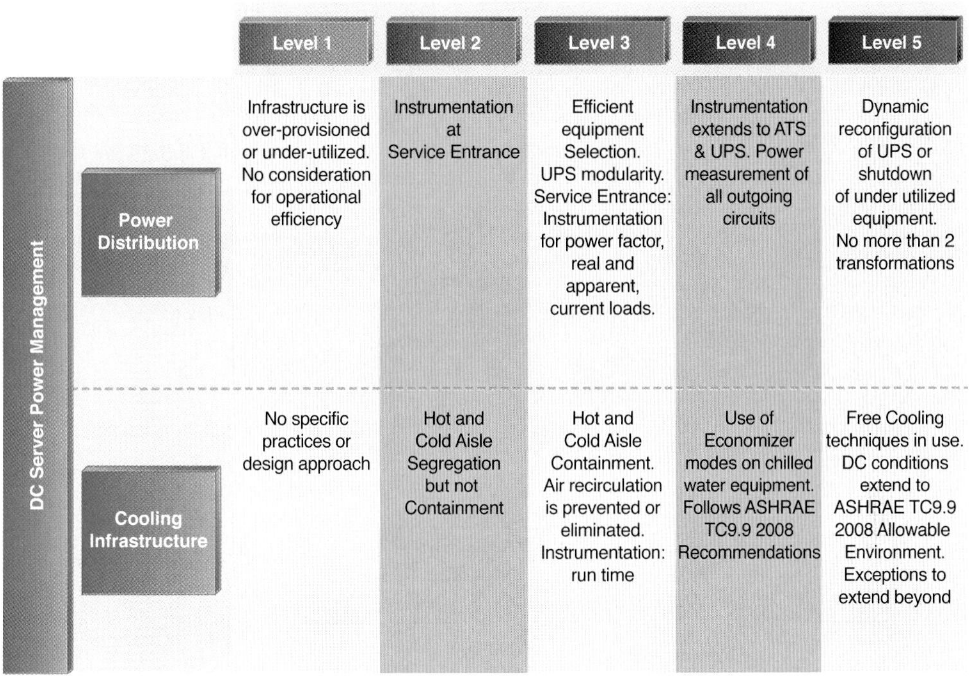
Level 1
Level 2
Level 3
Level 4
Level 5
DC Server Power Management
Power Distribution
Infrastructure is over-provisioned or under-utilized. No consideration for operational efficiency
Instrumentation at Service Entrance
Efficient equipment Selection. UPS modularity. Service Entrance: Instrumentation for power factor, real and apparent, current loads.
Instrumentation extends to ATS & UPS. Power measurement of all outgoing circuits
Dynamic reconfiguration of UPS or shutdown of under utilized equipment. No more than 2 transformations
Cooling Infrastructure
No specific practices or design approach
Hot and Cold Aisle Segregation but not Containment
Hot and Cold Aisle Containment. Air recirculation is prevented or eliminated. Instrumentation: run time
Use of Economizer modes on chilled water equipment. Follows ASHRAE TC9.9 2008 Recommendations
Free Cooling techniques in use. DC conditions extend to ASHRAE TC9.9 2008 Allowable Environment. Exceptions to extend beyond

Figure 19.11 Data Center Design for Efficiency Summary Maturity Curve

The capability maturity framework provides assessment tools that an organization can use to establish a baseline state along with specific recommendations and actions to be taken to allow the organization to advance to the next stage and at the same time establish an efficiency roadmap with progress targets over time. Progress is to be measured, preferably with metrics widely accepted in the industry. The Green Grid Forum Power Usage Effectiveness or PUE would be one such example. The targets shown in Figure 19.12 are still tentative. A number of experiments will need to be carried out to verify that these numbers are indeed realistic targets and attainable. One initial assumption is a tradeoff between redundancy and energy consumption. Higher data center tiers, as defined by the Uptime Institute are inherently more energy-intensive due to the larger amount of equipment needed to deliver a specific capability.

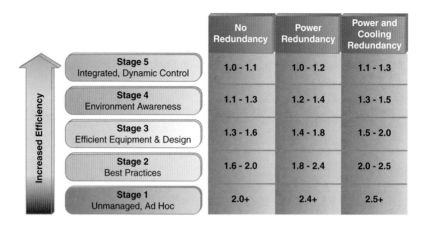

Figure 19.12 Data Center Design for Efficiency PUE Targets

About the Innovation Value Institute

The IVI IT-CMF was founded with the goal of creating a methodology for integrating approaches to enables CIOs and business management to optimize business value from IT investments and practices. The goals are achieved through research, development, and the dissemination of empirically proven and industry-validated information technology best practice models.

The IT-CMF

The IT Capability Maturity Framework (IT-CMF) is an emerging blueprint of end-to-end IT processes encapsulating the IT capability of an organization. A core function of the IT-CMF is to act as an assessment tool and a management system with associated improvement roadmaps to guide senior IT and business management in selecting strategies to continuously improve, develop, and manage the IT capability in support of optimized business value delivery.

IT-CMF is a systematic framework developed by the Innovation Value Institute (IVI), an open innovation consortium that spans academic, industry, public-sector, consulting, analyst, ISV, and professional bodies. The IVI currently has more than 30 members around the world, including Intel, which helped develop it.

The IT-CMF assists CIOs in better managing the integral complexities and tradeoffs required to continuously evolve an organization's IT capability to deliver more value. More than 200 companies around the world currently use it, including Intel IT.

It consists of a five-stage maturity model for improving IT capability, identifying and prioritizing opportunities, reducing costs, and optimizing the business value of IT investments. By using the IT-CMF, Intel IT has been able to systematically improve its capabilities year over year.

Research Focus

The IVI is supported by a global consortium of like-minded peers drawn from a community of public and private sector organizations, academia, analysts, professional associations, independent software vendors and professional services organizations.

The consortium draws expertise from its global footprint to integrate leading academic theory with the best of corporate experience to advance practices for managing information technology for business value and information technology enabled business innovation.

The IVI consortium's open-innovation model of collaboration ensures new perspectives on value-based IT management while validating that these approaches have a broad applicability across differing industries and contexts to optimize the business value of IT investments.

This unique collaboration provides the environment necessary for the synthesis of leading industry best practices and pioneering academic output, far beyond what any one entity could hope to achieve by itself.

The iterative refinement of this approach, operating at the intersection of academia and industry, by alternating inductive and deductive methods, means that the consortium can take advantage of the best practices at each juncture to design for success.

IVI offers a number of services drawn from empirically validated and industry proven best practice frameworks, management methodologies, case studies and assessment methods to guide organizations in delivering superior business value through the improvement of information technology management practices.

Chapter 20

Optimizing Service Level Agreements with Platform Power Management

Contributed by Xavier Simonart, Luc Provoost, and Enrique Castro-Leon

In Chapter 4 we discussed the complex relationship between the power control capability and performance. One school of thought to take advantage of this capability is to discover the circumstances and define the usage envelope where the Intel® Intelligent Power Node Manager technology can reduce server power consumption with negligible impact on performance. Another school of thought is to find mechanisms to maximize or at least neutralize the performance impact of power capping.

In this chapter we explore a third approach, perhaps more compatible with service applications deployed in the telecommunications sector. These services are usually subject to a service level agreement or SLA often enforced by industry or governmental organizations.

In case of applications whose quality of service is related to server performance the availability of power management enables operators to establish application key performance indicators or KPIs to match a target SLA. The goal for this exercise is to match the SLA exactly. Shorting the SLA can lead to customer complaints and enforcement actions. Exceeding the SLA for no particular business reason represents over-commitment of resources and unnecessary operational expenses.

The application of power management brings an economic benefit to operators, namely, the ability to operate under power limited situations, reduction of infrastructure requirements and with the right processes, a net reduction in energy costs. The experiment reported in this chapter exemplifies this approach.

Fine Tuning to Meet Service Level Agreements

We will conduct a conceptual exploration on a methodology for SLA optimization in the telecommunications industry segment through an experiment running an OpenSIPS SIPP proxy. We observe the relationship between power capping and performance in this environment. Under low or medium loads, those effects are usually minimal and can be neglected; on medium loads those effects are usually real in some aspects, like timings, but this is still far from impacting SLA; on high loads, the system performance is more heavily impacted, and the SLA might be in danger to be violated. We recommend a set of policies and strategies based on these behaviors.

Experimental Setup

The experiment was run on an Intel Server System with the S5520 Intel Server Board code named Urbanna and provisioned with two Intel® Xeon® X5660 processors. The operating system used was Red Hat Enterprise Linux version 5.4.

The system under test (SUT) is based on an open-source call control application. The server runs SIP call handling and can be considered as a core component of any SIP-based VoIP solution. It handles different use cases, including calling, messaging, registration, re-registration and de-registration. These scenarios represent typical usages for mobile users:

■ Calling, the mobile user making and receiving calls

■ Messaging, the mobile user sending and receiving SMS messages

■ Registration, mobile user powering on a mobile device

■ De-registration, switching off the mobile device

■ Re-registration. Re-registration messages are sent automatically when a mobile remains switched on for some time (depending of the networks this varies from half an hour to one hour).

For this environment, application performance is a function of CPU performance, memory bandwidth, and latency, as well as network bandwidth and latency.

Load Generation Setup

The load generated in the test system is based on another Open Source project, the IMS Bench SIPp tool. The IMS bench SIPp tool is an Open Source implementation of a test system conforming to IMS/NGN Performance Benchmark specification ETSI TS 186 008.

The IMS Bench SIPp tool consists of one manager and one or more SIPp load generators. As shown in Figure 20.1.

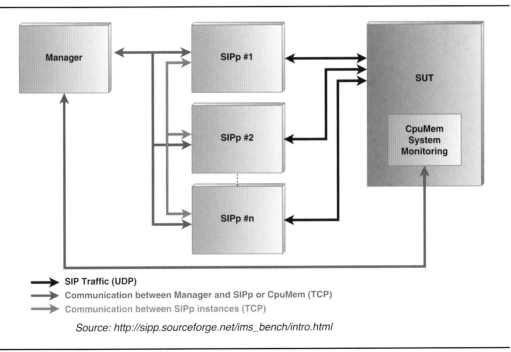

Source: http://sipp.sourceforge.net/ims_bench/intro.html

Figure 20.1   SIPp Tool Architecture

The manager reads configuration files to learn about the traffic set defining scenarios to be generated and the traffic profile defining the workload for specific scenarios, and how the workload must vary with the time. The tool was also developed to mimic real-life scenarios as accurately as possible. Hence, for instance, the load generated by the test systems is based on a Poisson distribution, the traffic mix is based on Poisson distribution, and all timings are based on negative exponentials. The IMS Bench SIPP tool can verify that the generated scenarios are handled correctly by the System Under Test given its capability to handle both parties in scenarios for calling and messaging.

As referenced in ETSI 186.008, the ETSI IMS benchmarking specification, a call for instance is not considered as handled properly if the time between the INVITE sent by UAC and received by the UAS is more than two seconds, or if the time between the INVITE and the ACK (less the ringing time) is more than two seconds, or if the time between the BYE and the OK is more than two seconds. Some similar timing measurements exist for the other scenarios such as messaging and registration. These timers are not the protocol timers; an INVITE message for instance is retransmitted if no response/acknowledge is being received after 500 msec. Those timers, part of the IMS benchmarking specification, are representative of an SLA.

Test Description

A first analysis consisted in checking whether one could have the server handle a fixed load, and reduce power consumption by using Intel® Intelligent Power Node Manager techniques.

Three workload tests were conducted:

- High load with 20,000 scenarios per second
- Medium load with 17,000 scenarios per second
- Low workload with 14,000 scenarios per second

The mix of scenarios for each workload is approximately

- Calling scenario (20%),
- Messaging (30%),
- Re-registration (46%),
- Registration (2%) and
- De-registration (2%).

The high load is similar in term of message handling to a load generated by around 15 million users, each of them switching on and off their mobile once a day, making 10 phones calls and sending 15 SMS per day.

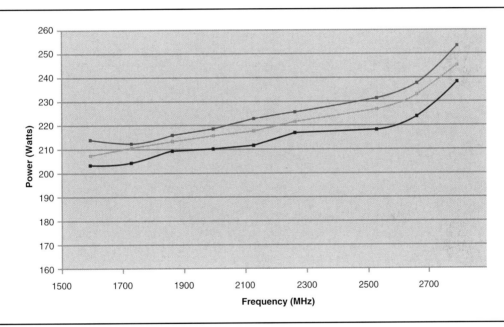

Figure 20.2   Power as Function of Frequency

The graphs in Figure 20.2 show the power consumed at different P-states, with the server always handling the same load (fixed externally by the test systems).

The graph shows a capping range of about 40 watts; that is, the value of $\rho_{capping}$ is about 1.2. The system was able to handle all three workload scenarios with no inadequately handled scenarios, or IHS, as defined by ETS 186.008).

While power capping did not impair the capacity for the system to handle calls, there were other performance parameters that needed a closer look, for instance response times, which, fortunately, the IMS Bench SIPp tool is capable of measuring. A key performance indicator or KPI is *response time,* the interval between the INVITE being sent by the caller, and the INVITE received by the call recipient. The average is shown in the Figure 20.3 for the same workload scenarios.

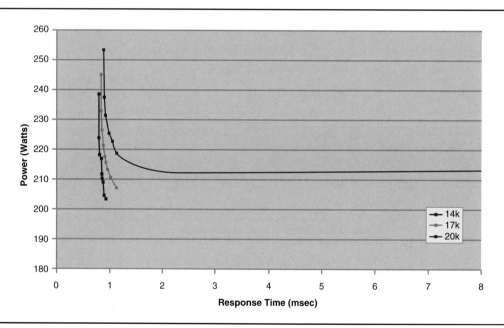

Figure 20.3   Response Time versus Power Consumption as Function of Workload

The experimental results show the following:

- The plot for the 14 K scenarios shows a minimal increase in response time, in the order of 0.1 milliseconds. These small variations would not be noticed by users, and hence do not impact at all the SLA.

- Response times under a 40-watt capping become larger for the 17 K scenarios per second, but at 1.2 milliseconds they are still well within the 2-second limit prescribed by ETSI.

- For the 20 K scenarios per seconds, the response times lengthen to about 10 milliseconds after a 40-watt cap is applied. However, the graph shows response times growing very rapidly after that threshold where response times can grow uncontrollably.

Summary

The infrastructure utilization is at its most efficient when it's applied to deliver the service demand at exactly the negotiated service level agreement. Exceeding the SLA indicates the service provider is over-spending and this is not a desirable situation. Neither is under-delivering on in terms of QoS because of the risk of negative reactions from customers or regulatory agencies.

Platform power management can be used as a knob to adjust the QoS level. Benchmarking and measurement is necessary to determine the sweet spot. These measurements can be estimated offline and monitored during operations. Through these experiments we discovered that the particular configuration tested can handle up to 20,000 call scenarios per second and it is possible to enforce a 40-watt power cap while keeping call response times within the SLA of 2 seconds. However, at the highest workload and most aggressive capping condition, response times are at risk of increasing uncontrollably, that is, there is a risk of unbounded degradation of service.

One possible policy to optimize operational costs is to have the system run with a 40-watt cap at all times. However, the application management console would monitor the call volume at all times and would begin to roll back the capping level if service demand gets close to 20,000 scenarios per second.

Chapter 21

Virtual User Environments for Clients

Contributed by Ed Jimison, David Buchholz and Jim Sutorka

Intel IT is developing a new computing approach that combines multiple emerging technologies, including client virtualization and streaming, to potentially transform the way we deliver computing to users.

Called the Virtual User Environment (VUE), it employs a virtualized IT container that could run on any client hardware capable of supporting virtualization. We manage the VUE according to IT policies and use streaming to deliver IT applications and data to it. The environment is protected because it runs within a virtual machine (VM), enabling employees to simultaneously use the client for personal applications and data without affecting the IT environment.

This usage could enable radically new business models with substantial benefits for IT and for employees:

- Employees can acquire the client platform of their choice, instead of being restricted to a few IT-qualified platforms.

- It frees Intel IT from having to build, distribute, or support client PCs.

- IT can focus on managing IT assets, not personal data and applications; employees are able to run their personal applications outside the VUE.

- Users could achieve device-independent mobility, accessing IT services through a wide variety of consumer and mobile devices.

Current PC Client Environment

The traditional client PC computing model has effectively supported Intel's increasingly mobile users. About 80 percent of our employees use laptops as their primary client PC hardware. This provides users with access to a full set of IT applications both in the office and while traveling or at home.

However, the traditional client PC model also has disadvantages and limitations, both for IT and for employees.

- To build a client PC, Intel IT purchases a laptop from a vendor, deletes all vendor-supplied software, replaces it with an IT-qualified build, and distributes the machine to the user. Intel IT has greatly streamlined this process over the years, but it is still time consuming and slows the delivery of new systems to users.

- To reduce total cost of ownership (TCO) and increase efficiency, Intel IT has standardized PCs on a few client hardware platforms and a number of software applications. While it helps keeping provisioning costs in check, this practice limits user choice and can constrain user productivity.

- Employees increasingly have their own personal computing devices, including mobile computing devices such as smart phones, yet they have limited ability to access corporate data and applications using these devices.

- Corporate and personal data may be interspersed throughout a client's storage devices. This makes it difficult to apply IT policies only to corporate data while letting users manage their personal data.

The emerging technology engineering team has been considering innovative client computing models to fundamentally address these issues. The team investigated many emerging technologies including application streaming, virtualization, open-source software, and hosted computing. During the course of the analysis it became clear that integrating these technologies to create a new computing environment could deliver even greater benefits than applying each technology individually.

The Benefits of Emerging Virtualization Technologies

The approach takes advantage of a virtualized IT environment capable of running on any client hardware. The use of streaming makes it possible to deliver IT applications and corporate data to this virtualized environment, with the environment managed remotely. Because the IT environment runs within a VM sandbox, it is protected, allowing employees to simultaneously use the rest of the client for personal applications and data. Users can choose from a variety of client devices and access their IT environment from each device. This approach enables new business models with deliver a range of benefits for IT and for users not attainable with more traditional methods. We call our concept the *virtual user environment* or *VUE*. Let's make a quick survey of the technological context that led to the virtual user environment.

Emerging Technologies and Shifting Computing Models

The virtual user environment concept takes advantage of technologies and models that have emerged over the past few years, as shown in Figure 21.1.

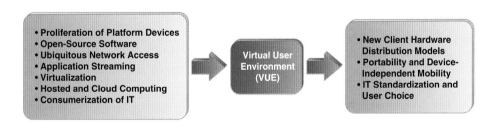

Figure 21.1 Technologies and Shifting Computing Models

Proliferation of Devices

In the past, the computer that Intel IT provided was often the only computer that an employee used. Now, many users have their own personal computers at home and may also carry small form factor computing devices such as smart phones and mobile Internet devices (MIDs). Today, employees have limited access to IT applications from these devices. With the virtual user environment, we could potentially deliver full IT services on these employee-owned devices.

Open-Source Software

Traditionally, enterprise software was supplied only by large software vendors. Today, there is an increasing amount of open-source or free software. It is entirely feasible to build a virtual user environment using Linux[†], an open-source browser, and open-source office productivity software, and reduce cost by streaming this environment to groups of users.

Ubiquitous Network Access.

Broadband Internet access is now available in most areas. With the proliferation of Wi-Fi[†] and the emergence of WiMAX, we are moving toward an *always connected* state.

Streaming Technologies

Streaming uses agents to deliver the operating environment and applications to clients, without the need to install the software locally on the client. The approach provides the benefits of centralized manageability and security, together with full client application capabilities.

Virtualization

Three types of virtualization are emerging: hardware, operating system, and application. Hardware virtualization, such as Intel® Virtualization Technology (Intel® VT), virtualizes parts of the platform and exposes them to the OS at different levels. This optimization allows direct access to hardware features from multiple OS environments, as well as the improved performance stemming from direct hardware access. Virtualizing the OS allows running the OS on other operating environments as well as cross-operating system isolation on the host. With application virtualization, the application is virtualized into a container that is then delivered to a host system. This helps ensure that the application runs within the same environment in which it was packaged and that it is isolated from other applications running on the same OS.

Hosted and Cloud Computing

Suppliers are increasingly offering software as a hosted service over the Internet. IT organizations can use hosted applications to deliver new services more quickly, without costly investment in infrastructure, and provide users with more choice.

Consumerization of IT

Traditionally, technology became available to enterprises first, then later spread to consumers. That trend continues with the spread of networks and shared storage into the home. However, a reverse trend is also emerging rapidly. Now, a variety of technologies that were first adopted by consumers are now spreading into the enterprise These include instant messaging, social media, small form factor platforms, wireless networking, and MIDs. This creates more choice for enterprise users and increases the possibility of using the same devices for both IT and personal use.

Benefits of the Virtual User Environment

As work proceeded in the development of the virtual user environment, the team identified substantial customer benefits in terms of client hardware distribution, portability and device-independent mobility and in spite of the apparent contradiction, in the economies brought by IT process and equipment standardization and user choice. Let's take a quick look at each of the three factors.

Client Hardware Distribution

In the present, IT distributes only a few qualified hardware platforms and supports a limited number of IT applications. Employees are not allowed to install some personal applications because of potential security threats.

BYOD.

With the virtual user environment, this situation could change completely. Potentially, Intel IT would not have to buy and distribute client hardware at all; employees could buy the platform they want.

Employees could use this platform to run their favorite consumer applications, such as photo and movie editing, Voice over IP (VoIP), and personal business software. IT applications would run in a protected "bubble." that is, a virtualized environment on the same platform.

IT would not be concerned with the personal applications employees use, because those applications would run outside the virtual user environment and would not interfere with it. Users would have the flexibility to run the virtual user environment and their personal applications on different operating systems.

Portability and Device-Independent Mobility

The research team realized that by virtualizing the IT environment, it was possible make it portable across many platforms. Potentially, any device capable of hosting a virtual machine could host a virtual user environment. Eventually, this usage model might include platforms other than traditional full-featured PC clients, such as the smaller *netbooks* and handheld-size MIDs based on Intel® Atom™ processors. When users travel, they enjoy the convenience of accessing the virtual user environment from any capable device, even if they chose not to carry their personal devices.

This realization made the team look at mobility in a new way and ultimately led to the idea of device-independent mobility. Traditionally, mobility has been defined as carrying your computer wherever you go. Our concept moves mobility up from the hardware platform itself to the application and data layer. We are redefining mobility as the ability to access IT applications and data from wherever you are, and from a variety of devices including full-featured desktop PCs at home or in Internet cafes, MIDs, and potentially televisions and computers built into cars.

IT Standardization and User Choice

Like other IT organizations, Intel IT reduces equipment total cost of ownership (TCO) through standardization. Today, this means standardizing on hardware platforms and operating environments. The virtual user environment suggests looking at client standardization from a totally different perspective. Rather than standardizing at the hardware and operating system level, standardization moves up in level of abstraction to the virtual user environment. Because of this, the end user would have a choice of hardware platform, OS, and consumer applications.

VUE Architecture

Figures 21.2 and 21.3 compare the traditional client architecture with the initial version of the virtual user environment. In the traditional architecture, IT applications and data are ingrained and bound to the platform. Personal and corporate data coexist as user data and can't be segregated. Figure 21.3 represents the evolved environment that can be achieved using technology that exists today or will become available during the next 12 to 18 months.

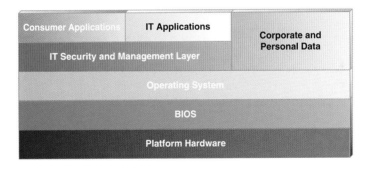

Figure 21.2 Today's IT Platform.

In our traditional client model, personal and corporate data are ingrained into the platform, where they coexist as user data. The two cannot be easily separated. In contrast, the virtual user environment clearly separates personal and corporate data. This means that through the VUE, we can easily apply Intel data retention and management policies singling out corporate-specific data only.

The VUE environment is encrypted to protect IT data and applications. Analogous to the hardware, users run their choice of security software to protect their personal environment.

IT uses virtual machine policy management software to control the virtual user environment. This lets us implement policies such as enabling access to the corporate network only from within the virtual user environment. It is also possible to determine when the bubble expires or whether users can, load data into the VUE from USB devices. Intel® vPro™ technology integrated into the platform also facilitates remote management, with Intel VT accelerating the performance of the virtualized software.

Even though this initial version of the virtual user environment represents, what can be achieved with technology that is readily available in the short term, yet it represents a radical departure from our traditional client architecture, shown in Figure 21.2.

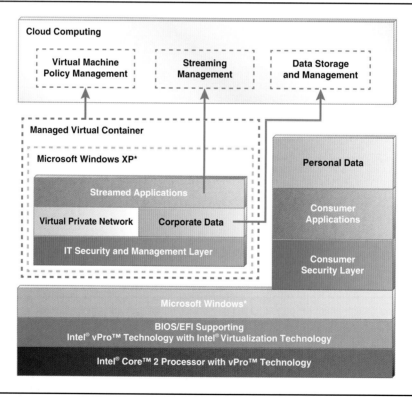

Figure 21.3 Virtual User Environment Reference Architecture.

On the user's client device, the VUE runs within a VM as a managed virtual container. We use a cloud computing approach, in which the OS, applications, and data may be stored remotely—whether on servers located at an Intel data center or hosted by a supplier—and streamed to the container as needed by the user, transported on a USB thumb drive or delivered by a combination of both methods.

Virtual User Environment Proof of Concept

At the time of writing the technology development team has implemented a prototype that includes key aspects of this initial architecture. In the prototype, the client systems are standard corporate and consumer PCs based on Intel® Core™2 Duo processors running Microsoft Windows† or Linux; the virtual user environment OS is Microsoft Windows XP†.

The environment uses a hypervisor and virtual machine policy management software from an established VM software supplier. The streaming capability is provided by a commercial, off-the-shelf application streaming product, with a client component within the virtual user environment communicating with a server component running on Intel's corporate servers.

For the current prototype, storage is provisioned from a commercial Internet-based data storage service, with an option to cache data locally as needed. For he current instantiation, the environment resides on removable memory. The environment can be moved between machines by the simple expedient of plugging the memory into the USB port on each machine. With these mechanisms in place, we have been able to transfer the prototype from a system at Intel to a consumer PC at home. All traditional client functionality is available within the virtual user environment. Also, the proof of concept demonstrated the feasibility of using the virtual user environment to access IT applications over the corporate network from both home and office locations.

Internal benchmarks indicate that hardware virtualization substantially accelerates performance of the virtual client. We tested a laptop equipped with Intel Intel® Centrino 2 with vPro™ technology, which includes Intel VT. The benchmarks indicate that a virtualized client environment on this platform can run approximately 60 percent faster than the native client environment on a current Intel IT-managed laptop model based on the 1.8 GHz Intel® Pentium™ M processor 750.

Evolution of the Virtual User Environment

The technologies underpinning the virtual user environment are evolving quickly. Hence it is not unreasonable to expect that the virtual user environment itself is to evolve accordingly. New capabilities will spring up as they are enabled by the available technologies. Extrapolating on current technology trends, Figure 21.4 shows what's possible within about two years.

Perhaps one important change is the addition of a client native hypervisor. This layer underlies the entire client environment, so that both the corporate and personal applications run within virtualized containers hosted by this hypervisor. This arrangement further protects the IT environment. The hypervisor provides each guest operating system with direct access to the client hardware resources. It would be possible to run multiple operating systems on a client platform simultaneously, yet keep them completely separate from each other.

With this arrangement, the performance and security of each guest OS are not dependent on a host OS. Security is enhanced because the guest OS cannot be manipulated through a host OS.

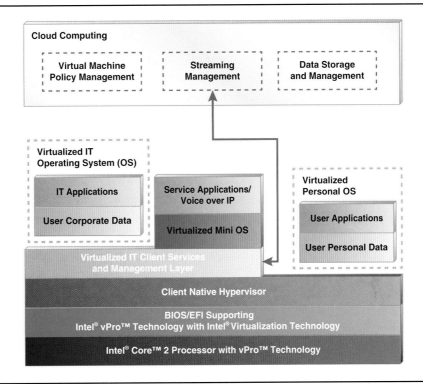

Figure 21.4 Virtual Client Architecture

In this future scenario, compute-intensive tasks initiated in the personal environment, such as malware scans, do not affect the performance of IT applications. Similarly, if the personal OS crashes, the IT container is unaffected. A service and management layer provides security services to the virtual user environment, independent of the virtual user environment operating system.

Reduced, small footprint operating systems specialized for specific purposes may become commonplace. This development is already occurring in server-based software. These lightweight operating systems enable the system to run without consuming more resources than necessary to perform a specific function. For example, we envision that such an OS might run VoIP. Another mini-OS might enable a PC to act as a DVD player without needing to boot the primary personal or corporate OS, resulting in faster startup and longer battery life.

Roadblocks to Virtual User Environment Adoption

A number of roadblocks exist today that stand in the way of pervasive adoption of virtual user environments.

To host a virtual user environment, *each device needs to be capable of running a virtualized environment.* This trend may accelerate as mobile and consumer devices incorporate more-powerful processors, such as Intel Atom processors.

Network bandwidth is still a limitation outside the corporate environment, though broadband availability and speed are improving rapidly.

Security is a concern. Virtual user environment data is stored within the cloud, requiring a new security support model to help ensure that a user can securely access the data from different clients. Another potential concern is that today, the virtual user environment client software runs on a host OS and thus could be vulnerable to attack from a non-managed host environment. In the future, the use of client native hypervisor could protect against these attacks.

Vendors need to tailor applications appropriately for each type of client environment, such as ultra-mobile devices. This is beginning to take place, but much more is needed. Vendors also need to make sure all applications run in virtualized environments, without requiring direct hardware access, and they need to develop better software licensing models for virtualized environments.

Benefits of the Virtual User Environment to the Business

IT organizations continually have to balance user preferences and corporate responsibility. Today, most IT organizations have swung toward corporate responsibility and favor treating clients primarily as corporate assets. This tends to restrict user capabilities. With the VUE, IT organizations do not have to make a choice; they can simultaneously fulfill corporate responsibilities and allow user preferences, as shown in Figure 21.5.

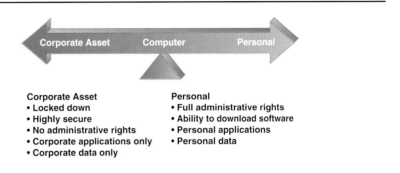

Corporate Asset
• Locked down
• Highly secure
• No administrative rights
• Corporate applications only
• Corporate data only

Personal
• Full administrative rights
• Ability to download software
• Personal applications
• Personal data

Figure 21.5 Using Virtual User Environments to Balance Business versus Personal Needs

The VUE concept could transform how we provide IT services and how employees use them. This could result in new IT business models that deliver significant benefits both for Intel IT and for employees.

Corporate Virtual User Environment Example

A typical usage model for virtual user environment is the on-demand IT corporate data delivery and management in a virtualized environment.

Usage Model

Dirk works as a Sales Manager for a pharmaceutical company who requires access to sensitive company documents while he travels. Since his company moved to providing a service for accessing documents, he is able to access sensitive company documents from his corporate PC, a hotel kiosk, or his mobile phone. Since the data is provided in a virtualized container, the company data is completely separate from the personal data that he keeps on his devices.

The virtual container or VUE is fully encrypted and secured from personal applications, and requires authentication for access to the files contained within it. If his laptop is lost or stolen, the corporate data is inaccessible to anyone but him.

The service offered by his IT group allows the flexibility of using the virtual user environment in offline mode as in the case when he's using his laptop or in "connected" mode in the case where he uses an unsecured shared computer. In the latter case, the data VUE is completely removed from the device when he requests it or he logs off. Since his data is always synched with the central repository there is no need for backup software on his devices. He doesn't need to copy it across multiple devices since the data files are accessible from all of these devices.

Problems and Needs Addressed

- Corporate data is spread across multiple devices and hard drives
- Corporate data is intertwined with personal data today requiring companies to encrypt the contents of the entire client hard drive.
- As a default, companies back up all files on the client hard drive including personal data files.
- Companies spend a lot of resources recovering files from clients for legal reasons.
- Users hoard their data for years to ensure that they have it in case they need it someday.

Benefits

■ Corporate data detached from platform device

■ IT can apply policies to data in the central repository

■ No need to back up data files as we do today since files are synchronized between platform and central repository

■ Virtual User Environment is secured from the rest of the platform

■ No need to have multiple copies of the document on different drives

Value

■ Reduces loss of sensitive data due to loss or theft

■ Increases security by isolating IT applications/data in virtual container.

Sequence of Events and Task Flow

■ User requests data virtual user environment by logging into the service with Active Directory credentials.

■ User is authenticated. Application detects user platform and provides custom IT data container for that platform. Data security is enabled.

■ If the user has cached changes on the platform he is logging in from, these are resolved with back-end store.

■ User works with applications and data. If data is modified, the changes are synchronized to the central repository.

■ When the user is finished, he submits a request to end the session. Session Manager closes out the virtual data session and removes data footprints from the target machine (if necessary).

Benefits of the Virtual User Environment to the IT

Virtual user environments enable new models for distributing client hardware, manageability, support, and security.

Distribution and Technology Adoption

IT could get out of the business of buying and distributing hardware, a radical idea. Surprisingly, doing so would accelerate technology adoption, allowing IT to get out of hardware sustaining and reallocate them to innovation. Employees could select their own hardware based on the latest technology available from vendors, rather than choosing from a traditionally constrained, pre-qualified list of IT platforms. This approach would also reduce the time required to deploy new client systems, enabling employees to use their new system immediately. The equipment becomes functional with the act of streaming a user's IT environment directly to it.

Various scenarios are possible under this environment:

- An employee might receive a stipend towards purchasing hardware of their choice, which would then be employee-owned.

- IT might specify that employees select from a small set of certified or preferred vendors, or it might be possible to let them buy from any vendor.

- IT could offer multiple OS options for the virtual user environment; because each of these would run within the virtual container, IT would not need to qualify each OS for every hardware platform.

Manageability

The virtual user environment approach facilitates changes in the way IT could manage its environment, which in turn would deliver a series of business benefits.

■ IT can focus on protecting and managing only IT assets. IT would not be responsible for managing personal data or hardware. In the traditional client environment, personal and corporate data are interspersed throughout a user's disk storage, making it difficult to enforce appropriate policies for management and retention of corporate and personal data. The virtual user environment will clearly separate corporate data from personal data making it easier to fulfill its mandate to manage corporate data only.

■ The virtual user environment can yield improved system utilization and performance by taking advantage of multi-core processors. Allocating one or more cores to the virtual user environment will yield predictable performance to corporate applications.

■ It will be possible for IT to distribute new applications faster because there would be no need to integrate them into each hardware platform and because the applications can be delivered immediately through streaming. It will be possible to integrate virtualized user environment container with other components in a service-oriented architecture (SOA) approach, resulting in faster development of new applications.

Support

Today, supporting IT clients and their users is one of our biggest IT costs. With the virtual user environment approach, the employee owns hardware, and IT would no longer be responsible for managing it. This could substantially reduce our overall hardware support costs.

There are many other potential benefits. IT would no longer have to recover PC client assets when employees leave the company; the hardware would already belong to the employee, and the rights to a virtual user environment can be revoked relatively easily. Today, IT provides and manages hardware used by on-site contractors; instead, IT could simply provide them with a bubble, allowing contractors to run on their systems. The virtual user environment can carry an expiration date set to coincide with the end of the contract. IT would no longer have to create custom reference builds for shared environments such as kiosks, because each environment could be delivered within the virtual user environment to the employee's personal device.

Security

Today, Intel IT's client hardware runs a single umbrella security solution that covers all corporate and personal data. With the virtual user environment on a native client hypervisor, the umbrella can be adjusted to protect the corporate environment and no more. By running a separate virtualized client, we can potentially shrink the footprint IT has to manage and protect. IT can now run applications and the OS as appropriate in their own virtualized spaces. Doing so, in turn, enables targeted security models in place for each environment rather than a one-size-fits-all solution for the whole platform.

Employee Benefits

The division of labor between corporate and personal assets increases the efficiency with which the assets are managed while reducing the risk of interference. The bubble concept could increase employee satisfaction and productivity by offering more choice, mobility, and reliability.

More Choice

Today, we support a limited number of PC configurations and applications. With the bubble, employees would be able to buy the platform that they want and run their choice of consumer applications on it and without IT imposing seemingly artificial limitations. Users could select platforms based on the most recent technology, rather than having to choose from a list of IT-qualified platforms.

Because the IT and personal environments are separate, users can select a preferred hardware support supplier, while continuing to get support from Intel IT. Users can select an operating system for personal use and yet another one for the virtual user environment. There is no requirement that a bubble be unique at all for a user. Users may pick from more than one bubble, enabling them to select best-of-breed applications that run only on a specific OS, as shown in Figure 21.6.

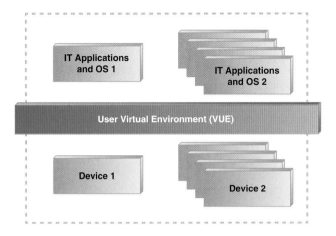

Figure 21.6 Virtual User Environment Supporting Multiple Bubbles.

Increased Mobility

With the virtual user environment, device-independent mobility becomes a practical proposition. The IT environment will no longer be bound to a specific piece of hardware; instead, the user will access IT services from any capable client hardware. Over time, employees might be able to use IT services from a growing range of mobile devices as well as home devices such as televisions. This can only increase user productivity and enhance business agility.

Increased Reliability

If an employee loses a PC or if a storage device fails, the potential impact to Intel will be greatly reduced. IT will be able to immediately restore the employee's virtual user environment to any new device, and terminate the virtual user environment on the old device. The system can also be engineered to be more stable and robust due to the separation of concerns. Also, given that IT and personal employee applications run in separate virtualized environments, there is a smaller risk for application conflicts.

Summary

Virtual user environments promise a new way to deliver computing. A technology development team demonstrated its feasibility by implementing a proof of concept. At the time of writing, the team is working with Intel business groups and external suppliers to define technology requirements and share these requirements with the industry. Within Intel, from the business side, the team is partnering with finance specialists to analyze return on investment (ROI) and with security teams to assess and document risks. Work is also taking place with other IT organizations to replicate and scale best known methods for client virtualization projects. Virtual user environments hold significant promise in transforming the way that IT delivers services, enabling new IT business models that will deliver substantial benefits both to IT organizations and their constituents.

Chapter **22**

Energy Management in a Virtualized Cloud Environment

*Contributed by Miguel Gómez Rodríguez, Ignacio Blasco López,
Telefónica Investigación y Desarrollo and Enrique Castro-Leon,
Intel Corporation*

Computing equipment has shown a notable improvement in performance over the past few decades thanks to Moore's Law. However, since the start of the twenty-first century, public demand for digital content has surged at an even higher pace. As a result, data centers keep proliferating in number and size to cope with rising demand1. Apart from increased investments in equipment, data center operators face higher operation and management costs as these facilities grow in size and complexity. Paradoxically, most of the provisioned capacity is actually wasted. The fluctuations in demand for service make it difficult to predict the capacity required.

In this chapter we present the results of a joint collaboration on energy management between Telefónica Investigación y Desarrollo and Intel. The goals for this investigation were threefold:

---

1   B. Schäppi, et al., "Energy efficient servers in Europe: Energy consumption, saving potentials, market barriers and measures. Part I: Energy consumption and saving potentials", Efficient Servers Project, Nov. 2007.

■ To assess the usability of emerging advanced technologies for power management with a currently deployed application in the industry.

■ To investigate composite usage models to derive benefits beyond what is possible when a technology is applied singly.

■ To investigate novel usage models taking advantage of the particularities of a virtualized cloud environment.

The two companies developed a proof of concept of a power and energy managed application by means of a realistic demonstrator of the target environment at Telefónica.

Motivation for Energy Efficiency

Under current management practices in the telecommunications industry, service availability and quality take a first seat. Hence equipment is provisioned for peak demand as well as in anticipation for future demand. Unfortunately this approach leads to gross over-provisioning. Analysts estimate that resource utilization of 15 to 20 percent is common in conventional data centers. Virtualization-based consolidation[2] has provided some relief to this trend allowing utilization factors to rise to the range of 40 to 70 percent depending on workload predictability.

Competitiveness and productivity considerations arising from low utilization factors notwithstanding, energy efficiency is yet another factor preventing the communication industry from fulfilling increasing demand for services at reasonable cost and low environmental impact. For example, servers are now providing 75 times more performance for the same hardware cost of eight years ago, but performance per watt has increased only 16 times during that period[3]. Thus, as the computational power of data centers grows to meet the requirements of corporations, governments, and individual consumers alike, the associated energy consumption increases at an even higher rate. Energy consumed by data centers in Europe, including cooling and power supply equipment, grew by 162 percent between 2000

---

2   W. Vogels, "Beyond server consolidation," ACM Queue, vol. 6, no. 1, pp. 20–26, Jan. 2008.

3   C. Belady, "In the data centre, power and cooling costs more than the IT equipment it supports," Electronics Cooling, Vol. 13, No. 1, Feb. 2007.

and 2006, rising from 15.1 to 39.6 terawatt-hours[1,4]. Moreover, information and communication technology (ICT) analysts expect this trend to continue, and forecast that the European data center energy consumption in 2011 will at least double the 2006 values[2].

Energy Management Considerations for the Data Center

The remarkable growth of data center energy consumption raises significant business, operational, environmental and regulatory issues that adversely affect ICT facilities individually and the ICT sector as a whole. In fact, energy efficiency has become one of the prime challenges for telecommunications operators.

The telecommunications infrastructure has experienced a significant evolution towards smaller form factors and greater density, thus multiplying by five the power demand per unit of area during the last 10 years[5].

Not surprisingly, facilities were not designed to cope with such a growth rate, with power and cooling technologies have evolving at a slower pace. Therefore, the amount of auxiliary equipment required to assist newer generations of telecommunications systems cannot be accommodated in current sites and, according to ICT analysts[6], 50 percent of data centers have suffered from power supply and cooling capacity limitations due to these factors.

In addition, electric utility companies are expected to start imposing power caps to such facilities[7] due to limitations in their transmission and distribution systems. Consequently, the adoption of energy efficiency improvement initiatives, allowing the growth of infrastructure capacity and performance levels while maintaining or even reducing power consumption, becomes a key element for making use of existing sites and extending their lifespan.

---

4   J. G. Koomey, "Estimating regional power consumption by servers: A technical note," Analytics Press, Oakland (U.S.A.), Dec. 2007.

5   Association of Heating, Refrigeration and Air-Conditioning Engineers, "Datacom Equipment Power Trends and Cooling Applications," 2005.

6   Gartner Inc., "Gartner Says 50 Percent of Data Centers Will Have Insufficient Power and Cooling Capacity by 2008" (press release), http://www.gartner.com/it/page.jsp?id=499090, Nov. 2006.

7   A. Barrett, "For PG&E customers, it pays to virtualize," SearchServerVirtualization.com, Oct. 2006.

Environmental Considerations

The telecommunications sector plays a dual role in reducing the impact of industrial activities on the environment. Telecommunications are perceived as a major tool in the fight against climate change, since they present an enormous potential to reduce greenhouse gas (GHG) emissions of other industrial sectors by optimizing production and logistics and reducing the need for transportation of people and goods. At the same time, telecommunications also constitute a major energy demand source, since recent studies estimate that ICTs account for 2 percent of global CO_2 emissions[8].

The contribution of data centers to ICT energy consumption is very significant, since they represent a remarkable 23 percent of the overall ICT CO_2 emissions[9]. Consequently, the environmental action plans undertaken by the telecommunications industry take into account these two facets, namely providing services that allow reducing the GHG emissions of other sectors while optimizing at the same time the energy consumption of telecommunications infrastructures in order to provide these services as efficiently as possible.

In order to foster this voluntary transformation of the telecommunications sector, the European Union is promoting the adoption of best practices and the endorsement of a series of codes of conduct. These initiatives are part of the EU's action plans against climate change based on the promotion of renewable energy sources and the reduction of energy consumption within the 2020 timeframe[10].

The Energy Management Proof of Concept

The main goal of this initiative is to demonstrate the application of intelligent management of infrastructure assets for attaining significant energy savings and a more rational utilization of the available energy resources, while preserving the service level of the managed platforms or the user perceived quality of the services hosted on them.

---

8   Gartner Inc., "Gartner Estimates ICT Industry Accounts for 2 Percent of Global CO2 Emissions" (Press release), http://www.gartner.com/it/page.jsp?id=503867, Apr. 2007.

9   Gartner Inc., "Gartner Says Data Centres Account for 23 Per Cent of Global ICT CO2 Emissions" (Press release), http://www.gartner.com/it/page.jsp?id=530912, Oct. 2007.

10 Commission of the European Communities, "20 20 by 2020: Europe's climate change opportunity," COM(2008) 30 final, Jan. 2008.

The two companies developed a proof of concept of an energy managed application by means of a realistic demonstrator of the target environment at Telefónica. The demonstrator comprises two main components:

■ A Dynamic Infrastructure Manager (DIM), assigned with the task of implementing the energy-aware infrastructure monitoring and control solution proposed in the context of this project.

■ A sample service infrastructure, implementing the test infrastructure to be administered by the dynamic manager.

The Telefónica Rate Plan application for premium mobile content (APC, for *Aplicación de Perfiles de Cobro*) was chosen as the sample workload. This application was deployed on a virtualized infrastructure based on VMware† ESX 4.0 and Intel® Xeon® 5500 servers.

Two separate use cases were applied concurrently to cover different operational scenarios for the infrastructure under control:

■ *Power-aware dynamic reconfiguration* for adjusting the infrastructure profile in real time to meet workload demand. The goal is in this case to fulfill the committed service level agreements (SLAs) with the minimum possible amount of resources.

■ *Power-constrained operation*, where the main goal of the dynamic management solution is to enforce the overall power or CO_2 emission restrictions of a certain facility.

The emission restrictions translate into power-limited operation. Under these conditions, the dynamic manager apportions power to the different services. The apportionment policies enforced maximize SLA compliance while taking into account the different priorities of the services hosted on the managed site.

The proof of concept involved the following activities:

■ *Deploying an actual production service* on top of the available infrastructure cluster. Measuring the baseline performance and power consumption of the sample workload on the advanced technology demonstrator, but without dynamic infrastructure management techniques. This phase also allowed identifying the prospective energy efficiency enhancements through the adoption of dynamic infrastructure management techniques and selecting specific energy-aware policies to be applied in subsequent phases.

■ *Implementing an advanced power management capability* through the integration of the technologies supplied by Intel and Telefónica Investigación y Desarrollo.

■ *Studying the power consumption and performance of the sample workload* in the improved execution environment, evaluating the operational flexibility, energy savings and the impact in performance due to the energy-aware dynamic infrastructure management.

Experimental Setup and Power Management

Figure 22.1 depicts the test bed infrastructure used in the use case evaluation tests described in this section. As shown in the diagram, we may distinguish between two main system groups:

■ The APC service infrastructure itself, based on the four Intel® Xeon® 5500 processor servers (iBOI1 to iBOI4) equipped with Intel® Intelligent Node Manager technology provided by Intel Corporation for this proof of concept.

■ Two auxiliary systems (HPM and iBOIx), where the management systems and simulators reside.

Additionally, a separate NAS storage volume for virtual machine storage completes the testing infrastructure.

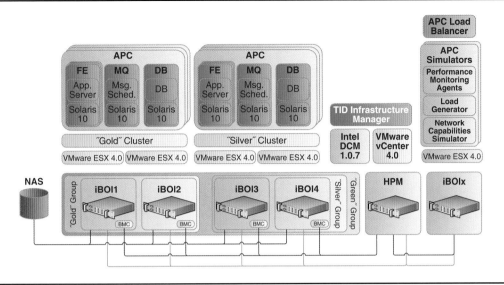

Figure 22.1   Experimental Setup

APC Service Infrastructure

As shown in Figure 22.1 the four Intel® Xeon® 5500 processor-based servers supporting the APC service infrastructure have been divided in two identical groups:

- A Gold group simulating the infrastructure for high-priority services, composed of the iBOI1 and iBOI2 servers.

- A *Silver* group simulating the infrastructure for standard services, composed of the iBOI3 and iBOI4 servers.

Additionally, these two server groups have been put together into a higher-level group, named *Green*, which represents the whole service facility.

Each of these servers has been provisioned with VMware* ESX* 4.0, and two separate server clusters have been created at virtualization level, one for each of the groups just mentioned,

- A Gold cluster simulating the virtualized infrastructure for high-priority services, composed of ESX hosts iBOI1 and iBOI2.

- A Silver cluster simulating the virtualized infrastructure for standard services, composed of ESX hosts iBOI3 and iBOI4.

An APC service instance has been deployed on each of these virtualized server clusters, simulating a high-priority and a standard workload respectively. Each instance is composed of four APC front-end nodes in a high-availability cluster configuration and a message queuing node for intra-cluster communication. Additionally, the Gold group includes an enterprise database node. Each of these APC nodes is an independent Solaris* 10 x86 virtual machine.

Management and Auxiliary Systems

A number of auxiliary systems are needed to complete the proof of concept setup. These include the APC simulators, a load balancer, and the management server.

APC Simulators

The APC simulators comprise a suite of validation and testing tools for the APC service. The tools include load injectors for generating signaling traffic, emulators to simulate the core network capacities with which the APC service communicates, and the performance monitoring agents.

The APC Performance Monitoring Agents are a group of tools responsible for generating reports on APC service behavior through log collection and analysis and the processing of service events. These components also provide a wide range of operational statistics, number of processed transactions per period such as transaction results, key performance indicators (KPIs), and so on. In this proof of concept, the service response time was selected as a KPI to drive dynamic infrastructure management. More specifically, the average response time observed in the HTTP-based rate profile interface was chosen, given that it represents the most stringent indicator in terms of response time.

As shown Figure 22.1, two APC simulators (*apc_sim1* and *apc_sim2*) were deployed in the test bed, running on a corresponding Solaris* 10 x86 virtual machine. The *apc_sim1* simulator injects traffic to the high-priority Gold APC instance, whereas the *apc_sim2* simulator feeds the standard-priority Silver instance. Both virtual machines run in the iBOIx server, virtualized with VMware ESX[†] 4.0.

Load Balancer

A software based load balancer performs the balancing of the traffic injected by the simulators to the APC front end service. The load balancer was installed and configured in an independent virtual machine and deployed in the iBOIx server along with the APC simulators.

The load balancer distributes the overall signaling load produced by the simulators across the active APC front-end instances. Moreover, it periodically monitors the availability of the different front-end nodes, routing traffic to them when they are available and removing them as traffic recipients as soon as it detects that they have been suspended by the DIM.

Management Server

The infrastructure management platform used in the proof of concept has been installed in an independent server (HPM) running Windows 2003 Server SP2. As shown in Figure 22.1, the software installed in this server includes:

■ Intel Datacenter Manager v1.0.7

■ VMware vCenter[†] v4.0.0

■ The Dynamic Infrastructure Manager provided by Telefónica Investigación y Desarrollo.

Figure 22.2 summarizes the logical architecture of the energy efficiency optimization solution evaluated in this proof of concept.

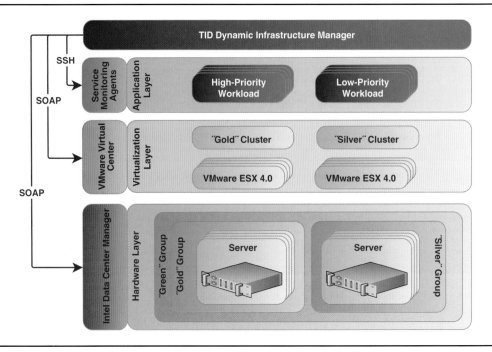

Figure 22.2   Test Bed Power Management Architecture.

As shown in Figure 22.2, the *Dynamic Infrastructure Manager*, in charge of enforcing the energy management policy, interacts with the systems under control at three different levels to gather a holistic infrastructure status view and apply appropriate infrastructure configuration according to the energy management policy and the current operational conditions:

■ *Hardware level*, for real-time power consumption monitoring, the management of the system power states, and any additional energy-saving features implemented by the computing elements such as power capping. These monitoring and control capabilities are based on the features offered by Intel's power management technologies.

■ *Virtualization level*, for monitoring guest-level resource utilization and the management of virtual system placement, reconfiguration, and the allocation of physical resources to virtual systems. These monitoring and control capabilities are based on the features offered by VMware vSphere[†] 4.

■ *Application level*, monitoring of service-specific KPIs and managing application scalability and workload placement. These monitoring and control capabilities exploit the features offered by the service monitoring agents supplied by Telefónica Investigación y Desarrollo.

A Hierarchical Framework for Power Management

As mentioned in the previous section, the environment used for the proof of concept, power management takes place concurrently at three logical levels, namely hardware, virtualization and application.

■ Hardware level

– Monitoring system power consumption and utilization, including CPU and memory utilization.

– Controlling system and performance states, for which two mechanisms are available:

■ DBS, an autonomic control scheme where the server operating system or hypervisor governs the system power and performance status through a policy based on hardware utilization thresholds.

■ Active power capping, where an external manager imposes a power restriction to the system. Such power restriction may have an effect on the processing capacity of the system under power proportional computing.

■ *Virtualization level*

– Monitoring virtual system resource utilization and hypervisor overhead.

– Managing virtual machine power states (S0, S5 and hypervisor-level suspension to disk).

– Virtual machine migration across a virtualized server pool.

■ *Application level*

– Monitoring application KPIs.

– In horizontally scalable applications, managing application topology (controlling the number of application nodes processing transactions in parallel).

Each of these mechanisms is appropriate for a certain goal under specific operational conditions. Let's see how we can apply this framework to the two main scenarios or use cases in this study.

Application Level Power Management

As previously mentioned, the sample workload chosen for this proof of concept was Telefónica's rate plan application for premium mobile content (APC, for *Aplicación de Perfiles de Cobro*). Whenever a mobile subscriber wants to access chargeable premium mobile content, such as ringtones, wallpapers, music, or videos, this service is contacted to find out the different rate plans under which such content is available, such as one-time payment, subscription, voucher for multiple uses, and so on. Once the subscriber selects the desired rate plan for content access, the APC sends a billing event to the charging system so that the appropriate fees are included in the user's regular billing and the customer is provided a token for content access.

The APC service in Telefónica's architecture is deployed in a high availability platform supporting horizontal scalability of the service front end and persistence layers. In the front end layer, the APC service publishes two SOAP interfaces and a HTTP-based interface. These interfaces are Java-based, deployed in separate servlet containers. User profiles and service information are stored in an enterprise database instance. The APC service logic uses the JDBC interface to communicate with the service persistence layer.

In order to provide a high availability solution, the APC service logic uses an internal communication layer under a mesh topology. This layer allows all APC front ends to publish execution environment checkpoints, enabling the recovery of the execution state if an instance or server fails. Thanks to this feature, it is also possible for us to continuously manage the number of active application nodes, given that the remaining nodes are able to finish processing active sessions in case of node shutdowns. Furthermore, nodes can also synchronize and start processing transactions on reactivation.

A secure shell wrapper allows connecting the APC monitoring agents with remotely executing commands as well as collecting APC KPI statistics. This wrapper library is the interface between the DIM and the APC monitoring agents.

Virtualization Level Power Management

In this section we present the power management features implemented by VMware vSphere 4: the operating system power management (OSPM) capabilities implemented by the VMware ESX 4 hypervisor and the VMware* Distributed Power Management solution that VMware vSphere 4 offers for virtualized server clusters.

Hypervisor-driven Power Management

To improve CPU power efficiency, VMware ESX hosts can be configured to dynamically switch CPU frequencies based on workload demand. If this feature is activated, as shown in Figure 22.3, the VMware ESX hypervisor makes use of the processor performance states (P-states) made available to the VMkernel through the ACPI interface to carry out dynamic processor voltage and frequency scaling.

Figure 22.3 shows the OSPM activation and configuration screen, available on the VMware vCenter management console under the advanced software settings for host configuration. By setting the *Power.CPUPolicy* property to *dynamic*, the VMkernel will start optimizing each CPU's frequency to match demand in order to improve power efficiency but not affect performance. When the CPU demand increases, this policy setting ensures that CPU frequencies also increase.

Two additional settings may be controlled. The *Power.MaxCpuLoad* property allows setting the CPU utilization threshold under which DVFS will be applied. Whenever CPU utilization surpasses that threshold, the processor will always operate at maximum frequency. The *Power.TimerHz* property allows configuring the CPU utilization polling interval. Higher timer frequencies will result into a finer-grained monitoring interval.

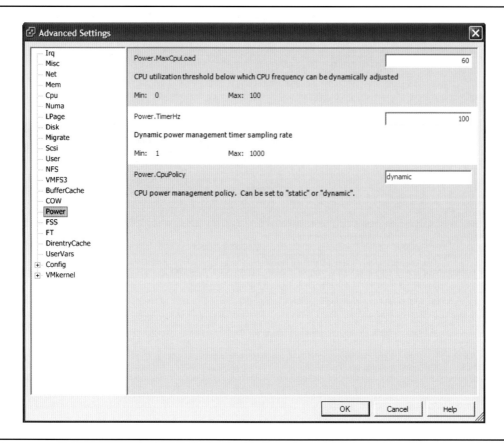

Figure 22.3 VMware[†] OSPM Activation and Configuration (Source VMware)

Distributed Power Management (DPM)

Starting with version 3.5, the VMware Distributed Resource Scheduling (DRS) tool set includes an energy saving feature named *Distributed Power Management* (DPM)[11]. As shown in Figure 22.4, this tool is based on the virtual machine migration and deployment optimization features implemented by DRS. The difference is that, in this case, instead of dispersing virtual machines to optimize cluster resource availability, DPM dynamically consolidates virtual

---

11 VMware Inc., "VMware DRS: Dynamic balancing and allocation of resources for virtual machines," Product datasheet VMW_09Q3_DS_DRS_USLET_EN_P3_R3, Sept. 2009, http://www.vmware.com/files/pdf/drs_datasheet.pdf.

machines in the minimum possible number of ESX servers required to supply the demanded resources, powering off idle cluster elements. When resource demand increases, DPM activates the required number of dormant servers through IPMI or Wake-on-LAN, migrating virtual machines to these hosts as soon as they become available.

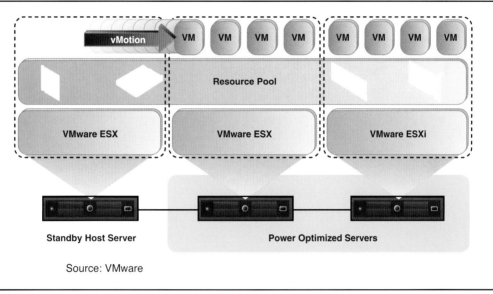

Source: VMware

Figure 22.4   VMware Distributed Resource Scheduling

The VMware* DPM behavior is governed by a series of heuristics, whose objective is to maintain the utilization level of active cluster members within a certain range (between 45 and 81 percent utilization, by default) by shutting down or activating VMware ESX hosts. Utilization is calculated as the quotient between resource demands (CPU and memory) and the capacity available on each node. The demand for resources does not only consider the actual resource usage of the virtual machines running on the hosts, but also an estimation of resource demands that are not being granted due to lack of available resources.

By default, DPM analyzes resource utilization every 5 minutes (DRS' polling interval) and issues management actions or recommendations (depending on the chosen DPM automation level) if necessary. It should be noted that, to avoid compulsive virtual machine migration and node power-off and reactivation in case of fast variations in infrastructure load, DPM does not evaluate instant utilization, but analyzes the average values during a certain interval. Node shutdown is much more conservative than node activation. By default, the average utilization value during the last 40 minutes is analyzed for taking node power-off decisions, whereas just 5 minutes of history are considered for node power-on. Once the necessity to increase or decrease cluster capacity has been detected, DPM makes use of DRS in "what if" mode to analyze all the possible configurations, recommending or applying the most efficient one in terms of the number of changes (virtual machines to be migrated and nodes to be started or powered-off) required to achieve the target utilization range.

Figure 22.5 shows the DPM settings screen on VMware vCenter. As shown in the in the figure, it is possible to choose between three different dynamic management configurations:

■ *Disabled (Off):* No power management is carried out by VMware vCenter. Even if some virtual machines have individual power management settings, these are not applied.

■ *Manual:* VMware vCenter provides virtual machine migration and node power on/off recommendations in order to optimize energy consumption, but these recommendations must be manually approved by the platform administrator prior to their application.

■ *Automatic:* VMware vCenter automatically migrates virtual machines and power servers on/off in order to optimize the platform's energy efficiency. In this configuration, users can also choose the desired automation level. The more conservative the automation threshold is, the higher the energy saving has to be to trigger the reduction of cluster capacity.

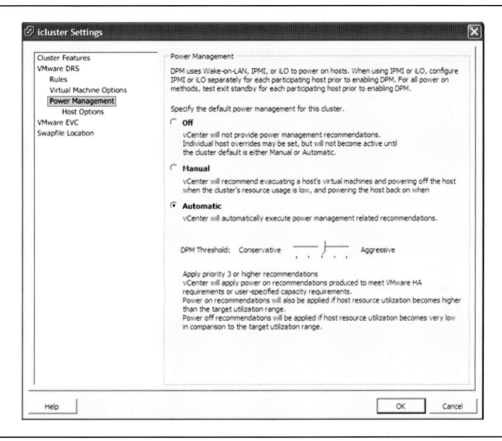

Figure 22.5   Configuring VMware† DPM Settings

Apart from choosing a global configuration for DPM, it is also possible to customize these settings for individual virtual machines, as shown in Figure 22.6. On this screen, it is possible to select whether the virtual machine will follow the default policy or rather is applied an inactive, manual or automatic configuration. As mentioned before, these individual settings are not taken into account if the global DPM configuration is set to "off."

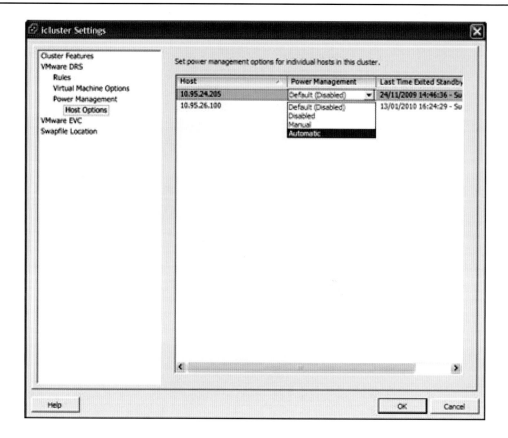

Figure 22.6   Setting Individual Host Options in VMware† DPM

VMware vCenter Interface

The VMware vCenter product includes a Java SDK that allows building third-party virtual infrastructure management applications. In order to operate the virtualized infrastructure and enable managing the APC nodes for application scale-in and scale-out, a group of Java libraries (VMware wrapper libraries) were developed in order to interact with vCenter.

Specifically, the VMware wrapper libraries implement the methods that allow executing the following actions:

- Connect with VMware vCenter.

- Search an entity managed by VMware vCenter.

- Get an entity object's (cluster, virtual machine, host and so on) state and properties.

- Get and update the power state of a virtual machine (power on, power off, suspend and so on

- Get and update the power state of a host (power on, power off, enter maintenance state and so on.).

- Migrate a virtual machine (cold and live migration).

- Get and update a cluster's DRS and DPM properties.

- Vertically scale a virtual machine by managing its CPU and memory limits.

- Reconfigure a virtual machine's hardware (disk, network interfaces, CPU and so on).

Hardware Level Power Management

Intel® Data Center Manager is architected as a software development kit to be used as a component for system integrators to build more sophisticated and valuable capabilities. For that purpose, it exports a Web Service interface that enables external management systems, like the one evaluated in this proof of concept, to make use of it for power and thermal server management.

Intel Data Center Manager in turn, uses the Intel® Intelligent Power Node Manager for monitoring and setting power targets for individual servers.

Intel® Data Center Manager Interface

In the context of the evaluation activities undertaken in this project, the Java language stubs for that Web Service interface were obtained from its WSDL definition by means of the Apache Axis2Java tool. A group of Java libraries was built with these stubs, the DCM Wrapper libraries, ready to be used and integrated with third party software, allowing easy operation and monitoring of the hardware elements managed by a DCM instance.

Specifically, the DCM Wrapper libraries implement the methods that allow executing the following actions:

- Connect with Intel DCM.

- Find an entity managed by Intel DCM.

- Get an entity's object properties.

- Get an entity's policies.

- Update or delete an entity's policies.

- Get the history of power consumption, temperature, and so on from an entity for a certain period.

The DCM wrapper libraries allowed easy integration of the DIM with DCM. Furthermore, an additional Java-based tool named Power Consumption Logger (DCMLogger) was developed in order to register the average power consumption of entities managed by Intel DCM during a certain period of time.

Use Cases for the Proof of Concept

As mentioned in the introductory section describing the energy management proof of concept, the usage scenarios covered for the experiments comprise two use cases: performing power management under dynamic reconfiguration and under global power constraints. The two use cases were run separately to assess the individual behaviors and in combination.

Power Management under Dynamic Reconfiguration

In this scenario, the policy applied by the dynamic infrastructure manager carries out the integrated management actions for all infrastructure layers in order to schedule platform capacity and utilization to the minimum level required to fulfill SLA commitments, thus optimizing energy consumption while fulfilling workload demands. The specific power use policies applicable to this use case are the following:

- Hardware level

  - Server power consumption and resource utilization monitoring, both at individual level and aggregated per cluster and facility.

  - Server power state management.

  - DVFS through OSPM.

- ■ Virtualization level
  - Virtual machine suspension to disk and reactivation.
  - Virtual machine migration across the virtualized server pool.
- ■ Application level
  - Application KPI monitoring.

As shown in the previous list, no hardware-level power capping is applied in this scenario, since we are assuming that infrastructure utilization levels are generally low. The most efficient management action is therefore shutting down the maximum possible number of active servers, rather than reducing their performance by means of power capping.

To better optimize platform power consumption, OSPM is used at hypervisor level in order to reduce processor frequency if a certain server is not required at full capacity. An entire physical server is the minimum unit of capacity we are able to manage. Accordingly, a server may need to be powered on to address resource requirements, yet it may not be needed at full capacity. In this case, the autonomous OSPM policy takes over, processor frequency is reduced whenever CPU utilization is below 60 percent, and utilization is sampled 100 times per second.

It is also worth noting that, although application KPIs are monitored, the number of active application nodes is not managed at service level in this case. This is so because, instead of shutting down nodes at application level, we have opted for suspending the virtual machines to disk and restoring them at hypervisor level in order to obtain a better response time when controlling the number of active application nodes.

Power Management under Global Power Constraints

In this scenario, the policy applied by the dynamic infrastructure manager carries out an integrated management of all infrastructure layers in order to enforce a global or facility-level power constraint while honoring different service classes. The service classes carry specific service priorities and SLAs. Here are the power management policies applicable to this use case.

- ■ Hardware level
  - – Server power consumption and resource utilization monitoring, both at individual level and aggregated per cluster and facility.
  - – Server power capping.
- ■ Virtualization level
  - – Virtual machine resource utilization and hypervisor overhead monitoring
- ■ Application level
  - – Application KPI monitoring.

Since the facility would exceed its power or emissions limitations if not controlled, a high degree of platform utilization is assumed in this scenario. Accordingly, no server power state management or OS-driven DVFS is carried out, since all servers are assumed to be active and presenting high CPU utilization rates. Similarly, the number of active application nodes is not controlled, since all available nodes are assumed to be active.

Proof of Concept Experimental Results

In this section we present the results from experiments performed on the system described in the previous section arranged in three subsections: operation under dynamic configuration, under global power constraints and a combined scenario.

Evaluation of Power-Aware Dynamic Reconfiguration

Assuming an environment where we operate under no power or CO_2 emission limitations, this set of tests intends to evaluate the energy-saving benefits derived from the adoption of a dynamic reconfiguration policy to adaptively reconfigure the equipment to track large variations in workload demand and the impact on service performance of such management approach.

Dynamic reconfiguration alone does reduce the number of servers necessary to meet periods of low demand and improves OpEx performance by extending power proportional computing range of a pool of servers for the pool as a group. The pool of active servers is maintained at its most efficient operating range even during periods of low workload demand. Equipment not needed to meet workload demand is turned off. This operating procedure leads to significant energy savings over more traditional methods that rely on the autonomic power management capabilities in the CPU only.

Baseline Scenario

The first group of tests intended to measure the baseline performance and power consumption of the APC sample workload in a state of the art environment (state of the art hardware, virtualization-based static consolidation, and so on) but without dynamic infrastructure management techniques applied. These experiments served also as benchmarking and calibration tests, allowing the selection of the different thresholds and parameters to be used in the energy-aware management policy.

In order to generate the signaling load required for these tests, the APC load injectors were configured with a load pattern following the typical APC service utilization during a working day. In order to speed up the execution of the tests, such signaling load was not injected in real time, but following a 3:1 acceleration factor. Consequently, the 24-hour test actually ran in eight hours, as shown in Figure 22.7.

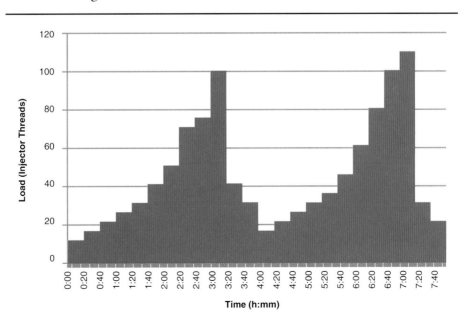

Figure 22.7 Load Pattern

Figure 22.8 shows the average host CPU utilization percentage of the Gold server group obtained during the execution of the test. It is close to 80 percent during the peak load intervals, and descends to 50 to 60 percent during the valley periods, with an average value of 64 percent for the full duration of the test.

If we consider the service response time, we can see that its evolution follows that of the load pattern as shown in Figure 22.9, apart from sporadic spikes. The APC service response time is lower than 200 milliseconds at low load, and rises above 600 milliseconds during peak load. The average response time measured during this test is 264 milliseconds.

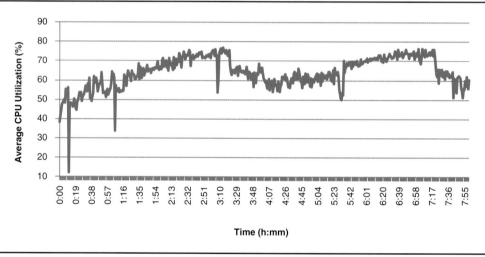

Figure 22.8   Average CPU Utilization

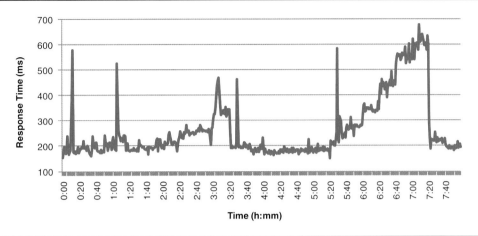

Figure 22.9   Service Response Time

Figure 22.10 shows the global power consumption of the "Gold" server group (two Intel Xeon processor 5500 series servers) during the execution of the test. The server power draw also follows very closely the signaling load pattern, since peak and valley power demand coincides with the maximum and minimum load intervals. The average power draw during this test is 462 watts, which represents an energy consumption of 3694 watt-hours in the 8 hours that takes this scenario to complete.

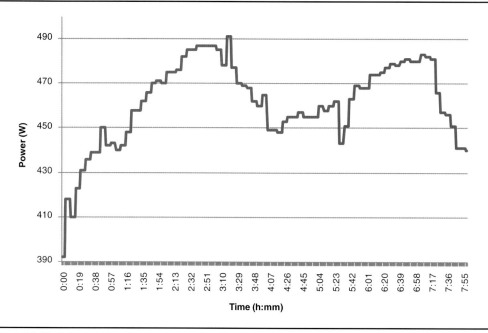

Figure 22.10   Server Group Power Consumption

Dynamic Reconfiguration

In this second group of tests we repeated the load injection pattern presented in the previous section, applying in this case the energy-aware dynamic reconfiguration policy.

Figure 22.11 shows the infrastructure management actions undertaken by the Dynamic Infrastructure Manager during scenario execution depending on the signaling load level. The number of active APC front end instances is tuned to match service demand, suspending unnecessary nodes to disk to free CPU and memory resources. Additionally, active application nodes are dynamically consolidated when possible in a single host by means of live migration, thus allowing to power down the vacant server.

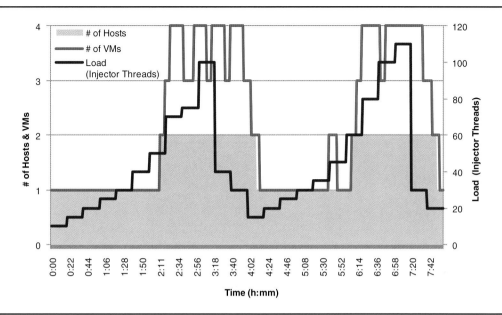

Figure 22.11 Power-aware Dynamic Reconfiguration Actions

If we have a look at the CPU utilization of the server group and the individual hosts composing it, we may appreciate the impact of the previously mentioned management actions. As shown in Figure 22.12, the average CPU utilization of the server group diminishes significantly during low load periods thanks to the powering-off of one of the hosts supporting the service infrastructure.

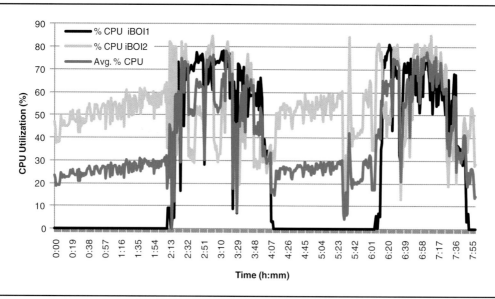

Figure 22.12 CPU Utilization

The benefits obtained are more evident if we compare the average CPU utilization of the server group in the baseline and dynamic reconfiguration scenarios. As shown in Figure 22.13, CPU utilization in the dynamic reconfiguration scenario is significantly lower at low and medium load levels, and only matches that of the baseline scenario during peak load periods. Average CPU utilization in the dynamic reconfiguration scenario is 39 percent, thus reducing by 39 percent the value obtained when not applying any power management policy.

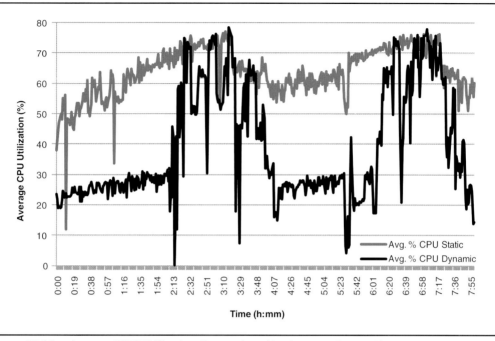

Figure 22.13 Average CPU Utilization Comparison (Static versus Dynamic)

If we consider the influence of the power management actions on service performance, we can see that there is a certain impact due to the direct relationship between service behavior, and infrastructure capacity and performance. Figure 22.14 presents a comparison between the service response time measured in the baseline and the dynamic reconfiguration scenarios.

It should be noted that the KPI thresholds depicted in the figure represent the triggers for dynamic management actions as configured in the policy, not the KPI objectives (note they were already exceeded when applying no dynamic management actions). This necessity to set KPI thresholds lower than the desired KPI targets comes from the management platform's response time, since node power on/off and virtual machine suspension/reactivation actions take minutes to complete.

Comparing the service performance results on both scenarios, we see that the average service response time when applying the energy-aware infrastructure management policy is 299 ms, 14 percent higher than the value obtained on the baseline scenario.

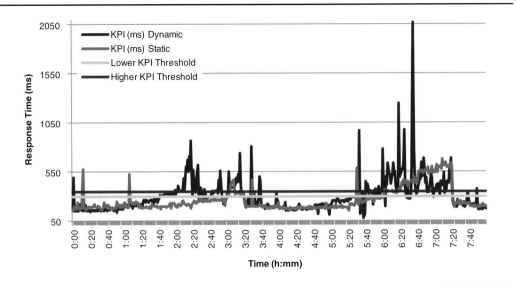

Figure 22.14   Service Response Time Comparison (Static versus Dynamic)

By having a look at the service infrastructure's power consumption, we may quantify the energy savings derived from the controlled degradation in service performance introduced by the application of the dynamic management policy. As shown in Figure 22.15, the global power consumption of the Gold server group follows very closely the previously mentioned reduction in CPU utilization, thus notably lowering the energy consumption measured in the baseline scenario.

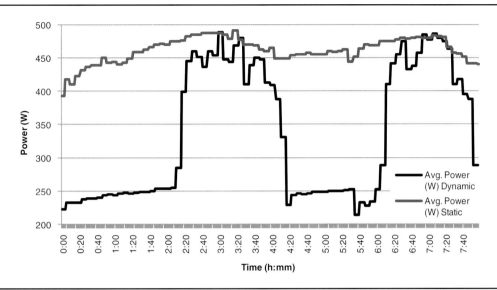

Figure 22.15 Server Group Power Draw Comparison (Static versus Dynamic)

The average power draw during this test is 335 watts, which leads to an energy consumption of 2684 watt-hours in the 8 hours that takes this scenario to complete. This represents consuming 1011 watt-hours less than in the power-unmanaged configuration or, in other words, reducing energy consumption by 27 percent.

Evaluation of Power-Constrained Operation

Assuming an environment where we operate under power or CO_2 emission limitations, this set of use case evaluation tests intended to analyze the management policy's capacity to enforce such limitations while administering the available power budget to maximize SLA compliance for top-priority services.

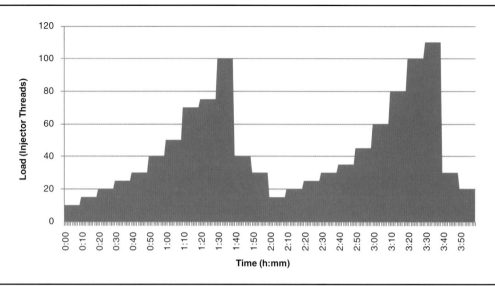

Figure 22.16   Signaling Load Pattern

As shown in Figure 22.16, this scenario corresponds to a 4 hour test that injects a variable amount of signaling traffic to the APC platform. This 4-hour time frame reproduces the typical 24-hour load pattern observed in the APC production environment in a working day. This signaling load profile is compressed by a factor of 6 instead of 4 as in the previous scenario. It is possible to run the power constrained scenario twice as fast as the dynamic reconfiguration scenario because the main control mechanism, power capping is much faster than the server shutdown and restarts used in the dynamic reconfiguration scenario.

Unrestricted Power Scenario

In order to evaluate the default platform behavior in terms of service performance and power consumption when no power restrictions are enforced, in this first set of tests we measured the power consumption and KPI values when no power management policies were applied.

The information obtained in this power-unlimited execution environment is required to compare and analyze the behavior of the *static* or *limited* and *managed* or *dynamic* use case tests that will be presented in the following sections.

Moreover, these experiments have also served as benchmarking tests, allowing the selection of the different thresholds and parameters to be used in the energy-aware management policy.

Figure 22.17 shows the service response time of the two APC service instances deployed in our test bed. The high-priority Gold instance presents slightly higher response time values than the standard service Silver instance (an average of 330 milliseconds vs. 278 milliseconds), despite the fact that they are both injected the same signaling load and have been deployed in an identical infrastructure. However, it should be noted that the Gold instance hosts the database node serving both applications, and therefore it bears a higher overall load.

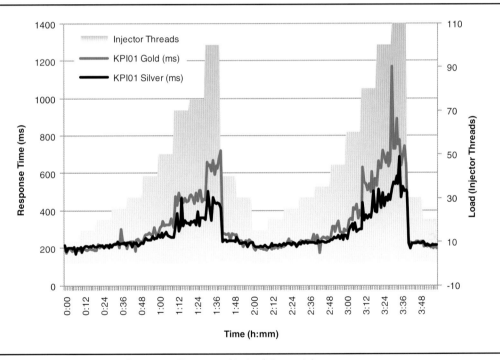

Figure 22.17   Service Performance (Power-unlimited Scenario)

As shown in Figure 22.18, the average overall power consumption ranges between 800 watts and 900 watts during the test, depending on the service load being injected to the platform. It is also worth noting that both service instances show a similar power consumption pattern, being the only difference that the Gold instance consumes a few watts more due to the impact of the database node.

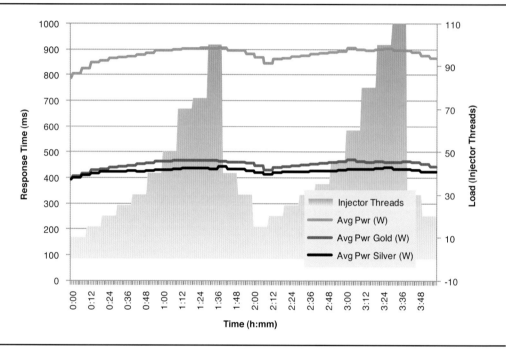

Figure 22.18   Power Consumption (Power-unlimited Scenario)

Static Scenario

In this scenario, the average power consumption for the whole facility, represented by the green server group described in the section *APC Service Infrastructure,* has been manually limited to 800 watts using Intel Data Center Manager.

The information obtained from this execution environment is useful to evaluate the impact of infrastructure power constraints on APC service performance when no priority and SLA-aware management policies are applied.

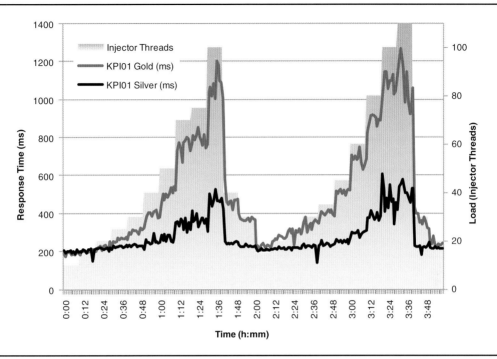

Figure 22.19   Service Performance, 800-Watt Static Global Cap without Compensating Policies

Figure 22.19 shows the service response time of the two APC service instances during this test. A key point of interest is to note the KPI degradation due to the introduction of the 800-watt global cap. This is shown in Figure 22.20, which combines the graphs of Figures 22.18 and 22.19. Also note how the Gold instance is affected to a larger extent (a 51 percent increase in average), since response times for the Silver instance show no significant differences (less than a 1 percent increase) when compared to those of the power-unlimited scenario.

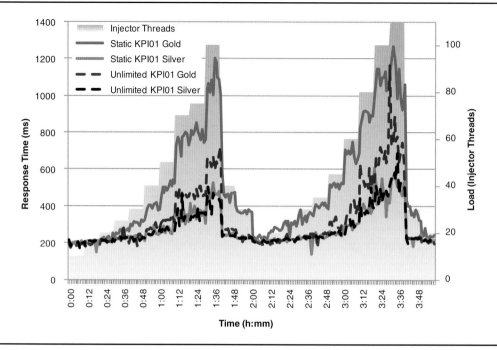

Figure 22.20 Service Performance (Static versus Power-unlimited Scenario)

This service performance behavior becomes obvious by looking at the power consumption of the overall facility and the different server groups. As shown in Figure 22.21, the overall power limitation of 800 watts is strictly enforced by Intel Data Center Manager by limiting the power draw of the Gold and Silver server groups. If we compare these values with those measured in the power-unlimited scenario as shown in Figure 22.22 we can observe that 84 percent of the power draw reduction is extracted from the Gold server group, thus explaining the previously presented service performance results.

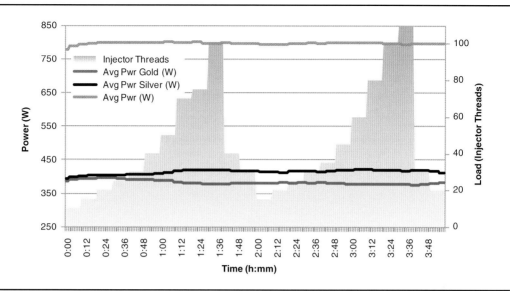

Figure 22.21   Power Consumption (Static Scenario)

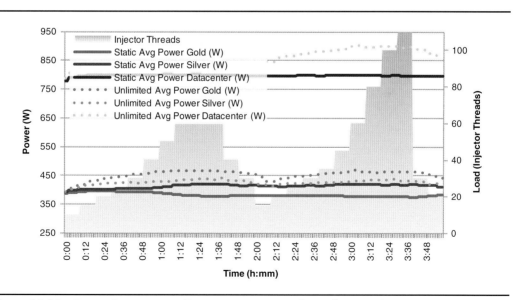

Figure 22.22   Power Consumption (Static versus Power-unlimited Scenario)

Dynamic Scenario

In this scenario, the Dynamic Infrastructure Manager (DIM) evaluates the platform power consumption and the APC KPIs in order to carry out an intelligent allocation of the available power budget that takes service priority into account and maximizes SLA compliance. The DIM software evaluates all the collected information every six minutes and provides Intel Data Center Manager power capping targets by service class according to policies in effect.

In this group of tests, we executed the use case with the same global power limitation of 800 watts for the whole facility, plus variable limitations (configured by the DIM) for the individual Gold and Silver server groups whenever power shifting across service instances was required.

If we consider the service performance results shown in Figure 22.23, we can observe how the service-aware energy management policy is able to prioritize the Gold service instance. From the moment when the high-priority service KPI exceeds the maximum SLA degradation threshold, the DIM starts imposing caps to the Gold and Silver servers groups, apportioning the power budget to make sure that the high-priority service instance gets the amount of resources it requires.

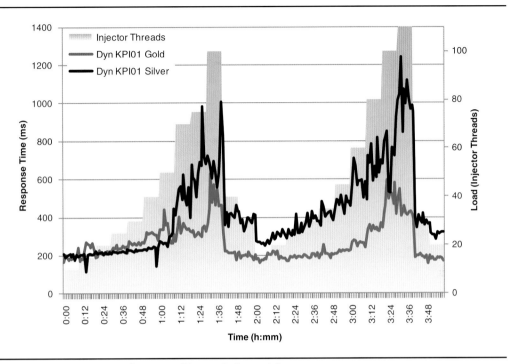

Figure 22.23   Service Performance (Dynamic Scenario)

This prioritization of the Gold service instance is clearer if we compare the results obtained on this test with those obtained on the Static use case. As shown in Figure 22.24, the service response time of the Gold APC instance is significantly lower than in the Static scenario, thanks to the power allocation policy adopted by the DIM. Specifically, the average service response time drops from 499 milliseconds in the Static scenario to 269 milliseconds in this test, thus registering a service performance improvement of 46 percent. Obviously, since this performance gain is obtained by taking resources out from the Silver server group, the response time of the low-priority service instance worsens in this environment. We measured an average response time of 427 milliseconds for the Silver APC instance, which represents a deterioration of 52 percent in service performance when compared to the Static scenario (280 milliseconds).

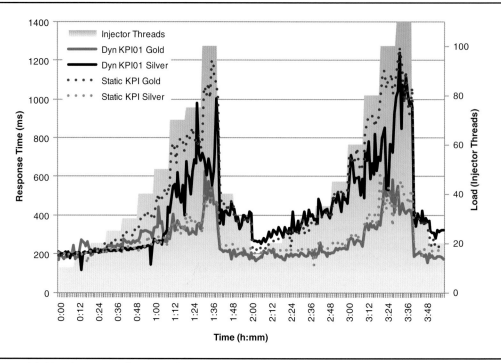

Figure 22.24 Service Performance (Dynamic vs. Static Scenario)

In Figure 22.25 we may appreciate the effect of the power management policy by observing how the 800 watt power budget is apportioned across the service instances. As shown in the figure, once the DIM starts managing the power allocation to the different server groups, the Gold Service instance is always favored with respect to the Silver instance. We may also perceive how, whenever the response time of the Gold service instance is faster than the committed service level, the resource unbalancing process is reverted and part of the power budget is taken out from the Gold server group.

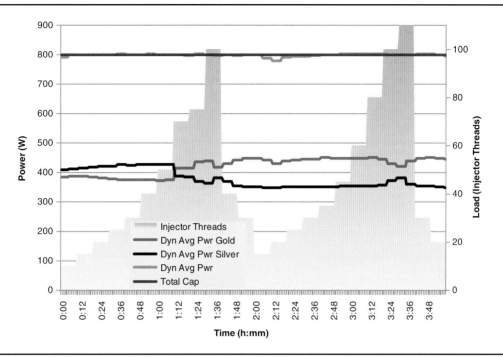

Figure 22.25   Power Consumption (Dynamic Scenario)

The effect of the power management policy becomes more evident if we compare the results obtained on these tests with those measured in the Static scenario, as shown in Figure 22.26. In the Static scenario, a total of 3190 watt-hours were consumed. Of this total, only 1532 watt-hours (48 percent) were consumed by the Gold server group, whereas 1658 watt-hours (52 percent) were spent by the Silver infrastructure. When applying the service-aware power management policy, such trend reverts. In this test, a total of 3196 watt-hours were consumed, of which 53 percent (1686 watt-hours) was apportioned to the Gold server group and 47 percent (1510 watt-hours) was apportioned to the Silver instance.

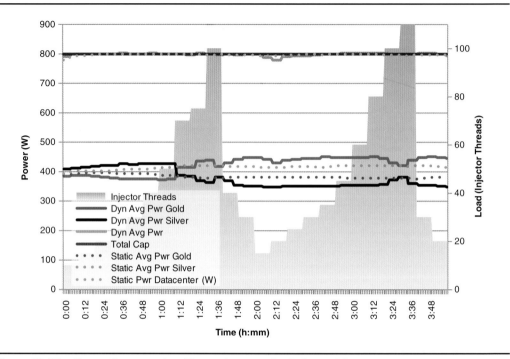

Figure 22.26 Power Consumption (Dynamic versus Static Scenario)

Evaluation of Combined Operation

The energy management policies evaluated in previous sections are not mutually exclusive. To the contrary, a facility can be run under a strategy that emphasizes reducing energy consumption through dynamic reconfiguration during low workload periods and operate under power restrictions during peak load intervals. In this situation, the Dynamic Infrastructure Manager is programmed to carry out a combined policy:

Whenever the facility's power draw is below its limit, a dynamic reconfiguration policy is applied to optimize energy consumption. When the overall power cap is reached, the facility enters into power-constrained operation mode.

In this group of tests we evaluated a variant of the Dynamic scenario described in the evaluation of power-constrained operation, executing the use case with power limitations for the whole facility and the Gold and Silver server groups. As in the original use case, server group limitations were dynamically configured by the DIM whenever power shifting across them was required. The main novelty was that the overall power cap was also dynamic in this case, taking a value up to 800 W that the DIM adjusted to obtain further energy savings on low utilization periods. Additionally, dynamic reconfiguration techniques were also applied to yield additional reductions in power consumption whenever the facility was not power-constrained.

Figure 22.27 shows the dynamic reconfiguration actions implemented by the DIM depending on the signaling load injected to the platform. As shown in the chart, the activation and parking of the second server is identical in the Gold and Silver server group. However, in terms of active application nodes, there is a slight shifting in node activation and deactivation. Since the Silver group presents lower performance results due to its higher power capping values, the application is scaled out earlier and the number of active application nodes is also higher over time (2.47 versus 2.18 active nodes in average).

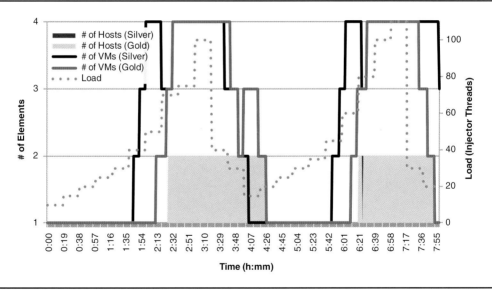

Figure 22.27   Dynamic Reconfiguration Actions

Figure 22.28 shows the service performance measurements driving these dynamic management actions. As shown in the figure, node and host activations correspond to periods where response times increase for each application type. As soon as response time values drop to minimum levels, nodes are suspended and servers are parked on the corresponding group. The figure also shows how the high-priority (Gold) application instance is favored during power-constrained operation on high signaling load periods. In average, the Gold service instance's response time is 23 percent lower than the Silver's.

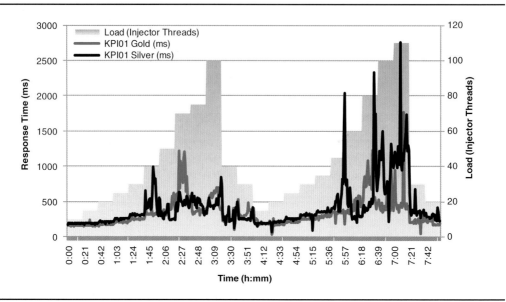

Figure 22.28 Service Performance (Combined Scenario)

Figure 22.29 compares the combined vs. dynamic reconfiguration scenarios. The Gold service instance's response time during low utilization intervals is almost identical to that measured on the dynamic reconfiguration scenario. However, performance degrades during power-constrained operation, leading to an average deterioration of 12 percent in Gold service performance. The low-priority service response time is generally worse due to the penalization in terms of power allocation that it suffers. When compared to the response time measured when only applying dynamic reconfiguration, we observe a 38 percent worsening.

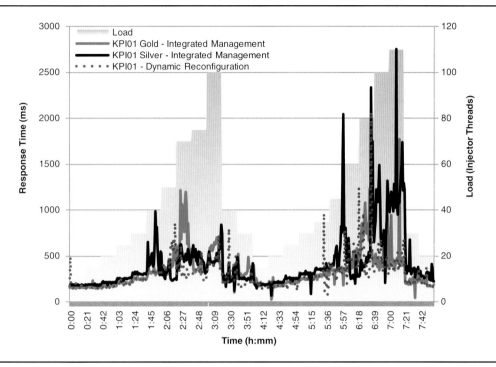

Figure 22.29 Service performance (Combined vs. Dynamic Reconfiguration)

Figure 22.30 depicts a comparison with the results measured when only applying intelligent power capping. The Gold service response time increases by 24 percent since the dynamic reconfiguration policy reduces platform capacity and performance on low-utilization periods to yield additional energy savings. On the other hand, Silver service performance improves slightly (3 percent), since the resources freed by the Gold instance become available to the low-priority service during the power-unconstrained intervals.

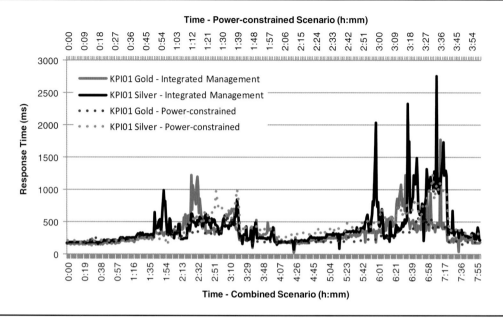

Figure 22.30   Service Performance (Combined vs. Power-constrained)

Figure 22.31 shows the effect of the dynamic power capping and reconfiguration actions on the platform's power consumption. The overall facility power cap is enforced, applying also more stringent caps on low-utilization intervals to reduce the power consumption further. Dynamic caps are also applied on the server groups as mandated by service performance, making sure that the high-priority service instance is favored whenever a competition for energy resources takes place. These caps, combined with the reconfiguration actions presented in Figure 22.27, introduce the correlation between signaling load and energy consumption that may be observed in the figure.

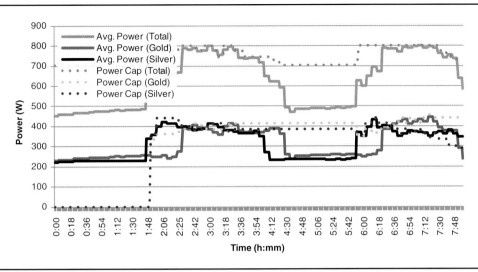

Figure 22.31 Power Consumption (Combined Scenario)

The effect of power-capping may be better singled out if we compare these results with those measured on the Dynamic Reconfiguration scenario, where that feature was not applied. As shown in Figure 22.32, the power consumption of the energy-favored (Gold) server group during low utilization periods is almost equal to that observed on dynamic reconfiguration, whereas the power consumption of the Silver server group is lower at all times due to the more stringent power policy applied to it. Logically, power consumption is lower on both server groups during peak load intervals due to the enforcement of the overall facility capping. Taking both effects into account, the overall power consumption of the Gold and Silver server group is respectively 7 percent and 6 percent lower than the dynamic reconfiguration values.

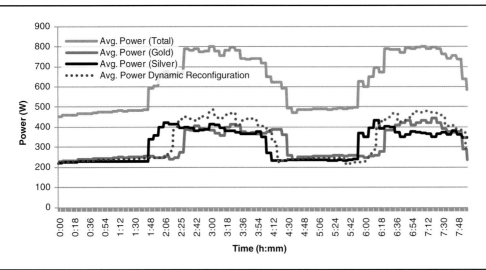

Figure 22.32 Power Consumption (Combined vs. Dynamic Reconfiguration)

Figure 22.33 we may better appreciate the highlights the behavior of dynamic reconfiguration by comparing the results measured in the Combined Scenario with those obtained in the Power-constrained Operation use case. Power consumption is now much more proportional to the signaling load being processed by the platform, thanks to the application scalability management, server parking and dynamic power cap management actions applied depending on service performance. Thanks to these measures, the energy consumption is 21 percent lower in the combined operation case.

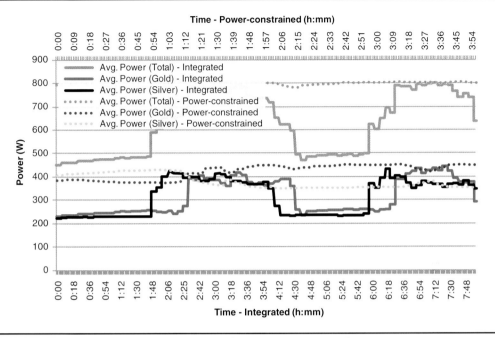

Figure 22.33 Power Consumption (Combined vs. Power-constrained)

Summary

As we mentioned in the introduction to this chapter, the main goal of this technology evaluation initiative was to demonstrate how the intelligent management of infrastructure assets may yield significant energy savings and a more rational utilization of the available energy resources with minimal impact on the service level of the managed platforms or the user-perceived quality of the services hosted on them.

According to the results obtained in our use case evaluation tests, we can consider the point well proven, since it becomes possible to achieve a notable reduction in energy consumption with a minimal and controlled reduction in service performance. In our tests we were able to reduce the energy consumption by 27 percent with only a 14 percent increase in the service response time, ensuring that the average service response time objectives were met. When analyzing these results, it is worth taking two considerations into account. First, that energy savings are strongly dependent on the horizontal scalability features of the target service and the differences in load intensity and duration between the peak and valley load periods. Shorter and higher-intensity peak load periods in comparison to the average service load will result into bigger energy savings. The second consideration is that the dynamic infrastructure management policy allows selecting the desired trade-off between service performance and energy savings. The higher the allowed service performance degradation is, the bigger the energy consumption reduction will be.

In our power-constrained operation tests we have been able to demonstrate how a data center-wide power cap is not a fair method for power budget apportioning. With an overall restriction, all services are treated equally, regardless of their priority level and the service level committed. It may even be the case that high-priority services are penalized in favor of standard services if these are more power-hungry.

Our tests show how, by taking into account service priority and SLAs when applying power caps, it becomes possible to prioritize services as desired, favoring them up to the maximum desired degradation in standard service performance.

Finally, the combined operation tests demonstrate how the two previous scenarios may coexist in the same facility, guaranteeing that overall power caps are enforced while improving energy efficiency on low utilization periods. In our tests, we measured a 21 percent reduction in energy consumption when compared to the standalone application of service-aware power capping.

The authors would like to thank Aitor Argomániz and Miguel A. Carrillio for their valuable contributions to the tests described in the chapter.

Chapter 23

Suspend-to-RAM Support in Servers

Contributed by William Carter, Mark Wright, Robert Villanueva and Enrique Castro-Leon

Platform architects often think of the support of hibernation or the suspend-to-RAM feature, defined as the ACPI S3 state, mainly as a desktop or workstation energy saving feature. The rationale is that since servers in a data center run 24–7, there is no need ever of having them hibernate. Our experience with dynamic reconfiguration as discussed in Chapter 22 challenges this basic assumption in the context of emerging virtualized cloud data center usages.

Recapping our discussion from Chapters 5 and 22, *server parking* stands for the action of shutting down servers for power management purposes. Desktop systems have been using the S3 (suspend) and S4 (hibernate) for a decade, and now it's time for servers to "wake up" to these server parking options.

As previously discussed, when we walk out of the office or leave our homes, we turn off the lights to save on our power bill. Data center operators can do the same with the servers in the building. Servers can be shut down and restarted under application control when they are not needed. This is the equivalent of turning lights off in a room. The capability for "dimming lights" in a server also exists. Enhanced Intel SpeedStep® technology and Intel® Intelligent Power Node Manager technology enables the system to run, trading off some performance. Enhanced Intel SpeedStep® technology reduces power consumption during periods of low workload and Intel Intelligent Power Node Manager can cap power, that is, reduce power consumption at high workload levels under application control.

There is a rich set of options for "turning off" the lights in the data center, figuratively, that is, talking about turning off server equipment, not the lighting equipment. The ACPI standard defines at least three states suitable for server parking: S3 (suspend to memory), S4 (hibernation where the server state is saved in a file) and S5 (soft off, where the server is powered down except for the circuitry to turn it on remotely under application control.) The specific choice depends on hardware support; not all states are supported by a specific implementation. It also depends on application requirements. A restart from S3, if supported by the hardware, can take place much faster than a restart from S4 or S5. The tradeoff is the extra power for the memory refresh needed to make S3 function.

A widespread use of server parking is not feasible in a traditional environment with the operating system running on the bare metal. In a virtualized cloud environment, virtual machines running the applications can be assigned to run in a pool of server hosts with a sub-pool of active hosts grown or shrunk to optimize utilization levels. Vacated hosts are parked, the equivalent of turning lights off in a room, and as in the lighting example, once a server is in parked state the server can't run applications.

Web hosting, gaming, search engines, and social networking utilize thousands of machines that are organized into a massive pool of resources all capable of performing similar work. The work is assigned by a set of supervisory machines acting as load balancers across the pool. These supervisory machines also support dynamic allocation of workloads and can keep track of servers that are in a parked state. The hard binding between servers is also relaxed in these server pools. The machine that performs the load balancing is now able to recognize when one of the hosts are turned off, and can rebalance across the remaining resources.

Overview of Suspend-to-RAM (STR)

The Advanced Configuration Peripheral Interface (ACPI) specification defines a computer system state where the system is completely suspended to the point that it appears to be shut off, but is able to quickly resume back to the exact point it was prior to the suspend operation. The system is able to resume very quickly because the processor content was saved to memory prior to the suspend operation, and the dynamic RAM context is maintained. The processors are not executing instructions: the processor-complex context including the cache content is not maintained. Devices that are enabled to wake the system can do so from this state and can initiate a hardware event that transitions the system state to operating. This state is defined as the S3 state and is called *Suspend-to-RAM* (STR).

Suspend-to-RAM (STR) has been a common feature in desktop, workstation, and laptop systems since the creation of the original ACPI specification in 1996. Suspend-to-RAM (STR) has *not* been a common feature in server systems.[1]

Hardware and Software Required for Supporting STR

Support for Suspend-to-RAM (STR) requires a computer system with a number of supporting features:

■ Power Supply. The power supply must provide auxiliary power to the memory subsystem even when the main outputs are turned off. This auxiliary power is typically called standby power and the power supply will provide 5 VSB[2] or 3.3 VSB output. The standby voltage is also used to power features that are always on, such as the baseboard management controller (BMC) and portions of the PCI devices or PCI controllers such as the NIC, IOH or the ICH3. The power supply must provide adequate current to operate all these devices and the maximum amount of memory even when the main power output is in the off state. The memory does consume less power in the S3 state.

---

1 Please refer to the ACPI Specification for a complete description of S3. The specification can be found at: http://www.acpi.info/

2 Volts standby.

3 Network interface controller; I/O and I/O controller hub.

■ The processor and chipset must provide the mechanism to copy processor content to main memory, and restore that content, when the system enters the STR state. The Intel processors and chipsets all support S3 as the same processors and chipsets are used in workstation designs.

■ The system BIOS must be able to respond to an OS request to enter S3 state. The BIOS is responsible for moving the processor content and all register data to main memory. Upon exit from the STR state, the BIOS performs the initialization of the PCI devices, restores register data previously saved to memory, and copies the processor content back into the processors. Once the BIOS completes this initialization, the control of the system is passed back to the operating system.

■ The operating system must recognize any of the actions that initiate entry into the S3 state. The operating system will perform a shutdown of its own processes in preparation for S3 state. Upon resume from S3 and after the BIOS has completed the initialization, the OS will reload the PCI device drivers and return to the exact state prior to suspend.

The Resume Process

The resume from the S3 state is similar to powering on the system from its off state. Resume can be initiated by the front panel button, a wake-on-LAN signal, a real-time-clock, or remotely through IPMI commands. Here are three alternative procedures to perform a remote resume from S3 without the physical intervention of pressing the power button in the front panel.

Resuming from S3 to S0 Using a Console:

■ Send an IPMI power on command to power on the system. This command can be issued out-of-band and the command is received by the BMC. The power on command for resume and on is the same. The BMC will interpret and act the same for the on command.

■ When the IPMI command is received by the BMC, the BMC assumes the system is completely off (that is, in S5 state), and uses the ICH10 to power on the system. The Intel ICH keeps track of the system state in nonvolatile memory and will take the appropriate actions to turn on the power supply and let the BIOS know that the system is resuming from S3.

Resuming a Server with a Wake-on-LAN Magic Packet

■ Magic packet arrives over the network. When the network adapter detects the packet, the adapter signals the ICH in the server.

■ The ICH, knowing which state the system is in at this point, will turn on the power supply and let the BIOS know that the system is resuming from S3.

Resuming with Intel® Intelligent Power Node Manager

■ A policy is programmed into Intel Intelligent Power Node Manager to resume the system at a specific time. When Intel Intelligent Power Node Manager determines it is time to resume the system, the Manageability Engine inside the IOH will signal the ICH to power on. Similarly, the real-time clock (RTC) may have a wakeup option that will wake the system at a preprogrammed time. The RTC also signals the ICH to wake the system.

■ The ICH, knowing which state the system is in at this point, will turn on the power supply and let the BIOS know that the system is resuming from S3.

Experimental Results

Four systems were used during the S3 testing. All four systems were a common configuration, except that three video options were used over the course of this testing: an nVidia GeForce 8300[†], an ATI Radeon HD 3650[†], and the integrated graphics controller.

■ Intel® S5520SC board based workstation system configured as follows

  – 5 PCI slots (no PCIe add-in cards installed)

  – Integrated 6 SATA ports

  – Optional 4 port SAS controller installed

  – USB2.0 controller with 6 ports

  – Embedded dual port Intel® 82575EB Gigabit Ethernet Controller

  – Integrated graphics: Server Engine LLC Pilot II Controller with 64 megabytes of DDR2 memory

  – Integrated IPMI 2.0 baseboard management controller

  – 1394A port (disabled)

  – Integrated audio (disabled)

■ Intel® Xeon® 5520 processors (2)

■ Six DIMMs of 2-GB DDR3 memory DIMMs for a total of 12-gigabyte system memory

■ One 300-GB SATA hard disk drive

■ OpenSUSE release 11

Operating System Compatibility Findings

The tests spanned a number of operating systems. Table 23.1 summarizes the results.

Table 23.1 ACPI S3 Operating System Compatibility Findings

Operating System	Compatibility
Microsoft Windows Server 2003 Enterprise, 32-bit	STR supported
Ubuntu Linux, version 9.10 SUSE Release 11 Red Hat Release 5.4 and 6.5, 64-bit	S3 (STR) is supported and worked properly with the embedded video option and the ATI video. The nVidia GEForce video card and ATI video card did not have a Linux driver available for download.
Microsoft Windows Server 2008 Enterprise R2, 64-bit	No support
VMware	No support

Resume Latency

When a system resumes from the S3 state, there are 4 phases as shown in Figure 23.1. During the *power on* phase shown by the light green bar, the power supply must turn on its output and allow the power to stabilize. This can take from tens of milliseconds to about half a second for systems with large power supplies in the range of 1000–1500 watt output.

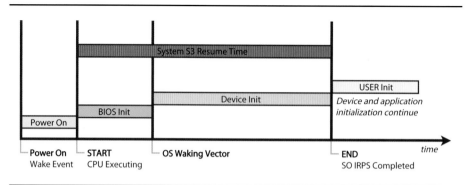

Figure 23.1 S3 Resume Sequence

After power is restored, the BIOS reloads processor context and performs hardware enumeration/initialization before handing off control to the operating system, which performs device initialization. Microsoft WHQL requirements state that the System S3 resume time period ends when the I/O request packets (IRPs) are completed. Even though the IRs are complete, devices such as the USB, RAID, or network controllers will likely take more time to complete their initialization process and any applications relying on those devices must wait until the devices are fully restored.

Per Microsoft's WHQL requirements, the resume time can be no more than 2 seconds.

Table 23.2 shows the resume times for the systems as configured. The stopwatch was started when the front panel button was pushed, and the stopwatch was stopped when the system was observed running a continuation of a script that had been started prior to entry to S3.

For purposes of comparison, the time to resume from the S3 state (Suspend-to-Disk) was also measured and shown in the table.

Table 23.2 ACPI Resume Times, S4 versus S3

Operating System	S4 Resume Time (s)	S3 Resume Time (s)
Microsoft Windows Server 2003 Enterprise	N/A	32
SUSE Linux Release 11	86	17
Ubuntu Linux Release 9.10	68	13
RedHat Linux Release 5.5	100	11

Note: All resume time measurements were taken with the full installation of the operating systems. The Linux operating systems are distributed with a set of default scripts that execute when Suspend-to-RAM is initiated. The default scripts were used for all measurements.

Power Consumption

Power measurements were taken using a Yokagawa WT210 power meter. The readings indicate the wall power consumed by the servers as configured. See table 23.3.

Table 23.3 Power Consumption at Various ACPI S-states

System State	Configuration: 1-socket server provisioned with 2 DIMMs (watts)	Configuration: 2-socket server provisioned with 6 DIMMs (watts)
S0 – Full load	N/A	187 - 217
S0 – Idle system	71	99
S3 – Suspended	10 - 14	22
S4 or S5 – Hibernation or Soft Off	10 - 13	15

Note: The 1 socket server was not used in any of the other S3 testing other than to measure power consumption for comparison purposes. Ranges represent variations across different operating systems.

Suspend and Resume Reliability

A common concern expressed in the industry is the reliability of the systems to enter and exit the STR state. There are three main concerns as captured in Table 23.4.

Table 23.4 Issues with Sleep-to-RAM Resumption

Component	Description of Concern
Application, system, and operating system Software	Maturity of software may not allow S3 to properly enter and restore the software context. Or the software stack may not reliability return to the prior pointer on exit from S3 state.
Hard disk drives	Spin up and spin down could adversely impact the endurance or reliability of the hard disk drives, creating a higher failure rate.
Power supply units	Switching between the primary output rails and the and standby rails could cause system crashes, induce hardware failures, or impact reliability

As part of this investigation, the research team conducted a simple reliability test to provide insight into these concerns. Over a four month period, two S3-enabled systems were cycled to test entry/exit to STR. The system configuration for both systems was the same as described in the section above.

The procedure was intended to collect reliability data on S3 suspend and resume but because of the size of the test population (one system exactly), this data is too subjective and cannot be used to predict reliability. However, the results suggest the reliability issues may not be as bad as perceived and that under controlled conditions (e.g. system hardware and software) the reliability can be managed and may be acceptable.

The first test was done using only systems running the same script. The system under test entered and exited S3 state using scripts to perform three steps:

1. The system under test (SUT) writes a time-of-day entry to a log file and then enters the S3 state. But before it enters S3, the system under test sets the real-time clock to wake up approximately 30 seconds after entering S3.

2. When the system under test wakes up, another time-of-day entry is made to the log.

3. The real-time clock is reset and the system shuts down after 30 seconds. The procedure is repeated from step 1.

For the next test, the two systems were set up in a network configuration as shown in Figure 23.2.

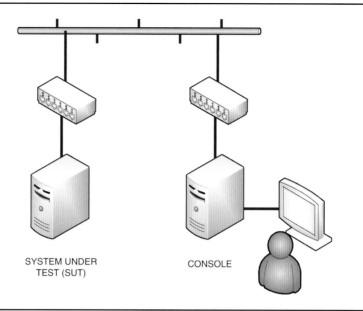

Figure 23.2 Reliability Test Setup

The system under test had the real-time clock enabled and a system management controller configured to accept out-of-band IPMI 2.0 commands from the Ethernet network. The console system was used to send IPMI commands to the system under test directing the system under test to shut down. A simple procedure was scripted on the two systems to perform the following steps:

1. The system under test writes a time-of-day entry to a log file and then enters the S3 state.

2. The console system writes a time-of-day entry to a log file and then sends an IPMI wake up command to the system under test.

3. When the system under test wakes up, another time-of-day entry is entered to the log.

4. The real time clock is reset and the system shuts down after 30 seconds. The procedure is repeated from step 1.

After four months of testing, the two systems were shut down, the log files compared, and the results tallied. System event logs were checked on a weekly basis to assure no abnormal reset or recoverable failure had occurred. At the completion of the tests, the results were:

- The system completed 43,718 STR cycles, of which 30,670 STR cycles were initiated by the console system via an IPMI command.

- No hard disk drive spin-up or power supply switching issues were observed during the testing.

- One observable failure occurred during the 4 months.

The log files indicated that the system failed to resume after a success entry in the S3 state. The actual cause of the failure could not be determined from the log files nor could the failure be repeated. A careful review of the log files found the failure occurred at the same time that the buildings' utility power was susceptible to line interruption (such as ½ sine wave dropout) or line quality problems (such as line droop or spikes). The site recorded power quality problems and power losses occurred in the immediate vicinity. If utility power was compromised while the system was in the S3 state, the context of memory would have been lost or corrupted, and the system could not resume successfully. Servers are typically tested to assure that the power supply can withstand AC surges and ½ sine wave dropout, but the secondary standby voltage rail may be undergo this testing. Therefore, the susceptibility of the standby voltage rail to voltage anomalies is not known.

Summary and Conclusions of the Investigation

A rich set of options exist for implementing server parking in the data center. Specific choices depend on hardware support and application requirements. In all cases where restart latency is not an issue, then powering down to the S5 state is the best choice.

- For usages where restart latency is a factor, this investigation shows that restart from S3 is much faster than a restart from S4 or S5, particularly with the Linux operating systems. By tuning the device drivers it may be possible to reduce the resume time and approach 2 seconds. Note that the total time for power up, BIOS initialization, and device initialization is already less than 2 seconds.

- Server power supply performance needs to be assessed to ensure that adequate power is available from the standby output rails to power memory, and that the regulator circuitry used for the standby power has the same robustness and protection from utility power anomalies such as voltage spikes and dropouts.

- S3 resume can be reliable when the hardware and software configuration is controlled.

- The energy saved is substantial, approximately 75 percent relative to idle ACPI S0.

- The same supervisory machines or load balancers in a Web server setting used to perform workload balancing across a server pool may also be used to initiate S3 entry and exit, using IPMI commands. These supervisory machines, which already can dynamically allocate workloads, could also keep track of servers that are in a parked state. And when bindings or connections between servers in the server pools needs to be established, the file structure used by Linux makes for easy implementation of scripts to reconnect the servers to other hosts, storage, or infrastructure resources.

Linux Files Used by Suspend-to-RAM

During the STR investigation on Linux operating systems, the files and paths shown in Table 23.5 were useful for making changes to the control and actions of the suspend operation.

Table 23.5 Issues with Sleep-to-RAM Resumption

Component	Description of Concern
`/etc/pm/config.d/rtcwake.config`	This configuration file enables the real-time clock wakeup and sets the time to wake.
`/etc/pm/config.d/s2ram.config`	This file sets the STR options. If STR does not work, try adding to this file: `S2RAM_OPTS = -f`
`/var/log/pm-suspend.log`	Log file of all the commands being executed by the operating system during the suspend and resume process.
`/usr/lib/pm-utils/defaults`	Primary config file for suspend. You should not edit this file, since after a package update it might be overwritten with the default settings. Put any config file changes into `/etc/pm/config.d/`
`/usr/lib/pm-utils/power.d`	Sets the power state. This is the default distribution package file when the OS was installed. Do not modify this file as it may get overwritten during an OS update.
`/usr/lib/pm-utils/sleep.d`	This is the default script that the OS runs to put the system to sleep. This is the default distribution package file when the OS was installed. Do not modify this file as it may get overwritten during a package update.
`/etc/pm/power.d`	Sets the power state. This script takes precedence over the script in `/usr/lib/pm-utils/`
`/etc/pm/sleep.d`	Puts system to sleep. This script takes precedence over the script in `/usr/lib/pm-utils/`

Any scripts saved in `/etc/pm/` take precedence over those in `/usr/lib/pm-utils/`, and hence the system administrator can override the defaults provided by the distribution.

Chapter **24**

Virtualized Low Cost Infrastructure for Small and Medium Businesses

Contributed by Chris Black

Legacy PC configurations with standalone, singularly managed, and individually updated OS and application components on local storage directly oppose scalability and low-cost ongoing support. Newer solutions exist that allow centralized management of PC images and application stacks returning a 1:1 reduction in maintenance time for each PC migrated to a centralized solution. This chapter explores the implementation of one such system at the Sacramento Boy's and Girl's Clubs beginning with a history of Intel's involvement with the nonprofit organization, the Intel IT Innovation team's goals with the project, and ongoing work at the Boy's and Girl's Clubs (BGC). The Intel work at the Sacramento BGC represents a framework and low TCO reference design for small and medium businesses and organizations.

Getting Involved

In the spring of 2008, BGC Sacramento staff contacted Intel IT Innovation and requested assistance in determining how BGC would spend an upcoming grant from the Buck Foundation[1]. IT Innovation formed a small, focused team

---

1   The Frank H. and Eva B. Buck Foundation. (2009). Foundation Home Page. Dedicated to Education in all its Aspects. Retrieved March 01, 2009 from http://www.buckfoundation.org/

to gather details, asses the current situation, engage with current IT support (Makely Enterprises), and formulate expenditure possibilities. The team's initial plans involved simple PC and equipment purchases but further investigation revealed an opportunity to do more than PO line-item recommendations. As is typical among small businesses and nonprofits, the IT infrastructure at BGC Sacramento was older, consisted of donations and ad-hoc purchases, and had changed support hands multiple times over the last 5–6 years. The systems were functional but what Intel Innovation noticed immediately was the large number of hours IT support spent on site just keeping BGC's 45 PCs and servers up and running.

Existing Infrastructure and Support

Three servers, 30 lab PCs for the children, and another 15 administrative PCs in the office area of the South Sacramento BGC location kept Makely Enterprises (ME) busy, along with another site in downtown Sacramento with another 30 machines. Like many nonprofit organizations, Makely Enterprise donated many support hours to BGC due to budget constraints. This brings to mind the nonprofit dilemma of volunteerism much akin to the corporate problem of work-life balance. The question they face is, how does an organization leverage volunteer hours among a limited population of persons and businesses willing to volunteer without eventually burning those volunteers out and losing their support completely? Managing this situation is difficult at best, and for IT volunteerism impossible without some form of low TCO infrastructure.

Planning

The Intel IT team saw immediate resolution potential for support issues at BGC Sacramento using recently developed technologies and some small donations. Through a number of joint planning sessions, BGC management, Intel Innovation, and Makely Enterprises addressed the major pain points around hours spent on support and stability with a design using streaming OS, appliance firewalls, and server donations. This left Buck Foundation grant funds available for other purchases such as Apple workstations, still and video cameras, and musical equipment and software. Intel IT invited participation from Citrix[2] in donating 150 licenses for the Provisioning Server for Desktops (PVS) streaming OS product, Astaro[†] in donating two Web-filtering firewall appliances, and Intel IT in donating a few servers based on the Intel® Xeon® processor. Both BGC locations had Category 5e cabling installed and some gigabit Ethernet, so the design took form in a new Windows[†] Server 2003 Active Directory (AD) domain controller, a second new AD domain controller with the Citrix[†] PVS software, and a later EOL of the two legacy Pentium® 3 servers. Figure 24.1 shows the single location proposed architecture with the two new servers donated from Intel, Citrix streaming OS for the kid's lab PCs, streaming OS for select office PCs, and new Astaro[3] firewall appliance. Replicating this setup at the second BGC location in Sacramento and erecting a point-to-point VPN tunnel finishes out the architecture connecting the two offices allowing direct sharing and printing.

---

2   Citrix Systems, Inc. (2009). Contacting Citrix Around the World. Retrieved March 01, 2009 from http://www.citrix.com/English/contact/index.asp

3   Astaro Internet Security. (2009). Astaro Security Gateway Homepage. Retrieved March 01, 2009 from http://www.astaro.com/

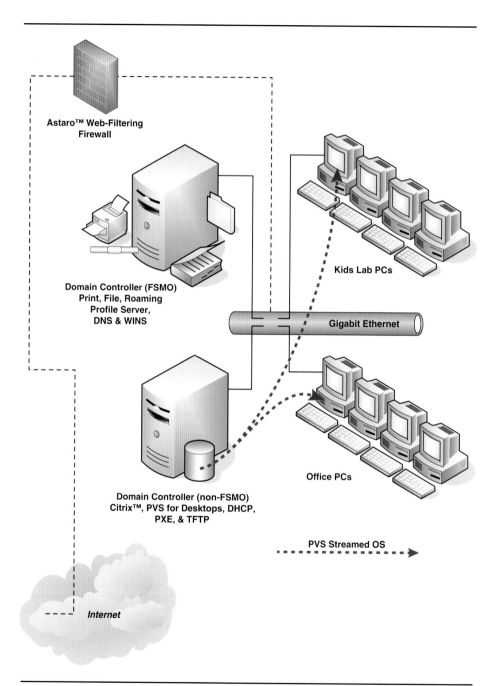

Figure 24.1 Proposed Architecture

Implementation

As with all implementations in IT, nothing ever goes as planned. Originally, attaching the new donated servers to the existing domain, migrating AD functions, bringing up the Citrix PVS server, and decommissioning the legacy servers seemed straightforward. Putting in the new servers went well. However, things went poorly for a time thereafter. A number of configuration issues prevented the original swap and roll cutover. First, the tendency of the existing Linux freeware firewall to "scavenge" the PXE broadcast and direct clients to the wrong TFTP server forced co-location of the DHCP server, primary DNS, and WINS services on the same server as PVS. Second, nested group policy within the existing domain caused multiple errors with FSMO role relocation to the new "primary" AD domain controller. Finally, this same nested group policy prevented printing to any other server than the legacy print server even though the team deleted that group policy. After several weeks of stymied progress, the team made the decision to move forward with a parallel AD installation and BGC's new domain came to life over the course of a very long weekend.

Lessons Learned

A number of best known methods (BKMs) came out of the implementation at BGC Sacramento. BKMs include:

- When working on a small AD domain of under 100 users sometimes it is best to start from scratch rather than incorporate unknown legacy AD settings.

- Never use roaming profiles and offline files together.

- The end user always forgets to tell the implementation team about at least one critical application.

- Allow approximately twice the time required to accomplish tasks while in the field.

- Never underestimate the value of e-mail, printing, and Quick Books to small businesses.

- At 4:00 a.m., coffee is a very valuable commodity.

Moving Forward

At this point, the new servers were in place and the Teichert BGC location stabilized. After many weeks of interruptions, the team decided limited and deliberate changes were in order. They started by first decommissioning the old servers and temporary servers, leaving them in place and off until achieving four consecutive weeks of stability. During this time, BGC placed the order for 50 new PCs that would replace their older Pentium 4 systems and the Intel team placed the new Astaro firewall in addition to tuning the existing OS Streaming images for the kid's lab. One of the reasons the team picked Astaro was the ability to hook to an Active Directory domain and apply Web filter policies granularly by Office User, group, or account. This particular feature allowed minimally restricted Web access to BGC Staff while still allowing well-protected Web access for the children in the kid's computer lab without excessive software overhead.

Today

Today, the Intel team is planning for the deployment of the 50 new PCs using the Citrix streaming OS solution, deployment of a new virtual server at the Ralley's location housing both domain controllers and streaming OS server, and the arrival of multimedia and creativity software/equipment for the kids labs as shown in Figure 24.2. The new streaming solution requires approximately 3–4 hours of maintenance to update the streaming images every month, along with a few hours for miscellaneous PCs, and an hour or two for patches and updates to the servers. A full day once per month from Makely Enterprises and an occasional remote check is sufficient to keep all systems up, patched, and running for 4 servers and 75 PCs at two separate locations. This differs greatly from the previous situation where 20 percent of the PCs were down for various reasons at any given time, excessive slowness caused 15-minute delays in login, and Makely Enterprises spent between 8 and 12 hours on-site every week repairing, patching, and recovering from unexpected PC incidents. Were BGC to purchase this solution outright, USD 20,000 in new PCs, USD 1,500 for Citrix licensing, USD 3,000 for an additional server, and USD 5,000 in Web-blocking firewalls totals less than

USD 30,000 in expenditure, a few thousand more than the nonstreaming solution. Using a traditional local disk based infrastructure, running support costs at 80 percent availability totaled almost USD 20,000 per year compared with USD 4,800 per year in support costs for the Citrix-based solution at 95 percent availability.

Summary

The solution the Intel team used at the Boy's and Girl's Club represents a viable alternative to the locally installed OS and individual PC. This reference architecture for small and medium business provides a scalable centrally managed IT system with a 75-percent reduction in ongoing support costs. For the BGC and their limited budget, this allows the club to use the IT support hours and monetary grants on activities and equipment for their kids instead of infrastructure maintenance and upkeep. Further, testing at Intel indicates that an Intel Xeon uni-processor dual-core server with 2 GB of RAM and 4 disks in a RAID array can support up to 200 streamed PCs on a single gigabit subnet with a heavy office workload [Intel, 2008]. Many thanks to the donations from Astaro, Citrix, and the employees at Intel for making this Intel Involved in the Community project possible.

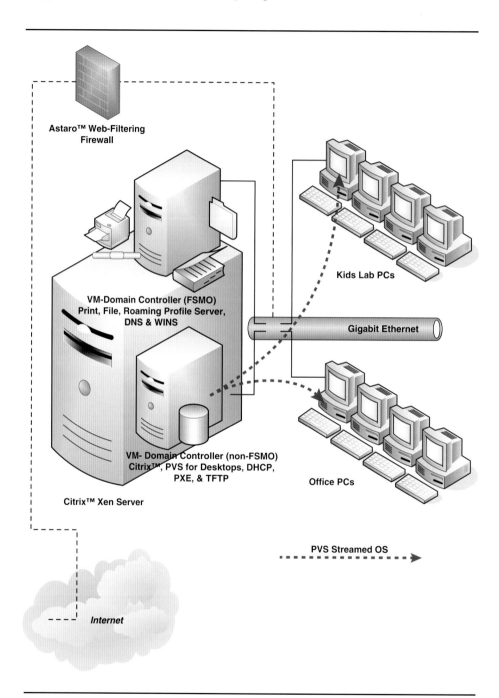

Figure 24.2 Location Network Diagram

Chapter **25**

Migrating Applications to the Cloud with Amazon Web Services

Contributed by Bernard Golden

The Silicon Valley Education Foundation serves 13,500 teachers and 260,000 students throughout Santa Clara County, located in the heart of Silicon Valley. To help teachers collaborate and enable peer learning, SVEF created Lessonopoly, a Web 2.0 application that offers lesson plan creation, modification, and sharing, thereby fostering improved education. A key feature of Lessonopoly is its round-the-clock accessibility, making it easy for teachers to work on lesson plans at their convenience.

The infrastructure that Lessonopoly was originally deployed upon offers no redundancy; exposing SVEF to the risk of an extended outage should any hardware fail. After examining the option of deploying duplicate hardware along with high availability virtualization, SVEF decided to pursue a different option: moving Lessonopoly into the cloud.

The application migration was highly successful, with the result of better application robustness. In addition, monthly hosting charges were reduced by moving the application into the cloud. This chapter discusses the migration process for Lessonopoly, including:

■ Motivations for considering cloud computing

■ Technical aspects of the effort

■ Key cloud migration issues

■ Lessonopoly migration project TCO

Overview of SVEF and Lessonopoly

The Silicon Valley Education Foundation (SVEF) supports education throughout the Santa Clara Valley, a large and diverse collection of school districts. Serving 34 school districts, with 13,500 teachers and 260,000 students, SVEF delivers a range of programs, including:

■ Teacher grants to support supplemental learning opportunities

■ Intensive tutoring to students to enable greater success rates

■ A Science, Technology, Engineering, and Math program designed to give students the skills necessary for tomorrow's jobs in Silicon Valley

Lessonopoly Description

As part of its efforts to enable high-quality teaching, SVEF recognizes it needs to help teachers with technology-based solutions. After extensive research, SVEF concluded a valuable initiative would be to assist teachers with their lesson plans, which are the building blocks of individual class sessions. In the past, lesson plans have been paper-based, with no ability to contain or link to rich data sources that can be used in individual lessons. For example, video can be a rich resource for teaching many subjects, but paper-based lesson plans can, at best, list the online location of a relevant video. Furthermore, paper-based lesson plans are a poor medium for collaboration, making it difficult for experienced teachers to share knowledge and best practices with less-experienced colleagues.

Therefore, SVEF developed Lessonopoly, a Web 2.0 application facilitating lesson plan creation, modification, and sharing. Lessonopoly offers the ability to link rich data sources to lesson plans; these data sources may be stored within Lessonopoly itself or on another server located on the Internet. Lessonpoly offers users the ability to rate and comment upon individual lesson plans, thereby offering user-based quality control. In addition, it offers search functionality to allow users to seek lesson plans by title, content, or description. Finally, Lessonopoly allows creation of new lesson plans by editing one or more existing lesson plans and saving the updated document as a new lesson plan. This facilitates teacher customization of material to suit the needs of their classes.

Lessonopoly Architecture

Lessonopoly is a Web-based content management system based on the open source product Drupal. Lessonopoly is a three-tier application, with user interaction being funneled through the Apache Web server to Web pages served up by the Drupal engine, which in turn accesses a MySQL database where Drupal configuration and page definition data is stored.

As originally designed, Lessonopoly's three tiers all run on a single server. Upon launch, low user volumes made it possible to handle all load on one server. Drupal-based systems are very flexible in terms of deployment, making it easy to spread the individual tiers onto additional servers as load increases. Some options for addressing Lessonopoly system load and robustness in a cloud environment are discussed later.

Motivation for Considering Cloud Computing

As just noted, the original deployment topology of Lessonopoly was a three-tier system, all of which resided on the same machine, a 1U server hosted in a co-location hosting provider. While the hosting company is reputable and offers responsive service, a number of drawbacks exist with the arrangement.

Limited System Scalability

The single server that Lessonopoly ran on was limited in its ability to scale to meet potential traffic. Meeting potential scalability requirements would require purchase of additional servers, something SVEF wanted to avoid, particularly in light of the current economy. Moreover, since user load volumes are variable, purchasing enough hardware to meet peak demand would result in excess hardware during low-demand periods, thereby tying up capital in unneeded capacity.

Limited Storage Scalability

Lessonopoly offers the ability for teachers to upload large documents and digital media like audio and video, which require large amounts of storage. Since individual servers are typically limited to two drives, it is likely that Lessonopoly will eventually require more storage than is possible on a single server. One option to address this is to move system data to a specialized storage device, which can contain more drives. However, this would require additional hardware purchase and poses the same issue of over-provisioning capacity. This would have the effect of burdening SVEF with excess capacity until the amount of Lessonopoly storage grew sufficiently to take advantage of the storage device.

Vulnerability to Hardware Failure

Lessonopoly serves as a hub for teacher activity in lesson plan sharing and collaboration. It is critical that it be available at all times; system outages could hamper teachers in their ability to deliver education.

In its original configuration, Lessonopoly was installed on a single server. This poses a risk, since hardware failure could result in system unavailability until repairs were made. If a component like a network card or a motherboard were to fail, a day or more could pass before system availability was restored. If a disk drive were to fail, not only would the device need to be replaced, but the system would need to be restored from backup, taking even longer.

This vulnerability would be worse if system load required additional hardware to enable the application tiers to be spread across multiple servers. Each server poses hardware failure risk at its level, which impacts total application availability; in essence, moving to a multi-tier hardware topology raises overall system risk.

Cost

In its original configuration, hosting fees for Lessonopoly were USD 200 per month, a relatively modest cost structure. However, as previously noted, the original application topology posed unacceptable risk to system downtime due to hardware failure. SVEF engaged HyperStratus to evaluate the Lessonopoly architecture and propose an alternative to reduce downtime risk. One option examined was using virtualization software to implement high availability on redundant hardware. This effectively would address the risk of downtime, since any hardware failure would cause the virtualization management software to shift virtual machines to other hardware.

While use of virtualization software would address downtime risk, it would impose a significant cost. At least one and possibly three or four new servers would be required to implement this topology, each costing around USD 2000. Finally, an additional hosting fee of USD 200 per month would be required for each new server.

Evaluating Cloud Computing

Because reducing Lessonopoly risk via virtualization and additional hardware would cost more than SVEF wanted to spend, HyperStratus and SVEF agreed to evaluate whether a cloud implementation would be appropriate for Lessonopoly. Amazon Web Services (AWS) was selected as the target cloud implementation to evaluate.

Because AWS, as part of its internal architecture, uses virtualization, SVEF would be shielded from the risk of hardware failure. In addition, should individual instances of the SVEF application crash, restart is easy and therefore downtime is kept to a minimum.

AWS Architecture

Amazon describes AWS as "an infrastructure web services platform in the cloud. With AWS you can requisition compute power, storage, and other services—gaining access to a suite of elastic IT infrastructure services as your business demands them."

AWS can be characterized as "infrastructure as a service." This means that Amazon provides basic computing capability—a virtual machine container, reliable and redundant storage, and high performance networking—in a remote location. Users have no need to provision or pay for local hardware infrastructure—Amazon takes care of that. Users focus on the software assets (the application) that reside upon and uses AWS computing resources.

AWS is comprised of a number of individual services; the key services for the needs of Lessonopoly are these four:

- *Elastic Compute Cloud (EC2).* EC2 provides elastic computing capacity. In essence, EC2 provides empty virtual machines into which users install desired software assets: operating system, middleware, and application(s). EC2 instantiates the collection of these assets as an "Amazon Machine Image." Users can create their own AMIs from scratch, use pre-built AMIs available from the AWS Web site or use a pre-built AMI as a starting point and then add additional software assets to finalize the desired AMI.

- *Simple Storage Services (S3):* S3 provides the ability to store any amount of desired data in a reliable fashion. It's important to understand that S3 data is unstructured: S3 data is a "bag of bits." It is up to the end user to impose structure on an S3 data collection. EC2 AMIs are stored in S3 and are instantiated from their S3 location. S3 data is not only unstructured, it is not updated dynamically. Updating an EC2 AMI requires a full "burn" process and results in a second AMI, somewhat different than the original one.

- *Elastic IP Addresses*: A feature of AWS is that DNS addresses for running EC2 instances are dynamically assigned at runtime. For web-based applications that are user-facing, AWS offers "Elastic IP Addresses" that are permanently assigned to a particular AMI, available at a small charge. Elastic IP Addresses are rationed by Amazon; therefore, it is important for applications that have EC2 instances that run without end user interaction to register the dynamic IP addresses with a known DNS server to enable inter-application EC2 instance communication.

- *Elastic Block Storage:* AWS also offers the Elastic Block Storage Service (EBS), which is persistent storage that is attached to running EC2 instances. With EBS, applications can save data permanently without needing to burn an entire new AMI.

Project Migration to AWS

Lessonopoly is a Linux-based application; there are many Linux-based AMIs available on the AWS Web site. However, in order to ensure the security of SVEF's system, rather than use a Linux AMI of unknown provenance, HyperStratus created a new AMI.

The first step in the creation process was to install and configure the necessary software on a local physical server. New copies of CentOS, XAMPP (an aggregation of software including Apache, MySQL, and the Perl and PHP languages), and Drupal were obtained and installed.

The next step involved uploading and converting the local system into an AMI image. Amazon provides a suite of tools to accomplish this task. The process of creating what Amazon refers to as a "bundle" results in an object that can then be uploaded as an AMI stored within S3. Once this AMI is created, it may be registered with AWS and is then ready to run. The process of creating an EC2 instance from a local system is shown in Figure 25.1.

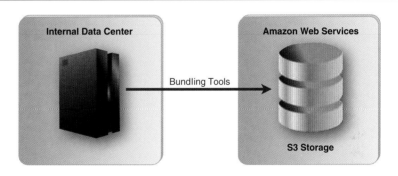

Figure 25.1 Creating an EC2 Instance

A third step involved creating a permanent IP address for Lessonopoly in AWS. An Elastic IP Address was obtained and assigned to the Lessonopoly AMI, thereby enabling consistent access via a domain name rather than requiring an ever-changing IP address, dynamically assigned each time Lessonopoly was started in AWS.

Key Cloud Computing Migration Issues

Once these three steps were performed, the Lessonopoly AMI was ready to run. Notwithstanding the relatively straightforward migration process, a number of issues present themselves in a typical migration process that must be understood and addressed. These issues include software licensing, management of dynamic data, system monitoring and management, and system backup.

Software Licensing

The Lessonopoly migration process was aided by the fact that the application is built entirely from open source software. This meant that no additional commercial licenses were needed during the initial system build. Furthermore, since open source licenses impose very few restrictions in terms of use, it was easy to run all the necessary software components in the Amazon cloud environment.

The terms of commercial software licenses are typically more restrictive, and may not allow deployment in a cloud environment. Moreover, many software vendors do not offer support for their products used in a cloud environment.

The issue of software licensing is likely to be a common challenge for many companies in their use of cloud computing. Most commercial software is licensed on a perpetual basis with a per-server licensing basis. No provision for transitory use with scaling across varying numbers of server instances is made. As organizations deploy cloud-based applications, matching system operational characteristics with commercial software licensing conditions will pose a challenge.

Dynamic Data Management

As noted earlier, the default behavior of AWS is that AMIs are stored in S3 and instantiated in EC2 when made operational. No dynamic storage capability is provided. Any changes made to a running EC2 instance are not automatically stored in the original S3 AMI; in effect, an AMI is a "gold master" that remains unchanged even if modifications are made to a running instance spawned from the original AMI. To permanently store new or modified data, a new AMI must be "burned" and stored; that leads to AMI sprawl as fresh

AMIs must be created each time an AMI is shut down with changed data contained within it. The process of launching, running, and then "burning" the updated EC2 instance is shown in Figure 25.2.

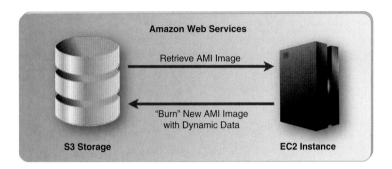

Figure 25.2 Launching, Running, and Burning an Updated EC2 Instance

One common practice to address this "gold master" issue is to capture changed files within an EC2 instance and save them to a separate S3 storage object. An example of changed files might be individual html files (such as Web pages). If an EC2 instance has new html files that need to be available when it runs, rather than burning a new AMI, the html files are stored to S3 prior to EC2 instance shutdown.

Subsequently, when the AMI is brought up, the separate S3 object is imported to the now-running EC2 instance and applied to its files. In this fashion, dynamic changes to an EC2 instances can be accommodated. This process is illustrated in Figure 25.3. This "gold master" plus incremental change incorporation process enables an application to incorporate dynamic data without requiring repeated complete AMI "burning." It does, however, impose some application complexity in that new S3 storage objects are created prior to each EC2 instance shutdown, thereby increasing the complexity of configuring and managing an application.

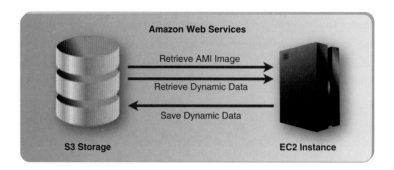

Figure 25.3   Accommodating Dynamic Changes in EC2 Instances

While the practice of separating dynamic data from base AMI can successfully accommodate dynamic data, it is less than satisfactory for applications that have large amounts of dynamic data, which tends to overload the flexibility of the "gold master plus incremental S3 storage object" approach. In addition, it is not appropriate for applications that require persistent and reliable SQL databases that can be recovered after a system failure.

Lessonopoly is an example of an application that does not map very well into this approach, as it is a very dynamic system. Drupal, which forms the heart of Lessonopoly, uses a MySQL database to store information about new users who register. As lesson plans are created or modified, they are stored, with metadata (for example, creation date, originating user) placed into Drupal, with associated documents or digital assets like video stored elsewhere in the Linux file system. In short, the application is constantly changing.

Rather than applying the "gold master plus incremental object" approach, Lessonopoly on AWS instead uses the Elastic Block Store (EBS) Service that Amazon provides. EBS enables assignment of all or part of an AMI's file system to a service that reliably stores dynamic data.

A common use of EBS is to map relational databases to EBS, enabling AWS-hosted applications to mirror common application architectures, which use a relational database for reliable data storage and queries. Non-database files and directories that hold dynamic data in the AMI's file system can also be mapped to the EBS resource. Figure 25.4 illustrates how Lessonopoly uses EBS as part of its AWS architecture.

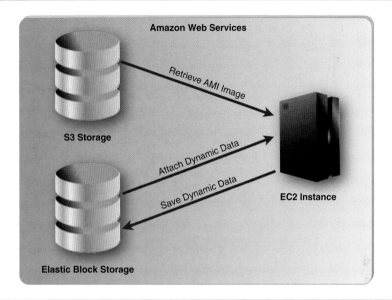

Figure 25.4 Using Elastic Block Storage.

EBS resources may only be attached to running AMI instances; any connection between an EBS resource and a specific AMI is lost when that image is stored in S3. This means that the EBS resource must be attached upon AMI startup. With Linux-based AMIs, this is typically implemented by mounting the EBS resource to a directory within the AMI's file system. (Note that EBS resources must be formatted prior to initial use; otherwise, attempting to mount the resource onto the AMI file system will fail). This mount process is accomplished via a script that is placed in the system bootup routine; each time the AMI is brought up, the script is executed, which attaches the EBS resource to the Lessonopoly file system, where system changes are stored persistently.

By using EBS, Lessonopoly can use the MySQL-based Drupal system without the need to burn a new S3 AMI image every time the system is brought down.

Application and System Management

Common application management processes must be modified when running systems in AWS. Most system management tools were originally developed to control the hardware resources of an IT organization. These tools were later extended to manage software assets as well. Notwithstanding their ability to manage software assets, they use hardware management as their primary reference to organizing assets; that is, they usually organize assets based on the hardware they are running on.

Since Amazon offers no hardware access to end users, common system management tools are inappropriate for this environment and other resources must be used for system management.

Amazon itself offers two different methods to manage AWS resources. The original tool is ElasticFox, a Firefox plug-in that lists and controls all AWS resources associated with a particular account.

A more recent tool that Amazon offers is an AJAX-enabled Web page that may be accessed by any browser, not just Firefox. It too lists and controls all AWS resources for a given account.

Two primary challenges lie within the system management tools Amazon provides.

■ Amazon tools manage Amazon resources, but require the user to separately manage the software assets running in EC2 instances. This means that two different management mechanisms must be used: one to manage the Amazon resources, and a second to manage the application software components running within the Amazon resources.

■ The Amazon tools manage the Amazon resources as discreet instances; this means that in a three-tier application running on three or more EC2 instances the application cannot be managed as a whole, but each EC2 instance must be managed separately. This can pose problems for applications with large load variability; manual intervention is required to add or subtract resources to the application to enable it to handle varied load. Far more preferable would be a management system that would allow a unified approach to the application as a whole; should additional resources be required to meet increased demand, an instruction to increase application capability by a certain percentage could be implemented by the management tool, which would then instantiate whatever additional Amazon resources would be necessary to increase processing capacity by that percentage.

A number of third-party vendors have released tools to offer more sophisticated system management capabilities for AWS. Some of these tools manage aggregations of EC2 instances as a single application instance that can be scaled up or down, cloned to allow separate test and development application instances, and offer application versioning at the aggregated level. Other of the tools focus on managing the software components within individual EC2 instances. Amazon itself is likely to increase the breadth and functionality of its management tools in the near future.

Since the Lessonopoly application today runs on a single EC2 instance, for the initial implementation the current Amazon tools were selected for system management. This decision will be revisited in the future as traffic increases or the application is partitioned across multiple EC2 instances.

Application and System Backup

Using redundant systems to prevent application unavailability due to hardware failure is useful; however, failing to have backups capable of restoring a system after database or hardware failure can literally make an application permanently unavailable. Consequently, reliable backups are critical to ensure long-term system availability.

Most organizations perform backups on machines in their data centers. They accomplish this either through manual activities like burning disks in machine DVD drives, or through automated solutions that copy system data out to disk or tape-based repositories.

Since AWS offers no access to hardware, the manual approach is unworkable for EC2-based systems. However, automated backups are possible by using S3 as a reliable disk repository. Backups to S3 consist of new S3 AMI images of the core EC2 instance (in effect creating new "gold master" images if the core operating system or configuration files have changed) and separate S3 backups files of the dynamic data.

Because the Lessonopoly architecture uses EBS to store dynamic data, it is necessary to back up the EBS-based data separately from the EC2 instance backup, since S3-based instance backup does not capture data stored on EBS storage. In other words, AWS treats EBS as separate from the EC2 instance, and "burning" a new AMI "gold master" instance misses any EBS-based data. EBS storage instances must be separately backed up to S3, which forces a dual-backup strategy: one for the overall EC2 instance, and a second for the EBS instance attached to the EC2 image.

Fortunately, the EBS service offers the ability to create snapshots of the data in the EBS instance, which are then stored in S3. Subsequent snapshots store only changed data since the previous snapshot, thereby reducing overall storage requirements. Use of EBS snapshots as a dynamic data backup strategy is a significant improvement over direct backup of the EBS data into S3 files.

In its previous hosted arrangement, Lessonopoly backups were performed manually on a regular basis. In the AWS-hosted version, backups are performed with native AWS functionality, driven by *cron* scripts placed in the operating system running Lessonopoly. As the application topology complexity or data volumes increase, one of the third-party tools will be used to simplify the backup procedure.

Lessonopoly AWS TCO

Calculating TCO for a cloud-based application is not necessarily a straightforward effort. Amazon pricing is public and easily understood, being based on units of resource consumption, like AMI instance use on a per-hour basis, Gigabyte of storage on a monthly basis, and so on. However, it is often impossible to know before deployment exactly how many resources will be consumed; this will affect the total cost of the system on a monthly basis. Furthermore, since system use may be highly variable, which would affect total resource use, the monthly cost of an AWS application may be highly variable as well.

On the other hand, it is often difficult to evaluate the cost of an application that is hosted in-house or at a hosting provider. The monthly hosting fees for a single machine may be known, which makes evaluation easier; however, if a general hosting contract is in place, it may be difficult to establish the cost for a single server, or the financial elements of the contract may be handled by a different part of the organization, making it hard to discover the actual cost for hosting a single server.

Establishing the cost for an internally hosted server (located in an organization's own data center) can be far more challenging. Most IT organizations track costs at a very high level, with no ability to assign costs at the single server granularity level. Moreover, many of the costs associated with a server, like power or the imputed capital cost of the data center itself that should be assigned on a pro rata basis to a server, are not available at all.

As cloud computing becomes more common, the lack of transparency with respect to the established alternatives like internal and external hosting will become a significant issue. Most IT organizations will come under pressure to provide much more clarity regarding their true costs on a highly granular basis to enable TCO comparison among alternatives, including cloud computing.

For Lessonopoly, a TCO comparison was important because SVEF is a budget-constrained nonprofit. Migrating the application to a cloud environment to improve system robustness was attractive, but if the cloud environment was not less than or equal to the equivalent cost of the hosted environment, SVEF would be forced to continue with the current hosting arrangement.

Fortunately, for the purposes of the Lessonopoly TCO comparison, the services offered by the hosting provider and Amazon are very similar: reliable machine support, with the ability to remotely power the machine on and off. The hosting provider offered no services beyond low-level machine support. All other support, like managing and patching the OS and ensuring the Lessonopoly application remained up and running, was left to SVEF. Therefore, the two environments—AWS and hosted—were very much alike and could be compared directly with respect to cost.

Because Lessonopoly is hosted on a single server today, but might expand to multi-tier or even multi-tier with one or more machines in each of the tiers, a number of TCO scenarios were evaluated. Each of the scenarios is described in the following sections, with an analysis of the cost for both alternatives.

Scenario 1: Single Server

This is the current scenario, as displayed in Figure 25.5.

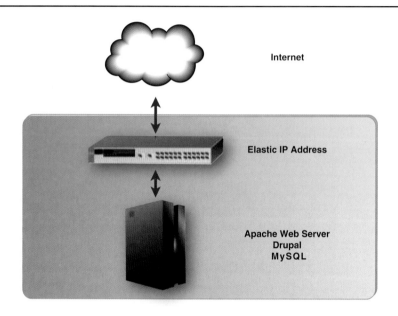

Figure 25.5 Single Server Scenario.

The costs of two alternatives can be seen in Table 25.1.

Table 25.1 Single-tier Hosted Cost versus AWS Cost

Hosted Cost		AWS Cost	
Server Monthly Hosting Fee	USD 200.00	AMI Monthly Hosting Fee (running 24 hours each day of the month)	USD 74.00
Monthly Data Storage Fee (included in Base Fee	USD 0.00	Monthly Data Storage Fee (50 GB)	USD 7.50
Monthly Data Transfer Fee (Included in Base Fee)	USD 0.00	Monthly Data Transfer Fee (20 GB)	USD 3.50
		Monthly EBS Storage (50 GB)	USD 5.00
Total Monthly Cost	USD 200.00	Total Monthly Cost	USD 90.00
		Total % AWS Savings	55%

Scenario 2: Multi-tier

If total traffic to the Lessonopoly Web site increases to the point at which performance of the system suffers due to load, the application could be partitioned to two machines, one hosting the Lessonopoly web server and Drupal instance, with the second hosting the Drupal database.

This scenario is displayed in Figure 25.6.

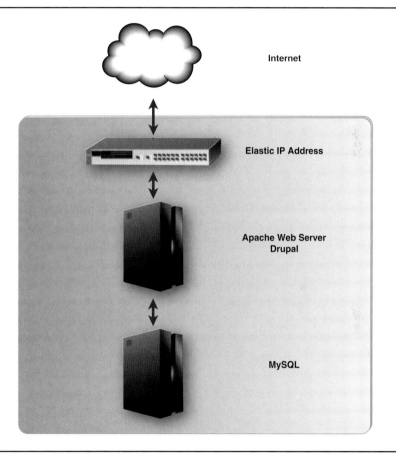

Figure 25.6 Multi-tier Scenario for High Workload Traffic

The costs of two alternatives can be seen in Table 25.2.

Table 25.2 Multi-tier Hosted versus AWS Cost

Hosted Cost		AWS Cost	
Server Monthly Hosting Fee (Two servers)	USD 400.00	AMI Monthly Hosting Fee (Two servers running 24 hours each day of month)	USD 148.00
Monthly Data Storage Fee (included in Base Fee	USD 0.00	Monthly Data Storage Fee (50 GB X 2)	USD 15.00
Monthly Data Transfer Fee (Included in Base Fee)	USD 0.00	Monthly Data Transfer Fee (20 GB X 2)	USD 19.00
		Monthly EBS Storage (50 GB X 2)	USD 10.00
Amortized Monthly Cost of New Hardware[1]	USD 55.00		
Total Monthly Cost	USD 455.00	Total Monthly Cost	USD 192.00
		Total % AWS Savings	57.00%

Note: 1. In addition to the monthly hosting fee, an additional machine would need to be purchased to be placed in the hosting facility. That machine would cost approximately USD 2000. Amortized over an expected three year lifespan, the monthly cost would be USD 55.

Scenario 3: Multi-machine, Multi-tier

If total traffic to the Lessonopoly Web site increases beyond the point at which partitioning of the two tiers onto individual machines is sufficient to support total application load, the application could be further partitioned to more machines, with two or more hosting the Lessonopoly web server and Drupal instance, and another machine hosting the Drupal database. To assess the TCO of this scenario, an application topology containing three web server machines was evaluated. In an application topology with multiple web server machines, a load balancer to distribute traffic among the web servers is necessary. Both hardware- and software-based load balancers are available in the market; since placing a hardware load balancer in the hosted environment would be difficult under the terms of the SVEF hosting agreement, and impossible in the AWS environment, this scenario assumes use of a software load balancing application. Because several open source load balancing packages are available, no software acquisition cost was factored into the evaluation. The load balancing software is run on a normal server; therefore, one additional server is placed into the scenario to host the load balancing software.

In summary, this scenario topology is:

■ One server to host load balancing software

■ Three servers to host Lessonopoly web servers

■ One server to host Drupal database server

This scenario is displayed in Figure 25.7.

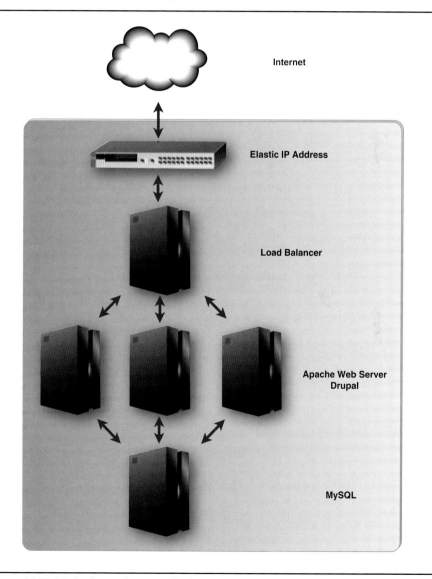

Figure 25.7 Multiple Machine, Multiple Tier Scenario.

The costs of two alternatives can be seen in Table 25.3.

Table 25.3 Multi-tier, Multi-machine Hosted versus AWS Cost

Hosted Cost		AWS Cost	
Server Monthly Hosting Fee (Five servers)	USD 1,000.00	AMI Monthly Hosting Fee (Five servers running 24 hours each day of month)[1]	USD 370.00
Monthly Data Storage Fee (included in Base Fee	USD 0.00	Monthly Data Storage Fee (1TB)	USD 150.00
Monthly Data Transfer Fee (Included in Base Fee)	USD 0.00	Monthly Data Transfer Fee (1.7TB)	USD 229.00
		Monthly EBS Storage (50GB X 5)	USD 25.00
Amortized Monthly Cost of New Hardware[2]	USD 222.00		
Total Monthly Cost	USD 1,222.00	Total Monthly Cost	USD 774.00
		Total % AWS Savings	36.00%

Notes: 1. Amazon was planning to offer load balancing as an AWS service in late 2009, which would obviate the need for one AMI instance.

2. In addition to the monthly hosting fee, four additional machines would need to be purchased to be placed in the hosting facility. Each machine would cost approximately USD 2000. Amortized over an expected three year lifespan, the monthly cost would be USD 222.

Lessonopoly TCO Analysis

In each scenario, hosting the application in AWS offers savings, which range from 36 percent to 57 percent. Note that Scenario 3, which is the multi-machine, multi-tier topology, assigns an extra EC2 instance to host the load balancing software.

With the release of the Amazon load balancing service in late 2009, this instance could be dropped and replaced with the Amazon service, which would reduce the cost of the AWS by USD 74 per month, and raise the AWS percentage savings for this scenario to 38 percent. Of course, Amazon charges for its load balancing service, so the savings would be somewhat less, but nevertheless, one could expect the percentage savings to be higher with substitution of the Amazon service for the load balancing software EC2 instance.

Factors Affecting TCO

The fees for the hosting provider as well as the costs for AWS EC2 instances are fixed; the cost for the hosting provider is a flat monthly fee, while the AWS EC2 instances are linear on a per-hour basis; running an EC2 instance every hour of the day for a full month sums to USD 74.

Also note that Amazon Web Services offers what are called "Reserved Instances," which, in return for an up-front payment, offer a lower per-hour cost. If an EC2 instance runs 24 hours per day, year-round, using Reserved Instances can reduce overall EC2 costs by approximately one-third. Reserved Instance costs were not factored into this TCO analysis, since this analysis is based on a monthly cost perspective; however, in a real world situation that assumes an always-on system, Reserved Instances would undoubtedly be used to reduce the overall cost of Amazon Web Services computing.

However, the amount of storage used by the application and network traffic between users and the data center where the application is hosted can affect the total monthly cost. In this TCO analysis, we have not assigned any charge for these factors to the existing hosting arrangement because the monthly fee includes a certain amount of network traffic, and storage is based on what is available on the SVEF-owned machine located in the hosting provider's data center.

For Amazon, S3 storage is priced on a sliding scale, according to volume, with the lowest volume tier costing USD 0.15/GB. EBS storage costs USD 0.10/GB as well as USD 0.10 per 1 million I/O requests in and out of an EBS instance. Network traffic in and out of Amazon's data center is also priced on a sliding scale. For network traffic in, cost is USD 0.10 per GB. For network traffic out, pricing at the lowest tier is USD 0.17/GB.

Scenario 1 represents current Lessonopoly use and so data storage and transfer volumes of 50 GB and 20 GB, respectively, were used in TCO calculations. The other two scenarios used forecasts of data storage and transfer, based on likely application traffic increases in the future. Note that the increased data transfer requirements would outstrip the amounts included in the current external hosting fee and would increase that fee beyond USD 200. The exact amount of increase was unavailable during the TCO analysis and was therefore not factored into the analysis; however, the increased fee would result in increasing the savings available through hosting the application in AWS.

In addition to the financial savings available to SVEF through using AWS to host its Lessonopoly application, AWS also offers increased application robustness by protecting SVEF from hardware failure. Using an external hosting provider avoids the need for SVEF to host machines in its own facilities and also avoids the need to manage service providers that supply resources like power and Internet connectivity.

However, the hosting provider expects SVEF to take responsibility for its own hardware. Because of budget limitations, SVEF is unable to purchase the redundant hardware necessary to protect itself from hardware failure.

Consequently, continuing the hosting arrangement exposes SVEF to the potential of application unavailability, which would affect the opportunity for teachers to improve their use of lesson plans and peer learning through the use of Lessonopoly. SVEF is particularly concerned about system uptime because if Lessonopoly is unavailable to any extent, teachers may conclude the application is too unreliable to depend on, and therefore avoid the use of the application altogether.

With the opportunity to save money as well as increase application reliability, SVEF will migrate the Lessonopoly application to AWS permanently. While this represents a change in the system hosting arrangements, with the potential for further change in the future, should system load require moving to a multi-tier system topology, end users are unaffected by the migration. Lessonopoly itself will continue to function in exactly the same fashion, with no discernible difference in user experience.

Summary

The SVEF initiative to move its Lessonopoly application from a co-located hosting service to Amazon Web Services illustrates much of the allure of cloud computing. By leveraging cloud computing, SVEF was able to:

■ Increase robustness: In the original hosting arrangement, the Lessonopoly application resided on a single hardware server. Even though good practices were followed regarding configuration management, source code management, and data backup, the application was still vulnerable to extended outages due to hardware failure. By migrating the application to AWS, SVEF mitigated its hardware vulnerability and increased the robustness of its application.

- ■ Increase flexibility: If system load increased in the original hosting environment, little could be done in a short timeframe to increase system resources. By migrating the application to AWS, additional system resources can be made available almost immediately. Moreover, if system load then diminishes, it is easy to release the additional resources, with no further operational or financial commitment.

- ■ Reduce costs: Even though the original hosting environment was relatively inexpensive, moving the Lessonopoly application reduced cost significantly. As the total application user base grows with additional traffic, the AWS infrastructure allows additional system resources to be deployed with linear scaling of costs. By contrast, if the original hosting infrastructure needed to have additional resources applied to the application, significant capital investment would be necessary, along with increasing hosting fees for each new piece of hardware.

While cloud computing may not be appropriate for every application or every computing environment, SVEF's experience with migrating Lessonopoly to AWS illustrates the very real benefits available to organizations that identify applications that are appropriate candidates for placement in cloud environments.

Index

[Handwritten annotations:]
—Intel DC mgr
—Intel Intelligent Power node mgr
—Intel VT.
—Intel TxT.
—Intel Cloud builder.

Continuing Education is Essential

It's a challenge we all face – keeping pace with constant change in information technology. Whether our formal training was recent or long ago, we must all find time to keep ourselves educated and up to date in spite of the daily time pressures of our profession.

Intel produces technical books to help the industry learn about the latest technologies. The focus of these publications spans the basic motivation and origin for a technology through its practical application.

Right books, right time, from the experts

These technical books are planned to synchronize with roadmaps for technology and platforms, in order to give the industry a head-start. They provide new insights, in an engineer-to-engineer voice, from named experts. Sharing proven insights and design methods is intended to make it more practical for you to embrace the latest technology with greater design freedom and reduced risks.

I encourage you to take full advantage of Intel Press books as a way to dive deeper into the latest technologies, as you plan and develop your next generation products. They are an essential tool for every practicing engineer or programmer. I hope you will make them a part of your continuing education tool box.

Sincerely,

Senior Fellow and Chief Technology Officer Intel Corporation

**Turn the page to learn about titles
from Intel Press for system developers**

Service Oriented Architecture Demystified

A pragmatic approach to SOA for the IT Executives

By Girish Juneja, Blake Dournaee, Joe Natoli, and Steve Birkel

ISBN 1-934053-02-3

The authors of this definitive book on SOA debunk the myths and demonstrate through examples from different vertical industries how a "crawl, walk, run" approach to deployment of SOA in an IT environment can lead to a successful return on investment.

One popular argument states that SOA is not a technology per se, but that it stands alone and can be implemented using a wide range of technologies. The authors believe that this definition, while attractive and elegant, doesn't necessarily pass pragmatic muster.

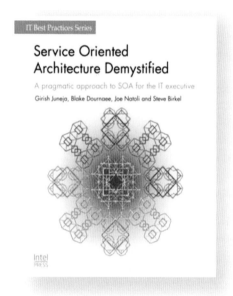

IT Best Practices Series

Service Oriented Architecture Demystified

A pragmatic approach to SOA for the IT executive

Girish Juneja, Blake Dournaee, Joe Natoli and Steve Birkel

Intel
PRESS

Service Oriented Architecture Demystified describes both the technical and organizational im-pacts of adopting SOA and the pursuant challenges. The authors demonstrate through real life deployments why and how different industry sectors are adopting SOA, the challenges they face, the advantages they have realized, and how they have (or have not) addressed the issues emerging from their adoption of SOA. This book strikes a careful balance between describing SOA as an enabler of business processes and presenting SOA as a blueprint for the design of software systems in general. Throughout the book, the authors attempt to cater to both technical and organizational viewpoints, and show how both are very different in terms of why SOA is useful. The IT software architect sees SOA as a business process enabler and the CTO sees SOA as a technology trend with powerful paradigms for software development and software integration.

SOA can be characterized in terms of different vertical markets. For each such market, achieving SOA means something different and involves different transformational shifts. The vertical markets covered include healthcare, government, manufacturing, finance, and telecommunications. SOA considerations are quite different across these vertical markets, and in some cases, the required organizational shifts and technology shifts are highly divergent and context dependent.

Whether you are a CTO, CIO, IT manager, or IT architect, this book provides you with the means to analyze the readiness of your internal IT organization and with technologies to adopt a service oriented approach to IT.

Active Platform Management Demystified
Unleashing the power of Intel® vPro™ Technology

By Arvind Kumar, Purushottam Goel and Ylian Saint-Hilare

ISBN 978-1-934053-19-5

"Has your IT organization been hampered by the need for faster, more accurate asset management, reduced downtime with fewer deskside maintenance and repair visits, and improved malware prevention and response?

Want a solution for out-of-band manageability and security when the PC is in a low-power state or even powered off, the operating system is unresponsive, or software agents are disabled?

Active Platform Management Demystified describes the manageability and security features in PCs equipped with Intel® vPro™ Technology which includes Intel® Active Management Technology (Intel® AMT). It "goes into detail about how Intel AMT eases the burden of maintaining, managing and protecting PCs in both the Enterprise and Small Business environments" according to Christoph Graham, Hewlett-Packard Technical Strategist, and "will be very useful to anyone delivering Intel AMT solutions."

Intel Active Management Technology provides an access point for the latest management consoles from Microsoft, Altiris, Cisco, LANDesk, HP and others so IT practitioners can access PCs over a wired or corporate wireless network—or even outside the corporate firewall through a wired LAN connection. "This book keeps things clear and simple, even when discussing out-of-band operational details on IDE-Redirect and heuristic filters. The explanations illustrated using the Developer's Tool Kit are especially useful" says Javier Caceres of Aranda Software Corporation.."

" *Active Platform Management Demystified provides a good balance between technology overview and implementation details, making it a great book for ISV product teams—including product managers, senior engineers, architects and support personnel—that are developing, supporting and selling client management software.* "

- Max Sokolov, Senior Director of Engineering, Symantec Corp.

Dynamics of a Trusted Platform
A Building Block Approach

By David Grawrock

ISBN 978-1-934053-08-9

In Dynamics of a Trusted Platform David Grawrock has updated his highly popular Intel Safer Computing Initiative with new topics covering the latest developments in secure computing. The reader is introduced to the concept of Trusted Computing and the building block approach to designing security into PC platforms. The Intel® Trusted Execution Technology† (Intel® TXT) is one of those building blocks that can be used to create a trusted platform by integrating new security features and capabilities into the processor, chipset, and other platform components.

"David finds analogies in everyday life to clearly explain many of the concepts in this book. I would highly recommended Dynamics of a Trusted Platform for researchers, architects, and designers who are serious about trusted computing." - Dr. Sigrid Gürgens Fraunhofer Institute for Secure Information Technology (SIT)

"The opportunity now exists to start building trusted systems, making this book very timely. It would be foolhardy to start without a thorough understanding of the concepts; and this is what Dynamics of a Trusted Platform gives you. The building blocks described here are certainly able to imbue the infrastructure with a higher level of trustworthiness, and we may all look forward to the many benefits flowing from that." - Andrew Martin Director, Oxford University Software Engineering Centre

Dynamics of
a Trusted Platform
A building block approach
David Grawrock

Intel PRESS
Books by Engineers, for Engineers
(intel)

"The chapters on Anatomy of an Attack and System Protection present useful, practical information that will help familiarize a person with the impacts of protection (or lack thereof) of system components and resources. Treatment of the topic of measurement is particularly useful for system designers and programmers."

- Amy C Nelson, Dell, Inc

Energy Efficiency for Information Technology
How to Reduce Power Consumption in Servers and Data Centers
By Lauri Minas and Brad Ellison

ISBN 978-1-934053-20-1

Minimizing power consumption is one of the primary technical challenges that today's IT organizations face. In Energy Efficiency for Information Technology, Lauri Minas and Brad Ellison point out, that the overall consumption of electrical power by data centers can be reduced by understanding the several sources of power consumption and minimizing each one. Drawing on their engineering experience within Intel Corporation and with the industry, they break down power consumption into its constituent parts and explain each in a bottom-up fashion. With energy consumption well defined, Minas and Ellison systematically provide guidance for minimizing each draw on electrical power.

YY Chow, Managing Director, Systems and Securities Services at Mitsubishi-UFJ Securities stated "In Energy Efficiency for Information Technology Minas and Ellison underscore the magnitude of increases in power consumption, they systematically suggest ways to minimize consumption and provide checklists and assessments tables that are particularly useful to gather or summarize the right information for the planning. This is a multidimensional book that addresses a serious challenge to IT departments around the globe."

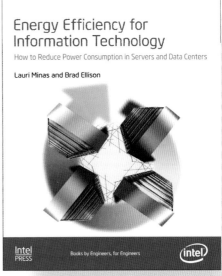

Energy Efficiency for
Information Technology
How to Reduce Power Consumption in Servers and Data Centers

Lauri Minas and Brad Ellison

Intel
PRESS
Books by Engineers, for Engineers
(intel)

"Energy Efficiency for Information Technology is a remarkable compilation of cutting-edge technical knowledge for addressing the critical issue of power and cooling in data centers. It shows how your data center can compute more but cost less, while also reducing energy use and environmental impacts."

*- Jonathan Koomey, Ph.D.,
Project Scientist ,
Lawrence Berkeley National
Laboratory*

The Business Value of Virtual Service Oriented Grids

Strategic Insights for Enterprise Decision Makers

By Enrique Castro-leon, Jackson He, Mark Chang, and Parviz Peiravi

ISBN 978-1-934053-20-1

The application of service-oriented architecture (SOA) for business will interest application developers looking for the latest advances in technology and ideas on how to utilize those advances to keep up in a global economy.

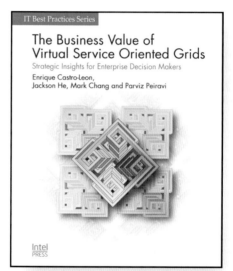

The Business Value of Virtual Service Oriented Grids provides a framework that describes how the convergence of three well-known technologies are defining a new information technology model that will fundamentally change the way we do business. The first step, say the authors, is the development of new applications for the consumer market. However, even bigger is the development of new applications in a federated fashion using services modules called *servicelets*. These federated or composite applications can be built in a fraction of the time it takes to develop traditional applications. This new environment will lower the bar for applications development, opening opportunities for thousands of smaller players worldwide.

The speed-up in application development and integration will accelerate the deployment of IT capabilities, which in turn will have a consequential effect on the organization's business agility. Corporate decision makers will enjoy the ability to pick and choose among capital and operations expenses to suit their organization's business goals. The book describes the business trends within which this convergence is taking place and provides insight on how these changes can affect your business. It clearly explains the interplay between technology, architectural considerations, and standards with illustrative examples. Finally, the book tells you how your organization can benefit from *servicelets*, alerts you about integration pitfalls, and describes approaches for putting together your technology adoption strategy for building your virtual SOA environment using *servicelets*.

Special Deals, Special Prices!

To ensure you have all the latest books
and enjoy aggressively priced discounts,
please go to this Web site:

www.intel.com/intelpress/bookbundles.htm

Bundles of our books are available,
selected especially to address the needs
of the developer. The bundles place
important complementary topics at
your fingertips, and the price for a
bundle is substantially less than
buying all the books individually.

About Intel Press

Intel Press is the authoritative source of timely, technical books
to help software and hardware developers speed up their development
process. We collaborate only with leading industry experts to deliver
reliable, first-to-market information about the latest
technologies, processes, and strategies.

Our products are planned with the help of many people in the developer
community and we encourage you to consider becoming a customer advisor.
If you would like to help us and gain additional advance insight to the latest
technologies, we encourage you to consider the Intel Press Customer
Advisor Program. You can **register** here:

www.intel.com/intelpress/register.htm

For information about bulk orders or corporate sales, please send email to
bulkbooksales@intel.com

Other Developer Resources from Intel

At these Web sites you can also find valuable technical information
and resources for developers:

www.intel.com/technology/rr	Recommended Reading list for books of interest to developers
www.intel.com/technology/itj	Intel Technology Journal
developer.intel.com	General information for developers
www.intel.com/software	Content, tools, training, and the Intel Early Access Program for software developers
www.intel.com/software/products	Programming tools to help you develop high-performance applications
www.intel.com/embedded	Solutions and resources for embedded and communications

6187-0112-7569-3141

If serial number is missing, please send an
e-mail to Intel Press at intelpress@intel.com

IMPORTANT

You can access the companion Web site for this book on
the Internet at:

www.intel.com/intelpress/virtn

Use the serial number located in the upper portion of
this page to register your book and access additional
material, including the Digital Edition of the book.